REVISITING HUMAN RIGHTS IN CANADIAN HISTORY

Human Rights and Social Justice Series

ISSN 2291-6024

Editors: Rhonda Hinther and Adele Perry

5 *Revisiting Human Rights in Canadian History*, edited by Jennifer Tunnicliffe and Stephanie Bangarth

4 *Laughing Back at Empire: The Grassroots Activism of* The Asianadian *Magazine, 1978–1985*, by Angie Wong

3 *Implicating the System: Judicial Discourses in the Sentencing of Indigenous Women*, by Elspeth Kaiser-Derrick

2 *Civilian Internment in Canada: Histories and Legacies*, edited by Rhonda Hinther and Jim Mochoruk

1 *The Idea of a Human Rights Museum*, edited by Karen Busby, Adam Muller, and Andrew Woolford

Revisiting Human Rights in Canadian History

Edited by
Jennifer Tunnicliffe
and Stephanie Bangarth

UNIVERSITY OF MANITOBA PRESS

Revisiting Human Rights in Canadian History

29 28 27 26 25 1 2 3 4 5

University of Manitoba Press
Winnipeg, Manitoba, Canada
Treaty 1 Territory
uofmpress.ca

For EU product safety concerns please contact Mare Nostrum Group B.V., Mauritskade 21D, 1091 GC Amsterdam, The Netherlands, gpsr@mare-nostrum.co.uk.

Cataloguing data available from Library and Archives Canada
Human Rights and Social Justice Series, ISSN 2291-6024 ; 5
ISBN 978-177284-126-8 (PAPER)
ISBN 978-177284-128-2 (PDF)
ISBN 978-177284-129-9 (EPUB)
ISBN 978-177284-127-5 (BOUND)

Cover design by Alexa Love
Interior Design by Galley Creative Co.

Printed in Canada

The University of Manitoba Press acknowledges the financial support for its publication program provided by the Government of Canada through the Canada Book Fund, the Canada Council for the Arts, the Manitoba Department of Sport, Culture, and Heritage, the Manitoba Arts Council, and the Manitoba Book Publishing Tax Credit.

This book has been published with the help of a grant from the Federation for the Humanities and Social Sciences, through the Awards to Scholarly Publications Program, using funds provided by the Social Sciences and Humanities Research Council of Canada.

Funded by the Government of Canada | Canadä

CERTIFIED CANADIAN PUBLISHER

Dedicated to James W.St.G Walker

CONTENTS

Contributors ix

Introduction *Jennifer Tunnicliffe and Stephanie Bangarth* 1

Chapter 1 Reflections: Trends in Historical Writing on Human Rights in Canada 14
James W.St.G. Walker

PART I HUMAN RIGHTS FOR WHOM?

Chapter 2 A Child's Right to Be Civilized? Human Rights, Children's Rights, and Indigenous Rights 35
Jasmine Holding Brown

Chapter 3 Whose Rights Count? Antiracist Activists, Feminists, and Canada's Human Rights Legislation from the Early 1950s to the Early 1970s 60
Ruth A. Frager

Chapter 4 On the Edge of Freedom: The Re-Enslavement of Elizabeth Watson in Nova Scotia 83
Franco Paz and Harvey Amani Whitfield

PART II INCARCERATION, CRIMINALIZATION, AND HUMAN RIGHTS IN CANADA

Chapter 5 Internment Is a Family Affair: One Pro-Communist Ukrainian Jewish Extended Family's Experiences with Political Incarceration in Second World War Canada 111
Rhonda L. Hinther

Chapter 6 "Injurious Effects on Mind and Body": Solitary Confinement and the Limitations of Rights in Canadian Penitentiaries 133
Janet Miron

Chapter 7	Performative Justice? Canada's Response to Alleged War Criminals in the Country: The Case of *Canada (Minister of Citizenship and Immigration) v. Vladimir Katriuk* *Katelyn Arac*	154
PART III	HUMAN RIGHTS ACTIVISTS AND ACTIVISM IN CANADA	
Chapter 8	The Battle of Church Street: Queers, Police, and the Streets of Toronto, 1981 *Tom Hooper*	179
Chapter 9	From Demanding Exclusion to Joining the Human Rights Community: Organized Labour and Human Rights in 1940s Canada *David Goutor*	201
Chapter 10	Universal Rights in Local Contexts: Postwar Human Rights Debates in Quebec (1940s–60s) *Paul-Etienne Rainville*	232
Chapter 11	Native Non-Governmental Organizations: Grassroots Constructions of Aboriginal Human Rights in Canada *María Cristina Manzano-Munguía, Dan Smoke, and Mary Lou Smoke*	256
PART IV	CANADA, FOREIGN POLICY, AND TRANSNATIONAL HUMAN RIGHTS APPROACHES	
Chapter 12	Inside Out: The Rights Revolution and Canadian Foreign Policy since 1948 *Asa McKercher*	283
Chapter 13	"Eyes on the Prize": Canada, Human Rights, and South African Apartheid in the Transition Years *Daniel Manulak*	307
Chapter 14	Pacific Flows: Asia, Canada, and Human Rights Norms Diffusion *David Webster*	324
Acknowledgements		348
Selected Bibliography		350

Contributors

EDITORS

JENNIFER TUNNICLIFFE is an Associate Professor in the Department of History at Toronto Metropolitan University. Her research interests include Canadian and international human rights history with a particular focus on how domestic and transnational activism shapes human rights policy. Tunnicliffe is the author of *Resisting Rights: Canada and the International Bill of Rights, 1947–76* (UBC Press, 2019) and a co-editor with Julien Mauduit of *Constant Struggle: Histories of Canadian Democratization* (McGill-Queen's University Press, 2021). Her current book project examines the evolution of Canada's hate speech laws through a human rights framework, situating Canadian policy in a global context.

STEPHANIE BANGARTH is a Professor in the Department of History at King's University College at Western University. She is the coordinator of the new human rights collaborative program at King's University College. Bangarth is the author of *Voices Raised in Protest: Defending North American Citizens of Japanese Ancestry, 1942–49* (UBC Press, 2008) and a co-editor with Roberta Lexier and Jon Weier of *Party of Conscience: The CCF, the NDP, and Social Democracy in Canada* (Between the Lines, 2018). She is the author of numerous book chapters and articles in journals such as the *American Review of Canadian Studies*, the *Canadian Historical Review*, the *International Journal*, and *Canadian Ethnic Studies*. Her work focuses on human rights activism, social movements, and immigration and refugee policy in Canadian history.

CONTRIBUTORS

KATELYN ARAC is a Postdoctoral Fellow in the Office of the UPA: Equity, Diversity, and Inclusion at Wilfrid Laurier University. Her research focuses on the immigration of Nazi war criminals into Canada after the Second World War and how reactions to their presence have shaped the national project. Multiculturalism and national identity were crucial concepts that the Commission of Inquiry on War Criminals was forced to address. Her work focuses on a broad analysis of this commission, from how the past informed the proceedings to how the commission influenced future actions. Her research interests include immigration and legal history, law and society, human rights, Indigenous studies, and First Nations history.

RUTH FRAGER is a Professor Emerita in the Department of History at McMaster University, where she taught Canadian history, American history, and women's studies. She has published two books: *Discounted Labour: Women Workers in Canada, 1870–1939* (University of Toronto Press, 2005, co-authored with Carmela Patrias), and *Sweatshop Strife: Class, Ethnicity, and Gender in the Jewish Labour Movement of Toronto, 1900–1939* (University of Toronto Press, 1992). More recently, she has published articles on aspects of Canada's human rights history in the *Canadian Historical Review, Histoire sociale/Social History*, and *Canadian Jewish Studies*.

DAVID GOUTOR is the Director of the School of Labour Studies at McMaster University. He teaches courses in labour history, theory, and technology and future of work. He pursues contemporary research on the living wage and the basic income guarantee and on historical research on unions, immigration, human rights campaigns, and international leftist political activism. His major publications include *Guarding the Gates: The Canadian Labour Movement and Immigration, 1872–1934* (UBC Press, 2007), *Taking Liberties: A History of Human Rights in Canada* (Oxford University Press, 2013, co-edited with Stephen Heathorn), and *A Chance to Fight Hitler: A Canadian Volunteer in the Spanish Civil War* (Between the Lines, 2018).

RHONDA HINTHER is a Professor in the Department of History at Brandon University and an active public historian. She is a co-editor with Jim Mochoruk of *Civilian Internment in Canada: Histories and Legacies* (University of Manitoba Press, 2020) and a co-editor with Mochoruk and Jim Naylor of *For a Better World: The Winnipeg General Strike & The Workers' Revolt* (University of Manitoba Press, 2022). She is also the author of *Perogies and Politics: Canada's Ukrainian Left, 1891–1991* (University of Toronto Press, 2018), a Wilson Prize finalist in 2019. Hinther is currently writing a book on the extended Walsh-Weir-Boyd-Steele family's Second World War internment experiences, and researching North American brothel museums and their treatment of sex worker histories from the mid-nineteenth to late-twentieth centuries.

JASMINE HOLDING BROWN graduated from the University of Hull in 2024 with a PhD in Sociology and Social Anthropology. Her doctoral research examined connections between two highly exploitative child "care" systems—British child migration and Canada's residential school system. Her thesis traced the transmission of ideas, practices, and children through colonial circuits that underpinned the building of Britain's "white" empire from its inception into the mid-twentieth century. She currently works part-time as a lecturer in the School of Humanities and Cultural Studies at Leeds Beckett University and as a teaching assistant in special needs education. She is developing a project exploring care justice in communities where grassroots activism has built radical alternatives to mainstream provisions.

TOM HOOPER is an Assistant Professor in the Department of Equity Studies at York University. He is a historian of 2SLGBTQ+ communities in Canada. His research has explored the 5 February 1981 bathhouse raids, in which over 300 gay men were arrested and criminally charged for their sexuality, with a focus on the community resistance to these raids both on the streets and in the courts. Hooper critically examines the construction of dominant queer historical narratives, including the myth that legal changes in 1969 represented the decriminalization of homosexuality in Canada. He also investigates the use and misuse of heritage grants provided to 2SLGBTQ+ organizations.

DANIEL MANULAK is a SSHRC Postdoctoral Fellow in the Department of History at the University of Toronto. His research interests include contemporary international and global history, modern Canada, modern Africa, decolonization, human rights, emotions, and race. His first book, *Canada, Apartheid, and the Defence of the Liberal Order*, is forthcoming with UBC Press in 2026. His recent work has appeared in *Diplomatic History*, the *American Review of Canadian Studies*, and the *Canadian Historical Review*.

MARÍA CRISTINA MANZANO-MUNGUÍA is a Research Professor in the Institute of Social Sciences and Humanities at the Benemérita Universidad Autónoma de Puebla in Puebla, Mexico and Adjunct Professor of the Department of Canadian and Indigenous Studies at Mount Allison University. She received her PhD from Western University in 2009. Her research explores decolonization and the politics of settler state and Indigenous relations. Manzano-Munguía is a member of the National Research Council and belongs to the academic research group Racism, Identities, and Modes of Subjectivity. She has published work on issues related to Indigenous forced transnationalism across borderlands, First Nations transnationalism, Indian diaspora, Indian policy and legislation in Canada, and Indigenous mobility. Her current research interests include Indigenous transnationalism, return migrant students' citizenship, and Indigenous intercultural education.

ASA MCKERCHER is Steven K. Hudson Research Chair in Canada-US Relations and an associate professor at St. Francis Xavier University. His books include *Canada First, Nor Canada Alone: A History of Canadian Foreign Policy* (Oxford, 2024) and *Canada and the World since 1867* (Bloomsbury, 2019). Editor-in-Chief of *International Journal*, he is a Senior Fellow at the Bill Graham Centre for Contemporary International History.

JANET MIRON is an Associate Professor in the Department of History at Trent University. Her research interests include medical and criminal history, asylums and prisons, the history of suicide in Canada, and Indigenous-settler relations. Miron is the author of *Prisons, Asylums, and the Public: Institutional Visiting in the Nineteenth Century* (University of Toronto Press, 2011) and the editor of the collection *A History of Human Rights in Canada: Essential Issues* (Canadian Scholars Press, 2009). She is currently working on a history of suicide in Canada from the late eighteenth century to the twentieth century.

FRANCO PAZ is a doctoral candidate at Harvard University. He completed his MA at the University of Vermont. His forthcoming book, *The Ends of the Earth: A Global History of Capitalism and Slavery*, will be published in 2025 with Penguin.

PAUL-ETIENNE RAINVILLE is an Adjunct Professor in the Department of History at Carleton University. He completed his doctoral dissertation in 2018 on the history of the struggle for human rights in Quebec from the postwar period to the Quiet Revolution (1945–60). His research interests include the history of citizenship, the state, interethnic relations, colonialism and identity, social movements, and human rights. Rainville is the recipient of the Prize for the Best Article (French) from the Groupe d'histoire politique of the Canadian Historical Association (2019) and the Political Book Prize from the Assemblée nationale du Québec (2019). He is also Scientific Coordinator of the Montreal History Group (Université du Québec à Montréal) and of the group Penser et agir pour la paix au Québec (Université de Montréal), he is Co-Director of the axis Immigration, everyday life and religion at the Center for Interdisciplinary Research on Montreal (McGill University) and Human Rights Policy Officer at the Ligue des droits et libertés (LDL).

Dr. Asayenes is the Spirit name of **DR. DAN ISAAC SMOKE**, a member of the Seneca Nation (Six Nations). He received a Ph.D. (ad honorem) from Western University (2022) and attended Princeton University, class of '77. Dr. Smoke spent his 70 years as a committed learner, activist, journalist at the Oka Crisis in Kanesatake, knowledge keeper, elder, and professor at Western University. He was a trusted, uniting voice for people across Turtle Island with Smoke Signals (radio program). Dan held a firm commitment to the Indigenous notion of "All my relations." For him, it mattered to bring Indigenous and non-Indigenous people to a place of common understanding, unity, and relatedness through increasing accessibility of Indigenous education and worldview that will carry forth through his legacy. Dan, a proud member of the Six Nations of the Grand River territory, husband to Mary Lou Smoke, father to Shayne Smoke, and cherished grandfather to Ryan Mitreski and Angelique Belcourt.

DR. MARY LOU SMOKE is Anishinawbe Kwe from Batchawana Bay. She was very fortunate to share 53 years with the love of her life (Dr. Dan Smoke) while travelling, attending Ceremonies, learning about her own history, culture, protocols, and conducting Ceremonies for and of her people as told by her Elders. She is a point of reference for grassroots knowledge about First Nations and a decolonizer of what is written in the history books, which were mostly written by colonizers, and which were believed by many of her people. She is continuing the work that she and her husband, Dr. Dan Smoke, have been doing to help their people heal from intergenerational trauma.

JAMES W.ST.G. WALKER is a Distinguished Professor Emeritus of the Department of History at the University of Waterloo. He is a leading scholar of Canadian race relations, Black history, immigration history, and Canadian human rights history. His most well-known publications are *The Black Loyalists* (University of Toronto Press, 1976, 1992, 2017), *"Race," Rights and the Law in the Supreme Court of Canada* (The Osgoode Society for Canadian Legal History and Wilfrid Laurier University Press, 1997), and *Burnley "Rocky" Jones: Revolutionary* (Fernwood Publishing, 2016). Walker was a Bora Laskin National Fellow in Human Rights Research, is a Fellow of the Royal Society of Canada, and received the Order of Canada in 2016.

DAVID WEBSTER is a Professor of History and Global Studies at Bishop's University. His research interests include international and Asian history, with a focus on the twentieth century. His book *Fire and the Full Moon: Canada and Indonesia in a Decolonizing World* (UBC Press, 2009) examines Canada-Indonesia relations from 1945 to 1999 at both government and civil society levels. Webster also edited the collection *East Timor Testimony* (Between the Lines, 2004). His research concentrates on trans-Pacific interactions between Canada and Asia and on the diplomacy of independence movements in Asia.

HARVEY AMANI WHITFIELD is the Centennial Carnegie Chair in the History of Slavery in Canada at the University of King's College and Professor of History at Dalhousie University. He is the author of several books including *North to Bondage: Loyalist Slavery in the Maritimes* (UBC Press, 2016) and *Biographical Dictionary of Enslaved Black People in the Maritimes* (University of Toronto Press, 2022).

Introduction

Jennifer Tunnicliffe and Stephanie Bangarth

IN DECEMBER 2023, the global community commemorated the seventy-fifth anniversary of the United Nations Universal Declaration of Human Rights (UDHR). The UDHR was the first international instrument to set out a list of fundamental human rights to be universally protected. In recognizing this milestone, Canadian Minister of Heritage Pascale St-Onge claimed that, "throughout history, Canadians have stood at the forefront of the human rights movement, helping to shape a more inclusive Canada."[1] St-Onge presented the anniversary of the UDHR as an occasion for Canadians to learn more about their own history of human rights, including the activists who historically have fought to advance human rights protections and to acknowledge the inequalities that persist in Canada.

St-Onge's statement reflects a common government and public narrative of Canada's human rights history, one that recognizes the discrimination and inequality that have shaped Canada's past yet is overwhelmingly celebratory in tone, presenting Canada and Canadians as long-time advocates of human rights and advancing the idea of a "triumph" of human rights in Canadian society. The power of this narrative was reflected in a 2018 Environics survey that found that a strong majority of Canadians believe that support for human rights at home (historically and in the present) has been one of the most important areas in which Canada acts as a role model for other countries around the world.[2] This survey underscores the persistence of a sense of Canadian exceptionalism, which scholars Vinh Nguyen and Thy Phu describe as the "belief that what sets Canada apart from other nation-states is its distinct benevolence and commitment to human rights."[3]

Much work has been done to counter this understanding of Canada. Indigenous, Black, and other racialized communities continue to fight against persistent notions of Canadian history that celebrate tolerance, inclusion, and multiculturalism without recognizing histories of white supremacy, slavery, settler colonialism, and racist immigration policies. Scholars such as Robyn Maynard demonstrate how, rather than exposing injustice in Canada's past, Black history—in particular Canada's role as a "safe haven" for Black Americans fleeing slavery through the Underground Railroad—too often is used to reinforce myths about Canada as an "exemplar of human rights."[4] According to Deirdre McCorkindale, when Canada uses this narrative to "champion itself as a bastion of freedom it does so at the expense of community-level Black efforts to make that reality possible."[5] Similarly, Indigenous communities and activists have pushed for changes to how Indigenous history is understood and taught in Canada. Call to Action 62 from the Truth and Reconciliation Commission urges "education for reconciliation," calling for the insertion of an age-appropriate curriculum into schools to ensure that all students are taught the history of settler colonialism in Canada, including the devastating consequences of the residential school system, and to integrate Indigenous knowledge, teaching methods, and history into the classroom.[6]

Over the past twenty-five years, critical historical scholarship has expanded to focus on a wide range of rights-related topics, including children's rights, language rights, gender discrimination, disability rights, 2SLGBTQ+ rights, and human rights in Canadian international relations. This scholarship reflects trends in critical human rights theory by highlighting how triumphant narratives of human rights advances can be used to conceal histories of injustice or obscure the tensions and competing interests within understandings and practices of human rights. The work of Carmela Patrias and Ruth Frager, for example, illustrates how the question of sex discrimination in postwar Ontario was largely ignored by activists who campaigned against racist and religious discrimination in the early postwar period, allowing for "sex" to be excluded as a protected ground within many early human rights laws.[7] Tom Hooper's research debunks the myth that homosexuality was "decriminalized" in Canada in 1969, exposing how present-day celebrations of this "decriminalization" obstruct awareness of the continued persecution of and violence toward queer communities in Canada.[8] Historical studies such as these help to reveal the discrepancies and nuances in how "human rights" have been understood, fought for, practised, and remembered throughout Canada's past.

Notwithstanding the work of historians such as Ross Lambertson and Christopher MacLennan, who link Canada's formal civil liberties organizations to the 1930s, much of the historical scholarship on human rights in Canada to date emphasizes the post-1945 era.[9] This is partly because of the rise of sustained equal rights campaigns after the Second World War, but it also reflects debates in the broader (and global) historiography over "human rights" origins. Historian Samuel Moyn, in *The Last Utopia: Human Rights in History*, argues that today's concept of human rights—universally applicable and internationally protected—began in the 1970s with figures such as President Jimmy Carter, diverging from earlier claims rooted in the American and French Revolutions or post–Second World War humanitarianism.[10]

This perspective has influenced some Canadian human rights scholars who focus less on earlier rights conceptions in Canada's history. However, the exact use of terms such as "human rights" is less important than their presence and utility across contexts. Examining how people used rights language historically reveals its evolving role as a tool with diverse meanings across time. The contributors to this volume demonstrate that the discourse of human rights is the product of specific social and cultural contexts. If we see human rights as part of shifting cultural values, then assigning a particular decade—such as the 1970s—as a "watershed" is problematic. Today's human rights movement in Canada stems from a decades-long cultural transformation driven by activists and social movements rather than a sudden breakthrough. And more importantly, as this volume demonstrates, this cultural and political transformation continues and remains deeply contested.

Although there has been substantial growth in the scholarship on human rights in recent years, it has been more than a decade since the publication of the last edited collection of historical studies of human rights in Canada, *Taking Liberties: Historicizing Human Rights in the 20th Century English-Speaking World*, edited by David Goutor and Stephen Heathorn.[11] That collection explored the transition of civil liberties and other rights discourses to the universalism of human rights that emerged after the Second World War, highlighting the tensions and struggles that this transition caused both domestically and in Canada's relationship with the emerging international rights regime.

Not only has this field of historical study grown, but also the recent explosion of social movement activity demonstrates that the time is right for scholars to revisit Canada's human rights history. A host of forces—from #MeToo to Black Lives Matter and the Land Back movement, along with concerns engendered by the COVID-19 pandemic, the discoveries of unmarked graves at former residential school sites, legislative attempts to restrict trans youth from using their preferred names or pronouns at school without parental consent, and Canada's engagement in the conflicts in Ukraine and the Middle East—contribute to the need to reassess how human rights historically have been understood and mobilized, to deconstruct national narratives and myths of human rights, and to question critically to whom these rights have been applied and at what cost.

The idea for this collection emerged out of a workshop held jointly by King's University College and Toronto Metropolitan University in May 2022. Following two years of the pandemic, we conceived of the project both as an occasion to gather as a community of scholars after such prolonged isolation and as an opportunity to discuss how to connect Canada's human rights past with contemporary issues of rights that seemed to be so pressing. The workshop included participants from a variety of career stages, some who identified as human rights historians or scholars, others who newly oriented their work to the field. We invited the workshop participants to reassess human rights in Canadian history, both the history itself and how it has been approached by historians, hoping to provoke discussions about the strengths and limitations of Canada's history with human rights.

In addition to presenting research papers, workshop participants reflected on best practices of and approaches to teaching human rights in the classroom, considering how to connect scholarship on Canada's human rights history to lived experiences in ways meaningful to students, how to teach collaboratively, how to engage with contemporary challenges to the human rights framework, and how to reflect the interdisciplinary and transnational nature of the field. This pedagogical discussion led to the publication, in 2023, of a special issue of the *American Review of Canadian Studies*, which included a roundtable discussion of the teaching of human rights history and two research contributions that encourage us to think more critically about how we approach the study and teaching of human rights history.[12]

The chapters in this collection build upon the research and pedagogical discussions of the workshop and the journal issue. The contributors challenge the idea of Canadian exceptionalism in the area of human rights, at home and in Canada's dealings with other nations. Through histories that capture the personal and emotional stories of the denial of rights in Canada's past, the contributors highlight how "justice," "equality," and even "human rights" have been used inconsistently, at times to promote the rights and well-being of some above others. In doing so, they offer insights into the limitations of how human rights have been understood and practised in Canada, with several contributors urging a reassessment of the historical focus on liberal individualism within our human rights system. The chapters similarly highlight the key role of communities and individuals in resisting the inconsistencies and inequalities in Canada's human rights system, hoping to reshape understandings of human rights to promote a more egalitarian society. To varying degrees, they show that, although studying power often involves examining societal elites, a full understanding of how power operates requires looking at the cultural attitudes that shape it and exploring the relationship between these elites and the broader civil society. The chapters emphasize that, although the government has played an important role in advancing human rights in Canada (mainly through protective legislation), it has not been the primary driver of the human rights movement.

James Walker begins the collection with a historiographical analysis of the field of Canadian human rights history. Focusing on trends over the past two decades, he explores common themes and questions raised in the scholarship and situates them alongside parallel socio-political and cultural developments in Canadian society. As one of the first Canadian historians to engage with human rights history, Walker reflects on the place of human rights in the continuing reinterpretation of Canadian history.

The remainder of the collection is divided into four thematic sections. The first section—"Human Rights for Whom?"—questions whose rights have been conceptualized as human rights, how these conceptions have changed over time, and at what cost. The chapters in this section examine the histories of Black Canadians, Indigenous Peoples, women, and children to illustrate how certain groups were excluded from the rights and protections of Canada's emerging human rights state. They illustrate how discourses of rights and freedoms operated at times in tandem with, rather than counter to, the ideas of "civilization," "development," and "modernization" that characterized settler colonialism, white supremacy, and patriarchy in Canadian society.

Jasmine Holding Brown begins the section by examining the parallels and intersections between the forced migration of children from Britain to Canada, between 1869 and 1950, and the incarceration of Indigenous children in residential schools. She demonstrates how the "best interests" of these "uncivilized" (poor migrant and Indigenous) children were effectively tied to Britain's imperial agenda and the attainment of a "white Canada forever." A system of elimination (of Indigenous children) and replacement (with white British children) helped to consolidate the settler colony, and this process was legitimized by emerging humanitarian and human rights discourses focused on "saving" the child. As Holding-Brown demonstrates, not all children were viewed and treated equally in this early era of children's rights.

Ruth Frager also questions whose rights counted in her study of antiracist activists and feminists during the development of Ontario's early rights-related laws. She considers under which historical circumstances women's rights have been conceptualized as human rights. In focusing on changes to Ontario legislation, from antiracist laws in the 1950s that omitted sex discrimination to human rights laws that included sex as a prohibited ground for discrimination in the 1970s, Frager points to shortcomings of the Canadian tradition of viewing rights through the lens of liberal individualism, which she argues promoted a narrow understanding of "equality of opportunity" that often excluded women.

Franco Paz and Harvey Amani Whitfield conclude this section by challenging well-known narratives of African American freedom in Canada through the brutal story of Elizabeth Watson, whose re-enslavement and death complicate our understanding of the relationship between freedom and slavery in the Atlantic world. In bringing Watson's story to light—a story that, like those of so many other enslaved peoples, has been silenced by the archive and erased from the history—Paz and Whitfield highlight the "world of unfreedom" experienced by those of African ancestry in what would become Canada.

The second section—"Incarceration, Criminalization, and Human Rights in Canada"—explores the uneven ways in which the nebulous concept of "justice" has been applied in Canada throughout its history, situating prisons, policing, and the courts as important sites of injustice. The contributors to this section expose how the criminal justice system has been used to regulate certain groups deemed dangerous to society, using their alleged "threat" as a justification for violating their basic human rights, while failing to act in other cases in ways that challenge the principle of equality before the law in Canada, past and present.

As Rhonda Hinther notes in Chapter 5, Canadian authorities have long employed a host of carceral strategies to contain "troublesome" communities (of racialized migrants, political dissenters, Indigenous Peoples). The Second World War was a particularly intensive period for the deployment of this strategy of containment, typically in the form of internment. The far left in Canada was a key target of this era of carceral repression. Hinther examines the experiences of an extended family of leftists, the various sides of which came out of the Ukrainian and Jewish lefts, and her chapter speaks to the personal, familial, and emotional consequences of violations of human rights.

Janet Miron explores the history of the use of isolation in Canadian penitentiaries and the persistence of the practice in the current correctional system, arguing that this practice demonstrates the inconsistent application of human rights and the ease with which certain populations (in this case prisoners) can be excluded from them. Similarly, Katelyn Arac highlights inconsistencies in how "justice" is dispensed by examining the subject of war criminals in Canada. The lack of scrutiny regarding their entry into Canada provides an excellent lens through which to critique Canada's national project, which came to be identified increasingly with the ideals of ethnic pluralism and multiculturalism while simultaneously adhering to and enforcing the edicts of settler colonialism and the ongoing oppression of Indigenous Peoples. Arac maintains that Canada's delayed legal action against alleged war criminals needs to be understood in conjunction with the state's inability to acknowledge its failures in national policy.

The third section—"Human Rights Activists and Activism in Canada"—explores grassroots, non-governmental organizations and their role in promoting human rights as a tool for greater social justice and equality. Building upon a strong literature on the role of community and citizen activists in promoting human rights, this section brings in new perspectives from queer activists, postwar labour activists, rights organizations in Quebec, and urban Indigenous populations to illustrate the variety of ways in which rights have been conceptualized in Canada, how the language of "universal human rights" has worked at local levels, and the key role of non-state actors in constructing ideas of and policies on human rights in Canada.

Tom Hooper opens this section by revisiting the history of the 1981 bathhouse raids and the ensuing street protests by Toronto's queer community, challenging popular narratives of the protests and situating them within the evolution of Pride Toronto. His research exposes the continued criminalization of, and escalated police violence toward, 2SLGBTQ+ people in the early 1980s and showcases the building of broader coalitions both within the community and with straight, Black, Indigenous, and other activists within these resistance movements.

In Chapter 9, David Goutor explores the influence of human rights campaigns on Canadian labour leaders' views of immigration in the 1940s. From the start of the labour movement in the 1870s through the 1930s, unionists were among the most vocal and energetic opponents to large-scale immigration to Canada. By the 1940s, labour leaders abandoned most of this opposition and especially their explicitly racist and exclusionary rhetoric. Goutor shows that human rights activists—many of whom came from within the labour movement itself in the new wave of organizing during the Second World War—played a key role in driving this change. In particular, human rights campaigns convinced labour leaders that racism and anti-immigrant sentiment were social forces that mostly benefited conservatives and would empower social and political forces hostile to the mass unions emerging during the 1940s.

Paul-Etienne Rainville's chapter offers a more in-depth analysis of the debates that stirred Quebec civil society during the 1940s and 1950s concerning recognition of the principles enshrined in the 1948 UDHR. Based on a comparative study of local NGOs from various sectors of civil society (students, unions, Catholics, nationalists, ethnic and racialized groups, etc.), Rainville argues that human rights discourse became one of the main instruments of mobilization, contestation, and social change for the social movements active in the decade leading to the Quiet Revolution in Quebec in the 1960s. The chapter brings an untold perspective to the story of human rights since Quebec largely has remained on the margin of the human rights history and narratives in Canada.

Finally, this section acknowledges the failure of the national project when it comes to Indigenous people in Canada, and by incorporating research with an Indigenous lens, Maria Manzano-Munguía explores how First Nations non-governmental organizations advocate for and honour human rights for Indigenous people in Canada. She and her collaborators, Dan and Mary-Lou Smoke,[13] explore how the language of "universal human rights" works at the local level through First Nations organizations that serve as the cultural mediators for grassroots constructions of human rights. At the heart of this chapter is the acknowledgement that Indigenous people in Canada still resist and negotiate multiple experiences of genocide, poverty, violence, racism, political isolation, and economic inequality.

The final section—"Canada, Foreign Policy, and Transnational Human Rights Approaches"—places Canada's human rights history into a global context. Through either a comparative lens or by highlighting transnational connections and international influences, the authors of the chapters in this section ask how human rights shaped Canada's global relations (both governmental and citizen), question the relationship between national and international human rights regimes, and consider how human rights norms have diffused across the globe.

The section opens with Asa McKercher's chapter, which focuses on three broad themes: the place of rights promotion in government diplomacy, Canadian activists' rights promotion efforts as a form of citizen diplomacy, and how international human rights discourse exposed domestic rights abuses within Canada. McKercher's research problematizes the notion of the rights revolution and highlights the transnational connections and international influences of that revolution particularly as they pertain to Canadian foreign policy broadly conceived.

Through case studies, Daniel Manulak and David Webster show how human rights norms can adapt to shifts in international sentiment. Manulak examines South Africa to offer a more nuanced analysis of how human rights and national interest have interacted in shaping Canadian foreign policy. Meanwhile, Webster urges scholars to move beyond a Eurocentric perspective, emphasizing how Asian rights traditions have also influenced Canada's human rights culture.

Where to Go Next?

The goal of this collection is to continue to push the study of human rights history, not only to critique Canada's past and to consider how and why understandings of rights and legislative protection for human rights have changed, but also to question the system itself. The intention is that researchers will be moved to explore the tensions, question the underlying assumptions, and understand better how human rights can be used at cross-purposes sometimes to do harm. The study of human rights expands our view of who qualifies as "political actors" and deepens our understanding of how politics extends through law, the evolution of liberalism and its role in Canada's rights movement, and the impact of human rights principles on the system more broadly.

It seems to be apropos to return to the issue of Canadian exceptionalism that we mentioned earlier. If anything, the study of human rights in Canadian contexts has led the way in pushing back at the traditional narrative of the peaceable kingdom with a commitment to human rights. The world, including Canada, continues to be shaken by protests, both disruptive and peaceful, that speak to economic need and injustice as well as conflict, war, and genocide. Homelessness, poverty, and other forms of economic insecurity continue to challenge the human rights state. Although we maintain the principle that all human rights are indivisible and interdependent, it is fair to note that the approach to economic, social, and cultural rights is separated from the approach to civil and political rights. The degree of progress in civil and political rights, often referred to as the "first generation" of human rights, such as the right to religion, speech, and assembly, is mainly based on observing infractions (e.g., incidences of censorship), whereas progress in economic, social, and cultural rights, the "second generation" of human rights, is often realized over time. To complicate matters further, the emerging "third generation" of collective rights, such as the right to self-determination, the right to a healthy environment, and the rights to intergenerational equity and sustainability, among other examples of a broad spectrum of human rights, are often found in agreements that are not legally binding, such as the UDHR and the 1992 Rio Declaration on Environment and Development. This generation of rights finds greater challenge at the national level, but it has found better expression at the international level, for many of the issues are overlapping global concerns, fostering heightened awareness on a global level.

Will the next volume of human rights studies reflect the global interconnectedness of rights issues of poverty, environmental justice, and intergenerational equity? What will that look like from a Canadian perspective? How will Canadian exceptionalism compel us to challenge or prevent us from challenging these global issues? International human rights law has been central to the liberal international order despite Canada's complicated relationship with it. This international order continues to be under threat because of the challenges noted here. This collection demonstrates that Canadians, through grassroots and traditional measures, have done the heavy lifting of creating this perception of Canadian exceptionalism. But when our international partners come calling, what will our answer be?

Notes

1 Pascale St-Onge, "Commemorating the 75th Anniversary of the Universal Declaration of Human Rights," Government of Canada, 6 December 2023, https://www.canada.ca/en/canadian-heritage/campaigns/declaration-human-rights.html.

2 Environics Institute, *Canada's World Survey 2018: Final Report*, April 2018, 6, https://www.environicsinstitute.org/docs/default-source/project-documents/canada's-world-2018-survey/canada's-world-survey-2018---final-report.pdf.

3 Vinh Nguyen and Thy Phu, *Refugee States: Critical Refugee Studies in Canada* (Toronto: University of Toronto Press, 2021), 3.

4 Robyn Maynard, "The Struggle against Anti-Blackness in Canada," *Roar*, 3 July 2020, https://roarmag.org/essays/the-struggle-against-anti-blackness-in-canada/.

5 Deirdre McCorkindale, "Weaponized History: The Underground Railroad's Mythologized Legacy in Canada," *American Review of Canadian Studies* 53, no. 1 (2023): 75.

6 Truth and Reconciliation Commission of Canada, *Truth and Reconciliation Commission of Canada: Calls to Action*, https://ehprnh2mwo3.exactdn.com/wp-content/uploads/2021/01/Calls_to_Action_English2.pdf.

7 Ruth A. Frager and Carmela Patrias, "Human Rights Activists and the Question of Sex Discrimination in Postwar Ontario," *Canadian Historical Review* 93, no. 4 (2012): 583–610.

8 Tom Hooper, "Queering '69: The Recriminalization of Homosexuality in Canada," *Canadian Historical Review* 100, no. 2 (2019): 257–73.

9 Ross Lambertson, *Repression and Resistance: Canadian Human Rights Activists, 1930–1960* (Toronto: University of Toronto Press, 2005); and Christopher MacLennan,

Toward the Charter: Canadians and the Demand for a National Bill of Rights, 1929–1960 (Montreal and Kingston: McGill-Queen's University Press, 2004).

10 Samuel Moyn, *The Last Utopia: Human Rights in History* (Boston: Belknap Press, Harvard University Press, 2010).

11 David Goutor and Stephen Heathorn, *Taking Liberties: Historicizing Human Rights in the 20th Century English-Speaking World* (Toronto: Oxford University Press, 2013).

12 "Revisiting Human Rights: Reflections on the Teaching and Study of Human Rights in Canadian History," *American Review of Canadian Studies* 53, no. 1 (2023): 63–154.

13 On 4 November 2024, Dr. Dan Smoke, Indigenous Elder, educator, advocate, and activist, passed away. We are honoured to include his teaching in this volume.

CHAPTER 1

Reflections: Trends in Historical Writing on Human Rights in Canada

James W.St.G. Walker

IN 2002, I gave a paper at the University of Toronto Law School's Constitutional Roundtable.[1] Here is how it began:

> Pick up almost any text or commentary on human rights in Canada and you will find that politicians and governments, sometimes in league with the courts, are credited with the origin of our current human rights system. In one recent example, Howe and Johnson introduce their book *Restraining Equality* with the comment that "it has been state actors, and forces within the state, that have done most to develop and expand [Canadian human rights] legislation."[2] Charles Ungerleider, writing in *Canadian Ethnic Studies*, attributes the governmental initiative to international developments, particularly the Universal Declaration: "Unlike its neighbour to the south, Canada had neither a tradition of social justice . . . nor well-established groups of citizens advocating an expansion of that tradition. And, where the United States has had independent groups speaking out on behalf of disfranchised minorities, Canada's advocacy groups

> depend to a great extent upon the support of the state in order to change social policy and programs."[3]
>
> This interpretation is endorsed by a paper, "Human Rights and the Courts in Canada," issued by the Parliamentary Research Branch in June 1998. Because of its provenance, I take this version to be orthodoxy. It goes like this: Nazi atrocities led to the Universal Declaration of Human Rights, which in turn led governments to bring their own legislation into line with their international commitments. In Canada this process brought the 1960 *Bill of Rights*, but "unfortunately" the courts rendered it ineffective. "It is not surprising, then," this paper continues, that provinces brought in human rights codes of their own. Eventually, with the *Charter*, the federal government caught up, and the courts are finally protecting us as they should.[4] There is an organic quality to this whole sequence, as of something natural, inexorable, unfolding according to its own logic.

Things have changed since I wrote that paper in 2002.

In his 2021 article, "Reflections and Conjectures: Postcolonial Historical Practices,"[5] Andrew Nurse suggests that historical practice in Canada is in the process of changing. Partly, he argues, the recent attention to our narrative framework was prompted by Canadian and international events such as Black Lives Matter and the Truth and Reconciliation Commission. He notes that this reorientation is akin to a previous generation's "new social history movement," which displaced a "colony-to-nation" narrative focusing on political leadership.[6]

In a sense, the King's University College workshop and this subsequent volume of essays are a sequel to the 2012 Taking Liberties workshop, held at McMaster University and sponsored by the L.R. Wilson Institute for Canadian History. One of our current purposes is to examine whether and how rights-related historical literature written over the past decade has changed since 2012, which themes are most prominent in that literature, and the extent to which it reflects societal influences, as Nurse suggests.

A selection of the papers from the McMaster gathering was conveniently published in *Taking Liberties: A History of Human Rights in Canada*.[7] It can serve as a benchmark for our exploration of the state of the literature in 2012.

In his preface,[8] Michael Ignatieff wrote that the subject of "human rights has shaped our time because it is protean, because it can serve many masters and many purposes. Because it is protean, it is also deeply contested."[9] Editors David Goutor and Stephen Heathorn elaborated in their introduction:[10]

> human rights may be typically framed in terms of universal concepts, but they are in fact profoundly historical constructs. . . . There was little interest among historians in human rights up to almost the end of the twentieth century; [it was] primarily an area of interest for legal scholars and political scientists. . . . [Yet] it is currently one of the most vibrant areas of Canadian historiography. . . . The early literature not only lacked a historical dimension, it also focused on the state and the roles of political and legal elites in shaping policy. Recent historical scholarship has taken a much more bottom-up approach, focusing on the communities, organizations, and activists that helped create Canada's "rights revolution." . . . The flexible, subjective, and "inherently debatable" nature of rights talk has been another important theme of recent scholarship.[11]

The essays in *Taking Liberties* cover a variety of topics: citizens' campaigns for legal equality, individual contributions to the enhancement of rights, Canada and the United Nations human rights instruments, gender rights, children's rights, and Indigenous rights. But they all shared in the analytical orientation suggested by the editors' introduction, including social activism, bottom-up, civil society, contingency and context, a transnational perspective, bringing new interpretations, identifying agency, challenging myths, reassessing Canada's human rights record.

Since it came shortly after the McMaster workshop, Jennifer Tunnicliffe's 2014 "Canada and the Human Rights Framework: Historiographical Trends"[12] article can contribute to our benchmark. "Support for human rights is an increasingly important element of the Canadian identity,"[13] Tunnicliffe begins. She indicates that one important theme in the literature at that time was a "challenge to the characterization of Canada as a nation with a strong record of human rights protection."[14] Another theme was "the agency of individuals, minority groups, and rights organizations."[15] And she concludes that, "as the historiography reveals, Canadian human rights history is a vibrant field that offers more than a simple narrative of rights violations, resistance, and legislative change. It can be used to analyze structures of power and to dissect what patterns of discrimination and intolerance reveal about concepts of citizenship and belonging."[16]

About the time this article was published, Statscan released a "General Social Survey" on our shared national values and "What Makes Canadians Most Proud." Number one, with 92 percent agreeing, was human rights. Hockey came fifth with 77 percent.[17] So apparently Tunnicliffe was right: human rights are important to us, a part of our self-proclaimed identity.

Robin Winks suggested that one can learn more from the time in which a historian writes than the time about which the historian writes.[18] What happened in the past decade of relevance to human rights scholarship? What is *our* time?

In February 2012, about the time of the McMaster workshop, policeman George Zimmerman shot and killed teenager Trayvon Martin in Sanford, Florida. When a jury found Zimmerman not guilty, an international protest erupted that developed into the Black Lives Matter movement, denouncing police violence. There were newspaper headlines almost daily at the time. No one could have missed it.[19] Also in 2012, and closer to home for Canadians, was the Idle No More movement launched by Indigenous women on western reserves demanding Indigenous rights and a commitment to environmental stewardship. They also called, successfully, for a National Inquiry into Missing and Murdered Indigenous Women and

Girls (MMIWG). With demonstrations on Parliament Hill and in many parts of the country, no one could have missed this eruption either.[20]

The Truth and Reconciliation Commission (TRC) report came out in 2015, revealing the "cultural genocide" resulting from the Indian residential school system and issuing 94 Calls to Action addressing, *inter alia*, the writing and teaching of Indigenous history as part of a general revision of Canadian history.[21] This momentum was reinforced by the 2019 report of the National Inquiry into MMIWG, whose Calls for Justice highlighted the importance of historical education.[22] Then in May 2020 the murder of George Floyd sparked the largest protest marches in American history during the "summer of reckoning," deemed by some a second civil rights movement aimed at police violence and Black inequality.[23] And in 2021 came the discovery in Kamloops of unmarked children's graves near a former Indian residential school. Eventually, almost 2,000, and still counting, such graves were identified across the country, each report intensifying the concern felt by the Canadian population.[24]

The TRC report referred to "cultural genocide," but the unmarked graves gave powerful testimony to the interpretation of "actual genocide." The term remains controversial, but our own Canadian Historical Association (CHA) has issued a strong public statement confirming that the history of violence against Indigenous Peoples fully warrants its use.[25]

This cascade of public awareness has had an impact on our universities, reflected in an explosion of Black studies programs and "cohort" or "cluster" hires of Black and Indigenous faculty members;[26] diversity, equity, and inclusion (DEI) committees, policies, and officers have become ubiquitous at Canadian universities, often at the senior administrative levels;[27] more than forty institutions have signed on to the Scarborough Charter on Anti-Black Racism and Black Inclusion in Canadian Higher Education;[28] the Social Sciences and Humanities Research Council (SSHRC) has established an advisory committee to counteract racism and created an array of special awards for Indigenous students and others who conduct research on Indigenous topics;[29] and four of the five titles short-listed for the CHA 2022 Best Book in Canadian History Prize (formerly the John A. Macdonald

Prize) dealt with rights-related topics.[30] On 4 April 2022, the CHA hosted a webinar on the term "BIPOC"[31] (contested during the meeting), with Indigenous, South Asian, and African Canadian discussants. All of them spoke positively of the recent trends on university campuses, and though there were a few cautious remarks the tone of the discussion was encouraging. Also in April 2022, Toronto Metropolitan University arrived on the scene.

The obvious place to test historical scholarship in the period when all of this was happening would be our flagship journal, the *Canadian Historical Review*. The following discussion will proceed chronologically from volume 93, issue 1, in March 2012 to volume 103, issue 2, in June 2022.

Laura Madokoro led off the decade with her article on Chinese immigration in March 2012.[32] The 1947 repeal of the Chinese Immigration Act was "largely symbolic" because, among other things, the immigration of families of Chinese Canadians was severely restricted.[33] The Chinese Benevolent Association (CBA) launched an extended campaign for family reunification, with President Foon Sien Wong making annual trips to Ottawa to lobby for family sponsorship rights using arguments based on the new idiom of human rights. Government officials, however, resisted this pressure, fearing that the Chinese family structure would damage the Canadian ideal of a nuclear family, deemed essential for nurturing a democratic way of life. The CBA campaign became "fused" with a church-led movement in 1962 to demand the entry of refugees from mainland China sheltering in Hong Kong in crisis conditions.[34] The combined influence of the mainstream churches and Chinese Canadians led to amendments in immigration regulations, demonstrating the "critical role" of civil society in bringing about policy reforms.[35]

In the December issue of 2012, Ruth Frager and Carmela Patrias examined anti-discrimination legislation in Ontario.[36] Comparing the Fair Employment Practices Act and the Female Employees Fair Remuneration Act, both from 1951, they found a distinction between the rights of racialized minorities and women's rights. That this division seemed to be "artificial"[37] in 2012, they suggested, indicated "the fluidity of the concept of human rights and the need to understand this concept in specific historical contexts."[38] The understanding of equity in the postwar era accommodated very different views. The authors made an additional important innovation by examining implementation of the Acts, to demonstrate the persistence of discrimination, rather than focusing exclusively on the campaigns leading to the reforms. "The Canadian rights revolution," they concluded, "was yet to come."[39]

David Meren launched a discussion of Canadian international history in 2015.[40] Identifying a historiographical shift beginning about 2012, he saw growing awareness of the significance of Canada's place in world history. He lamented the omissions in earlier literature in three successive "tragedies."[41] The newer interpretations engaged with social and cultural issues of "race," class, and gender, as they shaped international activities, and they included analysis of civil society rather than simply governments in explaining transnational phenomena.[42] Continuing the international theme, Asa McKercher revisited John Diefenbaker's record with human rights and foreign policy.[43] As his main title, "Sound and Fury," suggests, McKercher challenged Diefenbaker's reputation as a domestic and an international force for human rights reform. Placing the former prime minister's initiatives in their international context, including the impact of colonial independence and North American civil rights movements, McKercher argued that Diefenbaker was a "vocal yet reluctant"[44] human rights crusader whose rhetoric remained largely symbolic. In Canada, "the main drivers of change," McKercher argued, "have been activists rather than state actors."[45] Still pursuing a transnational theme, Edward Dunsworth examined the seasonal migration of Southern Americans to work on Ontario tobacco farms.[46] Between 1920 and the 1960s, thousands of American workers went to Ontario, until 1966 all of them white. And the removal of the racist restriction, when it came, originated with the American officials who feared that it might violate the 1964 Civil Rights Act. Our own civil servants and employers neglected to record the racist character of the program, resulting in "archival silences." The article revealed Canadian collaboration in maintaining a transnational system of white supremacy, even during the very period when Canadian immigration regulations were being "deracialized"[47] by the Diefenbaker and Pearson governments.

Turning to domestic issues, in 2018 Paul-Etienne Rainville wrote on the Canadian Jewish Congress (CJC) in Quebec during the Duplessis years.[48] The fact that the provincial CJC was not active in major anti-government protests of the era illustrates the ideological, regional, and class divisions in Quebec's Jewish community and in the human rights community as well as tensions between Jews in Quebec and those in Ontario and western Canada. Rainville observed that human rights are a fluid discursive category that can be mobilized differently, according to the activists' ideologies, identities, and interests and the local context in which the activists operate.[49]

As part of a 2019 Historical Perspectives forum on "Reconsidering 1969" in Canadian public policy, Tom Hooper contributed a fiftieth-anniversary take on "Queering '69."[50] Like several of the authors discussed above, Hooper deconstructs a generally accepted historical interpretation. Although ostensibly Parliament had decriminalized sexual acts between same-sex individuals in the Criminal Law Amendment Act of 1969, homosexuality was recriminalized to an even greater extent with arrests and charges throughout the 1970s and 1980s for gross indecency and keeping or being found in a bawdy house, which had not been removed from the Criminal Code. Hooper asserted that the 1969 decriminalization was a myth that did not change the fundamental ways in which queers were treated in the Canadian justice system.[51]

In another important 2019 article, Stephanie Bangarth and Jennifer Tunnicliffe described a way to overcome some of the deficiencies of traditional historical interpretation in their article on "Writing Rights into the 'New' Political History."[52] "A focus on human rights has the potential to alter how we understand Canadian history," they announced, because "the study of human rights broadens whom we consider 'political actors.'"[53] They traced the move from "grand narratives and the great men"[54] to a bottom-up approach to history that analyzes how those "on the ground"[55] have conceptualized and used a language of rights, how rights have been employed as tools, and how they have taken on different meanings over time in different scenarios. The authors encouraged increased attention to the influence of human rights principles on foreign policy, and on corporate responsibility, areas that had been relatively neglected in the existing literature, and they reinforced an important point raised in several articles: "Human rights are an evolving concept."[56]

Reaching further back in historical time,[57] Harvey Amani Whitfield confronted the "dominant image of Canada as a land of freedom" by introducing the history of slavery in the Maritimes, "the most neglected aspect of pre-Confederation Canadian history."[58] This neglect is explained partly by inadequate archival documentation and partly because it goes against a cherished Canadian myth. Whitfield revealed the resources, though incomplete, that can be used to reconstruct the lives of enslaved African Canadians as he presented a sampling of six biographical sketches adapted from his newest book. He brought a transnational focus by describing links with the West Indies and the Southern United States, where further information can be discerned about individual lives. Whitfield maintained that the insights and details in biographical treatments provide one way to understand Canadian slavery more broadly.

Wendell Nii Laryea Adjetey's 2021 article "In Search of Ethiopia: Messianic Pan-Africanism and the Problem of the Promised Land, 1919–1931"[59] also stressed the transnational forces in African Canadian history, calling Canada an "integral site" in the Black Atlantic and African diaspora.[60] Pan-Africanism, and awareness of a heroic African past, Adjetey argued, promoted pride and "racial redemption" among those in the diaspora, leading to community building and Black liberation movements and culminating in decolonization in the Caribbean and Africa and the civil and human rights campaigns in Canada and the United States. In Canada during the interwar years, there was a "racial renaissance" when the Black Star of Marcus Garvey's Universal Negro Improvement Association (with twenty-eight Canadian chapters and some 5,000 members) eclipsed the North Star myth of the Underground Railroad.[61] The "fault lines of the Promised Land,"[62] Adjetey explained, were exposed during this period with "the birth of cross-border Ethiopianism,"[63] challenging not just Canada's venerated non-racist character but also the image of a docile African Canadian community so often ascribed to this era.

Focusing on the first international treaties regarding Indigenous rights in independent states, David Meren's "Safeguarding Settler Colonialism in Geneva: Canada, Indigenous Rights, and ILO Convention No. 107 on the Protection and Integration of Indigenous Peoples (1957)" compounded the challenge to the Canadian image of liberal internationalism while revealing the reality behind Canadian "Indian policy."[64] Meren characterized the ILO convention, establishing non-binding responsibilities for nation-states to "protect and integrate" their Indigenous populations, as "marked by settler colonialism and infused with assimilationist logic."[65] Although this was an era of independence movements in the overseas empires and the emerging international human rights system, Canada and other settler states persistently avoided their international commitments. Yet Meren contended more positively that the convention's resolutions were significant in "forcing Canada to respond to growing international interest in Indigenous rights and the 'development' of Indigenous Peoples."[66] His transnational approach offered a global perspective on an issue usually regarded as domestic.

A 2021 Historical Perspectives roundtable on "Commemoration and Memory" provided a viewpoint worth including in a discussion of Canadian human rights literature.[67] Considering the "heated debates about monuments and renaming swirling in Canadian society and well beyond," editor Matthew Hayday and his co-editors declared in their introduction that "just as historical writing is often informed by events unfolding as historians put pens to paper . . . monuments are reflections of the historiographical and methodological trends that were active in the discipline of history when they were created."[68] Monuments, they continued, "aim not just to teach about the past but also to instruct about desired political behaviour, establish collective identity, and reinforce the legitimacy of a particular political and social order."[69] Such is so often the case with expository writing that comes from the discipline of history.

In his second contribution to the decade of literature, Asa McKercher gave an analysis of the Edmund Burke Society in modern Canada, with its right-wing rejection of multiculturalism and the rights revolution.[70] He dubbed the society "a counter-counterculture" since it challenged the status quo and the New Left and its own critique of the way that things were. McKercher suggested that this story was "a reminder that the 1960s were not all Trudeaumania and flower power,"[71] that history is more complicated than its usual portrayal, and that the "progressive" social changes in the late twentieth century were not universally approved.

Crystal Gail Fraser and Allyson Stevenson reflected on how the Truth and Reconciliation Commission inspired a fundamental reckoning for the historical profession.[72] Noting that history was "front and centre" in the TRC report, they introduced the discovery of unmarked graves and the "genocidal nature" of the residential school system to conclude that "it is time to ask: how have history departments and historians taken up the Calls to Action and/or been directly engaged in efforts of reconciliation?"[73] This responsibility is especially pressing, they argued, while they also wondered provocatively whether our discipline "create[d] the ideological scaffolding upon which Canada and Canadians could build and sustain a nationwide system that incarcerated Indigenous children."[74] Fraser and Stevenson charged that, "as historians, we must immediately stop framing the history of Canada in nation-building narratives," because "this country was built on the destruction of sovereign Indigenous nations and the genocide of Indigenous peoples. Colonialism is the plot of the story, not a chapter."[75] This *cri de coeur* fits well with an analysis of how human rights, including Indigenous rights, have been interpreted in Canadian historical writing and why new interpretations are necessary to regenerate Canada's national narrative.

The final *Canadian Historical Review* entry in the decade from March 2012 to June 2022 was Daniel Manulak's retelling of Canada's role in South Africa's removal from the Commonwealth.[76] Appropriately, given its position at the end of the story, this article evoked and elaborated several themes that have arisen in the literature already discussed. The background facts are familiar. In a 1960 referendum, South Africans voted to adopt a republican style of government. But to remain in the Commonwealth as a republic, South Africa would have had to apply for permission from the other Commonwealth members. At first, Prime Minister John Diefenbaker was sympathetic to South Africa retaining its Commonwealth status. He said as much in the

House of Commons after the referendum, and even after the Sharpeville Massacre of 21 March 1961 the Canadian government condemned racism in general but omitted any direct criticism of South African apartheid.[77] The Afro-Asian Commonwealth members were unanimous in wanting to expel South Africa, whereas Britain and the "white dominions" were opposed. Components of Canadian civil society, including the Canadian Labour Congress and the mainstream churches, put pressure on the government to side with the Afro-Asians. Then, at the 1961 Commonwealth Conference, Diefenbaker played an "important if overstated" role: he moved that the Commonwealth adopt a set of common principles that would include racial equality.[78] Of course, South Africans could not agree to this provision and withdrew their application. The Commonwealth was saved, and division along lines of colour was avoided. Diefenbaker was lionized across the "new" Commonwealth and in Canada. For Canadians, his stand represented their national self-image of fairness and antiracism. Furthermore, to Diefenbaker and many of his fellow citizens, the Commonwealth was central to the liberal international order, which Canada loudly endorsed, whereas apartheid threatened to disrupt it. Two impressions emerge from this episode: first, of Canadians' featured image, at that time (and long afterward), as tolerant liberal internationalists; second, of the morally informed worldview that prompted civil society to mobilize for the rejection of apartheid South Africa and then to feel "proud" of Diefenbaker's "accomplishment."[79] And Manulak placed his narrative in the context of what he perceived as a historiographical shift during the very decade that serves as the focus of this reflection. In that period, Manulak wrote, historians were investigating Canada's interactions with the world "through the lens of race," in the process abandoning the "colour blind" interpretation of Canadian history and revealing that Canadian officials shared the attitudes of their Western partners, "casting non-white peoples as backward and uncivilized."[80] Some myths deserve to be shattered, as so many of the authors discussed above argued.

Overall, in the *Canadian Historical Review* from 2012 to 2022, there were seventeen articles on topics related to rights, thirteen on Indigenous topics, three roundtables or special issues, thirty-six reviews of books about rights, broadly understood, and ninety-one reviews of books on Indigenous topics, including two review essays. Material on rights, both articles and reviews, was scattered over the decade. Material on Indigenous topics increased over the years to a peak in 2021, with four articles, one special issue, and fifteen reviews.

In her review of Dominique Clément's *Human Rights in Canada: A History*, Laura Madokoro wrote that "these are interesting times for those studying the history of human rights."[81] The preceding description of articles in the *Canadian Historical Review* will have confirmed that observation. Topics included Indigenous rights, immigration, gender discrimination, movements for reform, foreign policy and other international topics, increasingly with a transnational orientation, 2SLGBTQ+ rights, Canadian slavery, politics, and societal issues. But regardless of the topic, the approaches taken by *Canadian Historical Review* authors were remarkably consistent. Certainly, "bottom up" comes immediately to mind, including attention to civil society and grassroots activism and resistance. No more elite leadership responsible for our rights advances. On the contrary, critiques of Canadian human rights practices and reforms, as established in earlier periods, comprised another theme. The fluidity of the rights concept and the diversity of interpretations were part of the sense of an exciting and expanding field of scholarship. Transnational cross-fertilization featured as a theme, and in the Indigenous literature settler colonialism became increasingly present, along with cultural genocide and outright, unqualified genocide in the most recent few years. And, finally, the linking to human rights of Canadians' self-image and national identity percolated throughout the literature of the decade.

Significantly, these thematic approaches were already noticed in 2012 in the essays in *Taking Liberties* and in the commentary by Jennifer Tunnicliffe. The direction taken by human rights reform processes in both of the articles in volume 93 (2012) would be carried forward until the end of the decade under examination, with volume 103 (2022). Does that mean that current events of dramatic proportions such as Black Lives Matter or Idle No More have had no impact on historical writing? Well, not exactly. The emphasis on grassroots initiatives had become reasonably well established even before these and the other events and movements occurred post-2012. The swell in writing about Indigenous issues since Idle No More, along with the calls for historical revision by the TRC and the National Inquiry into MMIWG, arguably have contributed an awareness inspiring scholarly as well as political and social attention. Both David Meren and Daniel Manulak identify a "historiographical shift" beginning about 2012 in the interpretation of Canada's international history, driven, to some extent at least, by Canadians' enlightenment about the power of "race" in determining domestic and overseas relations. The blinkers have been removed, as evidenced not only by this sampling of the literature but also by the public acceptance, for example, of the fact that people were once enslaved in Canada and that its legacy lives on in disadvantages experienced by African Canadians today. Some of the groundswell has been too recent to have a direct impact on historical scholarship that, as we all know, is a very slow operation. But it would be reasonable to conclude this review of the past decade's literature with the observation that "race," rights, social movements, citizen initiative, and myth busting now have prominent places in the continuing reinterpretation of Canadian history.

The essays in this volume both reflect and advance the trends and themes in the literature reviewed here. We see, for example, considerable attention to issues of justice—that is, *in*justice—revealing the duplicity and inconsistency of government officials and policies, police violence and arbitrary imprisonment, all of which contradict our self-image as a rights-respecting people. The "myth of the North Star," in particular, is a liability, for it carries a message that all is well in terms of race relations in Canada. Intervention or correction are unnecessary, or so it is understood. As the old adage put it, "if it ain't broke, don't fix it." Conventional wisdom is challenged in many of the chapters, and standard historiographical tropes are deconstructed and replaced. The newer narratives that appear here recognize grassroots activism, cooperation and solidarity among marginalized groups, and Canada's participation in the global phenomenon of settler colonialism.

Many of the themes found in the literature are displayed imaginatively here in different contexts, from residential schools to slavery, from children's rights to queer rights, with a lot of myth busting en route. Following the cue of Stephanie Bangarth and Jennifer Tunnicliffe's 2019 *Canadian Historical Review* article, there is a strong injection of international topics in this volume. It is clear that we are witnessing a growing, vibrant, and exciting field of historical scholarship, not only inherently interesting but also highly relevant to some of the dominant issues of the day.

It is worth remembering that history *as it is understood* enters a political discourse, it becomes a participant in a power dialectic, and it influences power relationships. The writing of history is a political act, and it deserves to be undertaken deliberately. This set of essays engages with just such a project. Progress is recognized, as are failed or partial efforts at reform. Significant lessons are presented here, instructive for activists as for citizens in a democratic society. The structural and historical roots of the inequality that persists in Canada are exposed, not for cynical purposes but to inspire intervention to close the gaps between ideals and reality. As the *Taking Liberties* volume did for its time, this collection can serve as a benchmark for the next decade's writing on the history of human rights in Canada.

Notes

1 James W.St.G. Walker, "Social Change and the Courts: The 'Race' Case," Constitutional Roundtable, University of Toronto Law School, 9 June 2002.

2 Brian Howe and David Johnson, *Restraining Equality: Human Rights Commissions in Canada* (Toronto: University of Toronto Press, 2000), xiv.

3 Charles S. Ungerleider, "Immigration, Multiculturalism, and Citizenship: The Development of the Canadian Social Justice Infrastructure," *Canadian Ethnic Studies* 24, no. 3 (1992): 18–19.

4 Nancy Holmes, "Human Rights and the Courts in Canada," Parliamentary Research Branch, Ottawa, 1998, 8–9.

5 Andrew Nurse, "Reflections and Conjectures: Postcolonial Historical Practices," *Scholarly and Research Communications* 12, no. 1 (2021): 1–12.

6 Nurse, 3.

7 David Goutor and Stephen Heathorn, eds., *Taking Liberties: A History of Human Rights in Canada* (Don Mills, ON: Oxford University Press, 2013).

8 Michael Ignatieff, preface to *Taking Liberties*, by David Goutor and Stephen Heathorn, v–ix.

9 Ignatieff, vi.

10 Goutor and Heathorn, introduction to *Taking Liberties*, 1–28.

11 Goutor and Heathorn, 1, 15–16.

12 Jennifer Tunnicliffe, "Canada and the Human Rights Framework: Historiographical Trends," *History Compass* 2, no. 10 (2014): 807–17.

13 Tunnicliffe, 807.

14 Tunnicliffe, 808.

15 Tunnicliffe, 809.

16 Tunnicliffe, 813.

17 Statistics Canada, "General Social Survey: What Makes Canadians Most Proud," 1 October 2013. As reported in: Denise Wong, "What makes Canadians proud? History tops the list in Statistics Canada survey," *City News*, 1 October 2015. https://vancouver.citynews.ca/2015/10/01/canadian-proud-history-statistics-canada.

18 Robin W. Winks, "Canada," in *The Historiography of the British Empire-Commonwealth: Trends, Interpretations and Resources*, ed. Robin W. Winks (Durham, NC: Duke University Press, 1966), 70.

19 See Black Lives Matter, https://blacklivesmatter.com/.

20 See Idle No More, https://idlenomore.ca/.

21 TRC, *Truth and Reconciliation Commission: Calls to Action*, Winnipeg: Truth and Reconciliation Commission of Canada, 2015. See especially Calls 27, 28, 62, 65, 86, and 93. https://ehprnh2mwo3.exactdn.com/wp-content/uploads/2021/01/Calls_to_Action_English2.pdf.

22 National Inquiry into MMIWG, *Reclaiming Power and Place*: *Final Report of the National Inquiry into MMIWG*, Vancouver, Privy Council Office, 2019. See especially Call for Justice 11.1, https://www.mmiwg-ffada.ca/final-report/.

23 "George Floyd," Wikipedia, https://en.wikipedia.org/wiki/George_Floyd.

24 Canadian Press, "Timeline of Events since Finding of Unmarked Graves in Kamloops," CTV News, 18 May 2022, https://www.ctvnews.ca/canada/timeline-of-events-since-finding-of-unmarked-graves-in-kamloops-1.5908292.

25 Canadian Historical Association, "The History of Violence against Indigenous Peoples Fully Warrants the Use of the Word 'Genocide,'" Canada Day Statement, 30 June 2021, https://cha-shc.ca/advocacy/the-history-of-violence-against-indigenous-peoples-fully-warrants-the-use-of-the-word-genocide/. Reflecting on his "penitential pilgrimage" to Canada in July 2022, Pope Francis confirmed to reporters during his return flight to Rome that Indigenous Peoples suffered genocide at residential schools. CTV News, 30 July 2022, https://www.ctvnews.ca/canada/article/pope-says-indigenous-people-suffered-genocide-at-residential-schools/.

26 Jenna Benchetrit, "Wave of Black Studies Programs at Canadian Universities," CBC News, 31 October 2021, https://www.cbc.ca/news/canada/new-black-studies-curriculums-1.6229321.

27 Leo Charbonneau, "Most universities report having equity, diversity and inclusion plans, but challenges remain," *University Affairs*, 5 November 2019, https://

universityaffairs.ca/news/most-universities-report-having-equity-diversity-and-inclusion-plans-but-challenges-remain/.

28 Tayo Bero, "Scarborough Charter Signals National Effort to Deal with Anti-Blackness on Campus," *University Affairs*, 2 December 2021, https://universityaffairs.ca/news/scarborough-charter-signals-national-effort-to-deal-with-anti-blackness-on-campus/.

29 SSHRC, *Advisory Committee to Address Anti-Black Racism in Research and Research Training: Final Reports and Recommendations*, 15 February 2022, https://www.sshrc-crsh.gc.ca/about-au_sujet/governance-gouvernance/committees-comites/racism-racisme/reports-rapports/2023/pdf/abr_report-rapport_rpn-eng.pdf.

30 Canadian Historical Association, "The CHA Best Scholarly Book in Canadian History Prize," 2022, https://cha-shc.ca/prize-winner/benjamin-hoy/.

31 BIPOC is the acronym for Black, Indigenous, and People of Colour.

32 Laura Madokoro, "'Slotting' Chinese Families and Refugees, 1947–1967," *Canadian Historical Review* 93, no. 1 (2012): 25–56.

33 Madokoro, 27.

34 Madokoro, 30.

35 Madokoro, 25.

36 Ruth A. Frager and Carmela Patrias, "Human Rights Activists and the Question of Sex Discrimination in Postwar Ontario," *Canadian Historical Review* 93, no. 4 (2012): 583–610, republished in 102, Supplement 3 (2021): 802–24.

37 Frager and Patrias, 584.

38 Frager and Patrias, 585.

39 Frager and Patrias, 610.

40 David Meren, "The Tragedies of Canadian International History," *Canadian Historical Review* 96, no. 4 (2015): 534–66. In a response to Meren, Dominique Marshall offered a different overview, arguing that Canadian historians indeed have studied transnational topics such as humanitarian aid, refugee policy, and the promotion of human rights, and she identified some authors who could have been included in Meren's article. Dominique Marshall, "Réponse à 'The Tragedies of Canadian International History': Un autre survol historiographique," *Canadian Historical Review* 96, no. 4 (2015): 583–89, part of a roundtable discussion on Meren's article.

41 Meren, 537.

42 Meren, 562.

43 Asa McKercher, "Sound and Fury: Diefenbaker, Human Rights, and Canadian Foreign Policy," *Canadian Historical Review* 97, no. 2 (2016): 165–94.

44 McKercher, 168.

45 McKercher, 169.

46 Edward Dunsworth, "Race, Exclusion, and Archival Silences in the Seasonal Migration of Tobacco Workers from the Southern United States to Ontario," *Canadian Historical Review* 99, no. 4 (2018): 563–93.

47 Dunsworth, 567, 591.

48 Paul-Etienne Rainville, "Au nom de l'ordre ou de la liberté? Le Congres juif canadien face à la répression des libertés civiles et des droits des minorités religieuses au Québec (1945–1954)," *Canadian Historical Review* 99, no. 2 (2018): 196–224.
49 Rainville, 197.
50 Tom Hooper, "Queering '69: The Recriminalization of Homosexuality in Canada," *Canadian Historical Review* 100, no. 2 (2019): 257–73. Also in the forum were reconsiderations of abortion reform, the White Paper on Indian policy, and the Official Languages Act. All of them challenged accepted interpretations, and all emphasized social movement activism.
51 Hooper, 258.
52 Stephanie Bangarth and Jennifer Tunnicliffe, "Writing Rights into the 'New' Political History," *Canadian Historical Review* 100, no. 4 (2019): 638–53.
53 Bangarth and Tunnicliffe, 638.
54 Bangarth and Tunnicliffe, 638.
55 Bangarth and Tunnicliffe, 641.
56 Bangarth and Tunnicliffe, 651.
57 Harvey Amani Whitfield, "White Archives, Black Fragments: Problems and Possibilities in Telling the Lives of Enslaved Black People in the Maritimes," *Canadian Historical Review* 101, no. 3 (2020): 323–45.
58 Whitfield, 324.
59 Wendell Nii Laryea Adjetey, "In Search of Ethiopia: Messianic Pan-Africanism and the Problem of the Promised Land, 1919–1931," *Canadian Historical Review* 102, no. 1 (2021): 53–78.
60 Adjetey, 53.
61 Adjetey, 56–57
62 Adjetey, 52.
63 Adjetey, 72.
64 David Meren, "Safeguarding Settler Colonialism in Geneva: Canada, Indigenous Rights, and ILO Convention No. 107 on the Protection and Integration of Indigenous Peoples (1957)," *Canadian Historical Review* 102, no. 2 (2021): 205–31.
65 Meren, 206.
66 Meren, 206.
67 Matthew Hayday, Tina Loo, and Catherine Desbarats, eds., "Introduction" to "I Wish It Were That Simple: Historical Perspectives on Commemoration and Memory" roundtable, *Canadian Historical Review* 102, no. 3 (2021): 414–16.
68 Hayday, Loo, and Desbarats, 414.
69 Hayday, Loo, and Desbarats, 415.
70 Asa McKercher, "The Edmund Burke Society and Right-Wing Extremism in Late 20th-Century Canada," *Canadian Historical Review* 103, no. 1 (2022): 75–99.
71 McKercher, 79.
72 Crystal Gail Fraser and Allyson Stevenson, "Reflecting on the Foundations of Our Discipline Inspired by the TRC: A Duty to Respond during this Age of Reconciliation," *Canadian Historical Review* 103, no. 1 (2022): 1–31.
73 Fraser and Stevenson, 2.

74 Fraser and Stevenson, 2.
75 Fraser and Stevenson, 26.
76 Daniel Manulak, "Blood Brothers: Race, the Afro-Asian-Canadian Bloc, and South Africa's Expulsion from the Commonwealth, 1960–61," *Canadian Historical Review* 103, no. 2 (2022): 252–76.
77 Manulak, 262.
78 Manulak, 268.
79 Manulak, 272.
80 Manulak, 254.
81 Laura Madokoro, review of *Human Rights in Canada: A History*, by Dominique Clément, *Canadian Historical Review* 97, no. 4 (2016): 599.

PART I

Human Rights for Whom?

CHAPTER 2

A Child's Right to Be Civilized? Human Rights, Children's Rights, and Indigenous Rights

Jasmine Holding Brown

"WESTERN CIVILIZATION"—Aimé Césaire's provocation on two centuries of colonial history declared—"is incapable of solving the two major problems to which its existence has given rise: the problem of the proletariat and the colonial problem."[1] Within the British Empire, managing these "problematic" populations led to egregious solutions in complementary settler-colonial projects: the forced migration of children from Britain to Canada, between 1869 and 1950, and the parallel incarceration of Indigenous children in residential schools. The settler-colonial prerogative—elimination and replacement—was well served by these synchronic arrangements.[2] Deprived populations were repatriated as white settlers to colonized lands, where indigeneity was being systematically erased and children were being resocialized, all in the name of progress.

In this chapter, I consider how, rather than hindering these efforts, emerging human rights discourses, specifically proto-conceptions of children as the bearers of rights, assisted these colonial projects. I begin with an examination of Britain's civilizing mission, directed at what were considered "problematic" populations, before turning to the "child-saving" movement and how it was used to whiten the empire. Beginning in the 1870s, this movement facilitated the statutory removal of children from harmful situations for their own protection. It also legitimized the mass removal of children from situations considered morally injurious, including presumed cultures of idle poverty and "heathen" indigeneity.

Civilizing the Empire circa 1830–1900

An intimate relationship has existed between Great Britain's domestic concerns and its colonial projects since the early nineteenth century.[3] Following the abolition of slavery in most parts of the British Empire in 1833, Britain—one of the world's pre-eminent beneficiaries of the transatlantic slave trade—sought to recast itself in the role of emancipator. Slavery was considered "something to be regretted and forgotten, best expunged in so far as was possible from public memory."[4] It was to be replaced by a colonial civilizing mission to justify the ongoing conquest of one-quarter of the world's population and land mass by 1920.[5] Integral to this chauvinistic mission was a calculated process of social engineering by which "civilized" conduct would be inculcated among Britain's pauper class, formerly enslaved peoples, and Indigenous Peoples in the British Empire—groups that, as Anne O'Connell argues, presented interrelated concerns.[6]

The stated aims of the British government's survey of Indigenous Peoples across its colonies in 1837 were: "to consider what Measures ought to be adopted with respect to the Native Inhabitants of Countries where British Settlements are made . . . to secure to them the due observance of Justice and the protection of their Rights; to promote the spread of Civilisation among them, and to lead them in peaceful and voluntary reception of the Christian Religion."[7] The Committee noted that these considerations must be balanced with another "benevolent and laudable object," namely, "the national necessity of finding some outlet for the superabundant population of Great Britain and Ireland[,] . . . to give encouragement to emigration, and to find a soil to which our surplus population may retreat."[8] Britain's colonial pursuits were tied to domestic anxieties—deemed righteous and pragmatic and envisioned benignly in terms of peaceful encouragement.

The report was reissued with comments from the newly formed Aborigines' Protection Society (APS), which noted that the survey was "replete with evidence as to the injustice and cruelty with which the Aborigines have hitherto been treated, and the pernicious effects which have resulted to them from their intercourse with European nations, [and] it abundantly proves the necessity of immediate legislative interference."[9] The APS determined that it was the responsibility of the British government and its colonial governors to alter their conduct toward those whom it had formerly classed "under the sweeping term of savages."[10] It was argued that this approach would also "materially contribute to promote the civil and commercial interests of Great Britain."[11] The APS, a Quaker-inspired pressure group that drew from the work of slavery abolitionists in its attempts to raise awareness of Indigenous Peoples' "degraded state," wrote that "the mere fact, that scarcely one of the native tribes in the British colonies has become civilised, is sufficiently discreditable to our national character."[12] To atone for past atrocities, the British state should protect those whom it previously showed little interest in, exterminated, or enslaved. The APS considered political intervention as perhaps the only way that Indigenous Peoples could be saved from what it suggested was an otherwise inevitable descent toward extinction.[13]

Krista Maxwell uses the term "settler-humanitarianism" to describe the link between liberal interventionism and colonialism.[14] Organizations such as the APS argued that it was incumbent on the authorities to systematize efforts previously pursued by Christian missionaries, with Indigenous Peoples imagined to have human potential and their European protectors to have a corresponding duty to raise them from their arrested stage of development, much like children.[15] In the colonial hierarchy of humanity, the product of European liberalism and enlightenment thinking—further legitimated in the latter half of the nineteenth century by the construction of scientific racism—"white" people of European descent positioned themselves at the apex of human civilization.[16] An infantilized construction of Indigenous

Peoples tied the realization of their "rights" to a reformed colonial project. The protection and improvement of "non-white subjects," O'Connell says, "anchored and legitimized racial thinking and white bourgeois standards" across the British Empire.[17]

Welfare and genocide are not, Maxwell suggests, "mutually exclusive categories" but historically intertwined under Western liberalism, as demonstrated by the aggressive policy of assimilation developed in the United States and replicated by Canada in the mid-nineteenth century.[18] Its rationale was distilled in the phrase "kill the Indian in him, and save the man," coined by champion of assimilation, and American military officer, Richard Henry Pratt in 1892.[19] As the superintendent of the influential Carlisle Indian Industrial School, Pratt promoted residential schools as places where civilized "language and habit" could be aggressively inculcated.[20] His argument centred on the pre-eminence of nurture over nature. He suggested that programs of assimilation were necessary to prove to white society that Indigenous Peoples were potentially worthy fellow citizens. The aim was not to "colonize" but to individualize. Individuals, once deprived of their "tribal communistic surroundings," could become industrious workers loyal "to the stars and stripes."[21]

Settler colonialism revitalized as social justice could also inspire allegiance, it was hoped, to the state and integration into the labour market. Beginning in the 1870s, children became a central target of these pseudo-humanist interventions.

"The Story of Mary Ellen: Which Started the Child Saving Crusade throughout the World"[22]

In a New York courthouse in 1874, ten-year-old Mary Ellen Wilson testified about the sadistic treatment that she had experienced by her legal guardian.[23] Mary Ellen had been indentured to her late father's ex-wife as an infant. Her foster parent was found guilty of assault and battery, and Mary Ellen was placed in institutional care and later fostered.[24] A concerned neighbour, Etta Wheeler, pursued the case for several years after failing to elicit interventions from the local church and police. Wheeler finally succeeded by persuading the American Society for the Prevention of Cruelty to Animals to take legal action, which ultimately facilitated Mary Ellen's removal on the ground of habeas corpus.[25] The case became notorious because of its serialization in the *New York Times* and because it prompted the creation of an agency devised solely to protect children. Established in 1874, the New York Society for the Prevention of Cruelty to Children was the first of its kind.[26]

Similarly, in Britain, organizations for the prevention of cruelty to animals predated those serving children by some fifty years.[27] England's first child protection agency was established in Liverpool in 1883. The National Society for the Prevention of Cruelty to Children followed, securing legislative changes to facilitate child removal by designated agents in cases of neglect, cruelty, and exploitation under the 1889 Children's Charter of Great Britain and Ireland.[28] These measures were replicated across the Atlantic by Irish-born social reformer J.J. Kelso, who helped to draft—as president of Toronto's Children's Aid Society (1891)—Ontario's first Children's Protection Act in 1893, and he was subsequently appointed as Canada's first provincial superintendent of neglected and dependent children.[29]

Prior to the emergence of professional social work and the arrival of state welfare in Britain in the 1940s, child welfare was largely the domain of the charity sector, religious institutions, and wealthy philanthropists.[30] Dominant among these groups were the child rescuers, as they were known in Britain, and their North American counterparts in the child-saving movement, who were instrumental in establishing "a new orthodoxy in child protection practice."[31] Beginning in the mid-nineteenth century, these groups became increasingly influential in shaping the lives of disadvantaged children. As Ian Hacking explains, "what was wanted was power: power to do good, of course."[32] Their efforts focused on the children of the poor and the marginalized, whose plight was now a public rather than a private affair and whose numbers had swelled dramatically because of industrialization and mass urban migration.[33]

Critically, the child-saving movement rarely focused on the economic and social conditions that also facilitated child neglect.[34] Isolating the welfare of children from that of their parents further demonized the survival strategies of the desperately poor and frequently sought to deprive them of basic parental rights.[35] Laura Peters says that during this time "the state was actively encouraged to make orphans of the children of the poor."[36] The movement encouraged the moral placing of deprived children within the category of the "deserving" poor, which, to legitimize their removal, required the co-construction of their parents (particularly their mothers), communities, and homes as dangerously uncivilized.[37] Working-class folks threw their children into fires, according to one piece of propaganda produced in England.[38] The "unprecedented opposition of children's interests to those of their parents," Maxwell argues, "had devastating implications for poor and marginalized families across Britain and the Empire."[39] The child-saving movement was "undoubtedly a conservative project," premised on the discursively powerful notion of working-class depravity and rooted in evangelical Christianity.[40] These ideas were challenged at the turn of the twentieth century by social reformers who argued that child welfare was related to limited resources rather than moral failings alone—principles that later provided the foundation for state welfare.[41]

The turn of the twentieth century saw the beginning of a radical reconfiguration of how the relationship among child, family, and state was conceptualized: the limiting of parental power, the idea that a child could have interests separate from—or even antithetical to—those of their caregivers, and the belief that outsiders could intercede on their behalf, and perhaps ought to do so, were foundational to modern conceptions of children's rights.[42] The child-saving movement set an important precedent in dissolving absolute parental rights by removing children from parents deemed unfit, bringing child abuse to wider attention, and augmenting the role of increasingly powerful child removal agents.

The British Child Migration Project

In its unprecedented commitment to sending deprived and looked-after children to British overseas territories, the child-saving movement converged seamlessly with Britain's ongoing settler-colonial projects. Most child migrants were sent to Canada in the late nineteenth century and early twentieth century, with ten times as many sent there compared with elsewhere in the British Empire.[43] The dominions provided ideal locations to offload domestic child poverty, echoing penal transportation routes, indenture schemes, and apprenticeship programs that similarly had relied on coerced migration and labour in previous centuries.[44] Children from British workhouses had been sent to Britain's penal colony in Bermuda as early as 1851. The scheme was short-lived and involved only three groups of children before the Board of Guardians decided "not to entertain so absurd and inhuman a proposition."[45] Yet it marked the beginning of mass child migration and provided a "prototype for the very substantial emigration scheme to Canada which started in the 1870s."[46]

From its inception under the British North America Act in 1867, the Dominion of Canada was utilized as the destination for approximately 118,000 children.[47] Through schemes initiated by Maria Rye and Annie Macpherson in 1869, children from British workhouses, children's homes, and other voluntary associations were sent to Canada to work as farm labourers and domestic servants.[48] The child migration scheme was later adopted most enthusiastically by Thomas Barnardo, a name synonymous with child poverty in the United Kingdom. He considered migration "the final stage of child rescue."[49] Diverting from his training as a medical missionary, Barnardo—like many of his contemporaries in the child-rescue movement—was compelled by evangelical Protestantism and London's growing population of impoverished children.[50] He built children's homes in London that endeavoured to provide open doors for any destitute child; Canada would become the back door that facilitated this policy.[51] In the early 1900s, it cost ten pounds to send a child to Canada and sixteen pounds per year to keep the child in one of his homes.[52] In 1886, Barnardo argued in his periodical, *Night and Day*, that "philanthropic abduction" was morally justifiable in cases in which the law would not otherwise permit the removal of children from parents who led "infamous or immoral lives."[53] It was normal, at that time, for parents suffering financial hardship to institutionalize their children temporarily.[54] Barnardo was responding to allegations made against him in court by numerous parents whose children were sent to Canada without their consent.[55] Consequently, the 1891 Custody of Children Act included clauses designed to deter parents from pursuing legal action.[56] It also legalized child migration without parental consent if the courts deemed a child deserted or the parents unfit.[57]

Little consideration was given, however, to the fitness of the children's new guardians or the agencies involved in their deportation. The British government became aware of the risks involved in sending children to Canada when a local government inspector, Andrew Doyle, produced his report on the "Emigration of Pauper Children to Canada" in 1875 after complaints regarding the children's living and working conditions reached England.[58] Doyle interviewed 400 child migrants in Canada, and his findings were highly critical of the lack of supervision, the impunity with which unscrupulous persons could easily profit from the traffic in children, and the casualness with which both migrants and their employers were selected. He noted that for most children, some of whom were sent as infants, fewer than 10 percent were adopted in the familial sense but taken on in "view of their future usefulness."[59] He highlighted one teenager's remarks: adoption, "sir, is when folks gets a girl to work without wages."[60] Doyle concluded that, "in no English town or village of about the same population and general character are children who are merely servants, and who are strangers and friendless, exposed to greater risks than in such a country as Canada."[61] He asserted that undoubtedly "great abuses" had ensued under the schemes and would continue to do so unless homes were properly selected and vetted with greater oversight of the children's training.[62]

Although Doyle was correct, his warnings were largely ignored and his recommendations rejected by Canadian government officials.[63] The scale of the mistreatment endured by these children is difficult to gauge, but it is telling that many recounted in subsequent UK government inquiries that they were treated like working animals and forced to live correspondingly; injuries caused by pitchforks to get children to work harder were apparently common.[64] One person's recollections submitted to an inquiry in 1998 noted, "I ate in the barn, I slept in the barn. I lived in the barn. I never saw the inside of the house, and when I ran away, nobody came looking for me."[65]

Unwanted Migrants: The Canadian View

The migration of children under fourteen was proscribed under Canadian law, following a three-year moratorium on the practice in 1925, made permanent in 1928.[66] This followed the suicides of three of Barnardo's boys in Ontario between 1923 and 1924—stories publicized in the British press—and the recommendations of a delegation sent from the United Kingdom in 1924 about concerns regarding exploitation.[67] The moratorium was also the result of concerted anti-migrant lobbying by various groups in Canada, including trade unions, prominent eugenicists, women's groups, medics, and the Canadian Council on Child Welfare.[68] Their motives were mixed, from fears about child labour, to worries about the degradation of the Canadian population, to more sympathetic views of the children themselves. At the First Annual Review of Social Workers in Toronto in 1926, a parody of the song "Rule Britannia," "Britons Never Shall Be Slaves—Being an Odiferous Ode on Juvenile Migration," mocked the willingness of the British to emigrate dependent children "of a feeble minded strain" for "a cash return."[69]

Among the long-standing critiques of child migration levelled from within Canada was fear regarding the importation of Old World degeneracy, and this fear was voiced by those within the Canadian child-saving movement.[70] As Doyle's report confirmed, however, fears about delinquency were not unfounded. Children largely untrained and unsupervised, and often taken directly from Britain's streets to Canada, were referred to as "gutter children" or the pointedly racialized "street Arabs," and often they ended up in the criminal justice system.[71] The English press noted that "any Canadian farmer who ventured publicly to express an opinion that a neighbour was overworking or ill-treating a British waif would be regarded as a traitor to his community, and in rural circles there is unfortunately a disposition to believe that the average British orphan is a child of original sin."[72] Although there remained a terrible stigma attached to being British "home children," there was also a persistent demand for their labour. In 1910, it was noted in England that "applications have been received from employers of child labour in Canada for seven times the number of children supplied."[73]

For this labouring underclass of young people, Canada was far from the classless utopia envisioned by Britain's early child savers.[74] Any presumed inherited Old World deficiencies were compounded when migrant children, from whom cheap or free labour could be readily extracted, outgrew their usefulness and drastically diminished in value. No longer contracted to their hosts, the children typically drifted from farms to cities, where they competed for scarce jobs and increasingly were seen, by the more established settler classes, as unworthy Canadians—a situation exacerbated by widespread unemployment during the Great Depression.[75] Former child migrants were deported back to Britain during the first half of the twentieth century, known as the migrant "exclusion era," after entering the criminal justice system, being classified as degenerate, or more often being liable to become a public charge (i.e., unemployed or infirm).[76] Poignantly, as Barbara Roberts notes, Canada adopted procedures that echoed nineteenth-century English Poor Laws, by which paupers could be expelled from a locality after becoming reliant on public funds.[77] An 1850 Act of Parliament had permitted the guardians of the Poor Law to utilize migration for similar purposes, to alleviate the costs of managing mass destitution and overcrowding in England's major cities, thus initiating child migration to Canada in the first place.[78] The same pretext that shovelled Britain's pauper class of children to Canada was later utilized to expel them.

Settling Canada with "Children of Sound Stock"

It is striking, then, that child migration to Canada resumed in 1935, albeit on a drastically reduced scale, having been essentially outlawed under Canadian law in 1928.[79] In the aftermath of the First World War, the UK government considered assisted migration to its dominions an expedient means of relieving domestic unemployment while strengthening its imperial ties under threat from American ascendency and dominion—especially Canadian—desires for increased autonomy.[80] This became official policy under the 1922 Empire Settlement Act, which provided financial incentives for white resettlement overseas.[81] The British were keen to stress the motivation "to distribute our white population more evenly between this country and the Dominions, thus building greater Britains overseas," while downplaying their objective to transfer Britain's "superfluous population which cannot find work at home."[82] Their approach evoked one of the rationales underpinning the Select Committee on Aboriginal Tribes in the 1830s.[83]

The case for continuing child migration—now as a distinctly imperialist project of white settlement—was made emphatically by the Fairbridge Society, an organization dedicated entirely to the cause, having been established in the University of Oxford's Colonial Club by Kingsley Fairbridge in 1909.[84] Widely respected in Britain, with patronage of its royal family and significant political influence, Fairbridge successfully reformulated the old child migration model to circumvent Canadian law and emerging norms in child welfare practice.[85] Much like Pratt's vision for civilizing Indigenous children in residential schools, the Fairbridge Society emphasized nurture over nature in the promotional literature for its scheme. The society argued that impoverished slum children from the United Kingdom could be moulded into worthy imperial subjects, especially if they were sent abroad at a younger age than had been the norm.[86]

The Prince of Wales Fairbridge Farm School opened on Vancouver Island in 1935.[87] Unlike previous iterations, Fairbridge children did not work initially on private farms and in households but were housed communally in purpose-built institutions. Yet they were still trained predominantly as farm labourers and domestic servants.[88] The farm school was the subject of sustained criticism from the BC Provincial Child Welfare Department, which increasingly considered the whole philosophy of child migration outdated, inappropriate, and un-Canadian.[89] Concerns were also raised that most Fairbridge children seemingly came from economically deprived rather than neglectful backgrounds and had living parents.[90] The superintendent of child welfare described the farm school in 1944 as "reminiscent of an orphanage of the last century."[91] The school closed in 1951.

The evolution of the Fairbridge Society—from an organization that unsuccessfully attempted to resettle poor white children from Britain's West Indian colonies to Canada in the 1940s[92] to one that opened a school in Rhodesia (Zimbabwe) in 1946 based on the apparent success of the Canadian and Australian schemes,[93] all the while continuing child migration to Australia until 1973 (including to institutions blacklisted as unfit in 1956)—reveals the relative weight of British imperialism versus an apparent commitment, in regard to the British, to protect the rights of children in care.[94] Expectations were outlined clearly in the 1946 Curtis Report and the resulting Children Act of 1948.[95]

Correspondence between the Fairbridge Society and various UK government departments confirms that imperial child migration was a political project of the British establishment. In the words of Fairbridge, this was "investment, not charity," and a project that—it was originally hoped in 1910—might stem "the multiplication of degenerates howling for debased Socialism. Farmers are never socialists."[96] The Fairbridge Society distinguished itself from its predecessors in that its methods, supposedly, were highly selective. To procure "sound stock," it utilized rigorous physical and psychological testing to appease, often unsuccessfully, increasingly restrictive Canadian immigration controls.[97] Its efforts complemented ethnonationalist sentiment within the dominions, proposed as "self-defence against [the] special dangers" of non-white and particularly Asian migration.[98] Canadian immigration officials typically disagreed, however, that the children whom Fairbridge presented were of "good blood." Canada House, responsible for vetting potential child migrants in the United Kingdom, rejected most children put forward in the 1930s, including children with "flat feet" and a "half-caste appearance."[99] It rejected one child for having once stolen apples from an orchard at age eight.[100]

The Fairbridge Society project was rooted in, and produced by, the British class system.[101] Poor children, the society asserted, were the "human material" that could consolidate an empire, "the waste of un-needed humanity converted to the husbandry of unpeopled areas."[102]

Civilizing Indigenous Peoples: Child Removal and "Intimate Colonial Governance"

The idea of Canada as a land without people was always a fiction.[103] The concept was enshrined in the Doctrine of Discovery that has legally justified Indigenous dispossession by Christian European settlers since the fifteenth century.[104] The occupation of land and the elimination of Indigenous Peoples remain, as Patrick Wolfe argues, settler colonialism's pre-eminent motivation.[105] They were consolidated in the nineteenth century under the 1857 Gradual Civilization Act and the 1876 Indian Act, which legally classified First Nations as "wards" of the Crown—wardship, in this context, meaning "protection" of those who lacked the capacity to protect their own interests.[106] Civilizing adults by treating them as children and civilizing children by separating them from their parents and homes were essential parts of the settler-colonial agenda: securing its permanence by eroding future claims against its sovereignty.[107] Civilizing Indigenous Peoples was the "white man's burden" and his children's inheritance.[108]

Child removal as a form of "intimate colonial governance" was utilized by European colonists among Indigenous populations in Scandinavia, North America, Africa, Asia, and Australasia throughout the late nineteenth century and well into the twentieth century.[109] The practice frequently targeted children considered illegitimate in both racialized and marital senses, particularly mixed-race and Indigenous children, in procedures that, to some extent, grew out of internal European child welfare practices, wherein the precedent for removal had been established.[110]

Indigenous child removal was systematized in Canada through the Indian residential school system. Established in the 1870s, contemporaneously with the onset of British child migration, it intended to make Indigenous children less Indigenous by destroying affective ties among children and their families, communities, and cultures, and it was part of the aggressive policy of assimilation pursued with a mandate to "kill the Indian in the child."[111] Residential schools were attended by more than 150,000 children between 1870 and 1996.[112] Resocializing Indigenous children derived from a set of suppositions similar to those contrived to uplift poor white children in Britain by removing them from the destructive influences of pauperism and sending them to the empire's supposedly empty spaces.[113] Both systems shared a heritage in Christian missionary activity and the attendant child-saving philosophy, a "fundamental conviction that in order for 'savage' children to be 'civilised' they needed to be 'rescued' from their parents."[114] The economic and material infrastructures that underpinned the two systems were also connected, including Indigenous and migrant children being housed in the same "distribution centre" in at least one documented case in the 1920s.[115] These child-saving impulses were not only comparable but also complementary features of the settler-colonial project (i.e., elimination and replacement) to dispense with cultures of Indigeneity and idle poverty and integrate the residual human "material" into the colonial economy.[116]

Indigenous Child Removal in Canada

Canada's Deputy Superintendent General of the Department of Indian Affairs Duncan Campbell Scott's solution to the country's "Indian problem" was compulsory residential schooling.[117] The amendments to the Indian Act in 1920 that Scott proposed made it illegal for First Nations children to attend anything other than a church-run residential or day school.[118] Indigenous children, unlike those of British stock, were understood to require religious conversion in addition to being made into productive workers. Residential schools, funded by the federal government and administered by the Christian churches, are now recognized as central proponents of cultural genocide, in which children were undereducated, exploited for their labour, abused, and experimented on.[119]

It is worth highlighting, however, that one of Canada's oldest and longest-running residential schools,[120] the Mohawk Institute, was founded by English missionaries half a century before the North American "blueprint" opened under Richard Henry Pratt, the Carlisle Indian Industrial School, and several decades before Confederation.[121] The Mohawk Institute was established in Brantford, Ontario, in 1828 by the royally chartered Protestant missionary society the New England Company.[122] As its missionaries stationed in Upper Canada relayed to their British benefactors in the 1830s, "while the ground-work of improvement must be laid amongst the young, that can be but imperfectly done if they are left to live and grow up at home."[123] The Mohawk Institute represents the materialization of Britain's civilizing mission as dreamed of and financed by pious men of wealth and power in the early nineteenth century.[124] Their aspirations for acculturating Indigenous Peoples, and children in particular, helped to lay the foundation for child removal on an industrial scale. The Canadian government effectively took over running the Mohawk Institute in the 1920s. In 1946, the conditions in it were described by a local women's organization as "abysmal and below any standard suitable to human living."[125] It closed in 1970.

As with child migration, the risks posed by residential schools to the children attending them were well known to those administering the policy. In 1907, Canada's first chief medical officer, Peter Henderson Bryce, exposed the state's culpability in the deaths of a quarter of all children who attended the schools; the cause of death was given almost invariably as tuberculosis.[126] Bryce was removed from public service, his investigations no longer necessary since the government did not intend to act on his findings.[127] Although his recommendations to set up emergency hospitals on reserves and to improve sanitation in schools were largely ignored, his findings became public knowledge when Ottawa's *Evening Citizen* ran a front-page story in November 1907 under the headline "Schools Aid White Plague—Startling Death Rolls Revealed among Indians—Absolute Inattention to the Bare Necessities of Health."[128] Bryce emphasized the structural inequalities underpinning the squalid conditions and extraordinary rates of death: Canadian citizens were allocated nearly triple the health funding that people with Indian Status received.[129]

The residential school system was not solely a provider of education; crucially, it also served as a welfare institution for children considered "not properly cared for" until at least the 1980s, a provision that continued after residential schooling was phased out and integrated into mainstream schooling, which began in the 1950s.[130] During the 1950s, Indigenous child welfare was devolved from the federal government to the provincial governments. Departments that formerly served non-Indigenous communities became responsible for filling the gaps in provision created by the dismantling of the residential school system. What followed was the wholesale removal of Indigenous children from their families during a period known as the Sixties Scoop. A social worker disclosed to researcher Patrick Johnston in the 1980s that "it was common practice in . . . the mid-sixties to 'scoop' from their mothers on reserves almost all newly born children."[131] Between the 1950s and the 1980s, approximately 20,000 Indigenous children were adopted or fostered out to predominantly white families in Canada and the United States.[132] Within Indigenous communities, where poverty and trauma were concentrated (due to the legacy of residential schooling in no small part), the "philanthropic abduction" of children resumed under new auspices.

Conclusion

In this chapter, I have constructed a dialectic between the colonizing (white) and the colonized (Indigenous) child subjects of British settler colonialism. To use the language of child migration innovator Kingsley Fairbridge, and the first principal of the Mohawk Institute, Reverend Robert Lugger, respectively, "little colonists" were meant to occupy the spaces cleared, literally and symbolically, via the assimilative processes inflicted on "little untutored savages."[133] This was a callous, unambiguous articulation of the "thingification" that Aimé Césaire argued underpinned colonialism.[134]

In 1924, both the United Kingdom and Canada signed the Geneva Declaration of the Rights of the Child, the first human rights instrument ratified by an intergovernmental body.[135] They also simultaneously pursued policies that facilitated gross violations of children's basic humanity despite clear indications that residential schooling and child migration served as repositories of misery over the previous half century. During the 1920s, residential schooling was expanded, and First Nations children could be compelled to attend the schools, while child migration was provided with additional taxpayer funding and establishment backing.

Firmly established in the late nineteenth century, these initiatives were designed to "civilize" children at the periphery of normative conceptions of humanity; they were not intended necessarily to confer them with rights.[136] Indeed, the 1924 declaration did not (yet) position the child as a rights holder but as "an object of the protection that the Declaration aimed to afford."[137] Beginning in the 1870s, the child-saving movement, which developed into the children's rights agenda, began to dismantle the assumption that children were essentially private property. That they were deemed worth "saving" and that their "protection" was of public concern comprise an important cultural milestone.

This precedent enabled interested parties not only to render services to children but also to serve other interests. In *loco parentis*, the state outsourced responsibility for its wards to corporate and Christian institutions and romanticized racist notions of New World civility. Settler colonialism was refashioned as a humanitarian exercise in child saving, part of a broader alignment of morality, through the promotion and protection of rights, with Western colonial capitalism.[138]

Although connected in various ways, the legacies of British child migration and Indian residential schooling are different. As Morgan Brie Johnson, a Canadian child migrant descendent, has written, "I rest on top of these generations of white settlers whose easy access to land was arranged by the same forces that removed and excluded so many others. . . . The injustice done to Home Children, while neither homogenous nor at all comparable to racialized oppressions, still stems from the same capitalist-colonial structures as the genocidal atrocities that continue to be enacted against BIPOC [Black, Indigenous, and People of Colour] bodies."[139] The procurement of "unwanted" children to whiten the colonies and exploit them for their labour, and the corresponding dehumanization of Indigenous children, ultimately served the same aim: consolidation of the settler colony. The appalling treatment that many suffered in British Canadian homes and institutions ought to dispel nostalgic visions of settler-colonial society while drawing attention to deep-rooted inequalities among settlers. For this largely institutional class of children, there are some striking parallels in their mistreatment that deserve further exploration. Connecting procedures that targeted poor and working-class communities in the United Kingdom and Indigenous Peoples in Canada exposes a mirroring of colonial statecraft between metropole and colony. To see their respective dispossessions as intimately connected, might also foster crucial solidarities between groups whose interests are often treated in opposition. Such opposition is a further inheritance, perhaps, of the divide and rule strategies implemented under British colonial rule.[140] Connection between these groups should also draw attention, not only to the historic alignment between the promotion of "rights" and colonial prerogatives within the anglophone world but to how progress is conceptualized, and whose dignity is sacrificed in its pursuit.

Notes

1 Aimé Césaire, *Discourse on Colonialism*, trans. Joan Pinkham (New York: NYU Press, 2000), 31.

2 Patrick Wolfe argues that settler colonialism does not seek "simply [to] replace native society *tout court*"; rather, it aims to eliminate Indigenous access to lands and resources, and on a symbolic level it attempts "to recuperate indigeneity in order to express its difference." Patrick Wolfe, "Settler Colonialism and the Elimination of the Native," *Journal of Genocide Research* 8, no. 4 (2006): 389–99.

3 Anne O'Connell, "The Pauper, Slave, and Aboriginal Subject: British Parliamentary Investigations and the Promotion of Civilized Conduct (1830s)," *Canadian Social Work Review* 26, no. 2 (2009): 172.

4 Catherine Hall, Nicholas Draper, and Keith McClelland, "Introduction," in *Emancipation and the Remaking of the British Imperial World*, ed. Catherine Hall, Nicholas Draper, and Keith McClelland (Manchester: Manchester University Press, 2014), 8.

5 Joel Quirk, *The Anti-Slavery Project from the Slave Trade to Human Trafficking* (Philadelphia: University of Pennsylvania Press, 2011), 82–110.

6 O'Connell, "The Pauper," 172–82.

7 Parliamentary Select Committee on Aborigines, *Report from the Select Committee on Aborigines, British Settlements: With the Minutes of Evidence, Appendix, and Index* (London: House of Commons, 1836), vol. 1, iii.

8 Parliamentary Select Committee on Aborigines, vol. 2, 75–76.

9 Parliamentary Select Committee on Aboriginal Tribes, *Report of the Parliamentary Select Committee on Aboriginal Tribes, British Settlements: Reprinted with Comments by the Aborigines Protection Society* (Paternoster Row: William Ball; Piccadilly: Hatchard and Son, 1837), v.

10 Parliamentary Select Committee on Aboriginal Tribes, 1.

11 Parliamentary Select Committee on Aboriginal Tribes, 4.

12 Kenneth Nworah, "The Aborigines Protection Society, 1889–1909: A Pressure-Group in Colonial Policy," *Canadian Journal of African Studies* 5 (1971): 79; Parliamentary Select Committee on Aboriginal Tribes, viii, iv.

13 Sven Lindqvist, *The Dead Do not Die: "Exterminate All the Brutes" and Terra Nullius* (New York: New Press, 2014), 132.

14 Krista Maxwell, "Settler-Humanitarianism: Healing the Indigenous Child-Victim," *Comparative Studies in Society and History* 59, no. 4 (2017): 975.

15 Gustav Jahoda, *Images of Savages: Ancient Roots of Modern Prejudice in Western Culture* (London: Routledge, 1999), 152.

16 Lindqvist, *The Dead*, 133.

17 O'Connell, "The Pauper," 180.

18 Maxwell, "Settler-Humanitarianism," 977; Derek Smith, "The 'Policy of Aggressive Civilization' and Projects of Governance in Roman Catholic Industrial Schools for Native Peoples in Canada, 1870–95," *Anthropologica* 43, no. 2 (2001): 254.

19 Richard Henry Pratt, "The Advantages of Mingling Indians with Whites," in *Proceedings of the National Conference of Charities and Correction at the Nineteenth Annual Session held in Denver, Colorado*, edited by I.C. Barrows (Boston: Press of Geo. H. Ellis, 1892), 45.

20 Tsianina K. Lomawaima and Jeffrey Ostler, "Reconsidering Richard Henry Pratt: Cultural Genocide and Native Liberation in an Era of Racial Oppression," *Journal of American Indian Education* 57, no. 1 (2018): 79.

21 Pratt, "The Advantages," 56–57.

22 This is the title of Etta Wheeler's keynote speech at the American Humane Association's Thirty-Seventh National Annual Conference in New York, October 1913. Wheeler took Mary Ellen to the conference; her speech was reprinted and widely distributed. See Lela Costin, "Unraveling the Mary Ellen Legend: Origins of the 'Cruelty Movement,'" *Social Service Review* 65, no. 1 (1991): 221.

23 "Mary Ellen Wilson: Further Testimony as to the Child's Ill Treatment by Her Guardians," *New York Times*, 12 April 1874, 12.

24 Sallie Watkins, "The Mary Ellen Myth: Correcting Child Welfare History," *Social Work* 35, no. 4 (1990): 500–03.

25 Watkins.

26 Alister Lamont and Leah Bromfield, *History of Child Protection Services* (Canberra: Australian Institute of Family Studies, 2010), 1–2.

27 Monica Flegel and Claudia Nelson, *Conceptualizing Cruelty to Children in Nineteenth-Century England: Literature, Representation, and the NSPCC* (Abingdon, UK: Taylor and Francis Group, 2009), 39.

28 Shurlee Swain and Margot Hillel, *Child, Nation, Race and Empire: Child Rescue Discourse, England, Canada and Australia, 1850–1915* (Manchester: Manchester University Press, 2010), 90.

29 Andre Jones and Leonard Rutman, *In the Children's Aid: J.J. Kelso and Child Welfare in Ontario* (Toronto: University of Toronto Press, 1981), vii–viii.

30 Harry Hendrick, *Child Welfare: Historical Dimensions, Contemporary Debates* (Bristol: Policy Press, 2003), 40–49.

31 Swain and Hillel, *Child, Nation, Race and Empire*, 140.

32 Ian Hacking, "The Making and Molding of Child Abuse," *Critical Inquiry* 17, no. 2 (1991): 284.

33 Hendrick, *Child Welfare*, 48.

34 Shurlee Swain, "But the Children . . . Indigenous Child Removal Policies Compared," in *Writing Colonial Histories: Comparative Perspectives*, ed. Tracey Banivanua Mar and Julie Evans (Melbourne: RMIT Publishing, 2002), 135.

35 Lydia Murdoch, *Imagined Orphans: Poor Families, Child Welfare, and Contested Citizenship in London* (New Brunswick, NJ: Rutgers University Press, 2006), 6.

36 Laura Peters, *Orphan Texts: Victorian Orphans, Culture and Empire* (Manchester: Manchester University Press, 2000), 13.

37 Marjorie Johnstone, "Settler Feminism, Race Making, and Early Social Work in Canada," *Affilia* 33, no. 3 (2018): 333; Swain, "But the Children," 134.

38 Swain and Hillel, *Child, Nation, Race and Empire*, 51.

39 Maxwell, "Settler-Humanitarianism," 982.

40 Swain and Hillel, *Child, Nation, Race and Empire*, 30.

41 Marilyn Callahan and Christopher Walmsley, "Rethinking Child Welfare Reform in British Columbia, 1900–60," in *People, Politics, and Child Welfare in British Columbia*, ed. Leslie Foster and Brian Wharf (Vancouver: UBC Press, 2007), 14.

42 Swain and Hillel, *Child, Nation, Race and Empire*, 17–35.

43 "Altogether about 150,000 children were 'exported' to outposts of the British Empire—to Canada, Australia, New Zealand and, to a lesser extent, South Africa, Rhodesia (now Zimbabwe) and the Caribbean." Phillip Bean and Joy Melville, *Lost Children of the Empire* (London: Routledge, 1989), 1.

44 Peters, *Orphan Texts*, 81; Shurlee Swain, "'Brighter Britain': Images of Empire in the International Child Rescue Movement, 1850–1915," in *Empires of Religion*, ed. Hilary Carey (Basingstoke, UK: Palgrave Macmillan, 2008), 168.

45 Peters, *Orphan Texts*, 81.

46 Peters, 85.

47 Patricia Skidmore, *A British Home Child in Canada* (Toronto: Dundurn, 2018), 13.

48 Patricia Rooke and R.L. Schnell, "Imperial Philanthropy and Colonial Response: British Juvenile Emigration to Canada, 1896–1930," *Historian* 46, no. 1 (1983): 56–77; see also Joy Parr, *Labouring Children: British Immigrant Apprentices to Canada, 1869–1924* (London: Croom-Helm, 1980).

49 Swain and Hillel, *Child, Nation, Race and Empire*, 112.

50 Gillian Wagner, "Barnardo, Thomas John (1845–1905), Philanthropist and Founder of Dr. Barnardo's Homes," in *Oxford Dictionary of Biography* (Oxford: Oxford University Press, 2017), https://doi.org/10.1093/ref:odnb/30600.

51 Alexis Jay, Malcolm Evans, Ivor Frank, and Drusilla Sharpling, *Child Migration Programmes: Investigation Report* (London: Independent Inquiry Child Sexual Abuse, 2018), 65.

52 Hendrick, *Child Welfare*, 47.

53 "Philanthropic Abduction: Is It Ever Justifiable?," *Sentinel* 7, no. 1 (1886): 14–16.

54 Parr, *Labouring Children*, 60–66; Callahan and Walmsley, "Rethinking Child Welfare," 14.

55 Roy Parker, *Uprooted: The Shipment of Poor Children to Canada, 1867–1917* (Bristol: Bristol University Press, 2008), 245–50; David Lorente, "Evidence Submitted by David Lorente of Home Children Canada," in *Health Select Committee on Child Migration*, 16 February 1998, Parliamentary Archives, London, HP/CP/16469/8.

56 Parker, *Uprooted*, 244–45.

57 Swain and Hillel, *Child, Nation, Race and Empire*, 113.

58 Andrew Doyle, "Pauper Children (Canada): A Report to the Right Honourable the President of the Local Government Board . . . as to the Emigration of Pauper Children to Canada," House of Commons, London, 8 February 1875; R.L. Schnell, "The Right Class of Boy: Youth Training Schemes and Assisted Emigration to Canada under the Empire Settlement Act, 1922–39," *History of Education* 24, no. 1 (1995): 74.

59 Doyle, "Pauper Children (Canada)," 13.

60 Doyle.

61 Doyle.

62 Doyle, 20.

63 Rooke and Schnell, "Imperial Philanthropy," 62.

64 Lorente, "Evidence Submitted," 20.

65 Lorente, 15.

66 Rooke and Schnell, "Imperial Philanthropy," 58.

67 "Barnardo Boy's Suicide in Canada: Smacked by Farmer's Wife," *Manchester Guardian*, 6 February 1924, 7; Madeline Engel, Norma Phillips, and Frances Della Cava, "Forced Migration and Immigration Programs for Children: The Emergence of a Social Movement," *International Journal of Children's Rights* 26, no. 3 (2018): 478.

68 Rooke and Schnell, "Imperial Philanthropy," 63.

69 David Lorente, "Britons Never Shall Be Slaves—Being an Odiferous Ode on Juvenile Migration at the First Annual Review of Social Workers of Toronto

April 16, 1926," in *Health Select Committee on Child Migration*, 16 February 1998, Parliamentary Archives, London, HP/CP/16469/8.

70 Rooke and Schnell, "Imperial Philanthropy," 58.

71 Doyle, "Pauper Children (Canada)," 14–16.

72 "The Orphan Immigrant in Canada: Employment Conditions," *Manchester Guardian*, 27 October 1924, 16.

73 Kingsley Fairbridge, *Juvenile Emigration and Farm School System: Reprinted from the Times of May 24th, 1910, with Additions* (London: John Parkinson Bland, 1910), 7; "Emigration of Children to Farm Schools in Australia and Canada: Fairbridge Society Emigration Scheme; Correspondence between Overseas Settlement Department, Ministry of Health and Child Emigration Society of Oxford," 1910–37, National Archives, Kew, UK, MH 102/1400.

74 Swain and Hillel, *Child, Nation, Race and Empire*, 117.

75 Schnell, "The Right Class," 85–88.

76 Barbara Roberts, *Whence They Came: Deportation from Canada 1900–1935* (Ottawa: University of Ottawa Press, 1988), 4–6.

77 Roberts, 4.

78 Engel, Phillips, and Della Cava, "Forced Migration," 475.

79 Rooke and Schnell, "Imperial Philanthropy," 58.

80 S.R. Ashton and S.E. Stockwell, eds., *Metropolitan Reorganisation, Defence and International Relations, Political Change and Constitutional Reform*, vol. 1 of *Imperial Policy and Colonial Practice 1925–1945* (London: University of London Institute for Commonwealth Studies, 1996), xxxiii.

81 Ashton and Stockwell, xii.

82 S.R. Ashton and S.E. Stockwell, eds., *Economic Policy, Social Policies and Colonial Research*, vol. 2 of *Imperial Policy and Colonial Practice 1925–1945* (London: University of London Institute for Commonwealth Studies, 1996), 8.

83 O'Connell, "The Pauper," 180.

84 Humphrey Milford, *The Autobiography of Kingsley Fairbridge* (London: Oxford University Press, 1927).

85 David Hill, *The Forgotten Children: Fairbridge Farm School and Its Betrayal of Britain's Child Migrants* (London: Atlantic Books, 2017), 29–34; Patrick Dunae, "Waifs: The Fairbridge Society in British Columbia, 1931–1951," *Social History* 21, no. 42 (1988): 225–26.

86 Fairbridge, *Juvenile Emigration*, 3–4; Swain and Hillel, *Child, Nation, Race and Empire*, 112.

87 Dunae, "Waifs," 238.

88 Dunae, 227.

89 Dunae, 240–41.

90 "Letter from George Davidson, Principal Director of British Columbia Social Welfare, to Harry Logan, Principal of the Prince of Wales Farm School," 6 July 1944, 1–6, British Columbia Provincial Archives, Victoria, MS-2045/1/14.

91 "Isobel Harvey's Report on Study Made of Fairbridge Farm School during the Month of August 1944," August 1944, 3, British Columbia Provincial Archives, Victoria, GR-0883/10/13.

92 "Admittance of West Indian Children to Fairbridge," 1944, National Archives, Kew, UK, CO 859/125/4.

93 "A Description of Kingsley Fairbridge Farm School Pinjarra, Western Australia, 1939," in *Health Select Committee on Child Migration*, 16 February 1998, 89, Parliamentary Archives, London, HP/CP/16469/7.

94 Hill, *The Forgotten Children*, 274.

95 Gordon Lynch, "Pathways to the 1946 Curtis Report and the Post-War Reconstruction of Children's Out-of-Home Care," *Contemporary British History* 34, no. 1 (2020): 22–24.

96 "Emigration of Children to Farm Schools in Australia and Canada: Fairbridge Society Emigration Scheme; Correspondence between Overseas Settlement Department, Ministry of Health and Child Emigration Society of Oxford," 1910, 21, National Archives, Kew, UK, MH 102/1400.

97 "A Description of Kingsley Fairbridge," 89; Peter Ward, *White Canada Forever: Popular Attitudes and Public Policy toward Orientals in British Columbia* (Montreal and Kingston: McGill-Queen's University Press, 2002), 118–25.

98 "Emigration of Children," 287.

99 Skidmore, *A British Home Child*, 165–66.

100 "Letter from Lord Lumley, Chairman of the Fairbridge Society, to Lord Stanley, Secretary of State for Dominion Affairs," 5 October 1935, 4, Fairbridge Society Archive, University of Liverpool Special Collections, D296/K1/2/6.

101 Hill, *The Forgotten Children*, 313.

102 "A Description of Kingsley Fairbridge," 151, 214.

103 Bonita Lawrence, "Rewriting Histories of the Land: Colonization and Indigenous Resistance in Eastern Canada," in *Race, Space and the Law: Unmapping a White Settler Society*, ed. Sherene Razack (Toronto: Sumach Press, 2002), 21–46.

104 Robert Miller et al., "The Doctrine of Discovery," in *Discovering Indigenous Lands: The Doctrine of Discovery in the English Colonies* (Oxford: Oxford University Press, 2010), 2.

105 Wolfe, "Settler Colonialism," 388.

106 Jo-Anne Fiske, "Political Status of Native Indian Women: Contradictory Implications of Canadian State Policy," in *The Days of Our Grandmothers: A Reader in Aboriginal Women's History in Canada*, ed. Mary-Ellen Kelm and Lorna Townsend (Toronto: University of Toronto Press, 2006), 339.

107 Kit Myers, "The Intimacy of Three Settler Nations: Colonialism, Race and Child Welfare," *Gazillion Voices* (November 2014): 4.

108 William Easterly, *The White Man's Burden* (London: Oxford University Press, 2007).

109 Christina Firpo and Margaret Jacobs, "Taking Children, Ruling Colonies: Child Removal and Colonial Subjugation in Australia, Canada, French Indochina, and the United States, 1870–1950s," *Journal of World History* 29, no. 4 (2018): 530–57, 562; Palo Annbritt, Lydia Kokkola, and Lena Manderstedt, "Forced Removal of

National Minority Children in the Swedish and Finnish Arctic through Schooling," *International Research in Children's Literature* 13, no. 2 (2020): 289.

110 Firpo and Jacobs, "Taking Children," 537; Swain, "But the Children," 133.

111 Bryanne Young, "'Killing the Indian in the Child': Death, Cruelty, and Subject-Formation in the Canadian Indian Residential School System," *Mosaic* 48, no. 4 (2015): 65.

112 Poitr Wilk, Alana Maltby, and Martin Cooke, "Residential Schools and the Effects on Indigenous Health and Well-Being in Canada: A Scoping Review," *Public Health Reviews* 38, no. 1 (2017): 8.

113 Gordon Lynch, "Saving the Child for the Sake of the Nation: Moral Framing and the Civic, Moral and Religious Redemption of Children," *American Journal of Cultural Sociology* 2, no. 2 (2014): 171; Swain, "But the Children," 133.

114 Swain, "But the Children," 133.

115 Eric Pouliot-Thisdale, "Pupils at Indian Residential Schools: 1911 Wikwemikong, 1921 Spanish and Carleton Ontario Census (Updated Edition)" (Montreal, 2016, 56–61), https://epe.lac-bac.gc.ca/100/200/300/eric_pouliot-thisdale/pupils_indian_residential_schools/Pupils_at_Indian_Residential_Schools_1911_1921_Wikwemikong_Spanish_Carleton_PDF_2016.pdf.

116 Wolfe, "Settler Colonialism," 391; Myers, "The Intimacy," 4.

117 Smith, "The 'Policy of Aggressive Civilization,'" 254.

118 Truth and Reconciliation Commission (TRC) of Canada, *A Knock on the Door: The Essential History of Residential Schools* (Winnipeg: University of Manitoba Press, 2016), 28–37.

119 TRC, 47–129.

120 The first residential schools for Indigenous children were established by the Récollets in the 1620s under French colonial rule. See Swain, "But the Children," 136.

121 David Stirrup, "The Toxic Legacy of the British Empire in Canada's Residential Schools," *Guardian*, 2 July 2021, https://www.theguardian.com/world/2021/jul/02/the-toxic-legacy-of-the-british-empire-in-canadas-residential-schools.

122 Cody Groat, "Commemoration and Reconciliation: The Mohawk Institute as a World Heritage Site," *British Journal of Canadian Studies* 31 (2018): 196–200.

123 "The History (Mohawk): The History of the Mohawk Institute Part One," 3, London Metropolitan Archives, 540/F/02/002.

124 Neil Hitchin, *"Come Over and Help Us": The New England Company and Its Mission 1649–2001* (Ely, UK: St Pancras Books, 2002), 40.

125 Wendy Fletcher, "The Canadian Experiment with Social Engineering, a Historical Case: The Mohawk Institute" (paper presented at the Canadian Society of Church History Annual Conference, University of Manitoba, 3–4 June 2024), 139. https://historicalpapers.journals.yorku.ca/index.php/historicalpapers/article/view/39276/35610.

126 Peter Henderson Bryce, *The Story of a National Crime* (Ottawa: James Hope and Sons, 1922), 1–18.

127 Travis Hay, Cindy Blackstock, and Michael Kirlew, "Dr. Peter Bryce (1853–1932): Whistleblower on Residential Schools," *Canadian Medical Association Journal* 192, no. 9 (2020): 224.

128 Hay, Blackstock, and Kirlew.

129 Bryce, *The Story of a National Crime*, 13.

130 Callahan and Walmsley, "Rethinking Child Welfare," 19.

131 Cited in Raven Sinclair, "Identity Lost and Found: Lessons from the Sixties Scoop," *First Peoples Child and Family Review* 3 (2020): 66.

132 Suzanne Fournier and Ernie Crey, *Stolen from Our Embrace: The Abduction of First Nations Children and the Restoration of Aboriginal Communities* (Vancouver: Douglas and McIntyre, 1997); Niigaanwewidam James Sinclair and Sharon Dainard, "Sixties Scoop," in *The Canadian Encyclopedia*, 21 June 2016, https://www.thecanadianencyclopedia.ca/en/article/sixties-scoop.

133 Lynch, "Saving the Child," 167; "The History (Mohawk)," 5.

134 Césaire, *Discourse on Colonialism*, 42.

135 Trevor Buck, *International Child Law* (London: Routledge, 2014), 89.

136 Caitlin Harvey, review of *Child, Nation, Race and Empire: Child Rescue Discourse, England, Canada and Australia, 1850–1915*, by Margot Hillel and Shurlee Swain, *Journal of Imperial and Commonwealth History* 42, no. 3 (2014): 587–89.

137 United Nations, *Legislative History of the Convention on the Rights of the Child* (Geneva: Office of the United Nations High Commissioner for Human Rights, 2007), 3.

138 Padraic Scanlan, "The Emancipated Empire," *Aeon*, 22 October 2021, https://aeon.co/essays/the-british-empire-was-built-on-slavery-then-grew-by-antislavery.

139 Morgan Brie Johnson, "Settler Colonial Structures of Domestication: British Home Children in Canada," *Genealogy* 5, no. 3 (2021): 77–78.

140 Aziz Rahman, Mary Anne Clarke, and Sean Byrne, "The Art of Breaking People Down: The British Colonial Model in Ireland and Canada," *Peace Research* 49, no. 2 (2017): 16.

CHAPTER 3

Whose Rights Count? Antiracist Activists, Feminists, and Canada's Human Rights Legislation from the Early 1950s to the Early 1970s

Ruth A. Frager

"IF IT IS essential that a declaration of tolerance be made," declared a *Globe and Mail* editorial on 27 February 1951, "it should most definitely include the most widespread form of discrimination between individuals and employers": that is, sex discrimination. "There is far more active discrimination against the female minority in business and industry than against all the other types of minority specified in the bill," the editorial continued. The editors were commenting on Ontario's Fair Employment Practices (FEP) bill, which would become the first law in Canada to prohibit employment discrimination on the basis of race, creed, and national origin. But they were not endorsing the bill, nor were they serious about prohibiting sex discrimination in employment. Instead, they were trying to make the bill look absurd by arguing that it should include the prohibition of sex discrimination. For the male editors, property rights trumped human rights—whether or not conceptions of human rights encompassed discrimination against women. From this point of view, if a person owned a business, his rights as the owner were paramount; thus, the editorial proclaimed that the employer "has the right to pick and choose his associates in any relationship, unless he is living *in a slave economy*."[1]

The editors of *Saturday Night* magazine highlighted the cynical strategy of this *Globe and Mail* editorial, adding their own emphasis on the alleged absurdity of forbidding sex discrimination in employment: "We cannot suspect the *Globe and Mail* of trying to be more progressive than Mr. Frost [the Conservative premier of Ontario] so we have to fall back on the theory that it is trying to make his F.E.P. legislation look ridiculous. To demand that for any job whatsoever the employer shall be prohibited from rejecting an applicant because he is a man or she is a woman is to threaten us with an epidemic of male hat-check 'girls' and female lumberjacks. We are against it."[2]

Yet, by the early 1970s, *Globe and Mail* editorials had changed, as had the Ontario government's position. Although the editors remained concerned about false accusations of discrimination,[3] they now supported measures against sex discrimination. In a 1972 editorial focusing on the proposal to amend the Ontario Human Rights Code by adding sex as one of the prohibited grounds of discrimination, for example, the editors approvingly quoted the Ontario labour minister: "We are particularly concerned about the problems of discrimination at the stage when people are finding employment. It is essential that they are able to get their foot in the door without regard to their race, creed, color, age, sex, marital status, nationality or place of origin." This editorial even condemned Ontario's Conservative premier for failing to fulfill his promise to appoint a woman to his cabinet.[4]

In fact, a 1970 *Globe and Mail* editorial lauded former Liberal Minister of National Health and Welfare Judy LaMarsh's *Memoirs of a Bird in a Gilded Cage*, stressing that LaMarsh "chronicles the little and big ways in which women are put down in the national Press Gallery, Government departments and the House of Commons itself." The editorial approvingly quoted an excerpt from her book: "Women will some day be equal in Canada and elsewhere in the Western world. We have come from being chattels or wards in the last hundred-odd years. . . . Each year we inch closer to true equality of opportunity. If the French Canadians can make it, if the Negroes and Indians can make it, then it is likely that women will make it, too." If the editors had any problem with her assumption that women's progress was a phenomenon of the Western world or her assumptions that French Canadians, African Canadians, and Indigenous Peoples were in fact achieving equality of opportunity in this country, they did not say.[5]

Although there were significant limits to this political transformation from the early 1950s to the early 1970s, this crucial change raises key questions about shifts in the conceptualization of the nature of human rights. Under which historical circumstances have women's rights been conceptualized as human rights? How have activists from disadvantaged groups—and their allies—shaped the conceptualization of human rights in key historical periods? What have been the advantages and disadvantages of conceptualizing women's rights in terms of human rights? How have various feminists reacted to the liberal framework of Canada's human rights legislation? Has there been a natural affinity—or, indeed, an alliance—between antiracist human rights activists and women's rights activists? In this chapter, I examine these questions in the specific Canadian context of the change from initial antiracist laws that omitted sex discrimination to the human rights laws that included sex as a prohibited ground of discrimination roughly twenty to twenty-five years later. I am particularly interested in employment discrimination and concentrate my discussion on Ontario.

To understand this change from the early 1950s to the early 1970s, it is important to stress that Canadian conceptions of human rights stemmed from a tradition that focused on liberal individualism in a historical context in which women were seldom seen as autonomous individuals because, unlike men, often they were defined exclusively in terms of their family functions.[6] As Lynn Hunt has emphasized in her examination of the roots of human rights in the Declaration of Independence (United States, 1776) and the Declaration of the Rights of Man and Citizen (France, 1789), "underpinning these notions of liberty and rights was a set of assumptions about individual autonomy." Hunt continues that, "to have human rights, people had to be perceived as separate individuals who were capable of exercising independent moral judgment."[7] But in this context, and of course for many decades to come, men—and many women themselves—typically viewed women as naturally dependent on their fathers and husbands.[8]

As Hunt explains further, "after 1789, many French revolutionaries would take public and vociferous stands in favor of rights for Protestants, Jews, free blacks, and even slaves, and at the same time actively oppose granting rights to women." The French, and their counterparts in the United States, "viewed women as dependents defined by their family status and thus by definition not fully capable of political autonomy."[9] Although there were a few exceptional feminist voices raised at the time, most notably Olympe de Gouges in France,[10] the common view of women as inherently dependent provided a crucial legacy for Canadian human rights development.

In Canada in the 1940s and 1950s, antiracist human rights activists typically did not think that women experienced discrimination based on their sex. When Carmela Patrias and I began researching the social origins of Canadian human rights campaigns, we asked Kalmen Kaplansky about this. He was the head of the Jewish Labour Committee from 1946 to 1957, at a time when the organization did pioneering antiracist work while totally ignoring women's issues. Kaplansky declared that the reasoning was straightforward: women were simply not considered equal at that time, for they were expected to be mothers and focus on looking after their families.[11] Many of these activists held deep convictions concerning the injustice of racist, ethnic, and religious discrimination while remaining blind to sex discrimination even though, as we shall see, there were a few exceptional feminist voices raised even then. In short, the vast majority of antiracist human rights activists reflected the sexism deeply entrenched in Canadian society at this time.[12]

By the early 1970s, however, it was harder to make the argument that women were defined by their roles as devoted daughters, wives, and mothers. As the dramatic postwar economic expansion created more "women's jobs," many more women were working outside the home, including more married women and more middle-class women. Then, too, the increasing divorce rate meant that newly single mothers often had to go out to work to support themselves and their children, thereby adding to the dramatic increase in women in the paid labour force. More specifically, census data indicate that the female labour force participation rate rose from 24 percent in 1951 to 29.5 percent in 1961 and then to 40 percent in 1971. At the same time, the proportion of employed people who were female rose from 22 percent in 1951 to 27 percent in 1961 and nearly to 35 percent in 1971.[13]

In this period, certain demographic trends were accelerating, particularly declining fertility rates and increasing life expectancy. Thus, women faced more years of life after their children reached adulthood. Increased access to birth control was facilitated not only by the availability of the pill in larger Canadian cities in the early 1960s but also by the 1969 legislation that finally rendered contraceptive devices legal. In addition, the increased use of labour-saving household devices played a role in freeing up some of the time that women needed to spend on domestic chores. However, as more young women graduated from universities, they found that many jobs nonetheless remained closed to them.[14]

In this context, the resurgence of the women's movement, often referred to as the Second Wave, was dramatic. Beginning in the mid-to-late 1960s, Canadian feminists—often newly minted—called loudly for women's rights. The establishment of the Royal Commission on the Status of Women in 1967 stemmed from the mounting feminist pressure on the government, especially from women's organizations that had existed for at least several decades. The commission itself acted as a catalyst for further feminist activism, especially when it conducted extensive hearings across the country and then issued its official report in 1970.[15]

Yet even in the late 1940s and early 1950s, there were a few rare calls to legislate against sex discrimination, particularly in employment, as Patrias and I explain in detail in an earlier article.[16] When the Fair Employment Practices Bill came before the Ontario legislature in 1951, Agnes Macphail—a member of the Cooperative Commonwealth Federation (CCF) and the sole female Member of the Provincial Parliament (MPP)—waxed indignant: "Today we have a Fair Employment Practices Act which gives everybody else equity, but does not give equity to women. . . . Anybody of any creed, anybody of any color, anybody of any nationality, anybody of any ancestry or anybody of any religion, so long as they are male will get equal treatment, but, if it is a woman involved, even if her ancestry is strictly Canadian, she has been here all her life and her family for generations, she can be discriminated against." Despite her plea that real Canadian women deserved better, her vigorous protest elicited no discussion in the legislature.[17]

The silence of the male CCF MPPs is particularly noteworthy, for, a few years earlier, the CCF Status of Women Committee had called for women's "full equality in all phases of life," including economic equality. In its 1948 report to the Ontario CCF, the committee asserted that discrimination against women "is subtle and far-reaching, and must be fought on a wider front [than equal pay]. Therefore we feel that laws or bills of rights emphasizing the general principles of equality should specifically ban discrimination because of sex as well as discrimination because of race or religion."[18]

Whereas the CCF had encompassed an antiracist commitment in its 1933 founding manifesto,[19] the Business and Professional Women's Clubs (BPWC) appeared to be indifferent to racist discrimination while promoting aspects of women's rights in the late 1940s and early 1950s. In 1951, when the Ontario government introduced the Female Employees Fair Remuneration Bill—a measure that would mandate equal pay for women who did the exact same jobs as men—the province's BPWC distributed copies of the United Nations' 1948 Universal Declaration of Human Rights (UDHR) to all MPPs, highlighting its inclusion of sex as one of the prohibited grounds of discrimination and the specific section of the declaration that called for equal pay. Margaret Hyndman, the BPWC's main leader, strongly supported the equal pay bill while pointedly reassuring the Ontario premier that the sex-typing of jobs meant that the province's economy would not suffer if this measure were enacted.[20] Yet she also declared that "a very real discrimination exists in the matter of employing women. The new fair employment practices bill . . . repudiates that part of the Declaration of Human Rights which would also prohibit discrimination on the grounds of sex."[21] Nevertheless, the BPWC had to settle for a narrow equal pay act that applied only to the woman doing the same exact job as a man for every minute of the day at the same workplace.[22]

Unlike the earlier provincial and federal anti-discrimination laws, the Canadian government's 1960 Bill of Rights encompassed sex discrimination. More specifically, the document affirmed "the right of the individual to equality before the law and the protection of the law," "without discrimination by reason of race, national origin, colour, religion or sex."[23] The Bill of Rights focused mainly on civil liberties, such as the right to habeas corpus as well as freedom of religion, freedom of speech, and freedom of assembly, among others. Although it did not call explicitly for an end to employment discrimination, some of the bill's supporters apparently hoped that this broad declaration could be used to fight various forms of discrimination against women as well as members of racialized groups.[24]

Many rights advocates at the time had pushed for a stronger Bill of Rights, to no avail, while stressing the many weaknesses of this formulation, especially that the bill was not embedded in the Constitution and that it was limited to areas of federal jurisdiction.[25] With the benefit of hindsight, it is clear that the Bill of Rights was useless in promoting women's rights and of limited use in promoting the rights of racialized groups.[26]

In the context of its feebleness, certain feminists pushed to add sex to existing human rights laws. Whereas most scholars who focus on the origins of human rights campaigns in Canada have neglected issues of sex discrimination, Dominique Clément's *Equality Deferred: Sex Discrimination and British Columbia's Human Rights State, 1953–84* is insightful. In 1951, Ontario had acted first not only to prohibit employment discrimination on the grounds of race, creed, and national origin but also to mandate equal pay for women doing the same jobs as men. By 1960, most provinces had followed this course of action, as had the federal government. As Clément stresses, in 1969 British Columbia became the first province to add sex to human rights legislation as one of the prohibited grounds of discrimination. A year later in Ontario, the Women's Equal Employment Opportunity Act prohibited sex discrimination, and in 1972 activists succeeded in adding sex discrimination to the Ontario Human Rights Code. By 1977, all other provinces, as well as the federal government, had made the same change.[27] Even though these measures had significant limitations, they were important milestones, and an examination of these changes sheds light on shifting conceptualizations of human rights.

Certain aspects of the 1970 *Report of the Royal Commission on the Status of Women in Canada* both reflected and reinforced the push to add the prohibition of sex discrimination to human rights legislation. In an initial section entitled "Criteria and Principles," the report began by asserting that the United Nations' 1948 Universal Declaration of Human Rights emphasized equality for women, and the report then asserted that "Canada is, therefore, committed to a principle that permits no distinction in rights and freedoms between women and men."[28] Soon thereafter, the report declared that "the main aspiration" expressed in the commission's extensive public hearings and in the hundreds of written submissions "was for elementary human rights and genuine equality." It stated that "we subscribe to the fundamental principle of equality of the sexes as human beings and as citizens and we believe that any action either legislative, corporate or individual which infringes on that equality violates a fundamental human right."[29]

In the official list of recommendations at the end of the report, some of the suggestions reinforced this expanded human rights orientation. One recommendation stipulated that "all provincial and territorial legislation dealing with equality of opportunity in employment specify that discrimination on the basis of sex and marital status be prohibited," and the next recommendation called for the same change to the federal Fair Employment Practices Act.[30] Another recommendation specified that all provincial and territorial jurisdictions, as well as the federal level, must have human rights commissions with strengthened powers of investigation and enforcement. In addition, each commission would include "a division dealing specifically with the protection of women's rights" for seven to ten years.[31]

In the immediate aftermath of the publication of the report, although many feminists criticized it for not going far enough,[32] many women's rights advocates also feared that it would just sit on the shelf, like so many other Royal Commission reports often did. These advocates therefore put together a group of activists to push for the implementation of the report's key recommendations. Established in January 1971 as the National Ad Hoc Action

Committee on the Status of Women, the group represented a wide variety of feminists, ranging from those from older organizations (e.g., the Imperial Order Daughters of the Empire, the Business and Professional Women's Clubs, the Federation of Women's Institutes of Canada, the Federation of Women Teachers' Associations of Ontario, as well as several religious women's groups) to female labour activists and women from newer, more radical groups such as the New Feminists and eventually Women's Liberation. The committee's leaders decided to focus initially on three issues: changes to human rights laws to include the prohibition of sex discrimination, expansion of daycare centres, and removal of abortion from the Criminal Code. When these leaders set up a much larger meeting in late March (based on representatives from forty national women's organizations that together represented a constituency of approximately 2 million women), the larger group unanimously endorsed the focus on human rights laws and approved the expansion of daycare centres but split over abortion rights.[33]

There was a strong affinity, of course, between liberal feminism and this human rights approach, as Monique Bégin has stressed. Bégin was the executive secretary of the Royal Commission, and, in reflecting on the commission's work approximately twenty years later, she explained that she and the commissioners "were liberal and pragmatic feminists." She maintained that "the commission did not have an explicit conceptual framework or a shared philosophy, other than its commitment to the 'equal rights' approach, which coexisted with general notions of the value of a specifically 'female culture.'" She contrasted the report's "reformist, moderate approach" with "the young women's liberation movement . . . with its radical concepts and dramatic demands."[34]

Indeed, some of the more radical feminists explicitly eschewed this kind of liberal individualistic human rights approach, which they dismissed as encompassing the shortcomings of liberal feminism. As the editors of *Women Unite!* declared in the introduction to their 1972 anthology, "the women's liberation movement . . . differs greatly from the middle class women's rights groups which consist mostly of professional and church women. Although the broad basis of both is the improvement of the quality of life for women in Canada, the philosophy of the women's rights groups is that civil liberty and equality can be achieved within the present system, while the underlying belief of women's liberation is that oppression can be overcome only through a radical and fundamental change in the structure of our society."[35]

In an article on radical feminism in *Women Unite!*, Bonnie Kreps (one of the founders of the New Feminists) declared that radical feminists necessarily opposed liberal feminists' goal of "some kind of integration of women into the main fabric of society." Hence, "*radical feminism . . . would not be particularly concerned with 'equal rights'* [and] 'equal pay for equal work.'" Calling for "really fundamental changes in our society," Kreps continued that "we, in this segment of the movement, do not believe that the oppression of women will be ended by giving them a bigger piece of the pie, as [American liberal feminist leader] Betty Friedan would have it. We believe that the pie itself is rotten."[36]

In another article in *Women Unite!*, entitled "Toward an Organization of Working Women," Jean Rands declared that, "because working women are both exploited as workers and oppressed as women, our struggle must shake this society to its very roots. . . . When women challenge the sex roles of this society, we will not merely ask for more women managers, more women principals, more women doctors. We will fight the fundamental division of labour between nurse and doctor, teacher and principal, secretary and boss." Rands also maintained that "working women must confront the corporations who benefit from our exploitation," for "we need an end to the division of labour into shitwork jobs and decision-making jobs—the division of labour that makes our jobs boring and justifies our lousy pay."[37]

Critiquing the Royal Commission's official recommendations for being "remarkably short-sighted," another article in the collection argued that the allegedly naive commissioners "failed somehow to understand the root causes of our oppression." From this socialist feminist point of view,

> the question to be asked is why a government closely inter-linked with business and industry would effect laws which will cut off a cheap pool of labour? Why equal pay? Why equal job

> opportunity? Big business is concerned about profit, not human equality. As women we are oppressed by the kind of society we live in—an economic system based on the exploitation of many by a few powerful owners and a social system dependent on racial, national, and sexual chauvinism. A few token women or even a significant minority of women sitting in corporation board rooms will not and cannot liberate women whose exploitation is the key to profits in quite a few industries.[38]

However, when assessing support for feminist human rights initiatives, it would be misleading to differentiate too schematically between liberal feminist groups, on the one hand, and radical feminist groups and socialist feminist groups, on the other hand. After all, there could be differences of opinion within a particular feminist organization at times, and the ideology of some organizations might have changed over time. Moreover, some groups, especially the New Feminists, helped to push for specific feminist changes to human rights codes even while advocating a far more radical ideology.

Appearing in 1969, the editorial in the first issue of the New Feminists' newsletter declared that "the first, fundamental step in the liberation of women is the rejection of a society" based on "separate but unequal sex-roles for men and women." It continued that, "a new society where pre-packaged sex-roles are irrelevant is our objective. . . . We must be humans before we are male or female, and society must be reconstituted to express this."[39] The New Feminists' newsletters in 1970 and 1971 affirmed the group's commitment to radical feminism and repeatedly warned that "there can be no stopping short of a revolutionary re-structuring of all of our society."[40] Hence, an article on the Royal Commission report declared that "society is so riddled with the cancer of woman's oppression that . . . every institution must be re-examined including marriage, the family, the church, the free-enterprise system, government, business, labour unions and the educational system. All of these have incorporated and in most cases derive direct benefits from the perpetuation of the exploitation of the female half of the human race. A few superficial changes in laws and in policies within institutions will not liberate women." This account went so far as to caution that "there is a danger, in fact, that temporary relief of symptoms could camouflage a real aggravation of the basic sickness." For example, "underlying the changes and proposed changes in divorce laws to make them more humane is a belief in the institution of marriage. This could postpone an analysis of the institution itself, which is probably the most oppressive institution of all for women."[41]

Yet, as we have seen, the New Feminists joined the National Ad Hoc Action Committee on the Status of Women, and they even co-sponsored a demonstration in April 1970 to pressure the Ontario government to add sex to the province's human rights code. They also called on their members to "PACK THE GALLERIES" on 28 May when the legislature was scheduled to debate New Democratic Party (NDP) MPP Cliff Pilkey's private member's bill calling for the prohibition of sex discrimination.[42] The New Feminists sent their own letter to all MPPs at that time, pushing them to support Pilkey's bill. Emphasizing the inclusion of sex as one of the prohibited grounds of discrimination in the United Nations' UDHR, the letter declared that "the glaring and obviously wilful omission of the word 'sex' from the Ontario code is we suggest an act of intolerable discrimination against one half of the citizens of the Province by a government which professes to be democratic. That women as a class are discriminated against more than any other class is beyond dispute. . . . There can be no moral or rational defense for not including 'sex' in the Ontario Human Rights Code" right away.[43]

The New Feminists expressed concern that attention to short-range, politically expedient goals should "not preclude the attainment of the long-range goals." In this context, one member declared that "perhaps . . . we should be wary of the dangers inherent even in grouping together and identifying ourselves as women—it may accentuate the sex categorization of people. For immediate political reasons, there is no other way than to develop a woman's identity but we must keep alert" since the real goal is to "get rid of the categorization of people by sex."[44]

Although this was a dilemma that could especially affect this type of radical feminist, it corresponds to what Joan Wallach Scott has labelled a central paradox for feminist activists. Focusing on feminists fighting for full political citizenship in France from 1789 to 1944, Scott explains that "feminism was a protest against women's political exclusion; its goal was to eliminate 'sexual difference' in politics, but it had to make its claims on behalf of 'women' (who were discursively produced through 'sexual difference'). To the extent that it acted for 'women,' feminism produced the 'sexual difference' it sought to eliminate. This paradox—the need both to accept *and* to refuse 'sexual difference'—was the constitutive condition of feminism as a political movement throughout its long history."[45] Although Scott focuses on French history over approximately 150 years, her point applies more broadly. In the Canadian context, even though equality between women and men has been further complicated as differences among women have been increasingly emphasized (especially since the 1980s),[46] this paradox remains important.

In the 1960s and early 1970s, Canadian feminists tended to believe that the oppression of women was different from the oppression of racialized groups. Although they sometimes drew quick parallels between women's liberation and Black liberation, for example, many feminists insisted on the unique nature of women's oppression.[47] Thus, there seem to have been few significant alliances between antiracist human rights advocates and feminist human rights advocates in this period. Of course, there were many feminists in these years, as well as many related articles in the mass media, that did not discuss feminist concerns within a human rights framework. However, for feminists who did focus significantly on human rights issues, there could have been, at least in theory, an alliance with certain antiracists on strengthening the powers of human rights commissions in Canada.

But there could be tensions linked to potential competition for scarce resources, as Joan Sangster has revealed in her examination of the development of the Women's Equal Employment Opportunity Act of 1970. The Ontario Women's Bureau, established in 1963, had pushed for the enactment of this provincial legislation. The Act prohibited sex discrimination in employment at a time when the Ontario Human Rights Code focused on race, creed, and national origin. Apparently, members of the Ontario Human Rights Commission were reluctant to add sex discrimination to their responsibilities, fearing that doing so would strain their limited resources and leave them too little time to combat racism. Yet some members of the NDP and representatives of organized labour were concerned that sex discrimination would not receive the prominence that it needed if it were not under the jurisdiction of the province's Human Rights Commission. However, according to Lita-Rose Betcherman, the director of the Women's Bureau at that time, feminists like her really wanted women's issues to be tackled separately, fearing that, if they were under the Human Rights Commission's authority, those issues might be subordinated to the commission's long-standing concerns.[48]

Meanwhile, the National Council of Jewish Women of Canada (NCJW) had evolved from a non-feminist orientation in the late 1940s and early 1950s to become part of the Steering Committee of the National Ad Hoc Action Committee on the Status of Women in the early 1970s. Founded in Toronto in 1897, this organization of middle-class volunteers focused for many decades on helping Canada's Jewish immigrants, especially girls and women. The organization provided a variety of social services, including English classes, recreational programs for girls, and aid for the elderly and sick.[49]

Jews were active in the 1940s and 1950s in pushing for human rights legislation, especially in the campaigns for the pioneering Fair Employment Practices Act (FEPA) in Ontario, but these efforts were largely by Jewish men who worked through the androcentric Jewish Labour Committee and the similarly androcentric Canadian Jewish Congress.[50] The NCJW's most notable contribution to the campaigns for FEPA took shape when the Toronto branch sponsored a large public meeting on this issue in mid-1949. Acting as the moderator of the meeting, Rabbi Abraham Feinberg started it by asserting "the right to work without handicap of race, religion or colour and also without handicap of sex." Yet apparently no one else at this meeting expressed concern about sex discrimination.[51] When the NCJW's Toronto section subsequently sent a resolution to the premier of Ontario calling on the government to find ways to end employment discrimination, its resolution focused on "race, color or creed" and omitted sex discrimination altogether.[52] In the immediate aftermath of the Holocaust, no doubt the intense dread of anti-Semitism was paramount.

Although Rabbi Feinberg continued to be one of the foremost antiracist human rights activists in the province, apparently he dropped the consideration of sex discrimination. In fact, an article that he submitted to *Chatelaine* in 1962 was rejected because the magazine's editors deemed his views on women too traditional.[53] As for the Jewish Labour Committee, apparently it did not join the eventual mobilization to broaden human rights codes to prohibit sex discrimination, and in fact the committee was fading by the early 1970s.[54]

In contrast, the NCJW's embrace of women's rights had become apparent by the late 1960s. In its brief to the Royal Commission on the Status of Women, the organization's national office called on the federal and provincial governments to implement the principles of the United Nations' Declaration on the Elimination of Discrimination against Women (1967). The brief specifically quoted the section of the declaration that called to "abolish existing laws, customs, regulations and practices which are discriminatory against women and establish adequate legal protection for equal rights of men and women."[55] Two other Jewish women's organizations, B'nai B'rith Women and Pioneer Women's Organization, also submitted feminist briefs. The latter asserted a woman's "human right to employment without discrimination" and called on the Canadian government "to educate public opinion and direct national aspirations toward elimination of prejudice and practices based on the idea of the inferiority of women."[56]

Meanwhile, the feminist campaign to amend the Ontario Human Rights Code had gained much momentum by 1970. The Women's Coalition for Inclusion of the Word Sex in the Ontario Human Rights Code consisted of a wide range of groups, including the Federation of Women Teachers' Associations of Ontario, the Toronto and Oshawa New Feminists, the Ontario branch of the Voice of Women, and several groups from organized labour.[57] Prominent women who pushed for adding sex to human rights codes, especially in Ontario, included former Liberal minister Judy LaMarsh and the feminist editor of *Chatelaine*, Doris Anderson.[58]

The Women's Coalition held a demonstration at Queen's Park in October 1970 to press for this change. Although the premier told coalition leaders that he did not think that women faced discrimination, the coalition's press release pointed out that the new Women's Equal Employment Opportunity Act contained "many loopholes," and "there are still areas of discrimination against women . . . in the fields of education, religion, housing and apartment accommodation, welfare, consumer credit, and others. The Human Rights Code MUST be changed to cover these." One of the leaders of the coalition was Patricia Proctor, the associate secretary of the Ontario Federation of Labour's Human Rights Committee, who also became one of organized labour's two representatives on the Steering Committee of the National Ad Hoc Action Committee on the Status of Women.[59] In fact, the labour movement's important role had also been highlighted in an earlier demonstration, for the Women's Committee of the Oshawa local of the United Auto Workers had been particularly active in promoting a protest at Queen's Park to advocate adding sex to the Human Rights Code in April 1970.[60]

Within the trade union movement more broadly, complex dynamics unfolded even as women continued to face significant barriers within their unions. Key labour groups, often prodded by activist female members, came to advocate officially for women's rights, especially for extending human rights laws to cover sex discrimination, particularly in employment.[61]

As for the NDP, a lot had changed since the Ontario CCF MPPs had failed to support Agnes Macphail's plea in 1951. Although the party officially supported groups such as the Women's Coalition for Inclusion of the Word Sex in the Ontario Human Rights Code and, as we have seen with regard to Cliff Pilkey, NDP politicians could play important roles in these efforts, some NDP members explicitly took issue with the liberal approach to women's rights. In a pamphlet entitled *Women in Canada—In Society, in Public Life, in the NDP*, the federal treasurer of the party, Mary Eady, promoted women's liberation while arguing that only a more collective approach would make it possible. She called for the "urban Kibbutz" whereby "family living would change, a housing development would contain apartments or units, but many things now owned privately would be co-operatively owned," such as restaurants and daycare centres. Furthermore, Eady argued, "we must change the basic premise of our society from one based on exploitation and materialism and owning things in private, to one based on human fulfillment and doing things co-operatively. Only in this way can we even begin to hope for liberation of those in our society who are not now free."[62]

Krista Maeots Laxer, one of the founders of the Waffle (a left-wing caucus established within the NDP in 1969), made similar arguments in another article in this pamphlet. In fact, Laxer boldly declared that "the small-l liberal position of our party—that a woman's place is wherever she wants it to be, in the home or in the work force—becomes an extremely reactionary position." She called for "socializing what is now called woman's work," for women would not have real choices without such measures. Thus, Laxer promoted "the community taking responsibility for many tasks now performed in the home," such as child care, meal services, cleaning services, et cetera. Women's liberation was an intrinsic part of "a new vision of a society organized for human fulfilment, rather than for more efficient human exploitation."[63]

Looking back at the 1940s and 1950s, we see that key segments of the Canadian labour movement, often led by the Jewish Labour Committee and African Canadian union activists, had championed human rights legislation that would prohibit discrimination on the basis of race, creed, and national origin, especially with respect to employment. David Goutor's chapter in this volume explains the factors that led key labour activists to combat racist discrimination in the aftermath of the Second World War. Paul-Etienne Rainville's chapter adds considerably to our understanding of these developments by focusing on the antiracist labour activists in Quebec as they also grappled with the prejudice and discrimination that French Canadians themselves faced in these years. At this time, human rights campaigns were also undertaken by middle-class Jewish activists as well as activists from a few other minority groups, along with key Anglo-Celtic allies, some of whom were well placed to influence government policies. As we have seen, these antiracist activists typically did not think that women needed human rights, even though a few feminists raised their voices back then. In the 1950s, the government of Ontario agreed, as did most other provincial governments as well as the federal government. The one concession that most of these governments made to women workers at that time was to bring in narrow equal pay laws that applied only to a woman doing the exact same job as a man.

By the mid-to-late 1960s, however, the women's movement surged forth in the wake of key demographic and economic changes. Whereas some feminists eschewed a liberal individualist human rights approach, many others demanded that antiracist human rights codes be changed to add sex as one of the prohibited grounds of discrimination. This was reflected in the liberal feminist orientation of the Royal Commission on the Status of Women, which emphasized the need for such change. As we have seen, the National Ad Hoc Action Committee on the Status of Women (which represented a wide variety of women's groups) prioritized the call to amend human rights legislation. In fact, the Women's Coalition for Inclusion of the Word Sex in the Ontario Human Rights Code gained support from labour activists as well as liberal feminists and even some of the more radical feminists who nonetheless supported such change. By the late 1970s, all of the provincial governments as well as the federal government had made these changes to human rights laws.

On the whole, the antiracist human rights campaigns and the feminist human rights campaigns apparently had proceeded separately, along different time frames, although certain labour leaders and leading politicians eventually came to endorse both causes officially. Although significant legislative gains were eventually made on both fronts, we must eschew a whiggish view of the development of Canada's allegedly deep commitment to human rights. As Jennifer Tunnicliffe and Stephanie Bangarth's introduction to this volume makes clear, the celebratory narrative of the ultimate triumph of Canada's human rights regime is mistaken. As so many of the chapters in this volume stress, key groups have been largely left out. However, even if Canada's human rights laws stretch to encompass more disadvantaged groups, and even if the enforcement of human rights legislation were to improve dramatically, all still would not be well.

Canada's human rights ethos remains rooted in a liberal orientation that stresses a short-sighted version of equality of opportunity while seldom encompassing the kinds of social and economic rights included as early as 1948 in the UDHR. This is a reflection, of course, of Canada's broader—and dominant—commitment to liberal ideology. However, even if women and members of minority groups were to become truly represented in the upper echelons of our economy and society in proportion to their percentages of the population, Canada still would be dramatically unequal.[64] Hence, we need to move beyond a limited liberal orientation to adopt a more radical conception of fundamental human rights and true equality. As Thomas Piketty has emphasized recently in *A Brief History of Equality*, "we must . . . underline the limits of an approach that is focused on the top of the hierarchy," for we must tackle a "social system that is extremely hierarchized."[65]

Notes

1 Editorial, *Globe and Mail*, 27 February 1951, 6 (emphasis added). For a detailed account of the campaigns leading to Ontario's 1951 Fair Employment Practices Act, see Carmela Patrias and Ruth A. Frager, "'This Is Our Country, These Are Our Rights': Minorities and the Origins of Ontario's Human Rights Campaigns," *Canadian Historical Review* 82, no. 1 (2001): 1–35.

2 Editorial, *Saturday Night*, 20 March 1951, 6.

3 See, for example, editorial, *Globe and Mail*, 1 November 1969, 6.

4 Editorial, *Globe and Mail*, 26 June 1972, 6; see also editorial, *Globe and Mail*, 10 December 1970, 6.

5 Editorial, *Globe and Mail*, 31 January 1970, 6.

6 On liberal individualism, see, for example, Dominique Clément, *Human Rights in Canada: A History* (Waterloo, ON: Wilfrid Laurier University Press, 2016), 17.

7 Lynn Hunt, *Inventing Human Rights: A History* (New York: W.W. Norton and Company, 2007), 27.

8 Hunt, 28.

9 Hunt, 66–67.

10 Hunt, 171.

11 Kalmen Kaplansky, interview with Carmela Patrias and Ruth Frager, Ottawa, 30 June 1995.

12 See also Dominique Clément, *Equality Deferred: Sex Discrimination and British Columbia's Human Rights State, 1953–84* (Vancouver: UBC Press, 2014), 92.

13 Pat Armstrong and Hugh Armstrong, *The Double Ghetto: Canadian Women and Their Segregated Work* (Toronto: McClelland and Stewart, 1978), 1–42. For referenced statistics, see 17. See also Patricia Connelly, *Last Hired First Fired: Women and the Canadian Work Force* (Toronto: Women's Press, 1978), 84.

14 For a summary of these changes, see, for example, Gail Cuthbert Brandt et al., *Canadian Women: A History* (Toronto: Nelson Education, 2011), 437–40, 480–85. On the 1969 legislation, see Christopher Dummitt and Christabelle Sethna's introduction to their co-edited volume, *The Origins and Legacies of the 1969 Omnibus Bill* (Vancouver: UBC Press, 2020), 7.

15 On the Second Wave, see, for example, Nancy Adamson et al., *Feminist Organizing for Change: The Contemporary Women's Movement in Canada* (Toronto: Oxford University Press, 1988), 37–71.

16 Ruth A. Frager and Carmela Patrias, "Human Rights Activists and the Question of Sex Discrimination in Post-War Ontario," *Canadian Historical Review* 93, no. 4 (2012): 583–610.

17 Ontario, *Proceedings of the Third Session of the Twenty-Third Legislature*, vol. 29, 13 March 1951.

18 "Report from the Status of Women Committee to the Ontario CCF," 1948, Library and Archives Canada (LAC), Canadian Labour Congress Fonds, MG28 I103, vol. 459, file 22.

19 The CCF's founding manifesto called for "equal treatment before law of all residents of Canada irrespective of race, nationality or religious or political beliefs." CCF, Regina Manifesto, 7, Saskatchewan Archives, S-G2-1933.6, CCF Pamphlets, 1933.

20 Margaret Hyndman, report to Premier of Ontario Leslie Frost, 19 February 1951, 3, 10, LAC, Margaret Hyndman Collection, MG31 E98, vol. 1, file 17; Elizabeth Forbes, *With Enthusiasm and Faith: History of the Canadian Federation of Business and Professional Women's Clubs* (n.p.: CFBPWC, 1974), 75–76.

21 *Globe and Mail*, 9 March 1951, 16.

22 Frager and Patrias, "Human Rights Activists," 593–605.

23 The Bill of Rights is reprinted in Christopher MacLennan, *Toward the Charter: Canadians and the Demand for a National Bill of Rights, 1929–1960* (Montreal and Kingston: McGill-Queen's University Press, 2003), 175–77.

24 See, for example, MacLennan, 91–99, 109–12, 126–37. See also Ross Lambertson, *Repression and Resistance: Canadian Human Rights Activists, 1930–1960* (Toronto: University of Toronto Press, 2005), 240, 318–71.

25 MacLennan, *Toward the Charter*, 126–37, 148–50; Lambertson, *Repression and Resistance*, 362–71.

26 See, for example, editorial, *Globe and Mail*, 15 August 1972, 6; Clément, *Equality Deferred*, 44, 74; Lambertson, *Repression and Resistance*, 370–71; MacLennan, *Toward the Charter*, 151–61; and Brandt et al., *Canadian Women*, 567.

27 Walter Surma Tarnopolsky, *Discrimination and the Law in Canada* (Don Mills, ON: Richard de Boo, 1982), 27–29, 35; R. Brian Howe and David Johnson, *Restraining Equality: Human Rights Commissions in Canada* (Toronto: University of Toronto Press, 2000), 8; Clément, *Equality Deferred*, 73–74. On the 1970 and 1972 changes in Ontario, see, for example, *Globe and Mail*, 15 May 1970, 11; 15 August 1970, 13; 31 May 1972, 11; 23 June 1972, 1; and 18 August 1972, B2.

28 Royal Commission on the Status of Women (RCSW) in Canada, *Report of the Royal Commission on the Status of Women in Canada* (Ottawa: Information Canada, 1970), xi.

29 RCSW, 3 (quoting from Brief No. 441).

30 RCSW, 398; see also 98.

31 RCSW, 418.

32 See, for example, *Globe and Mail*, 8 December 1970, 15; *Toronto Star*, 21 December 1970, 49; and *Globe and Mail*, 29 March 1971, 11.

33 *Globe and Mail*, 23 February 1971, 11; *Globe and Mail*, 30 March 1971, 10; *Toronto Star*, 30 March 1971, 54; *Toronto Star*, 13 August 1971, 50.

34 Monique Bégin, "The Royal Commission on the Status of Women in Canada: Twenty Years Later," in *Challenging Times: The Women's Movement in Canada and the United States*, ed. Constance Backhouse and David H. Flaherty (Montreal and Kingston: McGill-Queen's University Press, 1992), 29, 34–35. See also Monique Bégin, *Ladies Upstairs! My Life in Politics and After* (Montreal and Kingston: McGill-Queen's University Press, 2019), 66–67.

35 Janice Acton et al., "Introduction," in *Women Unite! An Anthology of the Canadian Women's Movement* [hereafter *Women Unite!*], ed. Discussion Collective No. 6 (Toronto: Canadian Women's Educational Press, 1972), 9.

36 Bonnie Kreps, "Radical Feminism," in *Women Unite!*, 74–75 (emphasis added).

37 Jean Rands, "Toward an Organization of Working Women," in *Women Unite!*, 146.

38 "Pie in the Sky," in *Women Unite!*, 40–41.

39 Editorial, *New Feminist* [hereafter *NF*], 17 November 1969, 1.

40 Editorial, *NF*, January 1971, 1. See also editorial, *NF*, March 1970, 1.

41 Position Paper, *NF*, May 1971, 2–3.

42 *NF*, May 1970, 22, 25. The New Feminists' newsletter also called on its members to join a demonstration organized by Toronto Gay Action to add sexual orientation as one of the prohibited grounds of discrimination in the Ontario Human Rights Code. On this, see *NF*, October 1971, 17.

43 *NF*, May 1970, 2.

44 Position Paper, *NF*, May 1971, 6.

45 Joan Wallach Scott, *Only Paradoxes to Offer: French Feminists and the Rights of Man* (Cambridge, MA: Harvard University Press, 1996), 3–4.

46 On the increasing emphasis on the diversity of women, see, for example, Alexandra Dobrowolsky, "The Women's Movement in Flux: Feminism and Framing, Passion,

and Politics," in *Group Politics and Social Movements in Canada*, ed. Miriam Smith (Peterborough: Broadview Press, 2008), 170–71. Dobrowolsky goes so far as to characterize the Canadian women's movement of the 1960s and 1970s as a product of "false universalism."

47 See, for example, Peggy Morton, "Women's Work Is Never Done . . . ," in *Women Unite!*, 46–47.

48 Joan Sangster, "Doing Two Jobs: The Wage-Earning Mother, 1945–70," in *A Diversity of Women: Ontario, 1945–1980*, ed. Joy Parr (Toronto: University of Toronto Press, 1995), 107, 113–15; *Globe and Mail*, 15 May 1970, 11; 10 June 1970, 13; 11 November 1970, 11; 29 March 1971, 11; Lita-Rose Betcherman's conversation with Ruth Frager and Carmela Patrias, Ottawa, 15 June 1995.

49 Eliane Leslau Silverman, "The National Council of Jewish Women: Private Lives, Public People," *Canadian Woman Studies* 7, no. 4 (1986): 49–51; Gerald Tulchinsky, *Canada's Jews: A People's Journey* (Toronto: University of Toronto Press, 2008), 104; Adamson et al., *Feminist Organizing for Change*, 52.

50 On the central role of male Jewish activists in pressing the Ontario government to enact FEPA, see Patrias and Frager, "'This Is Our Country,'" 17–34.

51 Transcript of panel discussion, 21 April [1949], 1, LAC, Records of the Jewish Labour Committee (JLC), MG28 V75, vol. 15, file 14.

52 Bella Sanders to Mr. Tanaka, 30 May 1949, LAC, JLC, MG28 V75, vol. 15, file 14.

53 On his submission to *Chatelaine*, see Valerie J. Korinek, *Roughing It in the Suburbs: Reading* Chatelaine *Magazine in the Fifties and Sixties* (Toronto: University of Toronto Press, 2000), 330–31.

54 On the JLC in British Columbia, see Clément, *Equality Deferred*, 92. On the JLC's demise, see Dominique Clément, "Jewish Labour Committee," Canada's Human Rights History, https://historyofrights.ca/archives/jewish-labour-committee/.

55 Brief to the RCSW from the national office of the National Council of Jewish Women of Canada, May 1968 (Brief #361), 2–3. See also brief to the RCSW from the Vancouver office of the National Council of Jewish Women, [1968] (Brief #378), 2, 5, 7. These briefs are available in the Government Documents Section of McMaster University's Mills Library.

56 Brief to the RCSW from the Pioneer Women's Organization of Canada, 11 March 1968 (Brief #65), 3–4. See also brief to the RCSW from B'nai B'rith Women, [1968] (Brief #107). As for African Canadian women, apparently, they did not have an organization affiliated with the Women's Coalition for Inclusion of the Word Sex in the Ontario Human Rights Code or with the National Ad Hoc Action Committee on the Status of Women.

57 *Globe and Mail*, 13 April 1970, 13; *Globe and Mail*, 29 April 1970, 1; *Toronto Star*, 29 April 1970, 80; *Globe and Mail*, 30 October 1970, 11.

58 *Globe and Mail*, 16 April 1970, W3; *Toronto Star*, 15 May 1970, 12.

59 The quotation is from the Women's Coalition press release, 27 October 1970, LAC, Ontario Labour Committee for Human Rights Fonds [hereafter OLCHR], MG28

I173, vol. 23, file "'Sex' in Ontario Human Rights Code. Women's Coalition. 1970." See also *Globe and Mail*, 30 October 1970, 11; handwritten notes, LAC, OLCHR, MG28 I173, vol. 23, file "'Sex' in Ontario Human Rights Code. Women's Coalition. 1970"; Minutes of the Steering Committee of the National Ad Hoc Action Committee on the Status of Women, 17 May 1971, vol. 25, file "Women. National Ad Hoc Committee on the Status of Women. 1971–72"; and Patricia Proctor to Mrs. John Bird, 8 February 1971, vol. 20, file "Ontario Federation of Labour. Educational Conference. 'Sex Discrimination.' 1971."

60 *Globe and Mail*, 13 April 1970, 13; *Globe and Mail*, 29 April 1970, 1; *Toronto Star*, 29 April 1970, 80; *Globe and Mail*, 30 October 1970, 11.

61 See, for example, Pamela Sugiman, *Labour's Dilemma: The Gender Politics of Auto Workers in Canada, 1937–1979* (Toronto: University of Toronto Press, 1994), 137–70, 195; "Submission of the Ontario Federation of Labour to the Royal Commission on the Status of Women in Canada," 1968, 22–23, Rise Up! A Digital Archives of Feminist Activism, https://riseuptest.wpengine.com/activism/organizations/ontario-federation-of-labour/ofl-1968-submissionroyalcommissionstatuswomen/; "Submission by the Canadian Labour Congress to the Royal Commission on the Status of Women," 1968, 2–6, Rise Up! A Digital Archives of Feminist Activism, https://riseuptest.wpengine.com/activism/organizations/canadian-labour-congress-clc/clc-1968-submission_to_royal_commission_status_of_women/; and Joan Sangster, *Transforming Labour: Women and Work in Post-War Canada* (Toronto: University of Toronto Press, 2010), 247, 266.

62 Mary Eady, "For Independence and Opportunity," in *Women in Canada—In Society, in Public Life, in the NDP* [c. 1970; hereafter *Women in Canada*], 7, LAC, OLCHR, MG28 I173, vol. 25, file "Women. Miscellaneous. 1969–71."

63 Krista Maeots Laxer, "The Burdens of Discrimination," in *Women in Canada*, 10, 12. On her role in the founding of the Waffle, see, for example, NDP Socialist Caucus, "Remembering Jim Laxer," 26 February 2018, https://ndpsocialists.ca/remembering-jim-laxer/.

64 On the Jewish Labour Committee's socialist position, see Ruth A. Frager and Carmela Patrias, "Transnational Links and Citizens' Rights: Canadian Jewish Human Rights Activists and Their American Allies in the 1940s and 1950s," in *Taking Liberties: A History of Human Rights in Canada*, ed. David Goutor and Stephen Heathorn (Don Mills, ON: Oxford University Press, 2013), 150–51.

65 Thomas Piketty, *A Brief History of Equality* (Cambridge, MA: Harvard University Press, 2022), 187–88.

CHAPTER 4

On the Edge of Freedom: The Re-Enslavement of Elizabeth Watson in Nova Scotia[1]

Franco Paz and Harvey Amani Whitfield

IT WAS EARLY March 1778, seven o'clock in the morning. Elizabeth Watson lay shackled to the floor of a dark cellar.[2] She had been enslaved in Halifax, Nova Scotia, by Elias Marshall, master shipwright of the Royal Naval Dockyard.[3] Marshall had beaten her for six hours. Elizabeth Watson was pregnant. He had known for eight days.

Watson went into labour likely as a result of Marshall's assault. When she asked him for "help to have her [child] delivered," Marshall beat her once again. Hours later, Watson crawled out of the house toward a latrine inside the stable. In that outhouse, surrounded only by Marshall's cattle, she delivered her own child "without assistance from any earthly being."

Marshall found her there the following morning. He wanted Watson to work, ordered her to wash herself, but Watson told Marshall she was cold. "I will soon cure you," Marshall said. He sent Durdsly, another servant, to fill two buckets with snow and ice water, which Marshall emptied over her body. He left Watson there.[4]

The next day, Marshall took Watson back into the house, where his wife waited with a fire iron. When Watson entered the house, Marshall's wife seized her and split open her skull. Afterward, Marshall dragged her down the stairs and into the cellar once more, tied her hands and feet to a beam, and beat her for one hour. Then he walked upstairs to eat dinner.

Marshall went back to the cellar once he had finished eating. This time he beat Watson well into the night, until her body was no longer bound by skin. She could not even lie down. Her exposed flesh forced Watson to remain on her hands and knees. Realizing her life was in peril, Marshall was at last forced to call a doctor. When Halifax surgeon Phillips saw Watson, he fainted.[5]

The doctor pronounced Elizabeth Watson dead.

Elias Marshall did not accept this. He called a second, unnamed doctor, who was ultimately able to stabilize her, though this entailed severing large patches of skin and flesh from her body. Once Watson's life was no longer in immediate danger, Marshall refused to feed her anything but "peas or what [she] could get out of the Hog's Trough."[6]

Soon after, Marshall sold Elizabeth Watson to John Woodin.[7] Recognizing this opportunity to escape enslavement, Watson petitioned the Halifax Inferior Court of Common Pleas. She claimed she had been born a free woman in Boston and had been abducted there "under false pretense." As her witness she brought Elizabeth Reed, another Boston-born Halifax slave. Reed attested to the veracity of Watson's testimony, testifying that she "well knew . . . Elizabeth Watson to be a Free Woman." She added that Watson lived with a Mrs. Lobdell prior to her abduction. Following Reed's deposition, the court declared Watson a free woman.[8]

Watson's liberty only lasted thirty-one days. On 23 April 1779, Halifax butcher William Proud seized Elizabeth Watson and claimed she was his "Right and Property."[9]

The explicit portrayal of the violence Elizabeth Watson suffered at the hands of Elias Marshall might strike some readers as over the top, an altogether too graphic depiction of an event that constituted, at the end of the day, a shocking aberration in the generally "benign" form of slavery that existed in the Canadian Maritimes. This is simply not true.[10] But it is also beside the point. Whether or not this base brutality is indicative of the experience of the majority of Maritime bondspeople is incidental. This assault—this particular assault—happened. The account of it comes from Elizabeth Watson's deposition. These are her words. To omit or otherwise sanitize her story would have done her and others like her a disservice.[11]

Although the individual lives of enslaved people may have been erased by the archive's quiet tyranny, their presence in pre-Loyalist Nova Scotia remains evident. Beyond attesting to the brutal world in which she and others like her lived, Watson's story, particularly her petitioning of the lower court, reveals her keen understanding of the legal world she inhabited and of her rights as a British subject. But her actions alone do not account for the trial's occurrence. Watson's ability to stand in a court of law against white men suggests a legal apparatus that to some extent enabled Black people to assert themselves. A full ensemble of institutions, regulations, and customs must come together for such a trial to take place: lawyers willing to take a slave's case, judges inclined to hear it, juries amenable enough to not make the act futile. This apparatus is worth exploring, as is its role in regulating the conditions of possibility for both Black and white Maritime populations.

Watson's story is an early example of re-enslavement in the region.[12] Her story departs from well-known narratives of African American freedom in Canada. Likewise, it complicates and nuances historical analyses of the Black Atlantic world and reveals the porous, fragile nature of the boundary between slavery and freedom. Watson's protean story, time and again oscillating between freedom and slavery, is emblematic of this history. Elizabeth Watson was likely the first enslaved woman to seek her freedom in a Maritime court of law, but she was not the last. Watson's legal fight was followed by those of two other enslaved Black women: Mary Postell in 1791 and Nancy, with no surname, in New Brunswick nine years later.[13] Elizabeth Watson oscillated from slavery to freedom and back to slavery in the space of thirty-one days. Tracing the genealogy of her search for liberty and exploring her path to enslavement in Nova Scotia broaden our perception of the Maritime world's unique syntax. Elizabeth Watson brings this world of unfreedom into a fuller, more vivid light. Her life complicates our understanding of the threads that bound freedom and slavery in the Atlantic world.

Slavery in the Maritimes

Even as early as the seventeenth century, Africans had a presence in the Maritimes. Mathieu Da Costa, an early free Black man in colonial Canada, was a member of Pierre Dugua de Mons's 1605 exploratory party.[14] He likely worked as a translator between the French and Mi'kmaq, but it is unclear how Da Costa "might have travelled to North America, how long he stayed, for whom he worked, and with whom he interpreted."[15] His last name reveals some connection to Portugal. His story links him to the Atlantic Creoles, who were well versed in "the commerce of the Atlantic, fluent in its new languages, and intimate with its trade and cultures."[16] It is likely that Da Costa spoke multiple languages, including French and Mi'kmaq, and that he was familiar with the culture of the latter. Though his life remains obscured by a lack of extant sources, the known fragments of his life connote links between distant regions of the Atlantic world. Other Africans arrived in Nova Scotia during the seventeenth century. Little is known about their lives or whether they were enslaved. The archives hold a few scattered stories, most notably that of La Liberté, who lived in Cape Sable (an island off the southern coast of Nova Scotia) around 1686 and was likely "a slave who had escaped from one of the colonies to the south."[17]

Most enslaved Black Canadians during the first half of the eighteenth century lived in Île Royale, known eventually as Cape Breton.[18] At least 266 enslaved people populated Île Royale between 1713 and 1758, with the majority of them living in Louisbourg.[19] They came from a variety of backgrounds, including Africa, the West Indies, and the American colonies. In contrast to other areas of New France, where the enslaved were largely Indigenous, over 90 percent of Île Royale's enslaved population was Black.[20] They worked predominantly as domestic servants. They cleaned, cooked, nursed, gardened, and more.[21] Only nineteen of Île Royale's bondspeople worked outside the household: one fisherman, two cabin boys, fifteen sailors, and one executioner.[22] There were only a few enslaved people per household. The small-scale nature of Île Royale slavery, where close contact between slaveholders and the enslaved was the norm, led to a deep-rooted culture of sexual violence.[23]

In 1749, Edward Cornwallis and 2,500 settlers sailed into the waters of Chebucto on a sloop of war and thirteen transport ships. They disembarked along the harbour's spruce-lined shore and founded Halifax.[24] Enslaved Black people became a habitual sight soon thereafter, having made their way to Nova Scotia with Cornwallis's first settlers, as well as through the business dealings of early Halifax merchants. In 1750, Captain Bloss, a Royal Navy officer, brought sixteen bondspeople to Nova Scotia possibly from Antigua. They built him "a very good house."[25] It is likely that the people Bloss enslaved worked as agricultural labourers and domestic servants.[26]

In September 1751, the *Boston Post-Boy* advertised the sale of "ten strong hearty Negro men mostly tradesmen, such as caulkers, carpenters, sailmakers, and ropemakers."[27] This advertisement reveals the type of skilled labour that characterized Maritime slavery, as well as the existence of established trade routes between newly founded Halifax and Massachusetts. The following year, Thomas Thomas, "late of New York, but now of Halifax," wrote a will in which he bequeathed "all my plate and my negro servant Orange, that now lives with me at Halifax . . . to my son."[28]

The diversity of skills Maritime bondspeople possessed was once again displayed in merchant Joshua Mauger's 1752 sale notice in the *Halifax Gazette*. Mauger's advertisement was published shortly after his return from the West Indies and describes "several Negro slaves . . . a likely Negro Wench, of about thirty-five years of Age . . . capable of doing Needle-Work of all sorts . . . Washing, Ironing, Cookery and every other Thing that can be expected of such a Slave . . . Likewise two healthy Negro Slaves about 18 years of Age, of agreable [*sic*] Tempers, and fit for any kind of Business."[29] This advertisement indicates both the existence of a viable slave-trading market in Halifax—Mauger would likely have sold the slaves during the return voyage otherwise—and the city's growth as an urban centre, by then part of a larger Atlantic trading network between North America and the West Indies.[30] Coupled with the 1751 *Boston Post-Boy* sale notice, the advertisements display the versatile, multi-occupational nature of Maritime slavery and reveal labour patterns that would echo in the lives of the enslaved brought to the province by the New England Planters in 1760 and the Loyalists in 1783.[31]

Following the brutal expulsion of the Acadians from the Maritimes between 1755 and 1764, Governor Charles Lawrence offered land expropriated from the Acadians to English-speaking settlers from New England. The government granted an additional fifty acres of land to these settlers for each Black person they brought into the colony, encouraging slavery in the region. Between 1759 and 1774, approximately 8,000 Planters settled in Nova Scotia. Historians do not know the exact number of enslaved people who arrived in the Maritimes during this time, but it is clear that a number of prominent Planters were slaveholders.[32]

The New England Planters' use of enslaved labour and their efforts to strengthen slavery in the Maritime colonies underlined their similarity to other slaveholding areas throughout New England and New York. As in Île Royale, close contact between slaveholders and the enslaved was the norm. Most enslaved people worked in a range of tasks, such as planting crops, repairing fences, cooking, cleaning, and caring for children. Nova Scotia's Black population increased as a result of the New England Planters' arrival, but it remained small. For example, a colonial census taken in 1767 shows that Nova Scotia's Black population hardly exceeded 100, though this census almost certainly excluded the enslaved population.[33] The exact number of the enslaved population in Nova Scotia prior to the arrival of the Loyalists is impossible to calculate and will more than likely remain unknown.[34]

However, the experiences of the enslaved remain buried in the letters and diaries of white slaveholders and newspaper advertisements submitted by those who sought to buy or sell a person. In 1759, for example, a Halifax merchant named Malachy Salter wrote to his wife, Susanna Mulberry, and asked her to buy a slave while she was travelling in Boston. As Salter explained, a young, enslaved boy had proven troublesome. "Jack is Jack still," he wrote, "but rather worse. I am obliged [to beat him] almost every day."[35]

One year later, the *Halifax Gazette* advertised for the sale "at public auction on Monday the 3rd of November, at the house of Mr. John Rider, of two slaves, viz. a boy and a girl, about eleven years old."[36] Rider was a surveyor of highways who later managed—perhaps owned—the Wolfe Tavern, deemed in its day a "very elegant resort . . . [whose] wines were noted for excellence."[37] It is not known, however, whether Rider owned the two children sold at his home in the spring of 1760.

A Halifax assemblyman named Charles Proctor sold a "Mulatto girl" to Mary Wood of Annapolis, wife of missionary Reverend Thomas Wood, in the summer of 1767.[38] The girl's name was Louisa. She cost fifteen pounds. Mary Wood transferred ownership of Louisa to her daughter Mary Day, and Louisa then disappeared from history.[39] According to the January 1771 census, there were seven other bondspeople in Annapolis. Ebenezer Messenger owned one of them. Nothing is known about the man Ebenezer Messenger owned. Elsewhere in Annapolis, Magdalen Winniett owned a man, a woman, and a girl. Joseph Winniett owned a woman and a boy. Ann Williams owned one man. One is struck by how often all that remains of a Black life is the name of the white life that professed to own it.

Like those of Jack, Louisa, and other enslaved Black Canadians, the details surrounding Elizabeth Watson's arrival remain uncertain. Most likely, Watson arrived in Halifax sometime in the 1770s. Although the nature of slave labour in the region remained relatively unchanged following the arrival of the New England Planters, there is one contemporary local slave advertisement that denotes the particular skills Watson may have been expected to possess. In May 1776, a man published a notice in the *Nova Scotia Gazette and Weekly Chronicle*. He hoped to acquire "a Negro Woman, about 25 or 30 years of age, that understands country work . . . the management of a dairy . . . and domestic labor."[40] The breadth of skills that the enslaved—particularly women—were expected to have would likely have included "farming, cooking, cleaning, washing clothes, and looking after children."[41] Physical tasks might have been as diverse as "cutting, carting, threshing . . . milling wheat . . . husking corn . . . cutting cornstalks; mowing, raking, and carting hay; digging . . . sledding stones and building stone walls; building fences; cutting . . . wood; hoeing and picking peas, beans, and turnips."[42] Watson and others enslaved in Nova Scotia prior to the American Revolution would have experienced a form of slavery with many of the characteristics found in the province's New England counterpart.

Both New England and the Maritime region maintained slaveholding connections and trading relationships with the West Indies. Yet, the small number of bondspeople per household implies an inherent level of proximity between the enslaved and slaveholders that contrasts with the Caribbean and southern United States; low population density in turn indicates a greater difficulty in forming Black communities and producing distinct Black cultures compared to the large-scale plantations of the southern colonies and the Caribbean.[43] But this is not to say that the enslaved women and men of Nova Scotia were unable to develop communities or distinct cultures. Certain aspects of low-density, small-scale slavery with multi-occupational, semi-skilled, and skilled labour patterns might even have lent themselves to cultural diffusion in a way that large plantations did not. "Abroad" marriages and romantic relationships, for example, were likely far more common in Nova Scotia than South Carolina. In addition, skilled workers were often able to travel unsupervised. All of these represented valuable opportunities to network and build communities across large distances.[44]

Though the number of bondspeople brought to Nova Scotia by the New England Planters will almost certainly remain elusive, there are enough extant sources to suppose it was modest.[45] The New England Planters came largely from overcrowded areas of southern New England. They were above all else attracted to Nova Scotia by the promise of free developed land. They did not have much money; they likely would have bought land in New England if they had had the financial resources to do so.[46] Governor Lawrence's offer included subsidies to cover the cost of resettlement, further enticing New Englanders of lower socio-economic status.[47] All of this amounts to the unlikelihood that slaveholding was widespread among Planters. But slavery had an influence far more pervasive than bare numbers might suggest. Planters who had the greatest financial resources were likely to take on positions of leadership within the province. These same men were the most likely to enslave Black people. Slaveholders may have been a minority, but—as evidenced by Malachy Salter and others—they tended to have outsized influence over public and legislative policy. In outright political terms, it did not matter whether the New England Planters brought 20 or 2,000 bondspeople so long as the right people enslaved them.

Nova Scotia never had a statute law that recognized or regulated slavery.[48] Indeed, Prince Edward Island was the only Maritime province ever to enact slavery into law.[49] In 1762, Nova Scotia came as close as it ever would to acknowledging the existence of slavery within its territory. The Second Session of the Third General Assembly convened that year and passed the Innholders Act, which banned the sale of alcohol on credit for "any sum exceeding five shillings . . . to any soldier, sailor, servant, apprentice, bound servant, or negro slave."[50] It is not beyond reason to speculate that the language of the bill might have been engineered in such a way as to give slavery a legal footing in the province. After all, the Third General Assembly counted slaveholders among their rank. Slaveholders were present in the Nova Scotia Assembly as late as 1808.[51]

Lacking statute law, the legitimacy of slavery in Nova Scotia was predicated on the notion that custom attains the force of law and as such remained "implicitly lawful . . . until adjudged or legislated to be explicitly illegal."[52] This rationale began to be challenged in the 1780s following the arrival of the Loyalists. But even then these challenges were rare and often unsuccessful. Fruitful legal challenges on the basis of title defect did not become the norm until the 1792 exodus to Sierra Leone. Elizabeth Watson's court cases should not be confused with these actions, which were explicitly designed to test the legality of slavery within the province.

From Slavery to Freedom

When Elizabeth Watson petitioned the Halifax Inferior Court of Common Pleas in March 1778, she claimed she had been "brought from Boston [to Halifax]" and there, unknown to herself, had been sold to Elias Marshall as a slave. By petitioning the court, she became the first Black woman to seek possession of her freedom in a Nova Scotia court of law.[53] Elizabeth Watson's keen understanding of the legal world she inhabited and of her rights as a British subject may well point to her New England origins. Indeed, freedom suits were a well-established legal recourse for the enslaved population of New England around the time Elizabeth Watson likely arrived in Nova Scotia.[54]

In New England, Joan Jackson was the first Black woman to win her freedom through judicial proceedings. She was declared free in 1716 in Cambridge, Massachusetts, and spent the remainder of her life seeking freedom for her children.[55] By 1750, three other enslaved women had obtained their legal freedom—one in South Kingstown, Rhode Island, and two in Portsmouth, New Hampshire.[56] These women seized their liberty through "freedom suits," civil actions brought by bondspeople, which often culminated in a lower court trial.[57] In other words, New England's freedom suits were traditionally brought in the exact fashion that Elizabeth Watson sought her freedom in March 1778. Though freedom suits originated in colonial Virginia, where six such actions had been brought by 1670, the loopholes that allowed enslaved women and men to sue for freedom in the American South did not remain open for long.[58]

By the eighteenth century, New England's legal system was unique in granting judicial access for such actions to enslaved and free Black people. Even in the northern colonies, there were few freedom suits outside of New England. None occurred in Pennsylvania or New Jersey prior to the end of the American Revolution. Likewise, there is no record of a freedom suit brought by an enslaved woman or man in New York.[59] By contrast, fourteen Massachusetts women filed civil lawsuits to secure their freedom between 1716 and 1783.[60] All of this points to Elizabeth Watson's New England origins and establishes her case as a transnational example of New England's freedom suits.

Elizabeth Watson's petition and subsequent freedom, however brief, can be interpreted as the ultimate assertion of her rights as a British subject, as well as a powerful statement to her self-perception and identity.[61] It can also be interpreted as a violent reminder of the aporia that permeated Blackness and slavery in New England, which Elizabeth Watson embodied as she stood astride her status of legal personhood and chattel. On the other hand, her re-enslavement at the hands of Halifax butcher William Proud and the jury's decision to reaffirm her slave status can be interpreted as symbolic of the ideological battle over the meaning of freedom—and therefore the meaning of slavery—that seized British North America around the time of the Revolutionary War.[62] Indeed, the 1765 Stamp Act coincided with a sharp rise in the incidence of freedom suits. This has twofold importance: while Elizabeth Watson clearly knew about and was influenced by these suits, so were the Loyalist judges and lawyers who later proved instrumental to ending slavery in Nova Scotia during the 1790s.

The Re-Enslavement of Elizabeth Watson

Proceedings at the Supreme Court began on 13 July 1778.[63] George Thomson, in front of Chief Justice Bryan Finucane and his assistant justices, declared in a writ of replevin that "William Proud . . . alias Butcher" had unlawfully seized Elizabeth Watson on 24 April 1778, and held her captive still at that very moment. Thomson declared that Watson was suing Proud for damages of £100—almost £20,000 today. Richard Gibbons's avowry on behalf of William Proud admitted to "the force and Injury" Proud had used when he abducted Elizabeth Watson but nonetheless affirmed that he had been justified in his actions, as Watson was "a Negro Slave and Servant [who] . . . without the consent and against the Will of the Said William Proud did desert and abscond from his service." Gibbons went on to say that "the Said female Negro Slave and Servant [was] truly called and known by the name of Phillis but [is] falsely and pretendedly calling herself Elizabeth Watson." He finished his avowry by asserting that Elizabeth Watson was William Proud's "absolute Slave and Servant, Right and Property and part of the proper Goods Chattels and Estate of the said William Proud and not a good Lawful and Free Woman." Thomson's replication maintained that Proud could not have abducted Watson lawfully because "she was and Yet is a Good Lawful and Free Woman justly and truly named Elizabeth Watson." "Without this," Thomson finished, "She is a Slave and Servant." Once Gibbons and Thomson had finished laying out their respective cases, the court commanded that a jury of "twelve free and lawful Men" convene at a later date to decide Elizabeth Watson's fate.

On 1 August 1778, a Court of Special Sessions of the Peace sat for the trial.[64] The judges were John George Pyke, Thomas Bridge, George Smith, and John Newton, the first three of whom had heard Watson's original suit against Elias Marshall. Elizabeth Watson secured the services of George Thomson, the most junior attorney in the province.[65] William Proud, by contrast, was represented by Solicitor General Richard Gibbons Jr., the senior member of the bar and its most prominent attorney—which points, perhaps, to the potentially high-profile nature of the trial. Elizabeth Watson's sworn deposition, signed with an X, is quoted here:

> Justices. —
>
> Elizabeth Watson, being duly Sworn Deposeth and Saith that on, or about the 16th Day of July last, about three of the Clock in the Morning being Warm, and much fatigued by Cooking &ca. in the House of Mr. William Proud, she went out to the necessary, when said Mr. Proud came out thither with a Candle, and this Deponent being in the necessary ask'd who came there. And immediately [Proud] asked who this Deponent had with her, and Demanded her to open the Door, and come out Directly, and this Deponent came into the House accordingly, and one Mr. Barn being in the House much in Liquor with this Deponent taking Notice of by Expressing the same. Mrs. Proud the wife of the said William Proud immediately Struck this Deponent in the face with her Hand after which this Deponent went up the Stairs and said Mr. Proud and his Wife both follow'd this Deponent. And the said Mr. Proud flogged, or Beat, this Deponent Violently with a Horse Whipp he had brought with him until he broke it & after got another and continued to repeat the same for a long time, and then kicked her this Deponent with his feet down the Stairs, or some part thereof.[66]

The Supreme Court of Nova Scotia took over the case through a writ of certiorari filed by Richard Gibbons after Watson's assertion that she had suffered "damage to the value of One Hundred Pounds."[67]

George Thomson applied for and obtained a writ de homine replegiando. This writ is crucial to understanding the significance of Elizabeth Watson's trial. De homine replegiando is an old medieval writ—perhaps one of the oldest, first appearing in the pipe rolls of 1165–66.[68] The writ de homine replegiando "lies to replevy a man out of prison, or out of custody of any private person—in the same manner that chattels in distress may be replevied—upon giving security to the sheriff that the man shall be forthcoming to answer any charge against him."[69] The writ was "a popular remedy to obtain release from simple custodies" and evolved through medieval times into the customary common law method to replevy villeins seized by a lord by writ de nativo habendo.[70] By the eighteenth century, the writ de homine replegiando had long been rendered obsolete by habeas corpus.[71] The two writs worked in much the same fashion, and both could be brought on behalf of the detainee by a third party. But habeas corpus and de homine replegiando differed in one crucial point. Where the former called for a bench trial, the latter called for a jury trial.[72] That Watson sought to take an obsolete action that guaranteed her a trial by jury may well speak to Nova Scotia's ideological state at the time of the Revolutionary War. Clearly, she thought a jury would be more likely to grant her freedom than the Supreme Court justices, pointing, perhaps, to schisms between the political elite and the people likely to serve on a jury. Of course, the jury would still comprise land-owning white men, but it has already been established that this segment of Nova Scotia's population—prior to the arrival of the Loyalists—had, at least to some extent, been drawn from New England's lower socio-economic strata.[73]

The case's pivotal moment, however, came two months later. William Proud's key witness, Samuel Laha, was deposed by the court at the home of Chief Justice Finucane on 14 September 1778. Richard Gibbons questioned him:[74]

"Did you at any time . . . purchase a Negro woman by the name of Phillis in Boston and from whom and for what sum?" Gibbons asked.

"I did purchase such a woman from Nicholas Lobdell in Boston, but when I paid the money and received her Nicholas was not present. Do not recollect the time. Believe the sum to be twenty-seven pounds," Laha replied.

"When and to whom and where did you dispose of this Woman?"

"I disposed of her in Halifax to Mr. Elias Marshall."

"In the Bill of Sale now shown to you with a receipt signed with your name—a Bill of Sale transferring this woman from you to Elias Marshall—is the name Samuel Laha, here signed, your handwriting?"

"It is," Laha answered.

"Is the Bill of Sale now shown to you under seal, signed 'Agnes Lobdell on behalf of my husband Nicholas Lobdell,' the original Bill of Sale of this Negro woman to you?" Gibbons continued.

"It is."

"Did this Negro woman at or before the time of her sale to you or at any time afterward while she was with you declare herself to be a free woman and not a slave, or claim to be set free as such, or object to being sold by you to Mr. Marshall as a slave?"

"She expressed uneasiness at coming to Halifax, but neither she nor anybody else ever said that she pretended to be Free or that I had no right to dispose of her as my property until my arrival at this time in Halifax," Laha answered.

"How long have you known this Negro woman, and what reasons have you to believe her a slave and not a free woman?"

"I knew her as a servant in Mr. Lobdell's family for about six months before I purchased her. I was told by Mr. and Mrs.

Lobdell that they had bought her from one Ebenezer Gorham, from whom I have a Bill of Sale to Lobdell."

"Other than Phillis, did you ever hear or know of any other name by which this Negro woman was at any time called or known—if yes, what was the name and where, and when, and by whom was she so called?" Gibbons asked.

"Never heard of any other than Phillis," Laha replied.

"Did this Negro Woman at the time of being sold to you and at the time of your selling her to Mr. Marshall know she was being sold as a slave?"

"Yes."

"Did you ever hear or know that either of this Negro woman's parents were Free persons? What were their names and, if slaves, to whom were they or either of them slaves?"

"I do not know."

"Are you eventually interested in Phillis's freedom or slavery?"

"I am not interested," Laha said.

George Thomson declined to question Laha on Elizabeth Watson's behalf. Samuel Laha was in the end the only witness at the trial. Elizabeth Reed, on the strength of whose testimony Watson had secured her freedom one year earlier, was not summoned to appear before the court.[75]

The trial concluded on 20 October 1779. George Thomson's failure to act on Watson's behalf—in terms of questioning Samuel Laha, objecting to any part of his testimony, or bringing a witness of his own—meant that William Proud's attorney presented all the evidence that the jury would consider. Having heard no evidence to the contrary, the Supreme Court of Nova Scotia ruled that "said Elizabeth Watson is [William Proud's] property and slave." At least she won her name.[76]

From Freedom to Slavery

Elizabeth Watson's story is not the only story of re-enslavement in Nova Scotia.[77] The incidence of such kidnappings in Nova Scotia is well documented, particularly in the wake of the Loyalist diaspora.[78]

There was Mertilla Dixon, who fled her enslaver's Virginia home during the Revolutionary War and found her way to Nova Scotia, where again she was impelled to flee from an employer who "threatened to ship her to the West Indies, and . . . dispose of her as a Slave." Dixon took refuge with her father and invited her old employer to "prove his claim."[79]

There was Lydia Jackson, whose poverty forced her to indenture herself to a Loyalist. He took advantage of her illiteracy and signed her to a thirty-nine-year term instead of the one-year term she had agreed to. He later sold Jackson to Dr. William Bulman, who beat her "with tongs, sticks, pieces of rope about the head and face . . . [and] in the most inhuman manner stamped upon her whilst she lay upon the ground . . . though she was in the last month of pregnancy."[80] The courts did not help her, silenced as they were by Dr. Bulman's overbearing influence. For three more years Jackson lived with him, until at last she "made her escape in a wonderful way through the woods."[81]

And there was Mary Postell. Likely born enslaved in South Carolina, she fled to British lines during the American Revolution with her daughters Flora and Nell.[82] They were re-enslaved in 1785, when Jesse Gray destroyed Postell's certificate of freedom. He took her and her two daughters to Nova Scotia, where he forced them to "Work and Labour . . . as the Slave and Slaves of him."[83] Postell grew fearful that Gray intended to sell her away from Flora and Nell. They fled his home, and Postell went to court. Though he submitted paltry evidence—a bill of sale from his own brother Samuel—the court ordered that Postell and her daughters return to Gray's home "on condition that he give Security for not Selling her . . . in Twelve Months from this Day."[84] One year later, Gray sold Mary Postell for 100 bushels of potatoes. Three years later, he sold Flora south to North Carolina for five pounds.[85] Afraid that Nell would suffer the same fate, Postell returned to court and "complained against Jesse Gray . . . for taking away her children."[86]

Mary Postell had a much stronger case than Elizabeth Watson. Two separate witnesses testified to her freedom and her work for the Loyalist cause. But the court still decided that Postell had not proven her freedom, and it returned her to slavery.[87] Her bitter end should not cast a shadow over the fact that Postell fought tooth and nail for five years.

Mertilla Dixon, Lydia Jackson, Mary Postell, and Elizabeth Watson. These four admirable women stand for countless others of all ages and genders whose names are lost to history. Neither their names nor their number will ever be known with any degree of certainty. Nova Scotia may not have been a place of widespread slavery, but it was a place of rampant unfreedom.

Conclusion

Ultimately, it would be easy to blame Elizabeth Watson's wretched fate on George Thomson's inability or unwillingness to represent his client with any semblance of integrity. But there is another possibility, one to which much of the evidence points: Elizabeth Watson lied.

Say she did not. Say Samuel Laha conspired with William Proud to deliver false testimony. Say that together they falsified three bills of sale, the genealogy of her unfreedom: from Ebenezer Gorham to Nicholas Lobdell, to Samuel Laha, to Elias Marshall. Say Elizabeth Reed did in fact know her as Elizabeth Watson, a free woman born of a free mother.

Here is another version. A young enslaved woman named Phillis landed on the shores of a foreign land and sensed an opportunity to fashion herself anew. She had heard stories of women in Boston who had sued for their freedom and won. She used this knowledge and her natural intelligence to navigate Nova Scotia's fledgling legal system. She gave herself a new name.

Whether or not she lied in the end does not matter. These are questions without answers. And answers, of course, would not change a thing. This is what history is. Nothing could change what happened to Elizabeth Watson.

Here is all that we know with certainty. Elizabeth Watson arrived in Halifax from Boston sometime in the mid-1770s. In March 1778 she suffered an atrocious beating at the hands of Elias Marshall. The Halifax Court of Quarter Sessions granted her freedom on 23 March 1778. She was seized by the butcher William Proud thirty-one days later. The Supreme Court of Nova Scotia returned her to slavery on 20 October 1779.

Nothing else is certain. The archive silenced her, as it has done to so many others. Elizabeth Watson's story comes to us like a frantic, solitary shout amid a sea of silence, a light that flashed once and was never seen again. The child she carried almost certainly died.[88] Its body was likely buried somewhere on Elias Marshall's land—400 acres bounded by Washmill Lake to the east and Fox Lake to the west.[89] There are no plaques here, no memorials or remembrances, no markers or headstones.[90] Only the soil remains; still bucolic, by now idyllic, long reclaimed by balsam firs and red spruce. Past the western shore of Fox Lake there is primeval forest, taller and heavier—the sole reminder that people lived in this place.

Notes

1 This chapter was originally published in *In Search of Liberty: African American Internationalism in the Nineteenth-Century Atlantic World*, ed. Ronald Johnson and Ousmane K. Power-Greene (Athens, GA: University of Georgia Press, 2021), 17–39. Content was unrevised with exceptions of Canadian spellings, formatting of notes, and other elements to conform to University of Manitoba Press's house style.

2 The following account comes from Elizabeth Watson's sworn testimony in *Woodin v. Watson*, Nova Scotia Archives (hereafter NSA), Record Group (hereafter RG) 37, 22/45.

3 For details on Elias Marshall's employment, see W.A.B. Douglas, "COFFIN, Sir ISAAC," in *Dictionary of Canadian Biography*, ed. Francess G. Halpenny, vol. 7 (Toronto: University of Toronto Press, 1988), 196–97; and Julian Gwyn, *Ashore and Afloat: The British Navy and the Halifax Naval Yard before 1820* (Ottawa: University of Ottawa Press, 2004), 107.

4 Whether Durdsly was enslaved is unknown.

5 There were three surgeons in Halifax by the name of Phillips—George, John, and William. Which of the three men this incident involved is unknown. A.E. Marble,

Surgeons, Smallpox, and the Poor: A History of Medicine and Social Conditions in Nova Scotia, 1749–1799 (Montreal and Kingston: McGill-Queen's University Press, 1993), 86, 107.

6 *Woodin v. Watson*, NSA, RG 37, 22/45.

7 Woodin was then the keeper of the Halifax Poor House, which was essentially an early version of a Victorian workhouse. Thomas B. Akins, *History of Halifax City* (Halifax: Nova Scotia Historical Society, 1895), 78.

8 *Woodin v. Watson*, NSA, RG 37, 22/45.

9 *Watson v. Proud*, NSA, RG 37, C/21.

10 Thomas Peters, for example, related the story of a man who, once reduced to slavery, "did actually lose his Life by the Beating and Ill Treatment of his Master and another who fled the like cruelty was inhumanly shot and maimed." Thomas Peters to Lord Grenville, "The Humble Petition of Thomas Peters, a Negro," National Archives, London (hereafter NA), 1790, FO 4/1, C 308757.

11 For several examples of cruelty toward the Maritimes' enslaved population, see Harvey Amani Whitfield, *North to Bondage: Loyalist Slavery in the Maritimes* (Vancouver: UBC Press, 2016), 78–80; Harvey Amani Whitfield, ed., *Black Slavery in the Maritimes: A History in Documents* (Peterborough: Broadview Press, 2018), 106, 116.

12 For more on the fluidity of the unfree condition, see Jared Ross Hardesty, *Unfreedom: Slavery and Dependence in Eighteenth-Century Boston* (New York: New York University Press, 2016). For a discussion of the onerous methodological difficulties that a high rate of re-enslavement presents, see Whitfield, *North to Bondage*, 13–16.

13 On the Mary Postell and Nancy cases, see Whitfield, *Black Slavery in the Maritimes*, 107, 114.

14 Pierre Dugua de Mons, along with Samuel de Champlain, founded Acadia's first capital at Port-Royal. It was France's first North American colony. Aside from a few trading outposts, Port-Royal was then the only European settlement in Nova Scotia. See John G. Reid, ed., *The "Conquest" of Acadia, 1710: Imperial, Colonial, and Aboriginal Constructions* (Toronto: University of Toronto Press, 2004); Phillip Buckner, ed., *Canada and the British Empire* (Oxford: Oxford University Press, 2008); and Elizabeth Mancke, "Early Modern Imperial Governance and the Origins of Canadian Political Culture," *Canadian Journal of Political Science* 32, no. 1 (1999): 3–20.

15 A.B.J. Johnston, "Research Note: Mathieu Da Costa along the Coasts of Nova Scotia: Some Possibilities," *Journal of the Royal Nova Scotia Historical Society* 4 (2001): 152–64.

16 Ira Berlin, *Many Thousands Gone: The First Two Centuries of Slavery in North America* (Cambridge, MA: Harvard University Press, 1998), 17. For more on Atlantic Creoles, see Linda Heywood and John Thornton, *Central Africans, Atlantic Creoles and the Foundation of the Americas, 1585–1660* (New York: Cambridge University Press, 2007); Jane G. Landers, *Atlantic Creoles in the Age of Revolutions* (Cambridge, MA: Harvard University Press, 2010); James H. Sweet, *Domingos Alvares, African Healing, and the Intellectual History of the Atlantic World* (Chapel Hill: University of North

Carolina Press, 2011); and Ira Berlin, "From Creole to African: Atlantic Creoles and the Origins of African American Society in Mainland North America," *William and Mary Quarterly* 53, no. 2 (1996): 251–88.

17 See NSA, doc. 28, vol. II, in C.B. Fergusson, *A Documentary Study of the Negroes in Nova Scotia between the War of 1812 and the Winning of Responsible Government* (Halifax: Public Archives of Nova Scotia, 1948), 1.

18 Kenneth Joseph Donovan, "Slaves in Île Royale, 1713–1758," *French Colonial History* 5 (2004): 25–42.

19 Louisbourg was a cod fishing port and later a fortress of formidable reputation. It was founded after the Treaty of Utrecht forced the French out of Nova Scotia. See A.J.B. Johnston, "From Port de Peche to Ville Fortifiee: The Evolution of Urban Louisbourg, 1713–1758," *Proceedings of the Meeting of the French Colonial Historical Society* 17 (1993): 24–43; Robert Emmet Wall Jr., "Louisbourg, 1745," *New England Quarterly* 37, no. 1 (1964): 64–83; and A.J.B. Johnston, "To Mark and to Celebrate: Commemoration Efforts at Eighteenth-Century Louisbourg," *French Colonial History* 1 (2002): 161–75. For more on the Treaty of Utrecht, see Renger E. de Bruin et al., eds., *Performances of Peace: Utrecht 1713* (Leiden, the Netherlands: Brill, 2015).

20 Donovan, "Slaves in Île Royale."

21 Kenneth Donovan, "A Nominal List of Slaves and Their Owners in Île Royale, 1713–1760," *Nova Scotia Historical Review* 16, no. 1 (1996): 151–62; Kenneth Donovan, "Slaves in Cape Breton, 1713–1815," *Directions: Canadian Race Relations Foundation* 4, no. 1 (Summer 2007): 44–45.

22 Donovan, "Slaves in Île Royale," 26.

23 Kenneth Donovan, "Female Slaves as Sexual Victims in Île Royale," *Acadiensis* 43, no. 1 (2014): 147–56, https://journals.lib.unb.ca/index.php/Acadiensis/article/view/22043.

24 George T. Bates, "The Great Exodus of 1749: Or, The Cornwallis Settlers Who Didn't," *Collections of the Nova Scotia Historical Society* 38 (1973): 227–62; see also John Grenier, *The Far Reaches of Empire: War in Nova Scotia, 1710–1760* (Norman: University of Oklahoma Press, 2008).

25 Letter from Governor Cornwallis about Captain Bloss and his slaves, 22 September 1750, NSA, RG 1, vol. 35, doc. 25; Douglas Brymner, *Report on Canadian Archives* (Ottawa: S.E. Dawson, 1895), 280; Harvey Amani Whitfield, *Blacks on the Border: The Black Refugees in British North America, 1815–1860* (Burlington: University of Vermont Press, 2006), 15.

26 Letter from Governor Cornwallis about Captain Bloss, NSA, RG 1, vol. 35, doc. 25. Donovan, "Slaves in Île Royale," 32, notes that a schooner brought nine slave men, the property of Captain Bloss, to Nova Scotia from Antigua.

27 Advertisements, *Boston Post-Boy*, 8 August 1750, and 23 September 1751. It is clear that Captain Bloss and Benjamin Hallowell knew each other.

28 T. Watson Smith, *The Slave in Canada*, Collections of the Nova Scotia Historical Society, vol. 10 (Halifax: Nova Scotia Printing Company, 1899), 9.

29 Joshua Mauger, advertisement, *Halifax Gazette*, 30 May 1752.

30 See Gregory E. O'Malley, *Final Passages: The Intercolonial Slave Trade of British America, 1619–1807* (Chapel Hill: University of North Carolina Press, 2014).

31 Jerry Bannister, "Atlantic Canada in an Atlantic World? Northeastern North America in the Long 18th Century," *Acadiensis* 43, no. 2 (2014): 28. For a general overview of the major demographic shifts, see Margaret Conrad and James Hiller, *Atlantic Canada: A History* (Toronto: Oxford University Press, 2010), Chapters 6–8.

32 T. Stephen Henderson and Wendy G. Robicheau, eds., *Nova Scotia Planters in the Atlantic World, 1759–1830* (Fredericton, N.B.: Acadiensis Press, 2012); Lucille H. Campey, *Planters, Paupers, and Pioneers: English Settlers in Atlantic Canada* (Toronto: Dundurn Press, 2010); George Rawlyk and Gordon T. Stewart, *A People Highly Favoured of God: The Nova Scotia Yankees and the American Revolution* (Toronto: Macmillan, 1972); Margaret Conrad, ed., *Making Adjustments: Change and Continuity in Planter Nova Scotia, 1759–1800* (Fredericton: Acadiensis Press,1991); Conrad and Barry Moody, eds., *Planter Links: Community and Culture in Colonial Nova Scotia* (Fredericton: Acadiensis Press, 2001); Margaret Conrad, ed., *They Planted Well: New England Planters in Maritime Canada* (Fredericton: Acadiensis Press, 1988); Margaret Conrad, ed., *Intimate Relations: Family and Community in Planter Nova Scotia, 1759–1800* (Fredericton: Acadiensis Press, 1995).

33 1767 Nova Scotia Census, NSA, RG 12.

34 As Barry Cahill writes, the "collection of quantifiable data is complicated by Black people not being enumerated in extant early census records. Blacks as a rule were slaves, slaves were chattels (movable property), and personality was not censual." Barry Cahill, "Colchester Men: The Pro-Slavery Presbyterian Witness of the Reverends Daniel Cock of Truro and David Smith of Londonderry," in Conrad and Moody, *Planter Links*, 134.

35 Malachy Salter to Susanna Mulberry, 2 September 1759, NSA, MG 100, vol. 217, doc. 27. Malachy Salter was one of Halifax's most prominent early entrepreneurs. A ruthless businessman, he was described by contemporaries as "a Litigious troublesome Man . . . who has treated us in a Barbarous cruel manner." He was the most litigious man of his time, having been the "plaintiff in 110 actions and a defendant in 30." James Muir, *Law, Debt, and Merchant Power: The Civil Courts of Eighteenth-Century Halifax* (Toronto: Osgoode Society for Canadian Legal History, 2016), 38.

36 Advertisement, *Halifax Gazette*, 1 November 1760. The advertisement continues: "likewise [for sale] a puncheon of choice cherry brandy with sundry other articles." For more on the commodification of Black people, see Walter Johnson, *Soul by Soul: Life inside the Antebellum Slave Market* (Cambridge, MA: Harvard University Press, 1999). For a controversial look at the economics of slavery, see William Robert Fogel and Stanley L. Engerman, *Time on the Cross: The Economics of American Negro Slavery* (Toronto: Little, Brown and Company, 1974). For a lengthy rebuttal of Fogel and Engerman's methods and conclusions, see Herbert G. Gutman, *Slavery and the Numbers Game: A Critique of "Time on the Cross"* (Urbana: University of Illinois Press, 1975). For more recent studies, see Sven Beckert and Seth Rockman, eds., *Slavery's Capitalism: A New History of American Economic Development* (Philadelphia: University

of Pennsylvania Press, 2016); Christy Clark-Pujara, *Dark Work: The Business of Slavery in Rhode Island* (New York: New York University Press, 2016); and Edward Baptist, *The Half Has Never Been Told: Slavery and the Making of American Capitalism* (New York: Basic Books, 2014).

37 Akins, *History of Halifax City*, 63; James S. MacDonald, *Annals of the North British Society in Halifax, Nova Scotia with Portraits and Biographical Notes 1768–1903* (Halifax, N.S.: McAlpine Publishing Company Ltd., 1905), 17.

38 For background on Charles Proctor, see Ronald Rompkey, ed., *Expeditions of Honour: The Journal of John Salusbury in Halifax, Nova Scotia, 1749–53* (Montreal: McGill-Queen's University Press, 2011), 173. For Thomas Wood, see C.E. Thomas, "WOOD, THOMAS (1711–78)," in Halpenny, *Dictionary of Canadian Biography*, vol. 4.

39 See Smith, "The Slave in Canada," 15n2.

40 Advertisement, *Nova Scotia Gazette and Weekly Chronicle*, 28 May 1776.

41 Whitfield, *North to Bondage*, 41.

42 Joanne Pope Melish, *Disowning Slavery: Gradual Emancipation and "Race" in New England, 1780–1860* (Ithaca, NY: Cornell University Press, 1998), 14.

43 For slave culture in the North, see William D. Piersen, *Black Yankees: The Development of an Afro-American Subculture in Eighteenth-Century New England* (Amherst: University of Massachusetts Press, 1988); Gary B. Nash, *Forging Freedom: The Formation of Philadelphia's Black Community, 1720–1840* (Cambridge, MA: Harvard University Press, 1988); and Shane White, "'It Was a Proud Day': African Americans, Festivals, and Parades in the North, 1741–1834," *Journal of American History* 81 (1994): 13–50; for slave life and culture more broadly, see Sterling Stuckey, *Slave Culture: Nationalist Theory and the Foundations of Black America* (New York: Oxford University Press, 1987); John W. Blassingame, *The Slave Community: Plantation Life in the Antebellum South* (New York: Oxford University Press, 1972); and George P. Rawick, *From Sundown to Sunup: The Making of the Black Community* (Westport, CT: Greenwood Press, 1972). On slavery in New England, see Hardesty, *Unfreedom*; Jared Ross Hardesty, *Black Lives, Native Lands, White Worlds: A History of Slavery in New England* (Amherst: University of Massachusetts Press, 2019); Harvey Amani Whitfield, *The Problem of Slavery in Early Vermont, 1777–1810* (Barre: Vermont Historical Society, 2014); Allegra di Bonaventura, *For Adam's Sake: A Family Saga in Colonial New England* (New York: W.W. Norton, 2013); Clark-Pujara, *Dark Work*; Lorenzo J. Greene, *The Negro in Colonial New England* (1942; reprinted, New York: Atheneum, 1968); Berlin, *Many Thousands Gone*, 177–94; Robert K. Fitts, *Inventing New England's Slave Paradise: Master/Slave Relations in Eighteenth-Century Narragansett, Rhode Island* (New York: Garland, 1998); Melish, *Disowning Slavery*, 1–49; and Peter Benes, ed., *Slavery/Antislavery in New England: The Dublin Seminar for New England Folklife Annual Proceedings, 2003* (Boston: Boston University, 2005).

44 One can look at the American South itself for examples of these processes at work; indeed, the history of slavery in the mountains of southern Appalachia might well hold some promise for future comparative studies of Maritime slavery. See Wilma

A. Dunaway, *Slavery in the American Mountain South* (Cambridge, UK: Cambridge University Press, 2003); and John C. Inscoe, ed., *Appalachians and Race: The Mountain South from Slavery to Segregation* (Lexington: University Press of Kentucky, 2001).

45 Historian Karolyn Smardz Frost argues that there might have been as many as 200 enslaved Black people brought into the region by the New England Planters, though she notes that the enslaved continued to be brought in after the initial migration. Cited in Harvey Amani Whitfield, "The African Diaspora in Atlantic Canada: History, Historians, and Historiography," *Acadiensis* 46, no. 1 (2017): 213n1.

46 Graeme Wynn, "A Province Too Much Dependent on New England," *Canadian Geographer* 31, no. 2 (1987): 98–113.

47 Robert McLaughlin, "New England Planters Prior to Migration: The Case of Chatham, Massachusetts," in Conrad and Moody, *Planter Links*, 17.

48 See D.G. Bell, "Slavery and the Judges of Loyalist New Brunswick," *University of New Brunswick Law Journal* 31 (1982): 9–42; I. Allen Jack, *The Loyalists and Slavery in New Brunswick* ([Ottawa?]: Royal Society of Canada, 1898); Robin W. Winks, *Blacks in Canada: A History* (Montreal and Kingston: McGill-Queen's University Press, 1997), 24–60; Barry Cahill, "Slavery and the Judges of Loyalist Nova Scotia," *University of New Brunswick Law Journal* 43 (1994): 73–135; and Barry Cahill, "*Habeas Corpus* and Slavery in Nova Scotia," *University of New Brunswick Law Journal* 44 (1995): 179–209.

49 "An Act, Declaring that Baptism of Slaves Shall not Exempt Them from Bondage," 1781, Public Archives and Records Office of Prince Edward Island, CO 228, Colonial Office Acts No. 1, Prince Edward Island, 1770–81, MS 1–66. See also Harvey Amani Whitfield and Barry Cahill, "Slave Life and Slave Law in Colonial Prince Edward Island, 1769–1825," *Acadiensis*, 38 no. 32 (2009): 29–51.

50 "1762 Innholders Act," in *Statutes at Large, Nova Scotia* (Halifax: John Howe and Son, King's Printers, 1805), 77.

51 Whitfield, *North to Bondage*, 68–109.

52 Cahill, "Slavery and the Judges," 79.

53 *Woodin v. Watson*, NSA, RG 37, 22/45.

54 The date of her arrival is unknown, though it was likely sometime in the mid-1770s.

55 See Bonaventura, *For Adam's Sake*; and Allegra di Bonaventura, "It's Complicated," *Historically Speaking* 14, no. 3 (2013): 7–8.

56 Catherine Adams and Elizabeth H. Pleck, *Love of Freedom: Black Women in Colonial and Revolutionary New England* (New York: Oxford University Press, 2010), 127.

57 Graham Russell Hodges, *Root and Branch: African Americans in New York and East Jersey, 1613–1863* (Chapel Hill: University of North Carolina Press, 1999), 129–30.

58 For more on the history of freedom suits, see Paul Finkelman, *Slavery in the Courtroom: An Annotated Bibliography of American Cases* (Washington, DC: Library of Congress, 1985); Paul Finkelman, *Imperfect Union: Slavery, Federalism, and Comity* (Chapel Hill: University of North Carolina Press, 1981); Ariela Gross, *Double Character: Slavery and Mastery in the Antebellum Southern Courtroom* (Princeton, NJ: Princeton University Press, 2000); Edlie L. Wong, *Neither Fugitive nor Free: Atlantic Slavery, Freedom Suits, and the Legal Culture of Travel* (New York: New York University Press, 2009); William E.

Foley, "Slave Freedom Suits before Dred Scott: The Case of Marie Jean Scypion's Descendants," *Missouri Historical Review* 79 (1984): 1–23; Loren Schweninger, "Freedom Suits, African American Women, and the Genealogy of Slavery," *William and Mary Quarterly* 71, no. 1 (2014): 35–62; and Jason A. Gillmer, "Suing for Freedom: Interracial Sex, Slave Law, and Racial Identity in the Post-Revolutionary and Antebellum South," *North Carolina Law Review* 82, no. 2 (2004): 535–619. For a first-person account of a freedom suit, see Lucy Delaney, *From the Darkness Cometh the Light: Or, Struggles for Freedom* (St. Louis: J.T. Smith, 1891).

59 Hodges, *Root and Branch*, 129–30.

60 Adams and Pleck, *Love of Freedom*, 127.

61 See Van Gosse, "As a Nation, the English Are Our Friends: The Emergence of African American Politics in the British Atlantic World, 1772–1861," *American Historical Review* 113, no. 4 (2008): 1003–28.

62 See Edmund Morgan, *American Slavery, American Freedom: The Ordeal of Colonial Virginia* (New York: W. W. Norton, 1975); David Brion Davis, *The Problem of Slavery in the Age of Revolution, 1770–1823* (Ithaca, NY: Cornell University Press, 1975); Winthrop D. Jordan, *White over Black: American Attitudes toward the Negro, 1550–1812* (Chapel Hill: University of North Carolina Press, 1968); Jack P. Greene, *All Men Are Created Equal: Some Reflections on the Character of the American Revolution, an Inaugural Lecture* (New York: Oxford University Press, 1976); Greene, "Slavery or Independence: Some Reflections on the Relationship among Liberty, Black Bondage, and Equality in Revolutionary South Carolina," *South Carolina Historical Magazine* 80 (1979): 193–214; and Holly Brewer, "Slavery, Sovereignty, and 'Inheritable Blood': Reconsidering John Locke and the Origins of American Slavery," *American Historical Review* 122, no. 4 (2017): 1038–78.

63 The following account comes from *Watson v. Proud*, NSA, RG 37, C/21.

64 Justices typically held "special" sessions between regularly scheduled Courts of Quarter or General Sessions of the Peace; they were intended to prevent delays in the administration of justice. See J.H. Baker, "Criminal Courts and Procedure at Common Law 1550–1800," in *Crime in England 1550–1800*, ed. J.S. Cockburn (Princeton, NJ: Princeton University Press, 1977), 30.

65 For mentions of *Watson v. Proud*, see Cahill, "Slavery and the Judges," 80; and Julian Gwyn, "Female Litigants before the Civil Courts of Nova Scotia, 1749–1801," *Histoire sociale / Social History* 36, no. 72 (2003): 340–41.

66 *Watson v. Proud*, NSA, RG 37, C/21.

67 *Watson v. Proud*. For more on writs of certiorari (i.e., definitions and uses), see William Blackstone, *Commentaries on the Laws of England*, 4 vols. (Oxford: Clarendon Press, 1765–69), 4: xxiv.

68 Note that the earliest extant record of the continuous series dates to 1155–56. Elsa de Haas, *Antiquities of Bail: Origin and Historical Development in Criminal Cases to the Year 1275* (New York: Columbia University Press, 1940), 62; Christopher Corèdon, *A Dictionary of Medieval Terms and Phrases* (Woodbridge, UK: D.S. Brewer, 2004), 219.

69 Blackstone, *Commentaries*, 3: 129; see also Joseph Harrison, *The Practice of the Court of Chancery*, 2 vols. (London: A. Strahan, 1796), 1: 164–66.

70 Maxwell Cohen, "Some Considerations on the Origin of Habeas Corpus," *Canadian Bar Review* 16 (1938): 92, 96, 97; Phineas Pemberton Morris, *Practical Treatise on the Law of Replevin in the United States; with an Appendix of Forms, and a Digest of Statutes* (Philadelphia: Kay and Brother, 1878), 255–65. For more on the writ de nativo habendo, see Blackstone, *Commentaries*, 1: 26.

71 Bryan A. Garner, ed., *Black's Law Dictionary*, 9th ed. (Eagan, MN: West, 2009), see "De Homine Replegiando."

72 "Some Defects in the Law of Habeas Corpus," *Law Review and Quarterly Journal of British and Foreign Jurisprudence* 22 (1855): 149–68; James Kent, *Commentaries on American Law*, 4 vols. (Philadelphia: Blackstone Publishing, 1889), 26–33.

73 See Wynn, "A Province Too Much Dependent"; and McLaughlin, "New England Planters." For more on the history of jury trials in Canada specifically, see Regina Schuller and Neil Vidmar, "The Canadian Criminal Jury," *Chicago-Kent Law Review* 86, no. 2 (2011): 497–535; and R. Blake Brown, *A Trying Question: The Jury in Nineteenth-Century Canada* (Toronto: University of Toronto Press, 2009).

74 The language in the following account has been adapted slightly from the original deposition in order to retain clarity. *Watson v. Proud*, NSA, RG 37, C/21. In an earlier publication, we mistranslated Laha as Laka. The correct name is Samuel Laha, likely a mariner from Boston.

75 The reasons for this are unknown.

76 *Watson v. Proud*, NSA, RG 37, C/21.

77 The re-enslavement of free and allegedly free Black people became all too common in the wake of the Loyalist diaspora. The relative lack of surviving sources pertaining to re-enslavement in the Maritimes reveals a need for historians to look elsewhere for analogous historical processes. Alongside Nova Scotia, the Bahamas had the highest incidence of wrongful re-enslavement in the Loyalist diaspora. There the practice became pervasive enough that Governor Lord Dunmore established a succession of courts dedicated solely to hearing evidence regarding the legal freedom of Black people. The means of re-enslavement in the Bahamas mirrored those often seen in Nova Scotia: destruction of freedom papers, followed by sale to the West Indies. See Carole Watterson Troxler, "Uses of the Bahamas by Southern Loyalist Exiles," in *The Loyal Atlantic: Remaking the British Atlantic in the Revolutionary Era*, ed. Jerry Bannister and Liam Riordan (Toronto: University of Toronto Press, 2012), 185–208, especially 194–95, 199–200.

78 See, for example, the story of Sam Ives, in Book of Negroes, Guy Carleton, 1st Baron Dorchester: Papers, National Archives, Kew (PRO 30/55/100) 10427, p. 19; Thomas Clarkson, "Some Account of the New Colony at Sierra Leone," *American Museum: Or, Universal Magazine*, May 1792, 229–30; complaint of Mertilla Dixon, NSA, RG 34-321, file M97; C.B. Fergusson, ed., *Clarkson's Mission to America, 1791–1792* (Halifax: Public Archives of Nova Scotia, 1971), 90. See also Carole Watterson Troxler, "Re-Enslavement of Black Loyalists: Mary Postell in South Carolina, East Florida, and Nova Scotia," *Acadiensis* 37, no. 2 (2008): 70–85; and Troxler, "Uses of the Bahamas." For an attempted measure to curb the incidence of Black kidnappings in Nova Scotia, see "Unpassed Bills: 'A Bill Intituled an Act for

the Regulation and Relief of the Free Negroes within the Province of Nova Scotia,' 1789," NSA.

79 Complaint of Mertilla Dixon, NSA, RG 34-321, file M97.

80 Cumberland County Census 1785, NSA, RG 1, vol. 443, doc. 37; Cumberland County Census 1791, NSA, RG 1, vol. 444, doc. 1; Fergusson, *Clarkson's Mission*, 90.

81 Fergusson, *Clarkson's Mission*, 90.

82 See Troxler, "Re-Enslavement of Black Loyalists."

83 General Sessions at Shelburne, Nova Scotia, 8 July 1791, Shelburne Records, NSA, MG 4, vol. 141; King v. Jesse Gray, 9 November 1786, Shelburne, NSA, RG 60, vol. 27, doc. 27.2.

84 General Sessions at Shelburne, Nova Scotia, 10 April 1786, Shelburne Records, NSA, MG 4, vol. 141.

85 Troxler, "Re-Enslavement of Black Loyalists," 77.

86 General Sessions at Shelburne, Nova Scotia, 5 April 1791, Shelburne Records, NSA, MG 4, vol. 141.

87 Troxler, "Re-enslavement of Black Loyalists," 84.

88 She could not have been too far along in her pregnancy. She told Marshall she was pregnant eight days before the beating, and it is unlikely she would have told him unless it was necessary to do so. This points to the physical changes characteristic of pregnancy becoming too pronounced to hide, leading to an estimate that Watson may have been twenty-one weeks pregnant at most. Even with modern medicine, a preterm birth at this stage of pregnancy is not considered viable. See Barbara J. Stoll et al., "Causes and Timing of Death in Extremely Premature Infants from 2000 through 2011," *New England Journal of Medicine* 372 (2015): 331–40.

89 "Index Sheet 66," Halifax County Land Grants, Department of Lands and Forests, Crown Land Information Management Centre, Nova Scotia; G.L. Saunders, *Trees of Nova Scotia: A Guide to the Native and Exotic Species* (Halifax: Department of Lands and Forests, 1973), 1–37.

90 As prominent archaeologist Charles E. Orser Jr. wrote, "only archaeology has the power to resurrect the daily lives and cultural patterns of the invisible men and women of the past. By piecing together the often-scant evidence left behind by a people in their artifacts and building remains, archaeologists can construct pictures of the past that are unique, insightful, and intimately human." Charles E. Orser, Jr., *Images of the Recent Past: Readings in Historical Archaeology* (Walnut Creek, CA: Altamira Press, 1996), 10. For more on historical archaeology and what land can tell historians about the people who lived on it, see Heather Macleod-Leslie, "Archaeology and Atlantic Canada's African Diaspora," *Acadiensis* 43, no. 1 (2014): 137–45; Catherine M.A. Cottreau-Robbins, "Searching for the Enslaved in Nova Scotia's Loyalist Landscape," *Acadiensis* 43, no. 1 (2014): 129–31; Alexandra A. Chan, *Slavery in the Age of Reason: Archaeology at a New England Farm* (Knoxville: University of Tennessee Press, 2007); and James Deetz, *In Small Things Forgotten: The Archaeology of Early American Life* (New York: Anchor Press, 1977).

PART II

Incarceration, Criminalization, and Human Rights in Canada

CHAPTER 5

Internment Is a Family Affair: One Pro-Communist Ukrainian Jewish Extended Family's Experiences with Political Incarceration in Second World War Canada

Rhonda L. Hinther

IN THIS CHAPTER, I focus on the lives and internment experiences of one Ukrainian Jewish extended family, the Walsh-Steele-Weir-Boyd family. This is a history of internment. It is a history of wartime. It is a history of the Canadian security state. It is a history of Jewish and Ukrainian "ethnic hall" socialists, the labour movement, and social justice activism. It is a history of women and their ability to cope in dire circumstances. It is a history of tenacity and survival. It is a history of intimacy under conditions of state siege. Making it all the more interesting is that this extended family's story has all the trappings of a Hollywood blockbuster (and at times a soap opera), set against the backdrop of the Second World War, featuring themes of love, infidelity, loss, injustice, and intrigue. This family's experiences speak to the precarity of human rights and civil liberties in wartime, even and especially in places relatively untouched by the worst physical and violent aspects of war.

Resonance can be found in other pieces in this collection, notably those that speak to Canada's long-standing carceral tradition. The political policing of difference is a hallmark of the Canadian state, as Tom Hooper's chapter demonstrates. So, too, is the targeting of the Communist and pro-Communist left while affording far-right elements privileged access to Canada, even in the face of difficult-to-ignore wartime criminality. Katelyn Arac's chapter on alleged war criminals certainly speaks to this. Pro-Communists such as the Walsh-Steele-Weir-Boyd family have long found themselves on the wrong side of the law for exercising their civil liberties and expressing their politics.

Context

During the Second World War, the Canadian government imprisoned numerous Communist and pro-Communist activists, particularly those associated with the Communist Party of Canada (CPC), adjacent ethnic hall socialist organizations such as the Ukrainian Labour Farmer Temple Association, and certain labour unions as part of a broader campaign of political repression and intimidation. The government utilized the war—and the CPC's opposition to it following the Molotov-Ribbentrop non-aggression pact signed by Germany and the Soviet Union in 1939—as a pretext to criminalize their radical activism, resulting in the arrest and detention of over 130 individuals involved in socialist organizations, labour unions, and the CPC itself. Under the Defence of Canada Regulations (DOCR) implemented in 1940, many of these organizations were banned, and authorities were granted the power to seize their assets and apprehend their leaders.[1]

The detainees hailed from diverse ethnic backgrounds (mostly Jews, Finns, and Ukrainians), and all but one of the internees were men.[2] Some were criminally charged under the DOCR, convicted, sentenced at trial, and sent to jail. Most, however, faced indefinite incarceration without formal charges; two years behind bars or internment camp barbed wire were typical. Despite the violation of their civil liberties and vocal support for their release, the internees remained confined long after the Soviet Union joined the Allied cause in June 1941 and the CPC's position on the war changed. Resistance efforts within and outside the prison walls were crucial in sustaining morale and fostering political solidarity.

The internees' wives faced challenging and complex daily circumstances resulting from the absence of their husbands. Almost immediately, these women launched a public campaign advocating for the men's release. They organized themselves as the Committee for the Release of Labour Prisoners; their protest gained support and continued later through the National Council for Democratic Rights, formed in 1941 to replace the Canadian Labour Defence League, banned under the DOCR in 1940. By early 1942, their efforts had garnered public support from diverse quarters. This support included reinforcement, albeit uneven, from some in the fledgling civil liberties movement, which arose in direct response to the DOCR and other extraordinary wartime measures that threatened Canadians' freedoms beyond what some thought the wartime emergency warranted. This increasing pressure and the Soviet Union joining the Allies in 1941 strengthened the challenges to internment. As a result, the authorities began releasing the internees starting in 1942, and by October that year all of the leftist prisoners had regained their freedom.

Historians, community members, internees, and internee kin have well documented elements of this internment episode. Legal perspectives and personal accounts of time served abound. Some wives' experiences are likewise recorded, though they are more limited in number and less detailed.[3] Examining the Walsh-Steele-Weir-Boyd family allows us to explore the wartime carceral state's impact from multiple angles, permitting us to understand not only diverse experiences of confinement but also the varied ways in which different family members adjusted to, coped with, and responded to new political and personal realities. Bill and Anne Walsh, Dick and Ester Steele, John and Helen Weir, and John and Gladys Boyd—four couples connected by blood, marriage, and politics—experienced the war and the implications of the DOCR in distinct ways. All had grown up in either the Ukrainian left or the Jewish left in Canada, and each remained involved as adults, often with the men in key leadership positions in unions or organizations that straddled the CPC/ethnic hall socialist divide. Their individual and collective wartime experiences were shaped by their gender, parental status, position in the movement, region, and other factors, which I will explore in this chapter. As a case study of husbands and wives, extended kin, community, and the many forms that wartime repression took on Communist and pro-Communist leftists, then, this intimate examination expands our understanding of the complicated impact of political policing, taken to an extreme, on community, family, and intimate relations. This consideration, in turn, supports a broader discussion of internment generally, the impacts and risks of social activism, and potential discrimination and state persecution that activists, their families, and their communities risked in wartime.

Practical reasons also make this family an excellent case study: there is a rich body of archival and personal materials available with which to tell their story. These materials include much personal family correspondence—I have nearly complete collections of letters sent by and to each of these people during the internments and beyond, to the end of the war. RCMP surveillance files, memoirs, and legal documents are also plentiful and have been critical. This project is also grounded in oral history, including several new interviews that I conducted with internee kin, including John and Helen Weir's daughter, Lorna, and with John Boyd himself. This project, then, is blessed with an abundance—perhaps even an overabundance—of sources.[4]

The Family

Since their childhood, siblings Charlie, John, and Anne Weir were involved with the Ukrainian Labour Farmer Temple Association. Charlie and John were also members of the CPC. When the war broke out, their parents were living on a farm in the Niagara Peninsula. Anne was living in southern Ontario and worked in the service industry. Charlie was a party trade union activist, also in southern Ontario, and John was in Winnipeg working as a journalist for the party.

Shortly after the start of the war, Anne married Bill Walsh in a small cross-border ceremony in Toledo, Ohio, in October 1939. Bill was best friends with Dick Steele, and they had come up together in the Jewish left and CPC and were active trade union leaders. Dick was married to Ester

Slominsky, also of the Jewish left. She had worked in the Toronto office of the party and for several unions, including the Industrial Union of Needle Trades Workers during the 1930s. Dick and Ester lived in Toronto, where he was a driving force in the Steelworkers Organizing Committee.[5] They were the proud parents of twin boys, Michael and Johnny, born 15 August 1940. Ester gave up waged labour to look after them until just before their second birthday.

Figure 5.1. Dick Steele giving a speech to steel workers, c. late 1930s. Ontario Jewish Archives (hereafter OJA), accession 2017-2/12.

Figure 5.2. Dick, Ester, and the twins, Johnny and Michael. OJA, accession 2017-2/12.

Like the Weirs, sisters Helen and Gladys Kucherian grew up in the Ukrainian left, in their case in Alberta. Gladys was married to John Boyd, also a Ukrainian leftist (but from Winnipeg) and active in the CPC. At the party's request, John Weir, Dick Steele, Bill Walsh, and John Boyd had anglicized their names. This was a common practice geared to making the organization appear to be less driven by (possibly "dangerous") "foreigners" (as those of Eastern European descent were considered by many in Canada). By thus presenting as Anglo-Celtic, party officials hoped to appear more mainstream and respectable and to attract more Anglo-Celtic supporters. The name change is an especially important detail to remember about John Boyd for the wartime period, for he was born Ivan Boychuk.[6]

Helen was married to Anne Weir's brother, John Weir. When the war broke out, as a devoted party man and leader, he was the editor of the *Mid-West Clarion*, a CPC newspaper. He also had close ties to the Ukrainian labour temple in Winnipeg. John and Gladys and John and Helen lived in Winnipeg at the start of the war.

	The Extended Family (Start of the War)			
	John Boyd	MARRIED	Gladys Kucherian	Siblings
Siblings	John Weir	MARRIED	Helen Kucherian	
	Anne Weir	MARRIED	Bill Walsh	Best Friends
	Ester Slominsky	MARRIED	Dick Steele	

Figure 5.3. The Shape of the Family, 1939. Illustration provided by author.

Arrests and Confinements

Authorities' actions following the advent of the 1940 DOCR would soon render all of the husbands as wanted men. John Weir was the first to go down. He was picked up by police, along with friend and co-worker Bill Tuomi, during a raid of the offices of the CPC's *Mid-West Clarion* newspaper in Winnipeg on 5 March 1940. That spring, after remanding their cases several times, local authorities chose to intern the two. The main motivation was seemingly to circumvent due process, especially since finding a jury sympathetic to the state's perspective and not that of the defendants could prove to be a costly hassle. As I note elsewhere, A.A. Moffat, Crown prosecutor, explained in correspondence to Manitoba's attorney general, "there are a great many communists [in the region] and it would be unsafe to have a communist on the jury." Additional jurors would therefore need to be imported, adding expense. As such, Moffat preferred internment as "it would save a great deal of time and money if they were duly interned."[7] Pre-existing internment orders for both men were thus executed, and Tuomi and Weir soon found themselves on a train to the Kananaskis Internment Camp, located near Canmore, Alberta.[8]

Bill Walsh was the next husband captured. He and Anne lived apart but within driving distance of one another following their wedding. Bill was in Windsor, where he had been organizing auto workers for several months, and Anne lived and worked in London, Ontario. When the police began rounding up CPC activists on 11 November 1939, just weeks after their wedding, Bill was forced underground at the party's urging, camping out in a barn in Amherstburg, Ontario, not far from Windsor. He evaded capture for over a year until police finally nabbed him and brother-in-law Charlie Weir on New Year's Day 1941. The two had secretly been spending

Figure 5.4. John Weir mug shot, 1940. Winnipeg Police Museum Archives, Image 15115.

the holidays with Anne in London and had arranged for an area printshop recommended by a local party activist to prepare some antiwar leaflets and stickers. As they carried them out of the shop, police apprehended them.[9]

On 24 January 1941, Bill was convicted under the Defence of Canada Act for being a member of an illegal organization—the CPC. He was sentenced to six months in jail and given a $300 fine (or an additional three months, which he elected to serve).[10] He spent his nine months in the Guelph Reformatory.

Charlie fared better at his 24 January trial. *The Toronto Daily Star* reported that he was "acquitted on charges of being a member of the Communist party, making statements likely to cause disaffection [to the war effort], and having subversive literature."[11] However, immediately thereafter, RCMP officers took him into custody on an internment order, which saw him shipped off to the Petawawa Internment Camp. There he found himself in good company; many party supporters, ethnic hall socialists, and fellow travellers arrested east of the Ontario border were already interned there. By summer, Charlie was reunited with his brother, John, along with the other western Canadian Communist and pro-Communist internees when they were moved from Kananaskis to Petawawa. Some weeks later Charlie and the others were relocated to the Hull Jail internment facility after they protested against the intolerable conditions caused by the presence of fascist and pro-Nazi prisoners housed at Petawawa.

Upon completion of his nine-month sentence that summer, with an internment order for him still pending, the RCMP immediately whisked Bill away to join his comrades in the Hull Jail. His experience was typical of a number of leftists convicted of criminal charges; after they served jail time as a result of their convictions, the RCMP picked many of them up, often on the jailhouse steps, and squired them off to an internment camp. Indeed, as I have written elsewhere, authorities often put internment orders in place prior to criminal trials to ensure that suspects would end up immediately incarcerated regardless of trial outcomes, as seemed to have happened to Charlie.[12]

Knowing that he was a wanted man for his connections with the CPC, and by then ousted from his role at the Steelworkers Organizing Committee as Communist and anti-Communist activist factions vied for leadership supremacy,[13] Dick Steele had gone into hiding midway through 1940 to preserve his freedom. He managed to evade arrest for over fourteen months. Poor weather even saved him on one occasion; a snowstorm prevented him from meeting up with Charlie and Bill at the printshop on that fateful New Year's Day morning in 1941.[14] During this time, Dick managed to maintain his relationship with Ester through letters, friends and kin, and the occasional visit, though not without considerable personal sacrifice. Underground, for example, he missed the twins' birth on 15 August 1940, only secretly meeting the newborns in person about a month later.[15] He managed sporadic visits with them and Ester somewhat regularly during his time on the lam.

Following Hitler's surprise attack on the Soviet Union on 22 June 1941 and the CPC's resulting turnaround in support of the war, Dick hoped to do his part to fight fascism overseas. He was no stranger to anti-fascist bloodshed; his older brother, Jack Steele, was among those Canadians who died fighting in the Spanish Civil War, killed in action in July 1937.[16] In the fall of 1941, while still in hiding, Dick wrote to federal Minister of

Justice Raoul Lapointe for assurance that the outstanding internment order against him would not be executed should he enlist in the armed services: "As a young Canadian who has always actively opposed fascism, I can no longer remain silent in my enforced seclusion, which greatly restricts my contribution to our nation's war effort. I offer my services—my life if need be—to help Canada and her allies wipe Hitler and Hitlerism from the face of the earth. However, I can not [*sic*] translate my desire into action because of the information which convinces me that I shall suffer the unjust fate of other anti-fascist union leaders who have been interned without trial."[17] No such assurance was forthcoming, and eventually RCMP officers caught up with and arrested Dick on 31 March 1942 at a cottage where he had been staying in Rouge Hills, Ontario (now Scarborough) following what Ester described as "just one slip" while in hiding.[18]

His lawyer, J.L. Cohen, who represented many of the internees, the National Council for Democratic Rights, and several of the organizations banned under the Defence of Canada Regulations, tried to get Dick's incarceration overturned under a habeas corpus challenge. Cohen argued that the internment order should be declared invalid because Minister of Justice LaPointe, who had issued it, had since died. Magistrate John Andrew Hope rejected this position, letting the internment order stand. Regardless, Dick was going away; he was caught with two fake registration cards at the time of his arrest (his aliases, as per CPC protocol for underground functionaries). He was sentenced on 31 August 1942 "on two counts for infraction of the Registration Act. The Magistrate imposed the minimum sentence provided in these cases of six months in jail."[19] Dick was given credit for time served as he had been held in custody in the Toronto Jail since his arrest; shortly after his sentencing, he was transferred to serve the remaining weeks of his sentence in the space that Bill Walsh had just vacated in the Guelph Reformatory.[20]

On the Outside

Ester did what she could to keep Dick's spirits up and maintain a connection between him and their little boys, both while he was underground and after his arrest and conviction. The two tried to make life as normal and happy for the twins as possible. In one letter, for example, Dick thanks Ester for giving them a building set and saying that it was from him. He goes on to say, "I'm afraid when I return home at last, and you introduce them to Daddy Dick, the lads will think me a queer sort of creature. . . . It's a little cheering at any rate to know that Daddy Dick is something in their baby consciousness."[21] Ester carried out this affective labour under considerable emotional and financial duress. As a new mom and quasi-single parent of two active boys, she needed to provide for both herself and them, relying on a network of family members and friends to help out.[22]

Like Ester, Helen Kucherian Weir needed to support herself and her two young children, Charlie and Lorna, while John Weir was incarcerated. Having to work for wages meant that she needed reliable child care, so she sent the two children to live with family members in Alberta, Manitoba, and later Ontario while she worked, joining them at various times when work was available in the area.[23] Meanwhile, her sister Gladys's husband, John Boyd, escaped arrest thanks to a case of mistaken identity. Recall how he had anglicized his birth name, Ivan Boychuk, at the party's behest. Authorities, it seemed, had erroneously apprehended and interned another Ivan Boychuk. Existing in a grey area, then, Gladys and John spent most of the internment years hiding in plain sight in Minnedosa, Manitoba, where he ran the Ukrainian left–founded Co-op Dairy's recently acquired creamery. There, playing the roles of small-town captain of industry and corporate wife, John and Gladys socialized with the community elite, including, as he enjoyed recounting, his regular golf dates with the chief of police, who had no idea that he was a wanted man. The couple often provided child care for Helen and John's daughter, Lorna, who stayed with them in Minnedosa for extended periods.[24]

Helen eventually took up activism as a travelling organizer in the struggle for the internees' liberation. She would become a key figure in the National Council for Democratic Rights, the organization that in 1941 replaced the wartime-banned Canadian Labour Defence League. The National Council was the vanguard of the struggle for the internees' release. Complicating Helen's situation was her challenging relationship with John. A reputed womanizer and seemingly serial bigamist at the time of their union, apparently he had already amassed and abandoned several wives. He had married Mary Bilinsky in 1929 in Winnipeg; then he had gone to Moscow in the early 1930s, where he had taken another wife, Edya, apparently without legally dissolving his earlier union. The two had a daughter, Emma, born in 1931. They, too, never formally divorced. It is unclear whether Helen knew of Mary or Edya and Emma when she insisted that John marry her in 1932 (because she was pregnant) or by the time of his internment.[25]

A symptom of their problematic relationship was the affair that she began and continued with Walter Sawiak, the son of John's fellow internee Michael Sawiak. It started when the two were both in Minnedosa in the summer of 1941. Walter was there on business for the Co-op, along with his wife and son. Helen was recuperating from recent surgery and a hospital stay, and she and the children were staying with John and Gladys Boyd. As she later recounted in her unpublished memoirs, "after my visit to Minnedosa, I probably felt a little happier—just resting and relaxing—Walter became a very important secret lover." Soon after, Helen and son Charlie moved to Winnipeg, where Walter ran the People's Co-op's main operation, and their affair might have continued. Evidence is unclear whether John ever found out; their marriage endured until the early 1960s.[26]

Having no children, newlywed Anne Weir Walsh, Bill's wife, enjoyed a degree of independence and mobility at this time that Ester and Helen did not. Anne did not feel the need to relocate or stay near kin or established friendship and neighbourhood connections in this context of crisis. She did need to work to support herself materially and emotionally, and she did so, taking up a variety of service industry jobs. A major benefit, beyond that to her mental health, was that they were relatively easy to take up or abandon, thus supporting her mobility to relocate to where Bill was incarcerated.[27] Because he had been convicted and jailed, as opposed to interned, initially he was allowed to have visitors. Living in the same locale as Bill meant that she was able to visit him regularly during his detention. By the time of his internment in the Hull Jail, the rules for internment camp visitation had relaxed (prior to then, no visitors had been allowed), and Anne, who by then had relocated to the Ottawa area, and the other wives were able to see their husbands, assuming that they had the means and ability to get to the internment facility. At that time, Anne would have been able to visit not only Bill but also her brothers, John and Charlie Weir. The stress of Bill's internment and the degree to which she had to work brought on or exacerbated a number of health issues. Her precarious health—she suffered from ulcers, migraine headaches, and other ailments—is a frequent subject in their personal and general family correspondence.[28]

Since John and Charlie Weir were internees, and visits to internment camps were not permitted for most of the internment period, Helen and her family went well over a year and a half without any in-person contact with them. Even for Ester and Anne, in-person contact was certainly less frequent than desired and always under circumstances of intense carceral regulation. Being far from family as they were in Minnedosa meant that in-person contact was limited for John and Gladys Boyd. Letters were especially critical, then, to maintaining a sense of connection, providing emotional and moral support for all parties, and keeping intact, however possible, vestiges of intimacy. For example, Ester's letters occasionally express romantic feelings. Before bed one evening, Ester wrote, "Our sons are asleep and all that is missing to complete the picture is you—here in person. Not merely in my thoughts. . . . I guess I've never told you that in all the time that we've had to be apart I've never, ever felt alone, I've always felt your presence near."[29] Dick, though his letters were warm and loving, was less comfortable sharing more intimate feelings, knowing that prison censors screened all correspondence. "Darling there are things I would like to write but I would rather share them with you in my thoughts," he notes on one occasion, continuing that "To write them under these circumstances would be to share them with others—which I must refuse to do."[30]

Self-censorship for this and other reasons was standard, especially to avoid the potential consequences that the contents of some letters could entail for prisoners. Italian fascist internee Antonio Rebaudengo cautioned his kin on many occasions about expressing their feelings in writing: "My criminal file is swollen like a leather bag, yes I know it, many of your letters and mine have contributed to that."[31] When writing to her interned leftist husband, Peter, Mary Prokop recalled writing in code; as historian and archivist Myron Momryk explains, "names and places were translated from English into Ukrainian or written in such a manner that the censor could not understand the message."[32] This allowed illicit information to slip past authorities and reach the internees without creating written evidence that could be used against them or incriminate other potentially at-risk community members.

Freedom

Eventually, the incarcerated men were released, thanks to the hard work and lobbying of their wives, their supporters, the National Council for Democratic Rights, diverse public support, and the change in geopolitics that brought the Soviet Union into the Allied camp. As Ian Radforth indicates, "after Hitler's invasion of the Soviet Union, the government's principal rationale for interning the Communists was gone completely, and so more and more people saw the injustice of the case and were willing to declare their position publicly."[33] Among the voices were those of Canada's emerging civil liberties groups, many founded in direct response to the threat that the DOCR and other extraordinary wartime measures posed to Canadians' freedoms, calling for the measures to be overhauled. Most of these civil libertarians did not explicitly defend or support the CPC or other leftist internees, as Ross Lambertson notes. Indeed, at least some of these groups, which existed in several cities across Canada, including Toronto, Vancouver, and Winnipeg, were anti-Communist in their outlook and membership.

Although, as Reg Whitaker explains, most Canadians remained silent on the matter, the rising chorus of voices of opposition, which also came to include elements of the mainstream press, some Liberal cabinet ministers, advisers in the Prime Minister's Office, and others from across the political spectrum, pushed authorities to move on the matter.[34] By the fall of 1942, all of the leftist internees were liberated.

The men of the family returned to their former activism in one way or another. John Weir, for example, went back to his leadership activities and journalism for the Ukrainian left and the Labor-Progressive Party, the replacement for the still-illegal CPC, which had outlaw status for several years. The younger men—John Boyd, Dick Steele, and Bill Walsh—expressed their activism through overseas service in the Canadian Forces.

Figure 5.5. Dick Steele enlists, 1942. OJA, accession 2017-2/12.

Bill did so under sudden and tragic circumstances. Mere months following his hard-fought release from the Hull Jail, Anne died suddenly in March 1943 from a brain hemorrhage. In the wake of Bill's tremendous loss and his overwhelming grief, he later recounted that "All I could think of doing was

Figure 5.6. Bill and Ester Steele Walsh pose with Michael and John Steele, late 1940s. OJA, accession 2017-2/12.

John Weir	DIVORCED	Helen Kucherian
Charlie Weir		
Anne Weir - DECEASED, 1942	MARRIED	Bill Walsh - WIDOWER
Ester Slominsky - WIDOW		Dick Steele - KILLED IN ACTION, 1944
John Boyd	MARRIED	Gladys Kucherian

Figure 5.7. The couples after the war. Illustration provided by author.

going overseas to fight the Nazis. What did I have to lose?"[35] By summer, he was headed to Europe in uniform for the Canadian Forces.

Home for only a few weeks after his release from the Guelph Reformatory, Dick enlisted and trained as a tank driver. Further separation from Ester and the twins was likely softened by his anti-fascist belief that he was fighting for a valuable cause.[36] Sadly, they would never see him again; Dick died in action nearly two years later on 17 August 1944.

Widower Bill, having promised his best friend, Dick, that he would look after Ester and the children should anything happen to him during the war, kept up an active correspondence with Ester, through which both processed their grief via overseas mail prior to his return to Canada. They eventually shifted to courtship. Ester debated remarriage, reluctant to surrender her independence. According to Bill's biography, "it was only settled, both of them agree, when Johnny blurted out, 'I want you for my daddy, uncle Bill.'" Ester and Bill were married in March 1946.[37]

Conclusion

It is possible to study this extended family because of the enormous volume of relevant source materials that they and others (especially state agents) generated during the Second World War and saw fit to preserve. In this extraordinary time, preserving intimacy and familial connection was a challenge. The only way to do so, in most instances, was through correspondence. We are privy to intimate conversations among husbands and wives, brothers and sisters, in-laws, other kin, and friends that otherwise might not have been put to paper had these individuals not been unexpectedly separated from each other. Writing under difficult and dangerous circumstances—notably under the gaze of government censors enforcing rules of appropriate and inappropriate information sharing and under threat of state harassment or worse—the letter writers were careful to avoid the creation of further suffering where possible. The kinship relations were critical to sustaining individuals and family units during this trying time.

The extended family's story offers insights into and expands our understanding of lived experiences of civil liberties and human rights struggles in wartime, particularly in the period before the post–Second World War "rights revolution" in Canada and elsewhere. It also highlights how states can legalize rights violations under extraordinary circumstances. As Ian Radforth asserts, "much vaunted civil liberties can be a fragile façade in wartime."[38] This is an important caution, reminding us of the need for constant vigilance. At the same time, this family's experiences and those of the other leftist internees underscore how challenging—and even threatening—it can be to speak truth to power.

Intimate stories like these, then, serve to humanize the struggle for human rights and the impacts of the violation of individual rights and civil liberties on spouses, children, broader kinship networks, and communities. Writing the Walsh-Steele-Weir-Boyd extended family's internment biography demonstrates the interconnectedness of the Jewish and Ukrainian lefts, these movements' national reach, their enduring but complicated connections with the Communist Party of Canada, the perceived threat that this activism posed to the capitalist social order, and the vulnerability of the movements' members to red-baiting, state surveillance, political policing, and other punitive measures, including incarceration. It also underscores the personal impacts of family members' commitments to left politics and social justice and the resulting outcomes and consequences, especially in times of crisis. Finally, this extended family case study shows the emotional, financial, and physical toll of criminalization and incarceration on confined individuals and their immediate and extended kinship networks. For all, no matter what side of the bars or barbed wire, internment is a family affair.

Notes

1 For a detailed discussion of the DOCR, how they affected civil liberties, and their pushback from Canadian civil liberties groups and others, see Ross Lambertson, "The Second World War: Civil Liberties at Risk," in *Repression and Resistance:*

Canadian Human Rights Activists, 1930–1960 (Toronto: University of Toronto Press, 2005), 68–105.

2 I have written about Gladys McDonald, the sole woman internee, and other pro-Communist women arrested under the DOCR during this period in "'Likely to Be Hampered and So She Prepared for the Worst': Far Left Women and Wartime Political Incarceration," in *Civilian Internment in Canada: Histories and Legacies*, ed. Rhonda L. Hinther and Jim Mochoruk (Winnipeg: University of Manitoba Press, 2020), 151–63; and in "'Thoroughly Impregnated With Bolshevik Philosophy': Annie Buller's Incarceration and Canadian Political Policing During World War II," *Labour / Le Travail* 94 (November 2024): 9–44. See also Michelle McBride, "The Curious Case of Female Internees," in *Enemies Within: Italian and Other Internees in Canada and Abroad*, ed. Franca Iacovetta, Roberto Perin, and Angelo Principe (Toronto: University of Toronto Press, 2000), 128–47.

3 Some examples of biographies, autobiographies, and personal accounts of this internment episode are Peter Krawchuk, *Interned without Cause* (Toronto: Kobzar, 1985); Peter Krawchuk, ed., *Reminiscences of Courage and Hope: Stories of Ukrainian Canadian Women Pioneers* (Toronto: Kobzar, 1991); Peter Krawchuk, "The War Years," in *Our History: The Ukrainian Labour-Farmer Movement in Canada, 1907–1991* (Toronto: Lugus, 1996); William Repka and Kathleen M. Repka, *Dangerous Patriots: Canada's Unknown Prisoners of War* (Vancouver: New Star Books, 1982); Ben Swankey, "Reflections of a Communist: Canadian Internment Camps," *Alberta History* 30, no. 2 (1982): 11–20; and Roland Penner, "Transition, Turmoil, and Trouble (1939–1943)," in *A Glowing Dream: A Memoir* (Winnipeg: J. Gordon Shillingford, 2007), 56–64.

For related works on state security, see Reg Whitaker, Gregory S. Kealey, and Andrew Parnaby, "Keep the Home Fires Burning, 1939–45," in *Secret Service: Political Policing in Canada: From the Fenians to Fortress America* (Toronto: University of Toronto Press, 2012), 145–76; Gregory S. Kealey, "State Repression of Labour and the Left in Canada, 1914–20: The Impact of the First World War," *Canadian Historical Review* 73, no. 3 (1992): 281–314; Daniel Robinson, "Planning for the 'Most Serious Contingency': Alien Internment, Arbitrary Detention, and the Canadian State, 1938–39," *Journal of Canadian Studies* 28, no. 2 (1993): 5–20; Reg Whitaker, "Official Repression of Communism during World War II," *Labour* 17 (1986): 135–66; Chris Frazer, "From Pariahs to Patriots: Canadian Communists and the Second World War," *Past Imperfect* 5 (1996): 3–36; and Reg Whitaker and Gregory S. Kealey, "A War on Ethnicity? The RCMP and Internment," in Iacovetta, Perin, and Principe, *Enemies Within*, 128–47.

For histories of the Communist Party of Canada that touch on this period, see Joan Sangster, *Dreams of Equality: Women on the Canadian Left, 1920–1950* (Toronto: McClelland and Stewart, 1989); Ivan Avakumovic, *The Communist Party in Canada: A History* (Toronto: McClelland and Stewart, 1975); Merrily Weisbord, "Underground" and "Total War" in *The Strangest Dream: Canadian Communists, the Spy Trials, and the Cold War* (Montreal: Véhicule Press, 1994), 103–10, 111–21;

A. Grenke, "From Dreams of the Worker State to Fighting Hitler: The German-Canadian Left from the Depression to the End of World War II," *Labour* 35 (1995): 65–105; Varpu Lindström, *From Heroes to Enemies: Finns in Canada, 1937–1947* (Beaverton, ON: Aspasia Books, 2000); Ian Radforth, "Political Prisoners: The Communist Internees," in Iacovetta, Perin, and Principe, *Enemies Within*, 194–224; Hinther, "'Likely to Be Hampered'"; Rhonda L. Hinther, "'Dear Kate! I Don't Know How You Manage!' The Ukrainian Left and WWII," in *Perogies and Politics: Radical Ukrainians in Canada, 1891–1991* (Toronto: University of Toronto Press, 2018), 101–32; Michael Martin, *The Red Patch: Political Imprisonment in Hull, Quebec, during World War II* (Gatineau: self-published, 2007); Michelle McBride, "The Curious Case of the Female Internees," in Iacovetta, Perin, and Principe, *Enemies Within*, 148–70; and Cy Gonick, "Chapter 6: Underground, Imprisoned, and Interned," in *A Very Red Life: The Story of Bill Walsh* (St. John's: Canadian Committee on Labour History, 2001), 125–50.

4 Given the volume and richness of the correspondence produced by each member of the extended Walsh-Steele-Weir-Boyd family, it is possible for large swaths of their stories to be told in their own words. I am presently focused on a more substantial written project, a monograph, that I am structuring using the various letters, cards, and other types of correspondence to allow the prisoners' contemporary voices and those of their loved ones and supporters to come through.

5 Gonick, "Underground, Imprisoned, and Interned," 129; "Biographical Information," Archives of Ontario (hereafter AO), Steele, Dick, Correspondence, 1942–44, reel 1 of 3, part 1, Ester and Bill Walsh Textual Records, Sub-series F 1405-85-44, MFN 627. For a detailed overview of Steele's Steelworkers Organizing Committee activities in the lead up to the war, see Irving Abella, "Chapter 4: The Steelworkers Organizing Committee," in *Nationalism, Communism, and Canadian Labour: The CIO, the Communist Party, and the Canadian Congress of Labour, 1935–1956* (Toronto: University of Toronto Press, 1973), 54–65.

6 Steele's name at birth was Moishe Kosowatsky, and Walsh's name was Moishe Wolofsky. See "Biographical Information," AO, Steele, Dick, Correspondence, 1942–44, reel 1 of 3, part 1, Ester and Bill Walsh Textual Collection. As Boyd later recalled in his memoir, in 1933, "when I was made organizer of the Young Communist League in Alberta" was "when I took on the name Boyd (I changed it legally in 1941). I did it at the suggestion of the Party leaders, as did many other active Ukrainian party members: John Vyviursky became John Weir. . . . When I became organizer of the Young Communist League in Alberta, it was supposed to be for Anglo-Saxon work. The irony is that the Party membership in Alberta was about 90 percent Ukrainian. (There were a few Finns around in Sylvan Lake.) It was the same in Saskatchewan." John Boyd, "A Noble Cause Betrayed . . . but Hope Lives On: Pages from a Political Life," Socialist History Project, https://www.socialisthistory.ca/Remember/Reminiscences/Boyd/B3.htm.

7 Hinther, "'Likely to Be Hampered,'" 160–61.

8 See the entries on 5 March 1940, Winnipeg Police Arrest Record Book, 1 December 1939–27 June 1941, Winnipeg Police Museum; and A.A. Moffat, Crown Prosecutor, to Attorney General Major, 29 August 1940, Library and Archives Canada (hereafter LAC), Bill Tuomi RCMP file, A201500408_2016-02-23_14-31-16; Hinther, "'Likely to Be Hampered,'" 160–61.

9 "Windsor Accountant Adjudged Communist," *Toronto Daily Star*, 24 January 1941, 3; Gonick, "Underground, Imprisoned, and Interned," 132–33.

10 "Windsor Accountant Adjudged Communist."

11 "Windsor Accountant Adjudged Communist."

12 See Hinther, "'Thoroughly Impregnated.'"

13 For details on his ouster and conflict between Communist and anti-Communist activists in the leadership of the Steelworkers Organizing Committee and the Congress for Industrial Organizations (CIO), see Abella, "The Steelworkers Organizing Committee," 54–65; and Gonick, "Underground, Imprisoned, and Interned," 124–50.

14 Gonick, "Underground, Imprisoned, and Interned," 132.

15 Dick Steele to newborns John and Michael, n.d. (likely late September 1940 from in hiding), AO, Steele, Dick, Correspondence, 1942–44, reel 1 of 3, Ester and Bill Walsh Textual Records.

16 Like Dick, Jack also anglicized his name. His birth name was Mortimer Kosowatski. For information on his service, see "Mortimer Kosowatski," Canada and the Spanish Civil War, https://spanishcivilwar.ca/volunteers/mortimer-kosowatski.

17 Dick Steele to Raoul Lapointe, Minister of Justice, 8 November 1941, AO, Steele, Dick, Correspondence, 1942–44, reel 1 of 3, part 1, Ester and Bill Walsh Textual Records; National Council for Democratic Rights, Correspondence, Notes, Trial Material re: Richard Steele, 1941–42, LAC, 2917 A, Cohen Fonds, MG 30 A 94, vol. 30.

18 Ester Steele to Dick Steele, 2 April 1942, AO, Steele, Dick, Correspondence, 1942–44, reel 2 of 3, part 1, Ester and Bill Walsh Textual Records; and "Arrest Steele under War Act," *Globe* [Toronto], 3 April 1942.

19 National Council for Democratic Rights, Information Bulletin, 1 September 1942, University of Toronto Library and Special Collections, Kenny Collection, Folder 18.

20 "Arrest Steele under War Act"; "*Habeas Corpus* Writs Granted," *Globe* [Toronto], 25 April 1942; "Osgoode Hall," *Globe* [Toronto], 16 May 1942.

21 Dick Steele to Ester Steele, 17 July 1942, AO, Steele, Dick, Correspondence, 1942–44, reel 1 of 3, part 1, Ester and Bill Walsh Textual Records.

22 Ester Steele to Mable Mayne, 6 June 1942, AO, Steele, Dick, Correspondence, 1942–44, reel 2 of 3, part 3 (Docs re Internment), Ester and Bill Walsh Textual Records.

23 Helen Weir, unpublished memoir, c. 1970s, Stavroff Private Collection, Toronto; see also her autobiography, "Helen Weir-Hale," in *Reminiscences of Courage and Hope: Stories of Ukrainian Canadian Women Pioneers*, ed. Peter Krawchuk (Toronto: Kobzar, 1991), 499–506.

24 John Boyd, interview with the author, 22 July 2015. For more information on the Co-op, consult Jim Mochoruk and Nancy Kardash, *The People's Co-op: The Life and Times of a North End Institution* (Halifax: Fernwood Publishing, 2002). John Boyd shares a description of his circumstances in a letter to interned John Weir, 26 July 1941, Stavroff Private Collection, folder "July to August 1941 Helen to John."

25 "Re John Weir Alias Wavurský [*sic*]," report dated 11 January 1939, LAC, Records of CSIS, RG 146, "Helen Weir"; and Lorna Clark, interview with the author, 26 April 2017.

26 Weir, unpublished memoir.

27 Anne describes the mental health benefits that she derived from paid work in a letter to Bill dated 12 February 1941, LAC, MG 31 B 27, vol. 47, file 3, "Correspondence from Anne Walsh, January–March 1941."

28 See, for example, Bill Walsh to Anne Walsh, AO, Steele, Dick, Correspondence, 1942–44, reel 2 of 3, part 4, Ester and Bill Walsh Textual Records. Gonick, *A Very Red Life*, 149, also describes some of her health problems.

29 Ester Steele to Dick Steele, n.d., AO, Steele, Dick, Correspondence, 1942–44, reel 2 of 3, part 1, Ester and Bill Walsh Textual Records.

30 Dick Steele, Don Jail, to Ester Steele, 13 April 1942, AO, Steele, Dick, Correspondence, 1942–44, reel 1 of 3, Bill and Ester Walsh Textual Records.

31 Antonio to Angelina, 9 January 1943, in Diary of Antonio Rebaudengo (translation), University of Calgary Archives, Angelina and Antonio Rebaudengo Fonds, CA ACU GBA F1531.

32 Myron Momryk, "Ukrainian Internment during the Second World War," in *Civilian Internment in Canada: Histories and Legacies*, ed. Rhonda L. Hinther and Jim Mochoruk (Winnipeg: University of Manitoba Press, 2020), 251.

33 Radforth, "Political Prisoners," 215, 220. See also Whitaker, "Official Repression of Communism," 146, 148–49, 165.

34 Lambertson, *Repression and Resistance*, 89–90; Whitaker, "Official Repression of Communism," 160. See also Hinther, "'Thoroughly Impregnated,'" 38–42.

35 Quoted in Gonick, *A Very Red Life*, 149.

36 Dick Steele to Reg Taylor, 30 October 1942, AO, Steele, Dick, Correspondence, 1942–44, reel 1 of 3, Ester and Bill Walsh Textual Records.

37 Gonick, *A Very Red Life*, 170.

38 Radforth, "Political Prisoners," 195.

CHAPTER 6

"Injurious Effects on Mind and Body":[1] Solitary Confinement and the Limitations of Rights in Canadian Penitentiaries

Janet Miron

SINCE THE ESTABLISHMENT of the first penitentiary in the region currently known as Canada, wardens have wielded isolation as a tool to discipline, control, and punish inmates considered "unruly," "recalcitrant," or "problematic." Whether via "the hole," purpose-built isolation wings, segregation cells, or dissociation units, solitary confinement has been justified, defended, and rationalized by prison officials who have presented it as an unavoidable, humane, and effective correctional measure. Although serious concerns were raised about the impact of isolation as early as the 1840s, and grew louder in the twentieth century, the correctional system in Canada has witnessed increasing reliance on isolation, with greater numbers of incarcerated individuals left in segregation for longer and longer periods of time.[2] In 1891, commissioners investigating Ontario's prisons condemned the practice as having "injurious effects on mind and body."[3] However, as scholars Kelly Hannah-Moffat and Amy Klassen argue, solitary confinement today is "becoming increasingly normalized in Canadian prisons."[4]

The history of the use of isolation in Canadian penitentiaries and the persistence of the practice in the contemporary correctional system offer important yet troubling insights into the inconsistent application of human rights and the ease with which certain populations can be excluded from them. In many ways, reconciling inmates' rights and mental and physical health with the impulse to punish and control has been elusive within Canada's penitentiaries when solitary confinement is considered. For almost two centuries, solitary segregation has existed inside Canada's penitentiaries, and for almost two centuries the practice has been condemned.[5] As critics both in the past and in the present have asserted, isolation, as a punitive response to violations of prison rules or as a means to "manage" inmates with mental illnesses, not only causes individual harm, but also undermines the objective of rehabilitation.[6] In sharp contrast to national and international condemnation of the practice as detrimental to mental health and a form of torture, the use of solitary segregation in Canadian penitentiaries highlights how idiosyncratic the extension of human rights discourses can be in regard to incarcerated populations, especially when those incarcerated are disproportionately Indigenous.

National and international movements have sought to define, defend, protect, and enshrine human rights, and there have been important and meaningful gestures, including the Universal Declaration of Human Rights (1948) and, on a national level, Canada's Bill of Rights (1960) and Charter of Rights and Freedoms (1982). Reflecting on contemporary Canada, historian Ross Lambertson writes that "we live in 'the age of rights.' . . . [S]upport for human rights is widespread and powerful."[7] Yet support for the rights of some populations, specifically incarcerated ones, has not been quite so widespread and powerful when the practice of isolation is considered. Solitary confinement has been used within Canadian penitentiaries for almost two centuries and persists today, and its history demonstrates how deeply engrained the practice is. As I discuss in this chapter, solitary confinement has been used since the beginning of penitentiary building in colonial Canada, yet its use has also been accompanied by voices that condemned it. If settler Canada is to continue its commitment to solitary confinement, then it cannot feign ignorance of its effects in the face of extensive study, commentary, and critique, now stretching over almost 200 years.

The Rise of the Penitentiary and the Use of Isolation in the Nineteenth Century

In early-nineteenth-century colonial Canada, reformers interested in new approaches to punishment followed discussions taking place in various countries on how to prevent crime and recidivism. At the centre of these discussions was the newly conceived institution, the penitentiary. Based on the view that human behaviour and morality could be reformed, the penitentiary was presented as embodying "purposeful" and "enlightened" punishment. Departing from earlier responses to crime that were swift, bloody, spectacular, and measured by increments of pain, the penitentiary was predicated on the optimistic notion that reform and rehabilitation could be accomplished in a carefully controlled environment.[8] Through discipline, work, routine, and isolation from corrupting influences, individuals would be remade from the inside out in the new penitentiary, and upon completion of their sentences they would be released as hard-working and law-abiding members of society. Kingston Penitentiary, or the Provincial Penitentiary of Upper Canada as it was then called, received its first inmates on 1 June 1835 and was established in this ideological burst of hopeful enthusiasm and expectation. Kingston quickly became the cornerstone of the colonial criminal justice system, and until it was decommissioned in 2013 it represented Canada's oldest federal penitentiary in operation.

In the minds of their advocates and founders, newly designed penitentiaries would help to resolve social problems by teaching inmates regularity, discipline, and conformity to the emerging industrial-capitalist system. In the British North American colonies or what would become Canada, those engaged with prison reform scrutinized minute details of prison design and management and followed with great interest debates on the merits of two influential prison systems that emerged in the United States: the congregate system, implemented in Auburn State Prison in New York, and the separate system, implemented in Eastern State Penitentiary in Pennsylvania. Although both designs enforced strict silence among inmates, the separate system sought to isolate inmates physically not only at night, but also in the day. In the separate system, inmates worked, ate, and slept alone in their cells, whereas in the congregate system they were allowed to eat and work together during the day. Although the degree of isolation was significantly greater in Eastern State Penitentiary or the solitary model, nineteenth-century penitentiaries, regardless of their design, embraced elements of isolation and sought to ensure that inmates had limited human interaction. For example, communicating with other inmates, including through eye contact, was prohibited during the first century of Kingston Penitentiary's existence. In this way, the penitentiary physically isolated inmates not only from the outside world, but from each other in the institution itself.

At Kingston Penitentiary, isolation as a tool to punish recalcitrant inmates quickly became part of the disciplinary regime, and many internal or in-house punishment practices involved inflicting even greater forms of isolation than enclosure behind the walls of the institution entailed. From the institution's earliest years and over the next century, wardens wielded isolation as punishment for defiant, disobedient, or refractory inmates whose offences ranged from refusing to work to dancing in their cells to unauthorized talking in a regime that enforced the rule of silence until the early 1930s.[9] In the nineteenth and early twentieth centuries, solitary confinement in Kingston Penitentiary could involve being placed in "the box" (a coffin-like contraption), isolation in one's own cell, or segregation in the "dark cell." Isolation furthermore was used in combination with an array of other punishments for in-house infractions, and wardens employed punishments that targeted not only the mind but also the body. Depending on the particular time period, they could order meals of bread and water, whipping, paddling, the ball and chain, the Oregon Boot, and various water punishments that inflicted a near-drowning experience or pressurized force on inmates.[10] However, though physical punishments were periodically questioned, modified, reduced, and gradually abolished at various times in federal penitentiaries, the history of solitary confinement followed a different trajectory.

In his book *American Notes for General Circulation*, published in 1842, Charles Dickens described his visit to Eastern State Penitentiary.[11] Of the isolation, segregation, and silence that characterized this institution, Dickens famously wrote, "very few men are capable of estimating the immense amount of torture and agony which this dreadful punishment, prolonged for years, inflicts upon the sufferers. . . . I hold this slow and daily tampering with the mysteries of the brain . . . to be immeasurably worse than any torture of the body: and because its ghastly signs and tokens are not so palpable to the eye [and] . . . because its wounds are not upon the surface, and it extorts few cries that human ears can hear; therefore I the more denounce it."[12] Aside from concerns about the financial cost of the separate system and the limited ability to profit from inmates' labour, Dickens and many others recognized that insanity was more pervasive in institutions that enforced prolonged isolation and deprived inmates of human interaction. Canadian prison officials were aware of Dickens's criticism, and several decades later they would have followed with interest a United States Supreme Court case in 1890 in which solitary confinement was described as leading to "a semi-fatuous condition, from which it was next to impossible to arouse" inmates. Prisoners, as argued in this case, "became violently insane; others still, committed suicide; while those who stood the ordeal better were not generally reformed, and in most cases did not recover sufficient mental activity to be of any subsequent service to the community."[13] Popular writers, lawyers, and a growing body of critics in the nineteenth century asserted that isolation constituted a form of torture, inflicted suffering, and caused or exacerbated mental illness. They also understood it as connected to suicide. Nevertheless, the separation of inmates from human interaction for the purposes of punishment remained a significant part of the prison system in Canada.

Although Kingston Penitentiary was founded upon the idea that the institution would not simply punish offenders but also rehabilitate them, institutional practices would easily tip to the side of the former, with prison officials often arguing that punishment or the threat of it was essential to ensure conformity, security, and control.[14] A little more than a decade after the penitentiary received its first inmates, an investigation of its management under Warden Henry Smith was launched. Commonly known as the Brown Report, the commission's findings were published in 1848. In hundreds of pages of evidence and testimony, the Brown Report detailed instances of abuse, corruption, favouritism, and mismanagement. As part of their investigation, the commissioners examined punishment practices for prison offences in detail, documenting, in one year alone, more than 6,000 meted out to prisoners. In 1847, for example, the commissioners found that punishments included 5,104 meals of bread and water, 58 whippings with the cat-o-nine tails, 759 confinements in the box, 73 confinements in the inmate's own cell, and 69 confinements in the dark cell.[15]

Troubled by the incarceration of children and youth alongside adults, the commissioners drew particular attention to the treatment of several young boys and girls, including Alexis Lafleur, who entered Kingston Penitentiary in 1842 at the age of eleven. Flogged with rawhide on the third day after his arrival at the institution, Lafleur was regularly punished in the months and years that followed. In one month alone, he was punished on ten separate occasions.[16] Of his treatment, the commissioners wrote that "it is horrifying to think of a child of 11 to 14 years of age . . . being lacerated with the lash before 500 grown men; to say nothing of the cruelty, the effect of such a scene, so often repeated, must have been to the last degree brutalizing."[17] In addition to flogging with rawhide, meals of bread and water, and confinement in the box, institutional officials used isolation in the dark cell when the boy was caught quarrelling, singing, talking, or being "insubordinate." However, though physical punishments galvanized outrage that led to policy recommendations and gradual modifications, the use of solitary confinement and its impact on the boy, or on other inmates for that matter, did not spark similar abhorrence and reform.

From the beginning of the institution, hundreds of punishments that involved isolation had taken place, and at several points in the Brown Report the commissioners explicitly acknowledged the impact of isolation on inmates. Referring to Eastern State Penitentiary in Philadelphia and its solitary system, they wrote that, "as to the effect of separation and seclusion on the minds of the Convicts, the Deputation were compelled to arrive at the conclusion . . . that the human mind cannot endure protracted imprisonment under this system; and that with all the care of the authorities, insanity, to a fearful extent, is to be found within the walls."[18] The commissioners included solitary confinement in their list of harsh punishments used at Kingston Penitentiary, and they concluded that such treatment was detrimental to rehabilitation:

> As in the construction of the Prison, in its internal economy and management, the idea of physical force alone has been kept in view; whilst the milder, but it is to be hoped the not less powerful influence of moral suasion, has been altogether lost sight of. Here indeed the Penitentiary system has been presented in its sternest aspect, and if the cat-o-nine-tails, the raw-hide, the box, the solitary cell, deprivation of food, or of the light of heaven, could ever have deterred the criminal from again preying on society, or violating its laws, here, at all events, the salutary effect would have been produced; but we cannot say that the experiment has proved successful or that the torture which the inmates endured within the walls of the Penitentiary . . . have rendered their returns to it a matter of less frequent occurrence than in similar Institutions, where a milder influence has prevailed. . . . [T]he only effect has been to render callous and to harden the offenders, and that each addition to the weight of punishment has increased the number of infractions of the Prison rules.[19]

Nevertheless, the Brown Report did not fundamentally question the use of solitary confinement at Kingston Penitentiary or recommend limitations on its use. Rather, what was deemed to be excessive corporal punishment, and the corruption and incompetence of specific institutional employees, constituted the focus of its recommendations. Indeed, the commissioners even argued that, moving forward, arrangements for solitary confinement should be expanded at Kingston Penitentiary.

Although they often discussed solitary confinement in the same context as corporal punishment, the commissioners recommended the construction of additional solitary confinement cells at Kingston Penitentiary, fifty to start, both to isolate newly admitted inmates and to punish inmates who had committed prison offences. They wrote that "we recommend that besides employing the separate cells on the first reception of the Convict, they be used as a means of discipline; not as a frequent punishment, but in the case of continued refractory conduct on the part of any Convict, to enable the Warden to deal with him individually and endeavour to produce a change."[20] Furthermore, they explained, "confinement in a dark cellar on bread and water . . . is perhaps better adapted to subdue refractory spirits, but this also requires care in the application, lest either the mind or body should sink under it. . . . [I]t will undoubtedly be a matter of necessity, sometimes, to inflict the severe punishment of the dark cell, or failing that, of the cat; but we conceive, that with proper management, the deprivation of comforts, and solitary confinement, and as little of these as possible, will be found sufficient aids to kindness and reason for the maintenance of good discipline."[21] In a pattern that would be repeated over the next 170 years, the ramifications of isolation for mental health and rehabilitation would be recognized, but the commitment to solitary confinement would remain unshaken. As long as it seemed to be "managed," regulated, and tempered with the caveat that it was used "only when necessary," solitary confinement was presented as an effective and palpable tool of prison discipline and management.

A Cycle of Indifference

The federal penitentiaries established in Canada after Kingston Penitentiary—the Stony Mountain in Manitoba (1877), New Westminster in British Columbia (1878), and a growing list of others—would rely not only on the threat of violent physical punishment and meals of bread and water, but also on solitary confinement, an approach to institutional management replicated in the expanding network of provincial and territorial prisons found across Canada. In the nineteenth century, Canadian wardens and others responsible for penitentiary design and discipline read prison literature that circulated widely and was frequently reprinted in newspapers and consumed by interested readers. Yet studies, criticism, and condemnation of the physical and psychological effects of isolation did not lead to reservation or hesitation among Canada's policy makers and would not lead to a retreat from solitary confinement. Although slight changes or modifications might be made, policies of segregation were increasingly incorporated into architectural design and management.

To expand opportunities for segregation beyond a group of below-ground cells at Kingston Penitentiary referred to as "the hole" by inmates, commitment to the use of solitary confinement gave rise to the construction of the Prison of Isolation on the penitentiary's grounds in 1894. It consisted of a separate building that aimed to segregate for "an indefinite period not to exceed the unexpired term of the convict's sentence" any male convict whose conduct "is found to be vicious, or who persists in disobedience to the Rules and Regulations of the prison, or who is found to exercise a pernicious influence on his fellow convicts."[22] Once built, the Prison of Isolation did not supplant the confinement of inmates in the below-ground segregation cells at Kingston Penitentiary, and both were used to punish inmates who violated prison rules.

Public criticism of the Prison of Isolation arose quickly in the years following its construction. In 1919, for example, the *Kingston Whig-Standard* published a scathing article that condemned the lengthy terms of solitary confinement imposed on inmates. Echoing the arguments of Dickens and presaging those that would be reiterated later in the twentieth and early twenty-first centuries, the author asserted that "the prison of isolation is still in operation and serious consideration should be given to abolishing it altogether, for no man can be confined in a solitary prison for any length of time without suffering serious mental and physical deterioration. . . . [T]he worst feature of the 'solitary' is the mental and moral effect, defeating the very purpose it was intended to serve. The isolation ward should only be used in pressing emergency and confinement therein should be limited to a few hours duration, not days, weeks and months, as insanity is the inevitable result of such treatment."[23] Very little would change. However, the building would be renamed the East Cell Block, and many of its cells would be repurposed to deal with overcrowding in the penitentiary in the 1930s.[24] Nevertheless, along with the cells beneath the keepers' hall, the building would continue to isolate inmates deemed refractory, and the use of solitary confinement for the violation of prison rules would continue. The Prison of Isolation represented merely one instance of the use of segregation in Canadian penitentiaries; it did not constitute the first use of isolation, nor was it the last.

In the twentieth century, concern about the effect of solitary confinement continued to be raised in Parliament and in newspapers, especially when riots brought institutional life into public view. Following a riot in October 1932, public attention to Kingston Penitentiary and its use of isolation intensified. During the subsequent investigation of the riot and the trial of those accused of leading it, one inmate claimed that he had been kept in solitary confinement for two years, and another insisted that he had been in solitary confinement for twenty-three years. Their claims sparked public outcry against the use of solitary confinement and contributed to extensive coverage in newspapers across Canada, compelling prison officials and government ministers to address accusations of cruelty and abuse.

Most notably, Minister of Justice Hugh Guthrie and Superintendent of Penitentiaries D.M. Ormond sought to defend the institution and its practices both in Parliament and in the popular press. Guthrie and Ormond responded to accusations and public concerns with denial and deflection. Ormond stated that the claims of inmates were "without foundation" and that "no convict is kept in solitary confinement in any penitentiary in Canada. Such confinement, either in the ordinary way or as a punishment, has been abolished for many years." Furthermore, he insisted, the eighteen "emergency segregation" or "close confinement" cells below the keepers' hall, referred to as "the hole" by inmates, did not constitute solitary confinement either. (These specific cells were described as being five feet wide, seven feet long, and eight feet high, with a double door that could shut out almost all light.)[25] Similarly, Guthrie explained, "there is no hole. . . . These are well ventilated airy cells which are used only for the purpose of punishment. If a prisoner got beyond control and had been tried and awarded punishment he was put in these cells. . . . The so-called hole had been examined by many competent and trustworthy authorities during the last 12 months." Nevertheless, he asserted, "there is no such thing in any Canadian penitentiary as solitary confinement and there has not been for at least 30 years."[26] Somehow the "close confinement cells" and the Prison of Isolation, to which Ormond described one inmate being sent for thirty days, did not constitute solitary confinement.

The contradictory statements made by officials did not go unnoticed by either the public or elected politicians. Criticizing government officials who argued that solitary confinement was not employed at Kingston Penitentiary, one newspaper writer sarcastically exclaimed "but please bear in mind that an inmate in a Prison of Isolation is not in solitary confinement. Oh dear no! A rose by any other name would smell as sweet!"[27] Agnes Macphail, a Member of Parliament who toured the institution following the riot, pressed Guthrie for clarification. "I would like to ask the Minister," she stated, "does he wonder that it is confusing to the people of this country when the Warden says that a man was in solitary confinement for a year and then the Minister stands up and says there was no such thing. . . . Just what does solitary confinement mean?"[28] In the midst of the confusion about what Guthrie and Ormond meant, one writer for the *Globe* emphasized the consequences of isolation on inmates and reflected that "it is not part of the sentence that they be broken in health and spirit." "The public of Canada," he argued, "will not tolerate inhuman treatment of convicted men."[29]

In the 1930s and following years, many commentators condemned the use of solitary confinement and recommended its abolition, understanding it as something that inflicted suffering that was both inhumane and detrimental to rehabilitation. Although often emphasizing opposition to any "coddling" inmates, they nevertheless understood that it was not in society's interest to make those who would be released eventually from the penitentiary worse than when they entered it. The Report of the Penitentiary Commission expressed in 1921 that penitentiaries needed to be aimed at reformation instead of repression; the commissioners recognized that most prisoners would be released and that "any system of punishment by imprisonment which decreases the prisoner's usefulness as a citizen must necessarily react adversely upon society." As a result, the commissioners recommended "the abolition of the present severely restrictive rules and the adoption instead of the idea of making the system such as to, as far as possible, turn prisoners into good citizens."[30] In many critical ways, Canada's correctional system today, at least in regard to its continued use of solitary confinement, has failed to accomplish this goal.

Solitary Confinement in a Time of Expanding Rights Discourses

Early advocates of the penitentiary prided themselves on departing from the physical and bloody punishments that preceded the move to incarceration. Subsequent generations of wardens and prison officials also touted their approach to punishment as "more progressive and modern" than that of their predecessors. After the Second World War, such claims were often made alongside an emphasis on the human rights of inmates. In 1965, for example, Kingston Penitentiary's assistant warden, E.L. Babcock, proclaimed that "today in Kingston Penitentiary, prisoners are people."[31] Similarly, the author of an article published in the magazine *Federal Corrections* stated in the same year that "we in the Canadian Penitentiary Service must not lose sight of the fact that we believe the correction of inmates is based on a humane approach towards the human being—a human being who has been deprived of his civil rights but retains his natural human rights and dignity."[32]

Beneath such laudatory claims lay a different reality. In the same year as Babcock's effusive claim, the federal government was making plans for the expansion of solitary confinement cells (or "detention units," as they were called at the time) at St. Vincent Penitentiary in Quebec. Stephen Cumas, executive director of the John Howard Society, condemned these units as a "diabolically custodial remanent [*sic*] of the past." Dr. Bruno Cormier, resident psychiatrist at the penitentiary and director of the McGill University Forensic Clinic, argued that the unit "presents the worst solution for the most severe problem in criminology."[33]

Cumas and Cormier were among a growing number of critics to put pressure on the federal government to enact fundamental changes to the correctional system. Although criticism and concern had been voiced by individuals since the early years of penitentiary building, the late twentieth and early twenty-first centuries witnessed increasing mobilization to push the government to mitigate the use of solitary confinement in Canadian prisons. Human rights advocates, scholars, lawyers, activists, various organizations, and individuals with first-hand experience of the effects of isolation have led this movement. Lawsuits have been launched, government commissions and inquiries conducted, policy recommendations made, studies published, testimonials shared, and documentaries produced to garner public attention and press for meaningful change.

Since the Second World War, pressure has also come from outside Canada. The Universal Declaration of Human Rights of 1948 did not address the treatment of prisoners specifically, but its prohibition of torture encompassed all people, including the incarcerated. Shortly thereafter, the First United Nations Congress on the Prevention of Crime and the Treatment of Offenders adopted in 1955 the Standard Minimum Rules for the Treatment of Prisoners, and more recently, in 2015, the United Nations General Assembly adopted additional rules that have become known as the "Nelson Mandela Rules."[34] The minimum requirements contained in the Nelson Mandela Rules include restrictions on the use of solitary confinement and the insistence that it "shall be a measure of last resort, for as short a time as possible." Condemning solitary confinement for more than fifteen consecutive days, the rules also prohibit the solitary confinement of persons with mental or physical disabilities "when their conditions would be exacerbated by such measures."[35] Nevertheless, despite such international change and pressure, Canada continues to defy the minimum requirements contained in the Nelson Mandela Rules and persists in contravening its own Charter of Rights and Freedoms.

The use of solitary confinement in Canadian prisons is not merely a matter of constitutional and human rights and not merely a matter of undermining any rehabilitative function that incarceration might serve. The practice is also implicated in racism, discrimination, and colonialism. Prisons in general have become another manifestation of the objectives at the heart of the genocidal residential school system in Canada. The Supreme Court of Canada determined in 1999 that the overrepresentation of Indigenous people in prison constituted a "crisis in the Canadian criminal justice system," and many, including Justice Murray Sinclair, have described Canada's prisons as the new residential schools and a continuation of colonial attempts to erase Indigenous cultures.[36] However, Indigenous people are not only overrepresented in Canadian prisons, but also more likely than their non-Indigenous counterparts to be subjected to segregation.

The overrepresentation of Indigenous people in solitary confinement units was recognized in the settler press as early as 1970. That year an article in the *Ottawa Journal* stated that, though the number of Indigenous people in Canadian penitentiaries was relatively small, "each one there, buried in the cell of an alien culture, has been sent to isolation for the duration of his sentence."[37] This pattern of discrimination has continued. According to one report in 2021, "Indigenous Peoples constitute about 4.2% of the adult Canadian population yet on 22 August 2021 constituted about 32% of the CSC [Correctional Service Canada] in-custody population. On that date, 48.9% of the SIU [Structured Intervention Units] population were Indigenous Peoples."[38] Moreover, not only are Indigenous people more likely to be inflicted with solitary confinement, but also they spend more time in segregation (approximately 16 percent more) than non-Indigenous inmates.[39]

Periodically tweaked, renamed, and modified, the practice of solitary confinement persists in Canada. According to Emilie Coyle and Jackie Omstead, "there is no humane way to hold someone in solitary confinement. Whatever the form of solitary confinement—SIUs, mental health monitoring, lockdowns, dry celling—all are characterized by constant observation, intense isolation, and severe mental health implications."[40] Officials might claim stricter oversight, greater accountability measures, clearer protocols, and due processes, yet the Correctional Service of Canada repeatedly has been found to treat inmates unconstitutionally and in violation of the

Charter of Rights and Freedoms.[41] At the heart of the matter are individuals whose health and well-being can be affected detrimentally by prison practices. Ashley Smith died from strangulation in 2007 while in solitary confinement and on twenty-four-hour suicide watch at a federal institution. Edward Snowshoe was a federal prisoner who spent 162 days in solitary confinement and eventually hanged himself in 2010.[42] Kinew James, who struggled with mental illness and self-harm, was kept in isolation for six years and died in 2013, a few months before the end of a fifteen-year sentence.[43] Many people have been inflicted with solitary confinement over the past almost 200 years, some of whom might be known to the public because of charter challenges, government commissions, or coroners' inquests. Although most who have been subjected to solitary confinement have survived, the impact of prolonged isolation does not simply dissolve once one is released.

Conclusion

In 1904, a letter to the editor was published in the *Kingston Daily Whig*. The letter was in response to the suicide of an inmate in Kingston's Prison of Isolation. In the letter, M.S. Burnette focused on the use of solitary confinement or what he described as "a refined system of cruelty and torture." Burnette stated that "I know not in how many of the so-called highly civilized nations of the world the prison of isolation is to be found, but I do know, at least to my own satisfaction, that any state that makes use of such a torture-house is not properly civilized. But some will say that human nature is so desperately bad and incorrigible that such a place exercises a deterrent effect upon the convicts, and so subserves a beneficial purpose. This may or may not be so, but if so . . . [it] is not a sufficient justification for the use of such a place." In contrast, he argued, "prison discipline should be made as easy and as humane as is consistent with the public safety." Furthermore, he argued, "no summary punishment like the torture of the dungeon-house should be permitted. . . . We have no right to torture a human being, and it matters not what he has done." Believing that prisons made individuals worse, not better, he concluded that, "whatever we do or not do, let us abolish the torture cells, as a feature that cannot commend itself to the enlightened conscience of the twentieth century."[44]

Although corporal punishments were questioned, modified, limited, and then abolished in 1972, solitary confinement persists. It continues to be used in the face of criticism and condemnation as constituting a form of torture: from Dickens's widely read book in 1842, to an ex-inmate who wrote a series of articles on Kingston Penitentiary in *Maclean's* in 1933,[45] to Supreme Court Justice Louise Arbour's determinations in "Commission of Inquiry into Certain Events at the Prison for Women in Kingston" (1996),[46] commentators and experts outside corrections have understood solitary confinement as cruel and connected to mental illness. The findings on the effects of solitary confinement have remained constant for almost 200 years, yet so has federal corrections' commitment to the practice. What differentiates contemporary practices of isolation from earlier forms in the nineteenth century? More elaborate details of procedures and processes? Electric lights, which could remain on in segregation cells for twenty-four hours a day? Periodically renamed by government officials in an effort to distinguish contemporary practices from older ones, solitary confinement has remained constant, but the label used by those who have experienced incarceration, whether today or almost 200 years ago, has remained "the hole."

In 2019, the Canadian government amended the Corrections and Conditional Release Act to implement a new SIU model. It claimed that prolonged solitary isolation had come to an end in federal correctional institutions. However, the Implementation Advisory Panel, which monitored the new units, found the claim to be hollow. In a 2020 newspaper article that had much in common with the criticism expressed in the 1930s, the author wrote that, "between November 30, 2019 and August 31, 2020, Canadian prisons held 268 individuals in a[n] SIU for periods ranging between 62 to 291 days. Straight. 291 days means somewhere in Canada, an individual sat in a 7-by-7-foot cell every single day since solitary confinement 'ended.' Perhaps Minister of Public Safety Bill Blair, who oversees the Correctional Service of Canada, could explain to this prisoner that, in fact, solitary [confinement] doesn't exist in Canada. I imagine this individual is a bit confused."[47] Institutional techniques to deny, defend, and distort the use of solitary confinement were apparent in the 1930s, and, sadly, the pattern seems yet to be broken.

Studies of the effects of isolation have a long history, and today literature on the topic is abundant. American psychologist Craig Haney wrote in 2018 that "research findings on the psychological effects of solitary confinement have been strikingly consistent since the early nineteenth century. Studies have identified a wide range of frequently occurring adverse psychological reactions that commonly affect prisoners in isolation units. The prevalence of psychological distress is extremely high."[48] Lawyer, advocate, and writer Michael Jackson has been challenging the use of isolation in Canadian prisons for decades and defending people who have been forced to endure it. He argues that solitary confinement is "the most individually destructive, psychologically crippling and socially alienating experience that could conceivably exist with[in] the borders of a country."[49] Nevertheless, despite extensive study, and despite almost two centuries of history to learn from, the Canadian government still argues that its practices are "different from and not analogous to the concept of solitary confinement referred to in many foreign jurisdictions and should not be confused with it." Believing that its practices are somehow different despite assertions to the contrary from experts (including those who have been incarcerated), the government claims that "inmates in administrative segregation do not suffer from the alleged effects as a result of their placement."[50]

Senator Kim Pate, an advocate for the rights of incarcerated people, recently argued that "we have a constitutional duty to uphold the Charter rights of Canadians, particularly those of minority and marginalized groups. The rule of law and constitutionally protected human rights of all Canadians are threatened when those in federal prisons are treated with cruelty and inhumanity and subjected to unlawful conditions."[51] Before we can no longer claim it to be "almost" 200 years, it is time for Canadian penitentiaries to break the historical cycle.

Notes

1 Commission Appointed to Enquire into the Prison and Reformatory System of Ontario, *Report of the Commissioners Appointed to Enquire into the Prison and Reformatory System of Ontario* (hereafter *Report of the Commissioners*) (Toronto: Warwick, 1891), 183.

2 For example, see Ivan Zinger, "Segregation in Canadian Federal Corrections: A Prison Ombudsman's Perspective," paper presented at Ending the Isolation: An International Conference on Human Rights and Solitary Confinement, Winnipeg, Manitoba, 22–23 March 2013, https://www.oci-bec.gc.ca/cnt/comm/presentations/presentations20130322-23-eng.aspx; and Diane Kelsall, "Cruel and Usual Punishment: Solitary Confinement in Canadian Prisons," *Canadian Medical Association Journal* 186, no. 18 (2014): 1345.

3 *Report of the Commissioners*, 183.

4 Kelly Hannah-Moffat and Amy Klassen, "Normalizing Exceptions: Solitary Confinement and the Micro-Politics of Risk/Need in Canada," in *Extreme Punishment: Comparative Studies in Detention, Incarceration and Solitary Confinement*, ed. Keramet Reiter and Alexa Koenig (Basingstoke, UK: Palgrave Macmillan, 2015), 135.

5 One of the most important figures in Canada who has argued against solitary confinement through his work as both a lawyer and a writer is Michael Jackson. His work stretches over several decades, highlighting the resistance of the correctional system to ensure that inmates are not treated in cruel or harmful ways. Two of his works are *Prisoners of Isolation: Solitary Confinement in Canada* (Toronto: University of Toronto Press, 2019) and "Reflections on 40 Years of Advocacy to End the Isolation of Canadian Prisoners," *Canadian Journal of Human Rights* 4, no. 1 (2015): 57–87. The latter article is part of an important issue of the *Canadian Journal of Human Rights*, edited by Debra Parkes. In particular, see Debra Parkes, "Ending the Isolation: An Introduction to the Special Volume on Human Rights and Solitary Confinement," *Canadian Journal of Human Rights* 4, no. 1 (2015): vii–xiv.

6 In this chapter, I concentrate on the use of solitary confinement to punish inmates or to manage inmates with mental illnesses. The line between the two is more blurry than distinct. I do not examine the issues of protective custody and the small number of inmates who voluntarily request solitary confinement.

7 Ross Lambertson, *Repression and Resistance: Canadian Human Rights Activists, 1930–1960* (Toronto: University of Toronto Press, 2005), 3.

8 Important early works on the rise of the prison include Michel Foucault, *Discipline and Punish: The Birth of the Prison*, trans. Alan Sheridan (New York: Vintage Books, 1977); and David J. Rothman, *The Discovery of the Asylum* (Boston: Little, Brown, and Company, 1971). The rise of the penitentiary in colonial Canada is examined in depth in Peter Oliver, *"Terror to Evil-Doers": Prisons and Punishments in Nineteenth-Century Ontario* (Toronto: University of Toronto Press, 1998); and Ted McCoy, *Reforming the Penitentiary in Nineteenth-Century Canada* (Edmonton: Athabasca

University Press, 2012). For work on the spectacular nature of punishment, see Petrus Cornelis Spierenburg, *The Spectacle of Suffering: Executions and the Evolution of Repression from a Preindustrial Metropolis to the European Experience* (Cambridge, UK: Cambridge University Press, 1984). In Canada, see Donald Fyson, "The Spectacle of State Violence: Executions in Quebec, 1759–1872," in *Violence, Order, and Unrest: A History of British North America, 1749–1876*, ed. Elizabeth Mancke et al. (Toronto: University of Toronto Press, 2019), 383–407.

9 See Canada, Legislative Assembly, *Reports of the Commissioners Appointed to Inquire into and Report upon the Conduct, Economy, Discipline, and Management of the Provincial Penitentiary* (Montreal: R. Campbell, 1849) (hereafter *Brown Report*).

10 Invented in the second half of the nineteenth century, the Oregon Boot or Gardiner Shackle was a heavy iron cuff worn on only one foot. It could weigh between six and twenty-eight pounds and was known to cause imbalance and physical suffering. See, for example, J.S. Murray, "Forty-Seven Years Prison Experience: Autobiography of J.S. Murray," [n.p., n.d.] https://sos.oregon.gov/archives/exhibits/prohibition/Documents/boot-murray.pdf.

11 Norman Johnston, *Forms of Constraint: A History of Prison Architecture* (Urbana: University of Illinois Press, 2000), 70–74.

12 Charles Dickens, *American Notes for General Circulation* (London: Chapman and Hall, 1842), 238–39.

13 United States Supreme Court in *Re Medley*, 134 US 160 (1890), https://supreme.justia.com/cases/federal/us/134/160/.

14 In particular, see Oliver, *"Terror to Evil-Doers"*; and Carolyn Strange, "The Undercurrents of Penal Culture: Punishment of the Body in Mid-Twentieth-Century Canada," *Law and History Review* 19, no. 2 (2001): 343–85.

15 *Brown Report*, 187.

16 *Brown Report*, 190–92.

17 *Brown Report*, 192.

18 *Brown Report*, 286.

19 *Brown Report*, 289.

20 *Brown Report*, 288.

21 *Brown Report*, 295.

22 Jackson, *Prisoners of Isolation*, 37.

23 "The Portsmouth Penitentiary," *Kingston Whig-Standard*, 17 October 1919, 7.

24 Superintendent of Penitentiaries, "Report of the Superintendent of Penitentiaries," in *Annual Report of the Superintendent of Penitentiaries for the Fiscal Year Ended March 31, 1933 and General Report to December 1, 1933* (Ottawa: J.O. Patenaude, 1934), 11; Jackson, *Prisoners of Isolation*, 39.

25 Superintendent of Penitentiaries, "Report of the Superintendent of Penitentiaries," 39–40.

26 Hugh Guthrie quoted in: "Justice Minister's Defence of Penitentiary," *Ottawa Citizen*, 4 July 1934, 16.

27 W.R. Givens, "W.R. Givens Writes on Penitentiary Reform," *Kingston Whig-Standard*, 31 August 1933, 3.

28 "W.M. Nickle's Letter to Canon Scott Denied by Hugh Guthrie," *Kingston Whig-Standard*, 4 July 1934, 2.
29 "Behind Prison Walls," *Globe* [Toronto], 14 July 1933, 4.
30 "Recommends Reformation Instead of Repression," *Weekly British Whig*, 16 May 1921, 3.
31 E.L. Babcock, *The History of the Kingston Penitentiary* (Ottawa: n.p., 1965), 9.
32 "New Year's Messages: From the Commissioner of Penitentiaries," *Federal Corrections* 3, no. 4 (1965): 12.
33 Bruno Cormier, quoted in: "Penal Reform Groups Oppose St. Vincent Detention Unit," *Gazette* [Montreal], 8 December 1965, 13.
34 United Nations Standard Minimum Rules for the Treatment of Prisoners (the Nelson Mandela Rules), resolution adopted by the General Assembly on 17 December 2015 on the report of the Third Committee (A/70/490) 70/175, https://documents-dds-ny.un.org/doc/UNDOC/GEN/N15/443/41/PDF/N1544341.pdf?OpenElement; Andrew Gilmour, "The Nelson Mandela Rules: Protecting the Rights of Persons Deprived of Liberty," United Nations, UN Chronicle, https://www.un.org/en/un-chronicle/nelson-mandela-rules-protecting-rights-persons-deprived-liberty#:~:text=to%20sentenced%20prisoners.-,The%20Rules%20are%20based%20on%20an%20obligation%20to%20treat%20all,disciplinary%20measures%20to%20medical%20services.
35 United Nations Standard Minimum Rules, 16–17.
36 *R. v. Gladue*, [1999] 1 SCR 688, https://decisions.scc-csc.ca/scc-csc/scc-csc/en/item/1695/index.do.
37 "Sentence to Isolation Unfair to Eskimos," *Ottawa Journal*, 8 September 1970, 6.
38 The Structured Intervention Unit Implementation Advisory Panel, "Preliminary Observations of the Operation of Correctional Service of Canada's Structured Intervention Units," 26 October 2021, Government of Canada, Public Safety Canada, https://www.publicsafety.gc.ca/cnt/rsrcs/pblctns/2022-siu-iap/index-en.aspx.
39 Nancy Macdonald, "Canada's Prisons Are the 'New Residential Schools,'" *Maclean's*, 18 February 2016, https://macleans.ca/news/canada/canadas-prisons-are-the-new-residential-schools/.
40 Emilie Coyle and Jackie Omstead, "The Use of Solitary Confinement Continues in Canada," *Policy Options*, 18 January 2022, https://policyoptions.irpp.org/magazines/january-2022/the-use-of-solitary-confinement-continues-in-canada/.
41 The reasons for Canada's reluctance to abolish segregation are difficult to comprehend since the practice is widely condemned and recognized as detrimental by both national and international bodies. According to Ivan Zinger, this pattern is partly connected to the fact that "correctional authorities can feel invulnerable to significant calls for reforms." Ivan Zinger, "Human Rights Compliance and the Role of External Prison Oversight," *Canadian Journal of Criminology and Criminal Justice* 48, no. 2 (2006): 130, https://doi.org/10.1353/ccj.2006.0023.

42 Martin Patriquin, "Why Adam Capay Spent 1,560 Days in Solitary," *Maclean's*, 2 November 2016, https://macleans.ca/news/canada/why-adam-capay-has-spent-1560-days-in-solitary/.

43 Macdonald, "Canada's Prisons."

44 M.S. Burnette, "In Isolation: A Modern and Refined System of Cruelty," letter to the editor, *Kingston Daily Whig*, 11 June 1904, 9.

45 Austin Campbell, "House of Hate," *Maclean's*, 15 August 1933, 16.

46 Louise Arbour, "Commission of Inquiry into Certain Events at the Prison for Women in Kingston," Solicitor General Canada, 1996, http://www.justicebehindthewalls.net/resources/arbour_report/arbour_rpt.htm.

47 Murray Fallis, "We Need a True End to Abusive Solitary Confinement," *Toronto Star*, 1 November 2020, https://www.thestar.com/opinion/contributors/2020/11/01/we-need-a-true-end-to-abusive-solitary-confinement.html.

48 Craig Haney, "The Psychological Effects of Solitary Confinement: A Systematic Critique," *Crime and Justice* 47, no. 1 (2018): 365.

49 West Coast Prison Justice Society, "Solitary: A Case for Abolition," November 2016, https://prisonjustice.org/wp-content/uploads/2018/11/solitary-confinement-report.pdf.

50 Cited in West Coast Prison Justice Society.

51 Kim Pate, "Corrections and Conditional Release Act, Bill to Amend—Second Reading—Debate Adjourned," 7 December 2021, Parliament of Canada, Senate of Canada, https://sencanada.ca/en/senators/pate-kim/interventions/566888/40.

CHAPTER 7

Performative Justice? Canada's Response to Alleged War Criminals in the Country: The Case of *Canada (Minister of Citizenship and Immigration) v. Vladimir Katriuk*

Katelyn Arac

IN 1983, an article published in the *Globe and Mail* estimated that between 100 and over 1,000 alleged Nazi war criminals[1] resided in Canada and that they ranged "from janitors to business executives, from Prairie residents to a Dachau camp guard turned Toronto real estate broker."[2] Such allegations were not new; they had troubled the nation since the end of the Second World War. Determining the veracity of such statements was one of the core objectives of the Commission of Inquiry on War Criminals, established in 1985 under the leadership of Judge Jules Deschênes. Alongside verifying whether alleged Nazi war criminals resided in Canada, the commission determined which legal options were available to the Canadian state to pursue justice in these cases and compiled a master list of names for further investigation and potential legal action. In leading the commission, Deschênes had to navigate the competing interests of and tensions among different ethnic groups and lobbyists in Canada while contending with a variety of opinions on how to define justice in the context of alleged war crimes.

The subject of Nazi war criminals in Canada provides an opportunity to discuss concepts of justice and judicial action and their relationship with human rights. As several chapters in this volume demonstrate, there is a long history of systemic discrimination in the Canadian criminal justice system. Rhonda Hinther and Janet Miron consider the devastating impacts of various forms of incarceration on "problematic" populations in Canada, and Tom Hooper explores the long (and continued) struggle of queer communities against police violence. In this chapter, I contribute to the discussion by arguing that Canada's judicial response to Nazi war criminals also demonstrates the inconsistencies of "justice" as it is enforced by the state.

Not only did the various groups involved in lobbying on the "Nazi war criminal issue" define justice differently based on their own positions, but also the idea of justice was further complicated by Canada's histories of settler colonialism and structural racism and its engagement with human rights discourses. How legal action has been used and against whom is integral to understanding the history of human rights in Canada; it provides a lens through which to critique Canada's national project, based on the perception that Canada has valued multiculturalism, equality, and human rights. Yet inherent to this project are a nation and a judicial system founded on policies of settler colonialism.

Legal action against alleged Nazi war criminals in Canada has been linked intrinsically to this history of settler colonialism since it is embedded within the judicial system and haunted by it.[3] In her monograph *Ghostly Matters: Haunting and the Sociological Imagination*, Avery Gordon proposes that, "in haunting, organized forces and systemic structures that appear removed from us make their impact felt in everyday life in a way that confounds our analytic separations and confounds the social separations themselves."[4] This idea of haunting can help to make visible the "ghosts" present within the legal system. Whether these ghosts are Canada's self-perception of its important role in advancing human rights or the structures of settler colonialism, thinking about them can elucidate how contours of justice are not neutral. Even in sincere attempts to administer justice, the Canadian legal system functions as a product and enforcement agent of settler colonialism: that is, as a tool to uphold hierarchies of difference and systemic racism by treating those deemed other differently before the law.[5]

By positioning Ottawa's delayed judicial action toward alleged Nazi war criminals living in Canada in conversation with both the biases present in the legal system because of settler colonialism and self-perceptions of justice and equality present in Canadian national identity, I argue that Canada's engagement with human rights, particularly in regard to justice and legal practice, is at times performative.[6] To assess this, I first discuss the case of *R. v. Finta* to explore the concerns associated with prosecuting alleged war crimes using Canada's criminal justice system and to consider why criminal cases have been quickly abandoned in favour of denaturalization and deportation proceedings. I then utilize the case of *Canada (Minister of Citizenship and Immigration) v. Vladimir Katriuk* to demonstrate the performative nature of human rights in Canada's judicial system. Katriuk was an ethnic Ukrainian who moved to Canada in 1951 with his wife and obtained citizenship in 1958. He was accused of having committed war crimes while serving in Byelorussia during the war, charges that he categorically denied. His case offers an opportunity to reflect on the complexities (and inconsistencies) of how justice has been understood and served in Canadian history.

Human Rights Developments

In the aftermath of the Second World War, the idea of human rights took on greater importance. The Universal Declaration of Human Rights (UDHR) was adopted in 1948 in the context of the United Nations War Crimes Commission (UNWCC) and the United States' and Allied war crimes prosecutions. Although the UDHR focused on an individual's right to justice, it did not define justice or provide a framework through which to discuss the tenuous nature of justice. It did introduce, however, the idea that human rights are a subject for international law. Yet, as Jennifer Tunnicliffe's work and Asa McKercher's contribution to this volume remind us, the Canadian government's engagement with the UDHR and other early international human rights instruments was reluctant and limited.[7]

Despite Ottawa's resistance, documents such as the UDHR influenced how many Canadians thought about themselves and the role of human rights in society. Human rights scholars have well documented the postwar growth of a human rights movement in Canada, efforts to lobby Canadian federal and provincial governments to adopt human rights laws, and the expansion of Canada's "human rights state." In its Constitution Act of 1982, the Canadian government reaffirmed its commitment to human rights by entrenching the Canadian Charter of Rights and Freedoms, which defined the political, civil, and legal rights of Canadians and people residing in Canada. Although the codification of these rights in both the UDHR and the charter shaped how Canadians conceptualized justice, a study of these instruments alone cannot explain why ideas and definitions of justice change and adapt over time or hold different meanings for different groups of people. The invocation of these rights in judicial action does provide greater insight into these questions, however, including in the investigation of and proceedings against suspected war criminals.

Alongside the postwar growth of a human rights ideology that entrenched rights discourse in the Canadian ethos, we must also consider the historical and political contexts of the Cold War in considering Canadian judicial responses to alleged Nazi war criminals. In early conversations about justice at Yalta in February 1945, the Allied powers discussed de-nazification and the executions of Nazi leaders. By July 1945, at the Potsdam Conference, the tone of justice had changed, and the Allied leaders decided to hold a series of trials against the Nazi regime and its leaders. This approach culminated in the International Military Tribunal at Nuremberg in 1945–46. Many of the Allied nations also conducted their own war crimes investigations and trials. Canada participated in the UNWCC alongside the United Kingdom and United States. Valentyna Polunina notes that the USSR found it more effective to establish its own commission to conduct investigations and solidify its position as the first power to prosecute Nazis, thus limiting foreign interference in USSR affairs.[8]

As the war drew to a close, Allied leaders scrambled to leverage German science and expertise through covert programs that gathered intelligence, documentation, and people. The American program was titled Operation Paperclip, the British program—of which Canada was a part—was titled Operation Matchbox, and the Soviet program was titled Operation Osoaviakhim.[9] These programs signalled the growing polarization of power and a sense of suspicion and rivalry, resulting in the collapse of diplomatic relations and the start of the Cold War. When the UNWCC disbanded in 1948, Canada and its British and American counterparts considered the topic of war crimes prosecution closed. In his report to the Canadian Commission of Inquiry on War Criminals, Assistant Commissioner R.R. Schramm of the RCMP made it clear that Canada had little interest in the prosecution of war criminals.[10] According to Schramm, between 1945 and 1962, there was no formal policy related to the investigation of war criminals.[11] National governments moved on to rebuilding after the war and to Cold War politics, and more effort was put into the surveillance of people with left-leaning or Communist political beliefs than into the allegations that Nazi war criminals had come to Canada.

During the Cold War, Canada developed a self-image linked to peacekeeping, multiculturalism, and rights activism. In her work on multiculturalism and nation building in Canada, Sunera Thobani challenges these national myths and contends that hegemonic accounts of a generous and welcoming Canadian national identity distort the nation's history given its self-image of tolerance and civility. In Canada, this has involved distorting and obscuring the effects of the ongoing settler-colonial project, which has contributed to the development of a complex racial hierarchy in Canadian society.[12] This directly influenced the development of Canada's criminal justice system since, through the colonial project, the state defined a system of hierarchy in the legal system by which a distinction existed based on racial classifications and settler-colonial ideals. In this way, settler colonialism has become a pervasive ghost present in the Canadian legal system that, when acknowledged, can help us to elucidate how the contours of justice are neither neutral nor temporally linear.

Examining the Katriuk case provides an opportunity to explore how structures of exclusion, settler colonialism, and perceptions of identity are embedded within Canadian legal practices and can be identified in court proceedings. There is an intrinsic irony in discussing the presence of Nazi war criminals in Canada—a state that actively and forcefully committed atrocities against Indigenous Peoples and continues those practices today.[13] It is only in conjunction with discussions about the pervasiveness of settler colonialism as an ongoing policy that the discourses of an "ideal immigrant" and a "good Canadian" present themselves. What justice means to whom is complex and made more so by the obfuscation of the fundamental inequalities of the Canadian justice system. The delayed response to allegations of Nazi war criminals in Canada, involving forty years of inaction, challenges the narrative of Canada as a protector and promoter of rights and contributes instead to the reality of settler-colonial judicial practice, which favours those who fit the image of an ideal Canadian, even those who have committed heinous crimes.

The presence of alleged Nazi war criminals in Canada also exposes tensions between different ethnic groups and in the judicial process. The histories of well-established Jewish and Ukrainian communities became entangled in the politics of postwar migration. For Jewish and Ukrainian displaced persons, the potential for migration to Canada was different. Ukrainians had a history of being welcomed as ideal immigrants to Canada in the early twentieth century, and, with the growing fear of Communism, those who refused to be repatriated into Soviet-occupied territories were welcomed more readily than Communist sympathizers. For Jewish migrants, gaining access to Canada remained difficult because of pervasive anti-Semitism.[14] These histories were entwined with discussions of justice and conversations about how the federal government should respond to allegations of Nazi war criminals in the country. The Jewish community in Canada gave high priority to the search for alleged Nazi war criminals and to the trials held to prosecute them; justice was imperative. For the Ukrainian community in Canada, the response was more complicated. Although the community understood the importance of justice, there was also the fear of Soviet propaganda and that the Soviet government would use such investigations to seek revenge against those who had fled from repatriation after the war.[15]

Investigations of alleged war criminals in Canada were therefore rife with complications.

The Canadian government was eventually forced into action. In January 1985, the *New York Times* printed an article claiming that infamous Nazi Dr. Josef Mengele might be hiding in Canada.[16] Speculation that Mengele—the notorious "Angel of Death" who conducted horrific experiments on the prisoners of Auschwitz under the guise of his role as a doctor—was in Canada was a serious matter. With pressure from the United States to investigate, the Canadian government had no choice but to respond to the accusation and, as a result, established a Commission of Inquiry on War Criminals on 30 December 1985.[17] Over the next year and a half, the commission investigated the presence of Nazi war criminals in Canada in sessions held across the country. It was tasked with identifying the number of war criminals in the country and providing a legal remedy for how to deal with them. When the commission concluded its work in 1986, it provided a list of recommendations to the federal government for further action.

The official mandate of the commission was to make "recommendations as to what legal means are available to bring to justice any such persons [war criminals] in Canada or whether and what legislation might be adopted by the Parliament of Canada to ensure that war criminals are brought to justice."[18] After requesting and receiving multiple perspectives from the public and private spheres of legal practice on the legal options available to the Canadian state, the commission determined that there were three options to pursue justice against alleged Nazi war criminals in Canada: extradition, prosecution in Canada, and denaturalization and deportation. Judge Deschênes viewed extradition as the most favourable legal option because, if it was requested and granted, then it afforded the opportunity of a trial in a country more intimately connected with the crimes of the alleged suspect. Extradition was not always possible, though; if no extradition treaty was in place with the country in which the crime was committed, then the next best legal option was criminal prosecution in Canada. To prosecute a suspected war criminal in Canada, amendments would have to be made to the Criminal Code, which was a possibility. Finally, the commission determined that the least popular legal option was denaturalization and deportation. It was ranked the lowest option because it was a lengthy process and because deportation would only transfer a suspect to another country, not allow for any substantive judicial conclusion.[19]

Subsequent tasks of the commission were to establish the alleged number of war criminals in Canada, undertake individual assessments, and then make recommendations on further action.[20] There was much controversy over the alleged number of war criminals in Canada. The commission came up with a master list of 774 names, investigating each case within Canada and with evidence from abroad (this later investigation proved to be controversial). Based on its initial research, the commission recommended that over 600 cases be closed since the suspects did not live in Canada, or had died in Canada, or since there was insufficient evidence. Ultimately, the commission closed 606 of the 774 cases on the master list and recommended further investigation of the cases that remained. By its conclusion, it put forward only fifty-nine names for further investigation and among them noted only twenty cases in which "steps should be taken toward either revocation of citizenship and deportation or criminal prosecution."[21]

The commission found that legal action should be taken in a small selection of cases, with several other cases requiring further investigation before the court could become fully involved. Deschênes, the commissioner, cautioned against the creation of a special department like the Office of Special Investigation established in the United States. The Canadian government determined that the best legal option to appease the division in Canadian society would be prosecution in Canada. It also took the advice of Deschênes and in 1987 passed the Canada War Crimes and Crimes Against Humanity Act to allow for the prosecution of foreign war crimes in Canadian courts.[22]

It took forty years from the end of the Second World War for the Canadian government to act and establish a commission to investigate the numerous allegations that Nazis were present in Canada. This inaction reflected a system of judicial and state power that passively enabled alleged war criminals to enter the country and then failed to respond adequately to assertions of their presence. Ideas of human rights and justice were present in the government's response to alleged war criminals. Lobby groups used the language of rights to formulate their arguments and referenced the newly minted Charter of Rights and Freedoms in their discussions about justice and judicial action.[23] In the trials of alleged war criminals, every interested party questioned and critiqued the idea of justice throughout the proceedings. Various challenges regarding the validity of such trials were raised, particularly by defence counsel, and legal challenges based on the charter were made to ensure that the rights of the accused were upheld. What justice meant and how it should be applied haunted judicial proceedings and made visible the many contradictions and biases of Canadian legal practice.

The Criminal Code and the Case of Imre Finta

Under the Canada War Crimes and Crimes Against Humanity Act of 1987, along with changes to the Criminal Code in 1987, Canadian courts were eligible to pursue legal action against the individuals listed in the commission's confidential report. The first of such cases was that of Imre Finta. He had immigrated to Canada in 1951 and was granted citizenship in 1956. In 1987, he was charged with unlawful confinement, robbery, kidnapping, and manslaughter under the war crimes provisions in the Criminal Code for allegedly committing said crimes while serving as a commander of a gendarmerie in Szeged, Hungary, and for assisting the Nazis during the Second World War.[24]

The Crown's case relied on witness testimony, and, though the witnesses were able to remember the events for which Finta was being tried, they were unable to identify him conclusively as the perpetrator. Defence counsel questioned the validity of the charges and used a series of applications to the court to challenge the constitutional validity of retroactive legislation. Finta was acquitted in a jury trial five years later since the Crown had failed to prove beyond a reasonable doubt that he had committed war crimes and crimes against humanity in 1944. On appeal, the courts again considered the jurisdiction of such a case and discussed whether the defence had the right to use the "peace officer" and "military orders" defence, which assesses whether the actions committed were done in obedience to superior orders or "manifestly unlawful."[25] In its final judgment, the Supreme Court of Canada acquitted Finta of the charges against him. The judgment clarified the jurisdictional questions related to legislation for war crimes and crimes against humanity by placing the charges firmly within conformity to international law, which allowed that, in the absence of an international court, a national court had the power to try the case for universal crimes, such as war crimes.[26]

In the appeal judgment of the Ontario Court of Appeals, two of the five appellate judges questioned the trial judge's instructions to the jury. In his charge to the jury, the trial judge reminded them that "on each count the Crown has to prove beyond a reasonable doubt . . . that the accused committed the Canadian offence, [and] the Crown has to prove beyond a reasonable doubt that the act of the accused and the knowledge of the accused rose up to that extra quality factually of a crime against humanity or a war crime."[27] This double burden of proof was viewed as problematic in the review conducted for the appeal and presented a "fundamental misdirection" of the legal definition of the offence.[28] For the appellate judge, Charles Dubin, this fundamentally prejudiced the trial. The other three appellate judges did not share his view, and the decision was made to dismiss the appeal. This decision set a precedent for the extent of the burden of proof required for the prosecution of war crimes cases (those tried over forty years after the crimes had been committed) and set a threshold so high that future legal action seemed to be unlikely. During the trial and especially evident in the appeal process were questions of how justice was best served and whether the legislation was fair and lawful.

The prosecution of war crimes under the Criminal Code came to an end when *R. v. Finta* resulted in an acquittal. When criminal proceedings proved to be unable to bring alleged war criminals to justice, authorities turned to civil proceedings—denaturalization and deportation—to strip those accused of their Canadian citizenship and deport them to the country where the alleged crimes had occurred. During the proceedings of the Commission of Inquiry on War Criminals, Judge Deschênes had found denaturalization and deportation to be the least favourable option to respond to war criminals. He asserted not only that proceedings of denaturalization were extremely lengthy but also that they did not "really deal with the substantive issue of war crimes," for the process "merely transfers the suspect to another country, provided there be one willing to accept the outcast."[29] The question of justice remained central to denaturalization and deportation proceedings. How Canada chose to pursue justice against war criminals and what justice meant to the different actors in such cases were complicated, as demonstrated in the Katriuk case.

The Case of Vladimir Katriuk

Katriuk was an ethnic Ukrainian born in 1921 in Lujeni, Cernăuți, in the Kingdom of Romania. The town was later renamed Luzhany, Chernivtsi Oblast, Ukraine, in 1940 when the Red Army occupied the territory and allotted it to Soviet Ukraine. The Romanian Army—allied with the Nazi regime—retook the city during the Second World War, and it was later reincorporated into the Ukrainian Soviet Socialist Republic in 1944. According to his own testimony, Katriuk worked in the meat-packing trade as a young man. With the arrival of Soviet troops in 1940, and continuing throughout the war, life was difficult for the local Ukrainians. In 1941, Katriuk joined a volunteer force that marched to Kyiv to attempt to liberate the city. Many of the leaders of this force were arrested, and some were executed. In 1942, the Germans formed Battalion 115—of which all members were Ukrainian—and later merged the military unit into Battalion 118; Katriuk was enlisted in both. The battalion was sent to Minsk in Byelorussia near the end of 1942, and in the spring of 1942 it was sent to Ivye, Poland ("Ivye" is the spelling used in the original court documents. The town is also spelled "Iwie" and is anglicized to Iwye), where it remained until the Russian advance in the spring of 1944.

When asked about the battalions' activities, Katriuk stated that in Kyiv he was stationed as a guard at a wheat mill. In Byelorussia, he stated, his unit was sent to maintain law and order and to protect villagers and their livestock from threatening partisan forces. He testified that "he had never participated in any major military operations and that he had never fired his gun."[30] In August 1944, his battalion was transported to France, where it became part of the 30th Waffen Grenadier Division of the SS. Soon after, Katriuk defected to the Forces françaises de l'intérieur (FFI)—the French underground—which was sent to the front to fight Germany. While at the front, the Ukrainian members of the FFI were told that they would be repatriated to the Soviet Union. To avoid this, Katriuk joined the French Foreign Legion (FFL) in September 1944 as a private. He was wounded at the front and spent a few months in an American hospital in France. He was at the Italian front in 1945 when the war came to an end and the FFL were sent to Paris to await reorganization. In Paris, Katriuk apparently had a poor relationship with his commanding officer and defected. He obtained a new identity paper as Nicolas Schpirka, the name of his brother-in-law back in Bukovina. Under his new identity, Katriuk worked in Paris as a butcher. He met and married Maria, a French citizen. In 1951, the couple decided to emigrate to Canada and obtained a visa. They arrived in Quebec City on 14 August 1951, travelling onward to Montreal. In 1958, they signed applications for citizenship. In his application, Katriuk applied to have his name changed back to Vladimir Katriuk. Both he and his wife were granted citizenship.

Although Katriuk's testimony at his trial presented a reasonable narrative of his experiences during the war and his immigration to Canada, the Crown presented a different narrative. Crown prosecutor David Lucas argued that Katriuk willingly volunteered for service in Battalions 115 and 118 and that he acted as a collaborator. In 1943, in Byelorussia—where Katriuk acknowledged that he was stationed—the Crown claimed that German forces and collaborators committed various war crimes and crimes against humanity against the civilians and prisoners of war in the area, in which Katriuk likely was involved. The Crown argued that, when he sought immigration to Canada, he not only used a false name but also had not been truthful when asked about how he had spent the war. The Crown argued that, if Katriuk had explained his activities during the war as he had in the trial, he would have been denied entry on the ground that he had participated in an enemy military force. The Crown's accusation that he had engaged in war crimes during his military service and that he had falsified the records used to obtain a visa for entry into Canada were used as grounds for revocation of his citizenship.

Ghosts were present in the trial of *Canada (Minister of Citizenship and Immigration) v. Katriuk*, in discussions about Katriuk's character, in frequent mentions of similar cases and the 1985 commission, in questions about legal procedure, and in divisions over what constituted justice. During the trial, both David Lucas and Orest Rudzik, attorney for the respondent (Katriuk), submitted immigration and security documents from 1945 and 1946 to the court that discussed specific details of how the Canadian government screened potential immigrants before their entry into Canada. These documents mentioned concerns about the potential entry of enemy aliens; however, they quickly turned toward how to streamline screening procedures to ensure the reopening of Canadian borders to immigrants and tourists alike. In a 5 July 1946 memorandum, A.L. Jolliffe, director of the Department of Mines and Resources, wrote about the importance of reopening Canadian borders: "Withholding of the visa[s] of Europeans pending security clearance would seriously curtail this important movement."[31] Instead, Jolliffe and his counterparts worked to reopen Canada to "good and desirable citizens."[32]

The idea of the desirable immigrant/good citizen was a ghost in the proceedings against alleged Nazi war criminals that invoked long-standing narratives about what constituted a good Canadian. Rudzik presented Katriuk as someone of good character, a good Canadian, and asserted that he had used a false identity only out of concern for his life. His 1958 application for citizenship even noted that Katriuk was "of good character."[33] Such phrases were used to obfuscate the reality of hierarchical preference in Canadian immigration policy. This language and further perceptions of equality in the Canadian mythos were carried forth into the trials of alleged Nazi war criminals.

The cases against alleged Nazi war criminals in Canada are intrinsically linked to each other. It is difficult to assess only one case since the trials are rife with mentions of the other trials. A case book of noteworthy legal precedent submitted prior to the Katriuk trial included lengthy references to the trials of other alleged war criminals, including Johann Dueck, Helmut Oberlander, Erichs Tobiass, Imre Finta, and Jacob Luitjens.[34] These earlier trials were more than precedents cited in the proceedings against Katriuk; they manifested as ghosts haunting his trial. In his opening statement to the court, Rudzik discussed the "family of these cases."[35] They shared legal precedents and practices, the respondents shared histories of their war experiences and immigration to Canada, and the cases even shared the testimonies of some expert witnesses. The shared body of case law established in this group of trials is evident in how the cases haunted each other and developed as a collective, denying their autonomy from one another.

Early in the proceedings against Katriuk, defence counsel Rudzik argued that the 1992 denaturalization and deportation proceedings against Jacob Luitjens (a Dutch collaborator during the Second World War) had intrinsically more concrete evidence against its defendant compared with the sparse evidence presented against Katriuk. This was because Luitjens had been tried in absentia in a court in the Netherlands in 1948 and convicted of war crimes. Such evidence did not exist in the case against Katriuk, making Rudzik's point that the burden of proof was more difficult to achieve alongside decades-old testimony and often sparse documentary records from the time period. This is one example of how previous trials were present in the courtrooms of later proceedings and how the evidence used in the cases held against alleged war criminals was a shared body of knowledge and to some extent prevented the trials from being autonomous. Moreover, the references enabled each trial to manifest discussions of justice and rights in later trials.

In 1999, Judge Marc Nadon presented his verdict that Katriuk "was not lawfully admitted to Canada for permanent residence," elaborating that he had obtained his Canadian citizenship by "false representation, or fraud, or by concealing material circumstances."[36] According to the decision, immigration processes in place would have led to the rejection of his application. In testimony from the trial, there was some debate about whether the immigration process was comprehensive given the Katriuks' application in Paris and because Maria Katriuk was a French citizen. However, if Vladimir Katriuk's service in the German forces was known, then it would have been enough to have his visa application rejected. On the question of culpability in war crimes, the court found that there was not enough evidence to make a determination of guilt. As the judge stated, "I find it difficult, if not impossible, to accept the respondent's evidence that he did not participate in any important military operation while his battalion was in Belorussia."[37] However, based on the evidence presented in the trial, the judge determined that there was not enough information to conclude that Katriuk had indeed participated in atrocities against the civilian population in Byelorussia. The Crown did not call any witness who could conclusively testify that he had participated in such crimes, and the court had to rely on an expert witness—a historian—to provide a broader view of events that took place. This was not enough to determine whether Katriuk had participated in such atrocities or not.

In the denaturalization and deportation trial against him, and in the other trials against alleged Nazi war criminals, we must consider one other ghost in those courtrooms—settler colonialism. Canada's legal system was founded upon an ongoing system of power that maintains the repression of Indigenous Peoples and cultures to establish a claim on the land. In thinking about the law broadly, but particularly when looking at cases regarding war crimes, crimes against humanity, and genocide, we must consider the parallels between the rhetoric surrounding the discussion of other people and other countries that commit such atrocities and how the Canadian state, past and present, has carried out policies of erasure against Indigenous Peoples. Although the case against Katriuk makes no mention of settler colonialism or Indigenous Peoples or their history, I find it impossible to reflect on this legal history without thinking about the systemic discrimination present in the justice system. Given these aforementioned parallels, the ideals of justice upheld by the Canadian legal system clearly reflect the performative nature of human rights. In *Ghostly Matters*, Gordon argues that "haunting is an animated state in which a repressed or unresolved social violence is making itself known, sometimes very directly, sometimes more obliquely."[38] Thinking about settler colonialism as a haunting, or a ghost, challenges perceptions of time and makes clear that law, justice, history, and memory are entangled in such a way that the past is ongoing in the present.

After the court decision in Katriuk, the procedure was for the cabinet of the federal government to review the matter and strip his citizenship. In 2007, the cabinet halted revocation proceedings, citing a lack of evidence, and allowed the ailing Katriuk to keep his citizenship and live the last years of his life on his bee farm in Quebec. He was not left in peace, however. Many people thought that there was no justice in the decision and that Katriuk and his battalion had committed atrocities in Byelorussia and needed to face proper justice for them. Groups such as the Friends of Simon Wiesenthal Center for Holocaust Studies and B'nai Brith Canada lobbied the federal government to re-examine the case. In 2012, historian P.R. Rudling published an article in *Holocaust and Genocide Studies* that elicited a strong response since it mentioned Katriuk by name in connection with the atrocities committed in Khatyn.[39] In the article, titled "The Khatyn Massacre in Belorussia," Rudling used archival material and recently released documents from the Soviet war crimes trials conducted in the 1970s and 1980s to discuss the political uses of history and shed light on collaboration among local militias in Eastern Europe and Nazi military units. In the transcripts from one Soviet trial, Battalion 118 was implicated in the events of the day. One of the witnesses, and later a defendant for his role in the massacre, Schutzmann Knap, testified that he had seen "Katriuk and Meleshko . . . shooting the people lying on the road."[40] Other witnesses mentioned in the trials corroborated and built upon the narrative of Katriuk's involvement in the massacre.

After the publication of Rudling's article, the press picked up the story. In several Canadian newspapers, including the *National Post*, the *Globe and Mail*, and the *Toronto Star*, articles appeared with headlines of "Accused Nazi Living as Quebec Beekeeper" and "Canadian Participated in 1943 Massacre."[41] The papers sensationalized the story, and dozens of articles were printed about the Katriuk case, first in the wake of his trial and then in 2012 with renewed interest in the case. His case, and the other cases of alleged war criminals in the country, sold papers.

Conclusion

Vladimir Katriuk died in 2015 in Quebec at the age of ninety-three. From his trial to his death, he immutably denied the allegations against him. Those in his community and his church remember him as a quiet man who enjoyed his bees.[42] His is a challenging case that provokes questions about justice and equal treatment under the law. As evident from the dismissal of the revocation of his citizenship, the Canadian government and its courts did not know how to achieve justice adequately for the various groups involved, including organizations such as B'nai Brith, the Canadian Jewish Congress, the Ukrainian Canadian Committee, and others interested in the outcomes of these cases. There was extensive lobbying from various groups, each interested in a different definition of justice. Some wanted men like Katriuk to be found guilty of charges of war crimes and crimes against humanity, and they continued to push for this outcome in cases in which the judicial system determined defendants not guilty.[43] Others—primarily individuals from Ukrainian and other Eastern European ethnic groups—argued that the trials spoke to a concerted effort against their communities, claiming that it was unjust to continue creating allegations even after trials concluded.[44] What is interesting in these competing conversations on justice—and in both the criminal and the civil proceedings—is the frequency with which both sides of the debate invoked the legal rights, and specifically the charter rights, of the accused.

Even while conducting these trials, there was a spectre of Canada's perceived furthering of rights and rights discourse that needs to be understood through a critical reflection on how settler colonialism was embedded in state policy and action in Canada's past and remains so in its present. Legal proceedings have been complicated and not free from the ghosts of the past or those created by an inflated sense of Canada's championing of human rights.

When considering the country's history of engagement with human rights, we must understand how concepts of justice and judicial action are critical to how the state has engaged in a performance in which policies of inclusion have been used to cover the reality of the unequal dispensing of justice. Canada's delayed legal action against alleged war criminals—prompted only after decades of activism—needs to be understood in conjunction with the state's inability to acknowledge its failures in national policy. The judicial system in Canada was built upon the premise of settler colonialism, and the delayed legal action against alleged Nazi war criminals in Canada further reflects a system designed to favour those who fit the ideals of the Canadian state. The judicial response to alleged Nazi war criminals indicates that Canada's record of engagement with human rights and concepts of justice has indeed been performative.

Notes

1 Throughout this chapter, I use the phrase "alleged Nazi war criminals" since the cases were never proven in criminal courts. My intention is not to embark on a discussion of culpability in the cases studied here but to engage in a discussion about how we can use these cases to examine critically the Canadian legal system.

2 David Lancashire, "Canada Powerless? The Lax Hunt for War Criminals," *Globe and Mail*, 21 July 1983.

3 For more on historical ghosts, see Avery Gordon, *Ghostly Matters: Haunting and the Sociological Imagination* (Minneapolis: University of Minnesota Press, 1997); and Christiane Wilke, "Enter Ghosts: Haunted Courts and Haunting Judgements in Transnational Justice," *Law and Critique* 21, no. 1 (2010): 73–92. For more on settler colonialism, see James Dashuk, *Clearing the Plains: Disease, Politics of Starvation, and the Loss of Aboriginal Life* (Regina: University of Regina Press, 2013); J.S. Frideres, *Arrows in a Quiver: Indigenous-Canadian Relations from Contact to the Courts* (Regina: University of Regina Press, 2019); Thomas King, *The Inconvenient Indian: A Curious Account of Native People in North America* (Minneapolis: University of Minnesota Press, 2013); and Scott Rutherford, *Canada's Other Red Scare: Indigenous Protest and Colonial Encounters during the Global Sixties* (Montreal and Kingston: McGill-Queen's University Press, 2020).

4 Gordon, *Ghostly Matters*, 19.

5 Literature on this topic is extensive and makes up the major argument of critical legal theory. Adherents to the school of critical legal studies showcase the ambiguity in supposedly impartial legal doctrines.

6 Commitment to human rights is a central component of Canadian identity since these rights were seen as a reasonable way to solve conflicts of ethnic identity and

inequality in the aftermath of the Second World War. Will Kymlicka, in *Multicultural Citizenship: A Liberal Theory of Minority Rights* (Oxford: Oxford University Press, 1995), argues that the concept of an ethnic mosaic "carries the connotation of respect," but in reality it requires conformity to the dominant culture (1). Eva Mackey, in *The House of Difference: Cultural Politics and National Identity in Canada* (Toronto: University of Toronto Press, 2002), argues that ideas of tolerance, pluralism, and multicultural state policies—all central to the human rights identity that Canada has espoused—have been mythologized in the narrative of nationhood as key features of Canadian identity. "Liberal inclusionary forms of national imagining" (18) work through the erasure of difference and construction of homogeneity. Sunera Thobani, in *Exalted Subjects: Studies in the Making of Race and Nation in Canada* (Toronto: University of Toronto Press, 2007), contends that hegemonic accounts of a generous and welcoming national identity obfuscate the reality of the nation's history, distorted through its own image of tolerance and civility.

7 Jennifer Tunnicliffe, *Resisting Rights: Canada and the International Bill of Rights, 1947–76* (Vancouver: UBC Press, 2019).

8 The UNWCC was constituted on 20 October 1943. It was made up of seventeen member nations, including Australia, Belgium, Canada, China, Czechoslovakia, Denmark, France, Greece, India, Luxembourg, the Netherlands, New Zealand, Norway, Poland, the United Kingdom, the United States, and Yugoslavia. The UNWCC aimed to investigate war crimes during the Second World War and to prosecute the Axis perpetrators of those crimes in an effective and efficient manner. The commission was operational from 1943 to 1948. Valentyna Polunina, "The Absent Player: The Soviet Union and the Genesis of the Allied War Crimes Trials Program, 1941–1943," *Journal of the History of International Law* 24 (2022): 354–72.

9 This was a covert program that the Allied powers used after the war to recruit experienced German scientists and technicians to subvert the average immigrant screening process for individuals deemed invaluable to the growth of industry in the Allied countries. In November 1946, the Canadian cabinet accepted the program and formally passed PC2047 in May 1947. This order legally provided for Operation Matchbox to be a joint British-Canadian endeavour. The project was kept far from the public eye. When asked by the press about Canadian involvement in it, the government responded that a small number of German personnel had been recruited to work in universities and industry. In 1945, the American forces recruited nearly 2,000 German scientific workers from German-occupied territories, and the British forces evacuated around 250, along with their families. This was the start of Operations Matchbox and Paperclip. Under the auspices of Operation Matchbox, Canada recruited 71 German scientists and technicians. Of that number, 41 definitely arrived in Canada. By late 1950, 461 German scientists had been recruited and screened by Operation Matchbox. By its conclusion, 469 scientific workers—1,000 people including their immediate family members—had been recruited by Operation Matchbox and brought outside the Soviet zone of influence. For further information on Operation Matchbox, see Galen R. Perras,

"The Triumph of the Politics of Economic Self-Interest? Operation Matchbox and Canada's Importation of German Scientists and Technicians, 1945–1950," *Journal of American and Canadian Studies* 13 (1995): 35–62; Paul Maddrell, "Operation Matchbox and the Scientific Containment of the USSR," in *Intelligence and Statecraft: The Use and Limits of Intelligence in International Society*, ed. Peter Jackson and Jennifer Siegel (Westport, CT: Praeger Publishers, 2005); and "Immigration Policy: Entry of German Scientists and Technicians," Cabinet Conclusions, 12 November 1946, Library and Archives Canada, RG2, vol. 2639, Item 305. *The Commission of Inquiry on War Criminals*, principal commissioner Judge Jules Deschênes (Ottawa: Library of Parliament, Research Branch, 1986).

10 *Commission of Inquiry on War Criminals*, 27.

11 *Commission of Inquiry on War Criminals*.

12 Thobani, *Exalted Subjects*.

13 The Canadian state projects an idealized and hegemonic image of the nation that minimizes consideration of how settler colonialism has influenced the construction, expansion, and current functioning of the country. Patrick Wolfe, in *Settler Colonialism and the Transformation of Anthropology* (London: Cassell, 1999), suggests that colonial "invasion is a structure not an event" (3). This notion refocuses the discussion of settler colonialism from an event that happened in the past and is now over to an ongoing process that still affects Indigenous Peoples. Canada was founded upon the principles of settler colonialism—the removal of Indigenous Peoples from the land, to be replaced by colonial subjects, and social, economic, and judicial practices—and those structures and practices remain operational today. Sherene Razack's work on the deaths of Indigenous people while in custody, and the role of the legal system and state actors in those deaths, reveals the flaws in Canada's self-perception of the value of human rights and equal justice. Mary Jane Logan McCallum and Adele Perry, in *Structures of Indifference: An Indigenous Life and Death in a Canadian City* (Winnipeg: University of Manitoba Press, 2018), show how both individual racism and structural racism form a devastating set of obstacles for Indigenous people in Canada. They argue that "a desire to mould Canada into a distinctly white settler state is evident, for example, in the dispossession, removal, and discipline of Indigenous people; the exclusion, segregation, and marginalization of people of colour; and the creation and repetition of pervasive national narratives about Canada that valorize white settlement and governance" (16).

14 Irving Abella and Harold Troper, *None Is Too Many: Canada and the Jews of Europe, 1933–1948* (Toronto: Lester and Orpen Dennys, 1982), 199.

15 Various articles were published during the era of the commission that highlighted the Ukrainian communities' concerns; see Stanley Oziewicz, "War-Crime Probe Ruined Reputation, Woman Complains," *Globe and Mail*, 2 May 1985; Jock Fergeson, "Ukrainian Veterans Expect Investigation by War Crimes Study," *Globe and Mail*, 12 April 1985; "Inquiry Slurs Ukrainian-Canadians—Group," *Edmonton Journal*, 30 May 1986; Ukrainian Canadian Committee, "Historical Note on the Ukrainian Division," press release, Toronto, 14 February 1985; Ron Vastokas, "Hunting Nazis: We Shouldn't Trust Soviet Evidence in Seeking Out War Criminals," *Kingston*

Whig-Standard, 5 October 1985; *House of Commons Debates,* 33rd Parliament, 1st Session, Vol. 2 (7 February 1985), 2113; and Lubomyr Luciuk, *Operation Payback: Soviet Disinformation and Alleged Nazi War Criminals in North America* (Kingston: Kashtan Press, 2022).

16 Ralph Blumenthal, "Papers Indicate Mengele May Have Been Held and Freed after War," *New York Times*, 23 January 1985.

17 In 1985, Sol Littman, a journalist for the *Toronto Star* and a representative of the Simon Wiesenthal Center, alleged that Mengele was living in Canada under an assumed identity. Littman sent this story to a contact with the *New York Times*, and the story was published as "Papers Indicate Mengele May Have Been Held and Freed after War." The article did not expressly state that Mengele was in Canada, yet the possibility remained. The West German government had maintained a warrant for his arrest since 1959, and the United States Office of Special Investigation listed Mengele as a priority. That he might have entered Canada prompted an immediate response.

18 *House of Commons Debates*, 33rd Parliament, 1st Session (7 February 1985), 2113.

19 *Commission of Inquiry on War Criminals*, 86. This option was used by the U.S. Department of Justice, but Canada found that this punishment did not offer the best answer to the evil of war crimes. The option of denaturalization and deportation was to be used as a last resort in chasing war criminals from Canada, and it was not considered the best way of bringing them to justice.

20 *Commission of Inquiry on War Criminals*, vii–ix.

21 *Commission of Inquiry on War Criminals*, 827.

22 Canada War Crimes and Crimes against Humanity Act, SC 2000, c. 24, 31 December 2002.

23 Franklin Bialystok, *Delayed Impact: The Holocaust and the Canadian Jewish Community* (Montreal and Kingston: McGill-Queen's University Press, 2000); Lawrence Douglas, *The Memory of Judgement: Making Law and History in the Trials of the Holocaust* (New Haven, CT: Yale University Press, 2001); Adara Goldberg, *Holocaust Survivors in Canada: Exclusion, Inclusion, Transformation, 1947–1955* (Winnipeg: University of Manitoba Press, 2015); Rhonda Hinther and Jim Mochoruk, eds., *Re-Imagining Ukrainian Canadians: History, Politics, and Identity* (Toronto: University of Toronto Press, 2011).

24 *R. v. Finta*, 1 SCR 701 (1994), 42, https://scc-csc.lexum.com/scc-csc/scc-csc/en/item/1124/index.do.

25 Under Canadian domestic law, the "peace officer" and "military orders" defences related to assessing whether the actions committed were done in obedience to superior orders or so "outrageous as to be manifestly unlawful." *R v. Finta* [1994] SCC, 811. A defendant thus had a valid defence in that he was following the orders of his superiors, as required in his role in a police unit.

26 *R. v. Finta*, [1989] OJ No. 1041, 31.

27 *R. v. Finta*, [1992] OJ No. 823, 14.

28 *R. v. Finta*, [1992] OJ No. 823, 15.

29 *Commission of Inquiry on War Criminals*, 86.

30 *Canada (Minister of Citizenship and Immigration) v. Katriuk*, FCJ 90 (1999).

31 "Federal Court of Canada, the Minister of Citizenship and Immigration, and Vladimir Katriuk," 1999, Queen's University Archives, Orest Rudzik Fonds, box 8, file 2, 28.

32 "Federal Court of Canada . . . and Vladimir Katriuk," 28.

33 *Canada . . . v. Katriuk.*

34 These cases include both criminal and civil proceedings against individuals who faced allegations similar to Katriuk.

35 *Canada . . . v. Katriuk.*

36 *Canada . . . v. Katriuk.*

37 *Canada . . . v. Katriuk.*

38 Gordon, *Ghostly Matters*, xvi.

39 Per Anders Rudling, "The Khatyn Massacre in Belorussia: A Historical Controversy Revisited," *Holocaust and Genocide Studies* 26, no. 1 (2012): 29–58.

40 Rudling, 11.

41 Andy Blatchford, "Accused Nazi Living as Quebec Beekeeper," *Toronto Star*, 26 April 2012; Stewart Bell, "Canadian Participated in 1943 Massacre," *National Post*, 25 April 2012.

42 Sam Roberts, "Vladimir Katriuk, Beekeeper Accused of Nazi War Crimes Is Dead at 93," *New York Times*, 29 May 2015.

43 Blatchford, "Accused Nazi"; Bialystok, *Delayed Impact*, 222–30, 240–50. Bialystok discusses how the Holocaust became important for the Canadian Jewish community and why lobbying for legal action against alleged war criminals was central to their identity, especially as Holocaust survivors immigrated to Canada and became part of the Canadian Jewish community and shared their experiences.

44 Blatchford, "Accused Nazi." Lobbying against the use of Soviet evidence was not new. It was a significant point of contention within and surrounding the commission and that sentiment continued in the later trials. Some examples of this contention include: Ron Vastokas, "Hunting Nazis: We Shouldn't Trust Soviet Evidence in Seeking Out War Criminals," *The Whig Standard*, 5 October 1985; Anna Ivasyk, "Reliable?" *Winnipeg Free Press*, 27 February 1986; and Ron Vastokas and Lubomyr Luciuk, "Soviet Villains Omitted: A Flaw in Canada's Search to Uncover War Criminals," *Globe and Mail*, 4 March 1986.

PART III

Human Rights Activists and Activism in Canada

CHAPTER 8

The Battle of Church Street: Queers, Police, and the Streets of Toronto, 1981

Tom Hooper

1981 WAS a remarkable year for street protests in Toronto. On 5 February, 200 police agents raided four gay bathhouses and arrested over 300 men. This was one of the largest mass arrests in Canadian history. Gay men were rounded up and charged with the Criminal Code offence of being found in a common bawdy house, and the bathhouse owners and employees were charged with keeping a common bawdy house. These raids were viewed as an attack on the emerging queer community. Queers (including two-spirit, lesbian, gay, bisexual, trans, and queer) took to the streets in resistance and built coalitions with feminists, union leaders, and Black and racialized communities. This chapter is dedicated to telling the story of these protests. They are important to study because they showcase the broad coalition that stood with gay men in this moment of crisis. These protests reveal how the queer community built the organizing capacity to resist police violence successfully. Although police went back into the baths with limited raids in June 1981 and April 1983, the resistance movement in 1981 essentially ended police raids on bathhouses in the city.

Studying the protests in 1981 contributes to a critical understanding of queer human rights history in Canada.[1] Queer history increasingly has become a topic of community and mainstream interest, and many queer organizations have sought to mobilize their histories and define their legacies. At the same time, queer history is susceptible to being oversimplified, co-opted, and even erased.[2] For example, to mark the fortieth anniversary of the bathhouse raids and the formation of pride, Pride Toronto issued a statement in the 2021 *Pride Guide*. This statement briefly mentioned the bathhouse raids on 5 February 1981 and then stated that "later in the year Pride Toronto was legally incorporated and an estimated 1,500 people celebrated Pride Day on Sunday, June 28th, 1981 at Grange Park."[3] This statement from Pride Toronto on its own history is a problem not only in its simplicity and brevity but also because substantial pieces of the historical narrative have been removed. Missing are the deep historical connections between queer activist groups with Black and racialized resistance movements against police violence. The statement ignores the central place of lesbian and heterosexual allies who went into the streets to defend gay men's bathhouses. Instead, it feeds a narrative that gay men were arrested, protested, and then won. According to this narrative, Pride is not about a continued struggle against police violence but about a celebration of dance parties, politicians, and corporate floats.

I propose a deeper understanding of what occurred in 1981. My research shows that there was not a simple path from the 5 February bathhouse raids to a sudden victory celebration that June. Instead, 5 February was part of a long battle between queers and the police. Groups such as the Right to Privacy Committee (RTPC), which formed after a raid in 1978 on the Barracks bathhouse, worked alongside civil rights leaders such as Bromley Armstrong, Dudley Laws, and Lemona Johnson to bring queers and Black communities into the streets together in resistance. Queers took to the streets in Leslieville when the Ku Klux Klan opened an office in the neighbourhood. When the police doubled down on bathhouse raids again in June 1981, a demonstration turned bloody. Named "the Battle of Church

Street," this was the climax, but not the conclusion, of a long struggle over police violence in Toronto.

By adopting an intersectional lens, in this chapter I emphasize the importance of addressing the intersecting forms of oppression facing 2SLGBTQ+ people, particularly those from marginalized communities. The chapter contributes to existing work in broader Canadian human rights history that essentializes the role of diverse coalitions in building the human rights state.[4] This approach seeks to ensure that efforts to advance gay rights are grounded in a broader commitment to social justice, liberation, and human rights for all, as the introduction to this volume asserts. Queer history is human rights history, and I contend that in revisiting what occurred in 1981 we also revisit human rights history in Canada.

6 February 1981: "No More Shit!"

The morning after the 5 February bathhouse raids various activists held a meeting at the offices of the *Body Politic*, Toronto's queer community news magazine. After a discussion about the motivations for the raids and possible next steps, the group decided to hold a demonstration that night. The plan was to assemble at the northeast corner of Yonge and Wellesley Streets. This location was known by Toronto's emerging queer community and used as a space for demonstrations throughout the 1970s. Among the activists speaking in favour of this idea, lesbian activist and journalist Chris Bearchell was the most insistent. To advertise the protest, activists relied on telephone trees, leaflets, and 4,000 flyers. They went into the bars and restaurants along Yonge Street that catered to queer customers. Ordinarily, but not on this occasion, these methods of interrupting dinner or bar service would be met with resistance from bouncers and business owners. Thousands gathered for this protest.[5]

At around midnight, a flatbed truck loaded with a sound system arrived to play music and allow for a series of speeches. The crowd began chanting with a common refrain from the 1970s: "Gay rights now!" As the crowd grew in both size and defiance, the chants turned more direct, including

"No more raids!" Among the loudest of these chants was "Fuck you 52!" This chant was in reference to the Toronto Police 52 Division, where some of the men arrested in the raids had been detained overnight. The selected speakers climbed onto the trailer and took turns at the microphone. Gay activist and former bathhouse owner Peter Maloney declared that "the first thing you got to know is that the Barracks and the Romans and the Club Toronto are open again," to thunderous cheers. Maloney continued, "they're open and operating, they're not going to be intimidated neither should we."[6] The final speech came from Bearchell, who yelled "They think that when they pick on us that they're picking on the weakest. Well, they made a mistake this time! We're going to show them just how strong we are. They can't get away with this shit anymore!" Concluding her speech, Bearchell shouted a phrase that has become iconic of the resistance to the bathhouse raids: "No more shit!"[7]

After the speeches, the crowd began to move. There was some deliberation among the activists about where to direct the protest. Initially, the plan was to march north in a route that would take them to police headquarters near Jarvis and Bloor Streets. According to *Body Politic* member Tim McCaskell, by that point the constant chants of "Fuck you 52!" were a sign that the crowd had a mind of its own. Instead of marching north, they headed south on Yonge Street toward 52 Division. Windsor gay activist Jim Monk was handed the microphone, and he announced to the crowd that this would be their destination. As the protesters proceeded south on Yonge Street, they were met with little resistance. There were a few homophobes who threatened violence. In response to the queer chant "No more raids!" the homophobes shouted "No more faggots!"[8] However, once they realized that they were outnumbered, they ran away. Police agents also moved in to remove queerbashers. The police established a barricade of cars at the intersection of Yonge and Dundas Streets, but the crowd simply manoeuvred around and over the vehicles. One protester jumped on the hood of a police car and urinated on the windshield, and the car's headlights were smashed. On the police radio, one officer "shouted frantically . . . they're smashing cars at Yonge and Dundas." Police were then ordered over the radio to park their cruisers in underground parking garages to prevent damage.[9]

A Toronto Transit Commission streetcar attempted to continue its route through the protest, but members of the crowd cracked several windows. At this point, organizers directed the crowd to turn west on Dundas Street toward 52 Division.

When the protesters crossed University Avenue and arrived at 52 Division, they were faced with a line of police officers guarding the building. The crowd approached the police line and began shouting "SIEG HEIL! SIEG HEIL!" while giving a Nazi salute, followed with "Fuck you 52! No more shit!" The protest marshals realized that they had very limited control over the crowd, and the standoff was tense. Monk had come from Windsor to assist with the protest. He remembers being on the sound truck with fellow activist Tom Warner from the Coalition for Gay Rights in Ontario. Because of police blockades, the truck was forced to take side roads to catch up with the crowd. Once they arrived opposite 52 Division, Monk and Warner made an announcement over the sound system that the crowd would head north on University Avenue to the Ontario legislature.[10]

The march north on University Avenue turned into a run. Protest marshals attempted to slow the crowd by locking arms, but ultimately they failed as hundreds ran ahead toward the front doors of Queen's Park, Ontario's Legislative Assembly. Several protesters ran up the front steps and began throwing themselves at the door. This concerned several organizers and activists. In the moment, Peter Zorzi thought, "if we rampage through this building it will do us no good."[11] A line of police arrived and pushed the crowd back from the doors, creating yet another face-to-face standoff. However, by this time, it was quite late, the protesters were tired, and they thought that the community had expressed its rage. Marshals encouraged remaining protesters to leave in groups for their own safety. The crowd slowly dispersed, but a group of dedicated protesters marched to the intersection of Yonge and Bloor Streets. Police and queerbashers were seen by members of the *Body Politic* beating one of the men charged in the raids. By about 2:30 a.m., the protest was over, and eleven people were arrested.[12]

20 February 1981: Enough Is Enough

In the weeks following the raids, the community refocused its efforts and used the momentum from the 6 February protest to bring hundreds of volunteers into the RTPC. On 10 February, about 1,000 people from the community met in the gymnasium at Jarvis Collegiate, a high school located close to the emerging gay neighbourhood near Church Street. George Smith, who became chair of the RTPC in the days after the bathhouse raids, opened the meeting by declaring that "What we see as the point of this meeting is to begin to organize a defense for the people who have been arrested."[13] After hearing from those arrested in the raids, the meeting divided into six classrooms, with each one dedicated to a new subcommittee of the RTPC.[14] Among these new committees was the Public Action Committee headed by Tim McCaskell. The immediate plan for the committee was to organize another street protest planned for 20 February. Bob Gallagher was chosen as the head marshal given his previous experience in Philadelphia as part of the antiwar movement.

Whereas the 6 February protest was organized over several hours, this time the RTPC could carefully plan its next protest action. Gallagher worked with fashion designer Charlie Grimes, who sewed a banner for the front of the protest. As 20 February approached, the Public Action Committee became increasingly concerned about confrontations between protesters and police. At a planning meeting on 15 February, activist Gary Kinsman recommended that the RTPC adopt a policy for dealing with police: namely, that there be no physical confrontations and that they do everything in their power to avoid arrests.[15] At the 6 February protest, there were reports of police removing their badges and engaging in violence against the crowd. The RTPC was also cognizant that, if it had more time to prepare for the next demonstration, then so did the police. In an attempt to mitigate potential conflict, Gallagher obtained a protest permit from the city. The marshalling team was trained on de-escalation tactics, and queer-friendly lawyers were invited to attend planning meetings to provide legal advice.

At the 15 February planning meeting, the Public Action Committee decided to reach out to various communities that had experienced police violence, inviting them to join the protest. Since 1979, the RTPC had worked with a broad coalition of groups that advocated for police reform, in particular the Working Group on Police-Minority Relations spearheaded by civil rights activist Bromley Armstrong. Building upon these connections, the Public Action Committee invited various speakers from beyond the queer community. They included members of the Working Group on Police-Minority Relations and Walter (Wally) Majesky from the Toronto Labour Council. The committee prioritized gender parity by planning an equal number of men and women speakers, including activist Pat Murphy from the group Women against Violence against Women.

The protest on 20 February began at 6:30 p.m. As the crowd assembled at Queen's Park, the marshals noticed more people showing up than had attended on 6 February. The weather was mild with a light drizzle. Majesky spoke first, stating that "we represent 180,000 trade unionists in the Toronto metropolitan area, [and] we in the trade union movement were appalled by the calculated vindictiveness and viciousness that took place a short while ago. We consider this an issue of human rights."[16] He was followed by Josephine Godlewski, a middle-aged Italian housewife who contacted the RTPC after being outraged at the injustice of the raids. In her speech, she stated, "First it was the Blacks. Now the gay people. Who is the next? Me?"[17] Mariana Valverde spoke on behalf of the International Women's Day Committee, stating that "many of us came out and joined you in the streets on 6 February and we're here now, we are here again tonight." Reverend Brent Hawkes, the senior pastor of Metropolitan Community Church, was on day five of a hunger strike demanding an inquiry into the raids. He stated in his speech that, "if others are harassed or discriminated against, we must come to their aid, not only because they need us but also because we could be next. We must join hands with one another, we must join hands with our Black sisters and our Black brothers, we must unite with all those who are oppressed because they are different."[18] After his speech, the crowd was instructed to begin the march with a planned destination of 52 Division.

The marshals set out to their assigned locations at the front, back, and sides of the crowd. Photojournalist Gerald Hannon was ready with his camera. Protest marshal and University of Toronto professor Ian Lumsden noticed an ominous sign: plainclothes police agents were spotted at the rally. Lumsden quickly asked Hannon to snap a picture of this group of men.[19]

Charlie Grimes's banner led the protest. It was about five metres long and in large print read "Enough Is Enough," with "Stop Police Violence" in smaller font underneath. The banner led the crowd away from Queen's Park east along College Street toward Yonge Street. Sewn into the top of the banner were five three-foot-long bamboo poles that allowed the front line of the protest to manoeuvre easily around corners and other potential obstacles in the path of the protest. When it was a block away from reaching Yonge Street, several activists and marshals noticed that a group of men moved to the front and were carrying the banner. Lynda Yanz was one of three people selected by the protest organizers to carry the banner for the entire march. She was among many straight allies who attended the protest and was involved with the International Women's Day Committee. In a signed affidavit following the protest, Yanz stated that she noticed two men had taken hold of the banner and "was concerned about their behavior. They were rowdy. In fact, I thought they were both drunk." Then she saw one of the men rip the banner: "I was holding onto the banner around one of the poles. Immediately after the banner was ripped, the pole I was holding was pulled from my hands by one of these men (officers) and removed through the rip he had made." Concerned, Yanz sought out the protest organizers and found head marshal Gary Kinsman, who was marching with Joanne Kates, a restaurant reviewer with the *Globe and Mail.* At the same time, David Smith, another straight ally tasked with holding the banner, noticed two other men. Four undercover police agents were carrying the "Enough Is Enough" banner.[20]

With one of the five bamboo poles removed, the banner reached Yonge Street, and the protest swung through the intersection, turning right to head south. The protest permit allowed the protesters to take over College Street and occupy the road, but it did not allow them to occupy Yonge Street.

Instead, they were supposed to march down its sidewalks.[21] This was an impossible task; with over 3,000 demonstrators, there was insufficient space to remain on the sidewalk. That was a handy excuse, for the activists had always intended to take over Yonge Street. As the protest continued south, instead of heading for the sidewalks, the protesters carrying the vandalized "Enough Is Enough" banner stretched it across the road with the massive crowd closely following. At the same time, the marshals were trying to figure out what to do about the group of undercover police agents who had taken the front of the line.

According to an affidavit signed by Kinsman after the protest, he conferred with a number of marshals to determine how best to respond: "We decided to get demonstrators we knew to replace them on the front banner. One of the marshals went off to collect some people for this task."[22] They also began pointing and staring at the men to make them feel uncomfortable and unwelcome. McCaskell stated in his affidavit that "several of the other marshals and myself then stayed very close and began to stare at them, making it clear that we recognized them as provocateurs and that we were ready if they began to cause any further trouble."[23] While Kinsman, Kates, McCaskell, and other marshals watched the men, Yanz and lesbian feminist Pat Leslie approached them and told them "we were now going to have women carrying the banner. The men then left the front of the march."[24] The protesters proceeded south on Yonge Street and then west on Dundas Street to 52 Division, where they were met with a line of police.

At 52 Division, more speeches were planned. Poet Allen Ginsberg read a greeting and was followed by Pat Murphy. "It's great to be outside this police department," Murphy declared sarcastically; "it's not the first time I've been outside or inside their great hallowed halls." She was arrested in 1974 after she was ejected by police from the Brunswick House, a tavern on Bloor Street. Alongside Adrienne Potts, Sue Wells, and Heather Elizabeth, Murphy sang a version of Rodgers and Hammerstein's "I Enjoy Being a Girl," replacing the lyrics with "I enjoy being a dyke." This act led to their arrest, and they became known as the "Brunswick Four."[25]

The most prominent speech was made by Lemona Johnson, the widow of Albert Johnson, a Black man killed by police in their family home in August 1979. Lemona later became an outspoken advocate against police violence alongside other Toronto civil rights activists, including Dudley Laws and Bromley Armstrong. They had worked with Toronto's queer community and the RTPC since 1979 in the Working Group on Police-Minority Relations. Armstrong was a trade union activist in addition to being an outspoken leader in the Black community, and he recalled in his memoir that, "when the need arose, I added my voice to those that were speaking about injustice in other ethnic communities to include also the gay and handicapped communities."[26] His activism came with personal consequences, he wrote, and his community advocacy hastened his departure as commissioner with the Ontario Human Rights Commission.[27] This was particularly the case in his intervention in Johnson's murder. In her speech, Lemona echoed Armstrong's solidarity with the queer community: "Together we have a duty, you and I, and all of us must coordinate our efforts, abilities, and strength to destroy all forms of discrimination in our society."[28] The response to her speech elicited the loudest applause of the protest.

During these speeches, scuffles broke out between protesters and undercover police agents. According to an affidavit by Hugh English, "I saw a man wearing a blue ski jacket with a dark moustache shove some other demonstrators. When the demonstrators responded, the man jumped into karate fighting stance with 'knife-blows' ready."[29] The marshals then formed a line in an attempt to protect the crowd, and it was then that Yanz realized the men holding the banner were police agents. According to her, "the next time I saw them was in front of 52 Division when the marshals linked arms to form a line between the uniformed police officers and the demonstrators in an attempt to prevent any violence. I saw these two men (officers) arrest several demonstrators and only then did I realize they were undercover police officers. Then someone who I have now identified as Officer Doyle . . . blew smoke in my face and in the faces of some of the marshals around me."[30] Marshal Ian Lumsden was at the back of the demonstration. He recalled that "approximately half-way through the speeches a violent scuffle broke out immediately alongside me."[31] Three marshals were arrested in the brawl, including marshals Bob Gallagher and James Chemerika. The three were standing together when they were "heavily spat upon" by undercover police agents. When one of the marshals yelled "What's going on?" Chemerika stated that he "saw the undercover cops roughly grab him by the jacket and drag him towards and through the police barrier." Unaware that they were undercover police officers, Gallagher tried to intervene and was arrested along with Chemerika. The protest ended at around 9:00 p.m., and six people were arrested. In the weeks that followed, various media outlets, including the *Toronto Star*, confirmed that at least four police agents grabbed hold of the "Enough Is Enough" banner during the protest.[32] The photojournalism of Gerald Hannon from the *Body Politic* and Ted Hebbes from the *Toronto Clarion* was essential to uncovering this infiltration.

7 May 1981: Riverdale Action Committee against Racism

The speeches by immigrants, labour activists, lesbians, feminists, and Black activists at the 20 February protest showed that there was a broader coalition in resisting attacks on gay men in the bathhouses. The protests on 6 and 20 February affirmed a key principle: policing and other systems of oppression cause harm to various intersecting communities. These ideas informed the protests that would follow. In the spring of 1981, the Ku Klux Klan opened an office at 1439 Dundas Street East near the neighbourhoods of Riverdale and Leslieville.[33] McCaskell was part of the Riverdale Action Committee against Racism, which canvassed door to door in the neighbourhood to raise awareness of the rise of this hate group.[34] On 31 May, the committee held a protest that gathered at Greenwood Park. Committee spokesperson Paul Pelletier criticized the lack of police response to the rise of the Klan in the city, stating that the police were "promoting racism by not acting."[35] One thousand people attended the protest in the park at 1:30 p.m., which included a festival atmosphere with food and music. The protesters then marched toward the Dundas Street home that housed the Klan.

Joining McCaskell in this action were several other queer groups, including the lesbian Amazon Motorcycle Club, the RTPC, Gay Asians of Toronto, and members of a new group called Gay Liberation against the Right Everywhere (GLARE). Ahead of the protest, GLARE distributed flyers in the queer community with the heading "Smash the Klan," urging queers to join the fight against racism. On the back of the flyer, GLARE outlined the connections between the Klan's obsession with both race and sex. The obsession with racial purity meant that "the only kind of sex accepted to the Klan is sex which serves to reproduce the 'white race.'" The flyer concluded that, since queer sex was "not aimed at producing babies, the Klan calls us 'race traitors' and demands our destruction."[36] The participation of these queer groups in this protest was important. When the protest reached the Dundas Street home of the Klan, several Klan members stood on the porch screaming at the crowd. McCaskell recalled that the Amazon Motorcycle Club revved their engines in response to deaden the racist noise. One protester threw an egg that smashed against the robe of one of the Klan members, but this was the only incident. The protest then returned to Greenwood Park.[37] According to historian Christine Sismondo, this public action forced the Klan to move their offices to Parkdale, where they were met with another community group called the Parkdale Action Committee against Racism.[38] Shortly after the community's battle with the Klan in Riverdale, activists were forced again into a confrontation with police.

12 June 1981: Convictions and the Pisces Raid

On 12 June, queers were back in the streets for two reasons. First, on 30 May, forty police officers in Edmonton raided the Pisces Health Spa, where sixty-two men were charged under the bawdy house law. Police kicked in the doors and punched holes in the walls as they stormed through the bathhouse. Most concerning to the community was the use of cameras to document the arrests. Police used a camcorder with a bright light to survey the bathhouse during the raid, finding men in the jacuzzi and in the showers. According to the report by Gerald Hannon, while naked "each man had his name, age and occupation written on a piece of paper and was told to hold it in front of him. He was photographed that way, and according to one found-in I talked to . . . everyone was photographed a second time after he was dressed." The raid had a direct connection to Toronto. As Edmonton police stated, "we picked Toronto's brains. We wanted to know the pitfalls they fell into with their raids and what they looked for."[39] An affiliated organization, RTPC Calgary, was formed to raise funds for the legal defence of the men charged.[40] The second reason that queers took to the streets was the final judgment in the court case stemming from a previous bathhouse raid on the Barracks in 1978. The charges against the owners and employees dragged out because of the legal appeals sponsored by the RTPC.

To prepare for the 12 June protest, queer activists distributed flyers calling for a 10:00 p.m. demonstration against the bawdy house law at the intersection of Yonge and Wellesley Streets. The flyer informed the community about the various charges that had been made by police, including in the 1978 Barracks raid, the 6 February raids, and the new cases in Edmonton. The flyer warned that, regardless of the verdict in the Barracks trial, "the result will have a direct bearing on the other Bawdy House trials."[41] That day, in a stunning move, the judge found the owners of the Barracks not guilty, but employees Andy Fabo and Paul Gaudet were convicted of being keepers of a common bawdy house.[42] This decision further galvanized the community, and 2,000 people showed up that night for the demonstration. The crowd was once again too large to be confined to the sidewalk, and the entire intersection was occupied. According to Hannon, "marchers created a deafening roar with whistles, noisemakers and cheers as speaker after speaker denounced the bawdyhouse laws and the invasion of privacy which they legitimize." The protest was generally peaceful. However, when a protester reportedly knocked off a police officer's hat, a group of police "waded into the crowd with billy clubs in hand."[43] One person was charged with breach of the peace, and another was charged with assault and theft for stealing the officer's hat. The protest then marched down Yonge Street to the offices of Attorney General Roy McMurtry located on Grenville Street a short distance away.

20 June 1981: The Battle of Church Street and the First Lesbian and Gay Pride Day

Despite this increasing pressure from the queer community and its allies, police in Toronto doubled down on their attacks by raiding two more bathhouses on 16 June. According to police records, the raids on the Back Door Club and the International Steambath were the culmination of a ten-month investigation of "acts of group sex, indecent acts, and buggery taking place between males" on the premises.[44] Twenty-one men were arrested, including four keepers and seventeen found-ins. A flyer produced by the RTPC stated that the "cops still haven't learned that we won't go away." The flyer advertised another protest at Yonge and Wellesley Streets on Saturday, 20 June: "Maybe they didn't hear us last time, [so] let's make sure they do this weekend! Bring a whistle!"[45]

At 10:00 p.m. on 20 June, thousands in the community were back on the streets. This was becoming familiar territory for the activists in the RTPC, whose ability to organize and implement street demonstrations was improving. This demonstration had various elements prepared, including planned speeches, a new protest route, and effigies of the attorney general and police chief that would be burned. The protest assembled at Yonge and Wellesley Streets, where Chris Bearchell and Brent Hawkes delivered rousing speeches. The atmosphere was loud since 2,500 people had gathered with many bringing their whistles. After the speeches, the crowd began to move, but not south, as in the other demonstrations. This time they were headed north to Bloor Street. They arrived at the intersection of Yonge and Bloor Streets at around 11:15 p.m., when suddenly a group of rogue marshals ordered the crowd to sit down and occupy the intersection. This was unplanned and represented an escalation of tactics that the organizers did not want. It also caused several marshals from the back of the protest to run forward to determine what had caused the crowd to sit down. After five minutes, the lead marshals, including McCaskell and Gallagher, regained some control, and the protest resumed heading east on Bloor Street toward Jarvis Street. A small but growing group of queerbashers began following the protest, taunting the crowd with homophobic slurs since there was not a large police presence. The marshals led the crowd south on Jarvis Street to the intersection of Jarvis and Charles Streets, the location of Toronto Police Headquarters.

By 11:45 p.m., the situation had become increasingly tense with threats of violence from the police and queerbashers, but the protesters carried on with their plans. There were various speeches, including from Toronto Alderman Dan Heap: "The people of Toronto do not fear the gay community, but when extreme right-wing groups target the gay community, and the police then attack it, the people of Toronto have good cause to fear the actions of the police."[46] During his speech, several marshals began to light the effigies of the attorney general (Roy McMurtry) and the police chief (Jack Ackroyd) on fire. The crowd loudly celebrated this action. As the scheduled speeches began to conclude, some marshals gathered and decided that they needed to direct the protest to return to the relative safety of the queer community at the intersection of Church and Wellesley Streets. The problem was that some of the protesters headed south on Jarvis Street, and others headed west on Charles Street. McCaskell was among those who headed south and then turned west on Wellesley Street and reached the assigned rallying point. At this moment, he and the others realized that a standoff had formed at the intersection of Church and Charles Streets. A group of queerbashers stood in their way. This did not deter McCaskell and the others; they angrily ran toward the queerbashers, who promptly fled.

When the protest regrouped at Church and Charles Streets at midnight, the situation was already becoming violent. As the second group left the Toronto Police Headquarters and proceeded west on Charles Street, they were followed by queerbashers, who taunted them the entire way. As they reached Church Street, a scuffle broke out when the protesters fought back against the queerbashers. Suddenly, police officers formed a line and placed crowd control fencing across Church Street. The queerbashers fled behind this line, and police hastily closed the gap. The standoff was set. When McCaskell and the others rejoined the group from the south, they found queer protesters rocking the police fence full of rage. Another group of rogue protesters found an empty police car a block south of the standoff. They began rocking the police car, at which point the police launched a full assault. McCaskell was at the Church-Charles police line facing forward when a police officer came forward and struck him on the head with a baton. Disoriented and bloody, McCaskell walked south back to Wellesley Street, where the driver of a passing car offered to take him to the Wellesley Hospital. He required six stitches to close the wound on his head.

As the police line continued pushing south on Church Street, other protesters suffered similar violence. Police knocked people to the ground and beat them. In a photograph taken by Hannon, a police officer used a baton to shove a woman from behind. Another woman had her leg broken. Brent Hawkes saw an older man being kicked as he was lying on the ground, so he jumped into action. However, he was then seized by two police officers who held him as a third punched him. As the police pushed south of the empty police car, a new marshalling line attempted to reform. It was at this moment that a police car, number 5210, drove toward the line and struck marshal and member of the *Body Politic* Ken Popert. He bounced off the passenger side of the hood and then hit the pavement. The police car quickly drove away. The melee continued, with police following the protesters back to Yonge and College Streets, where most of the arrests were made. By 1:00 a.m., both Popert and McCaskell were sitting in the emergency room at Wellesley Hospital full of people who were bruised, beaten, and bloody.[47] They compared notes. Popert labelled this moment "the Battle of Church Street."[48]

The direct confrontations with police in both February and June 1981 brought together gay men, lesbians, feminists, unions, and Black and South Asian communities. It was in this context that a new group was formed called the Lesbian and Gay Pride Day Committee, which later became Pride Toronto. The groups that formed this new organization included the RTPC, GLARE, and Lesbians against the Right.[49] Pride celebrations in various forms had occurred in Toronto during the 1970s, but in 1981 things were different. Previously, pride festivals were celebrated in August to commemorate the 1971 "We Demand" protest, the first queer protest in Canada. In

1981, the idea of a pride festival was moved to June to commemorate the 1969 police raids on the Stonewall Inn in New York City. This better aligned with the context of what was happening on the ground between communities and police in 1981. The pride march began on 28 June at Grange Park. At 2:00 p.m., the community gathered in the park and assembled for a march. The march headed east on Queen Street toward Yonge Street, where it turned north. It then went east on Dundas Street, where it arrived in front of 52 Division. There the Sisters of Perpetual Indulgence, a group of drag queen nuns, performed an exorcism on the police station. The march then returned to Grange Park with a more festive tone, including music, balloons, and art performances.[50]

The Don Franco Acquittal and Dykes in the Streets

In July and August 1981, the community of activists responsible for carrying forward this resistance needed a break. The RTPC held a few meetings generally dedicated to reflecting on the events of the previous months. For example, at an RTPC meeting on 6 July, much of the conversation was a debriefing of the 20 June demonstration. In particular, there was concern about the unapproved sit-down at Yonge and Bloor Streets, seen as an unnecessary escalation. The members also planned for a retreat to relax.[51] By the end of the summer, the RTPC would be back in the streets, this time with a more celebratory tone. On 24 September, RTPC activist Don Franco was acquitted of keeping a common bawdy house. Police had criminally charged him in 1979 after an undercover officer answered a personal ad in the *Body Politic*. When the officer arrived at Franco's home, he noticed that one of the bedrooms had been converted into a space designed for kinky sex. The officer arrested Franco and then searched his home. The court case was consequential for the community since it was unsure initially whether this decision would be in its favour. With his victory, the RTPC decided that the protest would instead be a celebration.[52]

On 25 September, the day after Franco's acquittal, the RTPC organized a "street party" that re-enacted the 20 June march. The Public Action

Committee organized booklets for the protest marshals that included legal advice and phone numbers for gay-friendly lawyers. The backs of the booklets included the planned protest chants—"Toronto gays are here to stay!" and "Gays unite, gays unite, all together we will fight!"—as well as the chants that came from the crowd on 6 February, "No more shit!" and "Fuck you 52!"[53] The crowd of about 850 began at Church and Wellesley Streets and followed the same route as the 20 June protest north to Bloor Street and then to Toronto Police Headquarters at Jarvis and Charles Streets. Writer Marcia Cannon performed "a wickedly funny skit" on the police infiltration of the queer community. The preparation that went into this march showcased the growing skills of the RTPC. The events of the previous months had trained this group of activists to respond quickly and organize in the streets. However, not everyone was impressed. Some in the crowd criticized the number and length of speeches.[54]

In the weeks that followed, the RTPC voted to attend and support another demonstration, the Dykes in the Street March organized by Lesbians against the Right.[55] On 17 October 1981, over 300 lesbians and other women rallied at the 519 Community Centre on Church Street and then marched through the city to various landmarks. The march was followed by a dance held at the Metropolitan Community Church at 730 Bathurst Street, near Bloor Street. The event was dedicated to promoting lesbian power, pride, and visibility. A flyer for the event declared that "You know how good it feels to be a strong, independent woman. When we share this strength with other lesbians, we know our collective power. We are here, and we have a right to be here."[56] The relationship between the RTPC and Lesbians against the Right was complicated. A few months later, on 6 February 1982, the RTPC organized a demonstration in commemoration of the 6 February 1981 protest against the bathhouse raids. This protest had many problems. The sound truck that accompanied the protest, led by men, played loud music while the lesbian contingent were trying to start their chants. In a letter from Lesbians against the Right to the RTPC, the problem that intersectionality had its limits was articulated: "All too frequently, our expected role at demonstrations has been to identify our issues with yours, and then to offer gay men unconditional support for our supposedly mutual struggles. This can leave us with the uneasy feeling of playing in to the self-oppressive script of women identifying with and selflessly nurturing male needs. Lesbian feminists do not relish the role of being cheerleaders at gay male rallies."[57]

1981 was a unique year for Toronto's emerging queer communities. First, in terms of resisting the bathhouse raids, these protests were a success. The RTPC enabled the successful legal defence of the vast majority of those who had been charged. Except for a limited raid in April 1983, police no longer harassed Toronto bathhouses. Second, gay men joined with lesbians, feminists, union leaders, and Black and racialized communities to protest in the streets. Although these connections were complicated and not always enduring, this resistance brought various communities together. Through grassroots activism, legal challenges, and public awareness campaigns, queer advocacy organizations have been central in pushing the boundaries of the framework of human rights, one of the goals of this collection.

Notes

1 I have argued elsewhere how the myth of decriminalization has contributed to a misunderstanding of the history of gay rights. Tom Hooper, "Queering '69: The Recriminalization of Homosexuality in Canada," *Canadian Historical Review* 100, no. 2 (2019): 257–63.

2 Gary Kinsman, *The Regulation of Desire: Queer Histories, Queer Struggles* (Montreal: Concordia University Press, 2024), xxxii.

3 Pride Toronto, *Pride Guide*, 2021.

4 See, for example, the work of the first generation of human rights scholars such as James W.St.G. Walker and Ross Lambertson.

5 The narrative of these raids is compiled from Peter Zorzi's website, "The 1981 Bathhouse Raids," https://onthebookshelves.com/raids.htm; see also Tim McCaskell, *Queer Progress: From Homophobia to Homonationalism* (Toronto: Between the Lines, 2016), 138–41.

6 *Track Two: Enough Is Enough*, YouTube, https://www.youtube.com/watch?v=iN4_8eurids.

7 Nancy Nicol, "Proud Lives: Chris Bearchell Tribute," 2016, ArQuives: Canada's LGBTQ2+ Archives (henceforth The ArQuives), https://digitalexhibitions.arquives.ca/items/show/678.

8 *1981 Toronto Bathhouse Raid Protests: Raw Footage*, 7 February 1981, CBC Archives, https://www.cbc.ca/player/play/1.3593935.

9 Don Dutton and Nicholas Pron, "3,000 Go on Rampage in Metro Riot," *Globe and Mail*, 7 February 1981, A1.

10 Jim Monk, interview with the author, 10 February 2021.

11 Peter Zorzi, "The 1981 Bathhouse Raids," https://onthebookshelves.com/raids.html.

12 "Taking It to the Streets," *Body Politic* no. 71 (1981): 8–12.

13 *Aftermath of the Toronto Bathhouse Raids of 1981*, 15 February 1981, CBC Radio Sunday Morning, https://www.cbc.ca/player/play/1.3333400.

14 "RTPC Minutes of Special Public Meeting," 10 February 1981, The ArQuives, Accession No. 1986-002, box 1, file "Minutes, Agendas, Meetings, Public."

15 "RTPC Minutes of Special Meeting," 15 February 1981, The ArQuives, Accession No. 1986-002, box 1, file "Minutes, Agendas, Meetings, Public," 1.

16 "Bath Raids Demonstration—Queen's Park" [recording], 20 February 1981, The ArQuives, Accession No. 2014-015.

17 McCaskell, *Queer Progress*, 143.

18 "Text of Speech by Brent Hawkes," 20 February 1981, The ArQuives, Accession No. 1983-009, box 3, file "Bath Raids: City Hall Report."

19 "Photograph of Crowd in Front of Queen's Park," 20 February 1981, The ArQuives, Accession No. 88-011, box 1, file 23; Affidavit by Ian Lumsden, 22 March 1981, The ArQuives, Accession No. 88-011, box 1, file 3.

20 Affidavit by David Smith, 22 March 1981, The ArQuives, Accession No. 88-011, box 1, file 3.

21 Margaret Mironowicz, "Supporters of Gay Rights Protest against Police Raids," *Globe and Mail*, 21 February 1981, 15.

22 Affidavit by Gary Kinsman, 22 March 1981, The ArQuives, Accession No. 88-011, box 1, file 3.

23 Affidavit by Tim McCaskell, 22 March 1981, The ArQuives, Accession No. 88-011, box 1, file 3.

24 Affidavit by Lynda Yanz, 22 March 1981, The ArQuives, Accession No. 88-011, box 1, file 3.

25 Andrea Houston, "Celebrating the 50th Anniversary of the Brunswick Four," 4 January 2024, DayofPink, https://www.dayofpink.org/brunswick-four.

26 Bromley Armstrong, *Tireless Champion for Just Causes: Memoirs of Bromley L. Armstrong* (Toronto: Vitabu Publications, 2000), 209.

27 Armstrong, 215.

28 "Bath Raids Demonstration."

29 Affidavit by Hugh English, 22 March 1981, The ArQuives, Accession No. 88-011, box 1, file 3.

30 Affidavit by Lynda Yanz, 22 March 1981, The ArQuives, Accession No. 88-011, box 1, file 3.
31 Affidavit by Ian Lumsden, 22 March 1981, The ArQuives, Accession No. 88-011, box 1, file 3.
32 Dale Brazao, "Police Led Homosexual March, *Star* Photos Show," *Toronto Star*, 16 March 1981, A3.
33 Myseum of Toronto, "Microhistories: The KKK in Toronto," http://www.myseumoftoronto.com/programming/microhistories-the-kkk-in-toronto/.
34 McCaskell, *Queer Progress*, 152.
35 "Anti-Klan Group Says Police Ignore Racism," *Toronto Star*, 31 May 1981, A9.
36 "Smash the Klan! Flyer by GLARE," 20 February 1981, The ArQuives, RTPC (88-011), box 1, file 23.
37 Peter Rickwood, "Anti-Racists Clash with Klansmen," *Toronto Star*, 1 June 1981, A2.
38 Christine Sismondo, "The KKK Has a History in Canada. And It Can Return," *Maclean's*, 18 August 2017, https://www.macleans.ca/news/canada/the-kkk-has-a-history-in-canada-and-it-can-return/.
39 Gerald Hannon, "Edmonton: Bath Raids Move West," *Body Politic*, July 1981, 14.
40 "RTPC Calgary—Anatomy of the Bawdy-House Laws," n.d., The ArQuives, RTPC (1986-002), box 1, file "Briefs."
41 "Flyer—Demonstrate against the Bawdy House Laws, Yonge and Wellesley," 12 June 1981, The ArQuives, *Body Politic* (1983-009), box 3, file "Gay Community Leaflets."
42 Paul Palango, "2 of 5 Convicted in Barracks Case," *Globe and Mail*, 13 June 1981, 5.
43 Gerald Hannon, "Judge Finds Group Sex Indecent: Two Found Guilty in Barracks Case," *Body Politic*, July 1981, 9.
44 "Metropolitan Toronto Police Press Release," 16 June 1981, The ArQuives, *Body Politic* (1983-009), box 3, file "Bath Raids—June 1981."
45 "RTPC Flyer—Blow the Whistle on the Cops," 20 June 1981, The ArQuives, *Body Politic* (1983-009), box 3, file "Gay Community Leaflets."
46 "Draft of Details of June 20, 1981 Protest," The ArQuives, *Body Politic* (1983-009), box 3, file "Bath Raids—June 1981."
47 McCaskell, *Queer Progress*, 150.
48 Remarks by Ken Popert, Centre for Sexual Diversity, University of Toronto, February 2011.
49 Kinsman, *The Regulation of Desire*, 259.
50 Peter Zorzi, "1981 Pride Parade, Toronto," https://onthebookshelves.com/1981pride.htm.
51 "RTPC Minutes of Executive Meeting," 6 July 1981, The ArQuives, Accession No. 1986-002, box 1, file "Minutes, Agendas, Meetings, Public."
52 "RTPC Minutes of Executive Meeting."
53 Marshal booklets, 25 September 1981, The ArQuives, Accession No. 88-011, box 1, file 22.

54 Gerald Hannon, "Bedroom, not Bawdyhouse," *Body Politic*, November 1981, 9.
55 "RTPC Minutes of General Meeting," 13 October 1981, The ArQuives, Accession No. 1986-002, box 1, file "Minutes, Agendas, Meetings, Public."
56 "Dykes in the Streets," Rise Up! A Digital Archive of Feminist Activism, https://riseupfeministarchive.ca/activism/organizations/lesbians-against-the-right/dykesinthestreet-lesbagainstright-march1981/.
57 Lesbians against the Right to RTPC, 6 March 1982, The ArQuives, RTPC (88-011), box 1, file 10.

CHAPTER 9

From Demanding Exclusion to Joining the Human Rights Community: Organized Labour and Human Rights in 1940s Canada

David Goutor

THE WAVE OF human rights campaigns that started in the 1940s had a major impact on Canadian society and produced the first important breakthroughs in anti-discrimination legislation. One of the strengths of this movement was its ability to bring together a wide coalition of groups and interests to support the cause of human rights. Stephanie Bangarth contends that by 1946 there was "an emerging human rights community" in Canada that included not only rights activists but also "political parties (especially the Co-operative Commonwealth Federation), certain liberal newspapers and periodicals (such as the *Toronto Star*, *Winnipeg Free Press*, *Canadian Forum*, and *Saturday Night*), several academics, Jewish groups, labour organizations, and the major churches of the day (such as the Roman Catholic Church, the United Church, and the Anglican Church)."[1]

As a number of historians (including Bangarth) have also shown, organized labour was a particularly important part of the coalition. James Walker, Ross Lambertson, and Ruth Frager and Carmela Patrias have emphasized that some of the main human rights activists and organizations of the era emerged from the union movement, particularly Kalmen Kaplansky and the Jewish Labour Committee.[2] Moreover, most mainstream labour leaders offered what Frager and Patrias describe as "steadfast support" for human rights campaigns late in the Second World War and in the postwar period.[3] For instance, at its convention in 1947, the Canadian Congress of Labour passed a resolution committing it to take "rigorous action" in support of the "fight for full equality of all peoples, regardless of race, colour, creed, or national origin."[4] Through the late 1940s, the labour movement put resources into and institutional strength behind these commitments. Both of the main labour congresses—the Trades and Labor Congress of Canada and the Canadian Congress of Labour—had standing committees to fight discrimination. By the end of the decade, most major Canadian cities outside Quebec had Joint Labour Committees to Combat Racial Intolerance, each with at least one paid staff member and including organizations affiliated with both congresses.[5]

As all of these scholars have noted, this support for human rights involved a massive shift in outlook for Canadian labour leaders. From the beginning of the labour movement in the 1870s and 1880s to the 1930s, Canadian unionists consistently made agitation for a restrictive and racially discriminatory immigration policy a top priority. In addition, labour leaders—especially in British Columbia—enthusiastically joined efforts to restrict the basic rights of Asians living within Canada, including rights to own property, testify in court, and participate in the political process. Union leaders consistently blamed immigrants for many of Canada's economic and social ills, be it unemployment, crime, urban blight, or strain on the family unit.[6] Yet, by the late 1940s, organized labour had undeniably become part of "the emerging postwar Canadian human rights community" that Bangarth and others describe.

Scholars of human rights activism have offered some insights into the causes of this shift in labour's views on human rights and racial discrimination. But their primary focus has been on human rights campaigns, and understandably they have treated labour as one group among many supporting them. Still needed is a deeper exploration of the extent of labour's change in position from advocating for exclusion to advocating for human rights and especially of the complex set of factors that drove the change. This chapter is meant to begin addressing these needs. I will explore the potent new forces—and the ironies and contradictions—at play in this period. I will also show that labour became open to new ideas about rights only when the gates to immigration were closed. I will explore, in greater depth than previous studies, the impact of the transformation of the labour movement due to the rise of industrial unionism and how it was profoundly connected to a new approach to race and rights. In addition, I will examine the impact of the broad shift in Canadian society's views on race, especially in the late stages of the war. I will emphasize throughout the central role of human rights activists—many of them coming from the ranks of labour—in convincing union leaders that they should support anti-discrimination campaigns not only because justice demanded it but because it was in labour's interest. Indeed, a careful analysis of the human rights discourse in the 1940s—both its pragmatic and its justice-oriented components—is crucial. Finally, the influence of new political forces on the left—namely, the Communists and the Cooperative Commonwealth Federation (CCF)—on labour's outlook is an important factor to consider.

In this chapter, I will focus on the two main labour congresses of the period and their affiliated unions. The older and more established one was the Trades and Labor Congress of Canada (TLC), affiliated with the American Federation of Labor (AFL). The newer organization was the Canadian Congress of Labour (CCL)—called the All-Canadian Congress of Labour until 1940—which became affiliated with America's Congress of Industrial Organizations (CIO). I will develop a fuller picture of these congresses throughout the chapter. But my first task is to delineate carefully the changes—and continuities—in labour's basic approach to race and rights.

Marking the Progress—and Its Limits

At the outset, it is essential to highlight that the change in labour's approach to human rights was not quite as sweeping and total as it might appear at first. In some areas, there was little progress at all; as Frager and Patrias observe, this wave of human rights activism focused on racism and xenophobia and ignored gender and other forms of discrimination.[7] Moreover, the change in labour's views on racial discrimination was decisive and clear in some instances but uneven, contradictory, and incomplete in others. Take, for example, labour's approach to Canada's discriminatory immigration policy. In the late 1940s, many unionists readily joined the successful campaign that demanded the repeal of the Chinese Immigration Act, which effectively had stopped all migration to Canada from China starting in 1923. The campaign succeeded in winning repeal of the act in 1949. However, the government still severely limited the number of Chinese and other Asian immigrants through other regulations. Some labour leaders, such as CCL President Aaron Mosher, complained about some of these restrictions, but for the most part unionists said little about them and continued to stand by their long-standing demands for ethnic and racial discrimination in immigration policy.[8]

This continuity in labour leaders' position was especially clear in their submissions to the Senate Committee on Immigration in 1946, when it conducted a major review with an eye toward reforming postwar admissions policies. In his submission to the Senate Committee, TLC President Percy Bengough reaffirmed the long-standing part of its platform demanding "the exclusion of all races that cannot be properly assimilated into the national life of Canada." Bengough then emphatically othered thousands of immigrants: "Experience has clearly demonstrated that . . . certain nationals who have in the past been admitted into Canada remain as a distinct race and will remain a problem for future generations."[9]

CCL leaders usually saught to present themselves as more progressive than the Trades and Labor Congress of Canada when it came to racial and ethnic relations. But they also generally demanded restrictive immigration policies that protected both Canadian standards of living and national "habits and character." In typically cushioned language, the CCL submission to the Senate Committee urged policy makers to "properly take into account . . . [that] people from some countries may, because of their background, education, and customs, fit into Canadian life more easily than people from some other countries."[10]

Hence, there was less an abandonment of the long-standing support for discriminatory admissions policy and more a shift in language, tone, and especially the perceived urgency of immigration as an issue. The amount of overt race baiting and vilification of particular immigrant groups diminished considerably. Labour publications through the late nineteenth and early twentieth centuries were full of heated invective against "docile" migrant workers undercutting white wages, "antisocial" Asian immigrants "driving out" white workers, or "wild" Eastern Europeans creating disorder on Canadian streets. However, by the late 1940s, this kind of rhetoric became hard to find in labour publications.[11]

Labour leaders also became defensive about supporting exclusionary policies, often going through contortions to insist that their positions were not "really" discriminatory. For instance, when Bengough reiterated to the Senate Committee the TLC demands for the exclusion of "unassimilative races," he also insisted that, "of course, we all subscribe to the principle that there should be no racial discrimination."[12] The Canadian Congress of Labour was more forceful in disavowing racism, making "no racial discrimination" one of the first policy principles of its submission to the Senate Committee. Yet it slipped into the middle of that "policy principle" the claim that "people from some countries may . . . fit into Canadian life more easily."[13]

In other words, the outcome of the campaign against the Chinese Immigration Act probably suited most of the labour movement just fine: a brazenly racist ban was removed, but the influx of a group that most unionists still viewed as "unassimilative" was limited by subtler means. Nevertheless, labour leaders' defensiveness and desire to avoid overt discrimination are clear departures from their approach in earlier decades when they openly, and often defiantly, positioned themselves as defenders of Canadian workers and communities against alleged immigrant menaces—and against other interests in Canada, especially political elites and the business lobby, who promoted more open immigration policies. Moreover, some organizations and labour leaders did shift positions regarding non-European immigration to a remarkable extent. The TLC deleted its demand for the exclusion of "unassimilative races" from its platform in 1948.[14] Another example was the British Columbia Federation of Labour, which since its founding in 1910 had been one of the organizations that agitated most energetically against Asian immigration. Yet, as Bangarth notes, in 1947 the executive director of the federation, Jack Greenhall, argued in a letter to the prime minister that the government should "place Chinese immigration on equal status with European immigration" as a response to the demand for new workers in the province.[15]

Moreover, in recognizing the limits of and contradictions in labour's position, it is important not to discount the achievements of the human rights activism in this period. One can appreciate the progress made without having to revisit the debate (which received considerable attention at the original Taking Liberties workshop in 2012) about the relative importance of this wave of human rights campaigns compared with those of later periods, especially starting in the 1960s.[16] The repeal of the Chinese Immigration Act allowed thousands of long-isolated Chinese immigrants to reunite (eventually) with their families.[17] The combination of the repeal and the changes to the Citizenship Act in 1946 significantly expanded the citizenship rights of marginalized groups living in Canada. As Walker notes, the BC legislature enfranchised Canadians of Chinese and Indian extraction by a unanimous vote in 1947.[18] Campaigns such as the one led by the Jewish Labor Committee in Dresden, Ontario, dented the myth that anti-Black racism was not a Canadian problem.[19] A persistent effort succeeded in leading to the creation of Fair Employment Practices Acts (the first passed in Ontario in 1951), which provided racialized workers with some protection in the workplace—at least against overt forms of discrimination. Similarly, the Fair Accommodation Practices Act (first passed in Ontario in 1955) outlawed discrimination in restaurants, hotels, sporting venues, and other public places. Another concerted campaign forced provincial authorities to file charges under the Act when it was brazenly violated in places such as Dresden.[20]

Changing Minds behind Closed Gates

An analysis of the causes of labour's shift in outlook starts with another surprising and somewhat counterintuitive factor: it happened during a period of minimal immigration. Indeed, this was not a period like the end of the twentieth century when Canada's demographics were clearly shifting, and the question was whether labour and other interest groups would accept or resist the change. The gates to Asian immigration were shut first, as one might expect since it had always received the most opposition from white Canadians. The influx of Japanese migrants was strictly limited to under forty annually by a diplomatic agreement made in the wake of the 1907 anti-Asian riot. The Chinese Immigration Act of 1923 was passed after another sustained wave of anti-Asian agitation after the First World War and reduced the annual influx from China to single digits for the rest of the 1920s.[21] Regarding all immigration, the onset of the Great Depression brought a radical shift in the government's approach. After John A. Macdonald launched the National Policy in 1878, a consensus endured for decades among business and political leaders that encouraging large-scale immigration was a key part of developing the economy and building the nation. But by 1931, barely a year into the economic crisis, that consensus collapsed with remarkably little discussion, and Prime Minister R.B. Bennett shut the gates into Canada.[22] This began a uniquely slow period in Canada's immigration history; the numbers from the 1930s and 1940s stand in stark contrast to those of the periods before and after. After annual influxes had exceeded 280,000 every year in the early 1910s (peaking at 400,000 in 1913) and over 135,000 through the late 1920s, rates dropped to 27,500 in 1931 and then to under 15,000 by 1933. Annual immigration averaged only about 16,000 through the 1930s, and for a brief period Canada became better known for its aggressive policy of deporting immigrants.[23] Immigration rates averaged less than 13,000 during the Second World War. As the war ended, government planning and public debate about a resumption of immigration promptly began, but the gates reopened only gradually in the late 1940s, with annual immigration remaining under 100,000 through the late 1940s (with the lone exception of 1948). Only in 1951 did large-scale immigration resume, when the influx reached 195,000, and the rate averaged just under 160,000 for the rest of the 1950s.[24]

When this period of reduced immigration began, labour's views did not immediately change in response. The shift in policy took time and developed in stages. It was first noticeable in the approach to Asian immigration after it was drastically curbed in 1923. By end of the 1920s, vitriol against Chinese and other Asian immigrants was harder to find in labour publications. Like many media commentators and community leaders in British Columbia, unionists noted that, since worries had abated about new waves of immigrants, "friendly feelings" had developed toward the Chinese living in the province. Initially, unionists seemed almost to be disoriented by the shift, and they had some jarring and curious responses. For instance, BC labour leaders asserted that, in order to maintain those "friendly feelings," the government should continue to ban all Chinese immigration.[25] The inherent problem with demanding exclusionary policies in the name of interracial harmony seemed to elude them.

By the early 1930s, labour leaders were open to more serious changes. They even expressed some solidarity with Asian workers, and in 1931 the Trades and Labor Congress of Canada chartered its first union local made up mostly of Asian (primarily Japanese) workers, the Vancouver and Vicinity Camp and Mill Workers. The new local did not take long to confront the congress about its racist policies, bringing a number of resolutions and a delegate to campaign to the convention in 1931.[26] The congress agreed to pass Camp and Mill's resolutions calling for Japanese Canadians to be naturalized and granted voting rights but would not go much further. Tellingly, it made only cosmetic changes to its position on new immigration from Asia.[27]

After Atlantic immigration was reduced to a trickle in 1931, further signs of softening of labour's stance started to appear. In 1932 and 1933, the *Trades and Labor Congress Journal* published several articles complaining about the government's rigorous pursuit of deportation policies, although it could not bring itself to oppose the deportations outright.[28] By 1934, labour leaders became more assured that new waves of immigration would not happen any time soon. They took immigration off the top of labour's agenda, and by the mid-1930s commentary on the issue became scarce in labour publications.[29]

But the extent of the trend toward greater openness to immigrant workers' rights in the 1930s should not be overstated. When the topic did arise, labour leaders insisted that they would "stand by our principles" in opposing open immigration policies. They also held on to immigration as one issue on which their voices were heard by Canadian governments during a bleak time for their movement.[30] A fuller embrace of human rights campaigns would require a transformation in the labour movement itself—and that is just what happened.

A New Labour Movement

At the start of the 1930s, craft unions representing skilled trades workers remained the predominant force in the labour movement, as they had been—with some notable exceptions—since the 1870s. But the 1930s and 1940s brought the emergence of industrial unions to North America, which sought to represent all workers in a given industry, regardless of their background or skill level. The rise of industrial unionism served to make the labour movement inherently more inclusive, for it involved a form of mass mobilization: it built strength in numbers by organizing the tens of thousands of workers, especially in new mass-production industries such as auto, steel, and rubber. Craft unions, in contrast, sought to protect the status of small numbers of skilled craft workers, who also tended to be overwhelmingly white, Anglo-Saxon men.[31]

Scholars of human rights in Canada have noted the importance of the growth of unions, but there has not been a full exploration of its impact. The profound connection between the new approach to labour organizing and a new approach to race and human rights especially demands greater appreciation. The organizing surge began in the United States in the mid-1930s, driven by ground-level enthusiasm among workers and the launch of the New Deal (a massive set of economic reforms forged in response to the

Depression). It eventually led to the creation of the Congress of Industrial Organizations (CIO), which allowed hundreds of thousands of immigrant workers—who had been cast not long before as "unorganizable" and threats to a "white standard of living"—to join as union members. Scores of African American workers also joined these new unions.[32]

Industrial unionism—and progressive policy reform—made little headway in Canada in the 1930s, but that changed with an unprecedented wave of organizing and a leftward shift in politics during the war. The unions that achieved breakthroughs in leading mass-production industries were part of the CIO-allied Canadian Congress of Labour, which counted just under 315,000 members after the war. Like the American Federation of Labor, the longer-established Trades and Labor Congress of Canada responded to the new competition by adopting the industrial model (or modified versions of it) and enjoyed a boom of its own. The Trades and Labor Congress of Canada stayed ahead of the Canadian Congress of Labour in terms of membership, with almost 360,000 members in 1946.[33]

By the time that this organizing spread to Canada, it had already seriously shifted America's social landscape and challenged some of its most deeply entrenched racial divides. According to Eric Schickler, the new industrial unions "came to represent the New Deal's boldest ambitions," which made it particularly important that they "placed civil rights alongside more traditional, economic concerns on the agenda for New Deal liberalism."[34] Organizing and empowering Black workers were also critical for the CIO's sizable radical left contingent—socialist and Communist—that drove much of the organizing.[35] By the late 1930s, Black organizations—which had long been justifiably skeptical of organized labour—gave their enthusiastic support, hailing the Congress of Industrial Organizations as the "lamp of democracy" in the Southern United States.[36]

The progress continued during the war when the American labour movement almost doubled in size again. The surging power and confidence of unions, and state policies to placate them, led to further gains for the most marginalized workers. Employers in the South saw their iron grip on their workplaces loosen noticeably. Workers' rights to organize expanded further, as did progressive wage policies and union bargaining powers. All of this led to unprecedented gains in the incomes of workers at the bottom of the wage scale—with Black wages rising at double the speed of white wages in important sectors.[37] African American organizations continued their support of organized labour during the war, with the National Association for the Advancement of Colored People (NAACP) Executive Secretary Walter White affirming that "the CIO has proved . . . it stands for Negro advancement. It has fought for our people within the unions and outside the unions."[38] According to historian Nelson Lichtenstein, "the fortunes of the movement for workers' rights and civil rights were linked in progressive and fruitful synthesis."[39]

Not surprisingly, then, the wave of organizing of CIO-affiliated unions was a major factor in the increased interest in protecting human rights and fighting discrimination. Canadian labour leaders embraced anti-discrimination as part of the "creed of equality" that they were convinced was central to their movement, especially in CIO unions.[40] Once again unions with a strong leftist—especially Communist—contingent were often the most outspoken against racism.[41] To be sure, the culture and outlook of the American CIO unions were not simply replicated north of the border; the Canadian CIO unions had a distinct, and decidedly British, culture of their own. As Wendy Cuthbertson shows, the leadership of the CIO/CCL unions in Canada was overwhelmingly Anglo-British—and their pride in their background showed. One union journal praised "the British way," which "workers believe is the best way," and another boasted that, when they signed their first collective agreement, both sides paused for "the good old English custom of tea."[42] The leadership of the TLC unions remained very Anglo-Canadian, as it had been for generations. Moreover, some of the forces encouraging labour to support human rights were distinctly Canadian, particularly the CCF (whose influence I will explore further below). According to Lambertson, labour's strongest supporters of human rights were the Canadian directors of CIO unions who were also committed CCFers, such as Charles Millard (United Steelworkers of America) and Fred Dowling (United Packinghouse Workers).[43]

More importantly, a generation of activists emerged from this wave of organizing of immigrant workers, many of whom would have been excluded in the past. The most prominent group of activists was the Jewish Labour Committee, led by Kaplansky, actually a member of one of the mainstay TLC organizations, the International Typographical Union.[44] Walker describes the Jewish Labour Committee as one of the "triumvirate" of Jewish-led organizations that drove human rights campaigns in this era (the others were the Association for Civil Liberties and the Joint Public Relations Committee [of the Canadian Jewish Congress and B'nai Brith]). The committee was heavily influenced by the American organization of the same name and would borrow many of its tactics and much of its material in campaigning for human rights in Canada.[45] As Frager and Patrias explain, it was Kaplansky who created an infrastructure of human rights advocacy organizations within the labour movement and consolidated support from the top union leadership: "Jewish activists convinced labour leaders . . . such as Percy Bengough . . . and A.R. Mosher . . . to write about these subjects, and then they published and distributed the pamphlets in tens of thousands of copies."[46]

Yet again progress would not prove to be smooth and even. As the labour movement and human rights campaigns gathered strength in Canada, they were hitting significant barriers in the United States. Within the American labour movement, the synthesis of workers' rights and civil rights was seriously fraying by late in the war. Increasing numbers of white workers were threatened by Black workers' progress and determined to maintain their own privileges both in the workplace and in society in general. The late 1940s saw a major counterattack from the political right, which sought to re-establish colour lines and contain union power. The labour movement still made some advances as the largest industrial unions—most with sizable contingents of racialized workers—consolidated their gains after the war mostly through new strikes. This consolidation in turn paved the way for further gains in members' standards of living for the next twenty-five years. But labour did not have a response to the Republican-led political backlash and the massive anti-Communist campaign with which it was associated;

they led to the passage of the Taft-Harley law, which made union officials swear oaths of loyalty and instigated the passage of the first right-to-work laws in many states. The major CIO drive to finally break the colour line and establish unions in the Old South, "Operation Dixie," ended in disastrous defeat. The liberal social programs launched or expanded in this postwar climate excluded racialized workers, especially African Americans.[47]

The Canadian context was different in the 1940s. As Frager and Patrias argue, Ottawa's restrictive immigration policies meant that the proportion of the labour force not considered white was small in the 1940s. Hence, in Canada, the risk of potential backlash, from either political opponents or union members, against the progress of Black and racialized workers was also small.[48] But Canadian unionists were certainly influenced by the crosscurrents at work in the United States. For instance, even when Canadian unions were surging in strength, there was not much heady rhetoric about a natural alliance between civil rights and human rights.[49] Frager and Patrias also note that "Canadian reliance on American anti-racist material was pronounced in the 1940s."[50] Hence, it is not surprising that much of its material—coming from American unions trying to mitigate the backlash—grappled with the dangers of workers' susceptibility to racism and xenophobia. At times, union leaders appealed to their members to resist racism for the sake of the union. I will discuss below some illustrations of this in a slightly different context, including a famous United Auto Workers pamphlet—which Canadian human rights activists also used widely—entitled *Discrimination Costs You Money*.[51] Some labour publications also sought to build up the image of immigrant workers as solid contributors to the movement. Canada's edition of United Auto Worker, for instance, ran a long profile in 1944 of Wen Kee, a trade unionist in China who immigrated to Canada and became active in his Toronto local. The profile highlighted that "many of Kee's fellow countrymen are keen unionists in other plants, such as Ford in Windsor."[52] At other times, union leaders took a different tack, showing notable resolve to press ahead with human rights initiatives, "regardless of the approval of any portion or all of the members of the local," as one journal put it.[53]

The backlash from some of the rank-and-file in the mid- to late 1940s should not be entirely surprising, for some of the limits to the alliance of labour rights and human rights were embedded in the rise of industrial unions from the beginning. In both Canada and the United States, industrial unions often took a more inclusive approach because they had to: if a large segment of the workforce in an industry was left unrepresented, marginalized, and exploited, then employers would give more of the work to them, thereby undercutting the union. Employers could also use them as strike-breakers. As Eric Arnesen shows, white unionists in America were haunted by "the spectre of the black strike-breaker" through the industrial age.[54]

Hence, fear and self-interest played a large part in the more inclusive approach to organizing. It was a new and different response, to be sure: instead of vilifying immigrant and Black workers and driving them out of skilled workforces as American Federation of Labor organizations usually did, industrial unions sought to organize them.[55] But even in the surge of early organizing, if American industrial unions could become established without breaking down colour barriers, then usually they were.[56] In Canada, Patrias has shown, even as unions were advancing, profound discrimination continued in wartime industries throughout the early 1940s.[57] Cuthbertson also notes that Canadian unions often fought against xenophobia and prejudice "if only for survival"—an instinct developed from management's continually vilifying union organizers as "foreign born."[58]

Self-Interest and Labour's Approach to Human Rights

Labour's self-interested approach translated directly into much of its human rights and anti-discrimination discourse in the 1940s. It further encouraged unions to cast discrimination as something that divided workers, broke solidarity in the ranks, and weakened unions when dealing with employers. The Trades and Labor Congress of Canada regularly declared that "prejudice and intolerance . . . can only cause disunity and we must fight to maintain the utmost cooperation as the sure road to success."[59] It was one position of mainstream union leaders that resonated with labour's left; for example, Jewish socialists had always viewed racial division as a key tool that employers used to divide the working class and maintain their class dominance.[60]

Hence, labour's sense of self-interest was another factor that worked in surprising ways in this period. As explained above, labour leaders' self-interested approach to racial and ethnic divisions left many inequities intact and helped to lead to a backlash. However, when union leaders urged rank-and-file workers to resist long-standing impulses toward discrimination, their favourite tactic was to appeal to the workers' self-interest, especially given the need to stand together against the employer. Kaplansky and the Jewish Labour Committee often led the way in deploying the rhetoric of worker unity against divisive racial and ethnic prejudice, and many union leaders followed them.[61] In one large Toronto United Auto Workers local, for instance, the chair of the education division contended that whenever "workers fall into the trap of harbouring racial prejudice they are doing just what anti-union employers want them to do." This in turn made the fight against discrimination "a life and death struggle for our unions."[62]

Labour leaders often cast the issue in simple, almost transactional, terms: reducing discrimination led to a stronger union, which in turn led to a better deal for workers. This was best expressed in the United Auto Workers pamphlet noted above, *Discrimination Costs You Money*.[63] In rhyming verse and graphic novel format, it tells the story of a newly hired white worker, named Joe, who causes trouble at a unionized factory. On his first day, Joe finds that his work team consists of a Jewish worker, Sidney Cohen, an Italian, Nick Petrone, and a Black man, Frederick Green. In the illustrations, a female worker appears at the edge of the scene (as she does in many others), though there is no reference to her in the text.[64] Joe's team is one "that worked with main and might," but Joe refuses to join it. As he declares,

> I won't work with Green or Cohen
> Or any guy named Nick Petrone.[65]

Then the union's shop steward, named Al (a massive white man usually drawn about twice the size as Joe), steps in to scold him:

> Don't talk and act so funny,
> Discrimination costs you money.

Joe is told that, before the union was established, many white workers "dumb as you" shut out immigrant and Black workers, compromising solidarity, and,

> When they counted up the cost,
> strikes were broken, battles lost.[66]

But then the industrial union was established "by Petrone and Green and Cohen and me," and only then

> No man would scab against his neighbor,
> for all of us were union labor.

Together they won the good conditions that new hires like Joe could now enjoy:

> Wages went up; hours went down
> We made this place a union town.

The giant steward Al crouches down and orders Joe to "go home and think that over!" And indeed Joe learns his lesson:

> Our Joey thought it over all right,
> Al's words stayed with him through the night.
> He dreamt of Cohens, Petrones and Greens,
> All putting money in his jeans.

The next day Joe comes back and admits that he was "a jerk":

> I didn't know—I could not see,
> That workers need their unity.[67]

Figure 9.1. *Discrimination Costs You Money*, n.d., Walter P. Reuther Library, Archives of Labor and Urban Affairs, Wayne State University.

Figure 9.2. *Discrimination Costs You Money*, 15, n.d., Walter P. Reuther Library, Archives of Labor and Urban Affairs, Wayne State University.

The cover of the pamphlet emphasized the message about the material costs of discrimination, showing Joe (clearly before he learned his lesson) counting coins from his pay packet, wondering where his money went.

At other times, union leaders portrayed the rejection of discrimination as a part of the labour movement as it entered a new stage of growth and strength. One particularly important editorial in the September 1947 edition of the *Trades and Labor Congress Journal* not only urged unionists to reject discrimination but also came close to acknowledging and repudiating its past approach to race relations. It is worth quoting at length: "We have advanced by a process of trial and error and we can now determine what has been good for us and what has been ineffective or disastrous. . . . The worst poisons of all are the nostrums that bring mistrust and disunity. The bitter feelings that result from racial, religious and political differences are the nasty poisonous medicines that members of the trade union movement must put and keep on the unfair list."[68]

Changes on the Homefront

Another critical factor affecting labour leaders' views was a shift in attitudes toward race during the Second World War. In a war meant to protect democracy and defeat an enemy steeped in murderous racism, discriminatory practices in Canada became much more open to challenge. As Walker puts it, the war—and especially the propaganda casting it as a struggle between freedom and race hate—lent "a moral base, and publicly recognizable reference point, for campaigns against racial discrimination."[69] Once again the social forces unleashed in this period did not all move in the same direction. In some ways, discrimination became worse, especially early in the war. There was a wave of animosity toward "enemy aliens" and hysteria about "alien subversion"; the biggest manifestation was the evacuation and internment of all Japanese Canadians and the seizure of their properties.[70] Canada accumulated a dismal record when it came to providing refuge for European Jews fleeing the Nazis—the worst of any Western democracy.[71] When immigrant (and other) women used government services, they faced pressure to conform to constructions of proper "Canadian habits and character" created by government officials and the emerging welfare state.[72] Feminist historians have also shown that, despite the major contribution of women to the war effort, traditional notions of jobs belonging to "Canadian working men" persisted through the 1940s.[73]

Nevertheless, the "moral base" that the war provided strengthened as the conflict went on, especially after the mass revulsion following the "discovery" of the Holocaust in mid-late 1944.[74] Most human rights discourses focused less on race and challenging stereotypes of certain peoples and more on rac*ism* and the problems created by discrimination. The most potent expression of this tendency was also the simplest: the argument that racism was the ideology of the enemy. By 1944, mainstream newspapers were warning that racism was "Hitler's creed" and that events in Europe had shown that Canada could be "no place for race or baiters."[75] Unionists were probably more ready than any other group to deploy this kind of rhetoric. They were early in seizing on propaganda casting the war as a defence of democracy and used it to counter accusations that labour activism disrupted essential wartime production. Instead of weakening the war effort, labour leaders insisted, they were fighting for democracy at home just as the soldiers were fighting for it abroad. According to Cuthbertson, they claimed that there was a "worker-warrior" alliance defending democracy on all fronts. As early as 1942, the United Auto Workers' main Canadian publication insisted that "any act or policy which denies the right of labour . . . is subversive of the war effort. We brand it as subterfuge akin to treason."[76] Speakers from the floor at a CCL convention dubbed union-busting employers as "Canadian Hitlers," compared aggressive foremen with "the gestapo," and likened the Pinkerton guards (private security that specialized in union busting) to the Nazi SS.[77]

Organized labour was also early in contending that fascism was the great enemy of both racialized people and labour unions. According to Schickler, the Congress of Industrial Organizations was forging this connection by the late 1930s, with one editorial cartoon in the CIO News drawing "Roosevelt and the CIO defending 'American democracy' from the Nazi 'wolf,' which had victimized both 'labor unions' and 'racial and religious minorities' in

Europe."[78] During the war, Canadian labour publications urged workers to understand that allowing racism to spread was to do "Hitler's bidding."[79]

Labour leaders again portrayed racism as divisive, and by 1944 the mainstream media were making similar complaints that racism divided the population and weakened the war effort in general. Some outlets even raised fears that bigots were doing "Hitler's bidding" in an almost literal sense. One *Toronto Star* editorial claimed that Hitler was trying to "sow the seeds of antisemitism" in Allied nations in order to destabilize them. The editorial explained that "antisemitism is indeed the most cunning of [the Nazis'] methods to undermine democratic nations."[80] Constructing racism as an outside plot was certainly convenient, for it underplayed Canada's own record of discrimination and oppression. But it was also remarkable to see much of the fearmongering about subversion by foreign elements being deployed in a new way: to raise alarms about the enemy undermining Canada by spreading racism and anti-Semitism.

The response to the "discovery" of the Holocaust was especially important in creating favourable conditions for human rights activists to consolidate broad support from labour. The reaction involved not just revulsion but also fear and a clear—and justified—sense that racism was both dangerous and powerful enough to unleash the most destructive social and political forces.[81] Publications by human rights campaigns drove home the point that unions would not be safe if these forces were let loose; they too would be devastated by the "single reactionary crusade of hatred and destruction" of which racism was a key part.[82] They also sought to tear down the complacency of even some supporters of human rights that these forces could not spread widely in Canada. As one report of the Jewish Labour Committee explained, "this fight is one that deeply concerns the trade union movement. History has shown that attempts to stir up prejudices against racial or religious minorities have always been accompanied by savage attacks on organized labour. Such has been the experience with Hitler's Germany and with the other fascist movements in Europe; such is our experience with the various hate groups that are extending their poisonous activities throughout the country today."[83] The message was also clear in many of the posters that human rights campaigns produced. One image, entitled "Hand in Glove," made the case bluntly: a "union-busting" arm and a glove dubbed "race hate" held a club that readers would recognize as commonly used by police or employers' thugs against strikers.

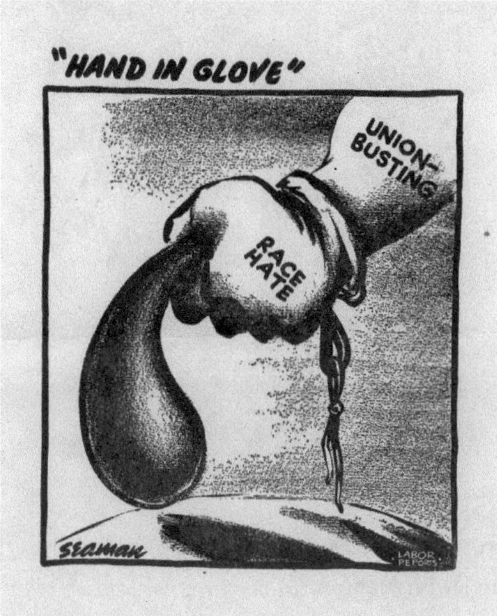

Figure 9.3. "Hand In Glove," *Canadian Labour Reports* 2, no. 2, February 1947, Canadian Jewish Archives.

Another image, entitled "The Real Target," similarly showed a "native fascist" hand driving a knife through a victim labelled "minority" before ultimately hitting a second victim labelled "labor unions."[84] Human rights campaigns thus argued that, in addition to the economic need for solidarity, there was a second way in which it was in labour's vital interest to join the fight against discrimination: to stop the growth of regressive forces that eventually would come for unions.

Figure 9.4. "The Real Target," *Canadian Labour Reports* 1, no. 1, September 1946, Canadian Jewish Archives.

Finding Allies to Support Human Rights

Up to the 1930s, union leaders liked to pose themselves as standing alone on the issue of immigration—as the only truly dedicated opponents. Labour viewed pro-immigration forces with contempt and deemed them (almost automatically) as hostile to labour's interests. In reality, labour leaders were hardly alone in their opposition, which was widespread across Canadian society, especially in the Pacific west. This opposition included officials in law enforcement, medical and other professionals, many politicians, and much of the mainstream press.[85] Yet union leaders were consistently mistrustful of other interest groups' commitment to exclusionary policies. One of the starkest examples was during the *Komagata Maru* affair in Vancouver in 1914, when the government took vigorous and sustained measures for two months to keep the ship from disembarking its 376 South Asian migrants.

The Vancouver Trades and Labour Council dismissed the government's actions—and the broad support for them—as unconvincing. It voted overwhelmingly to organize its own rally at the port because, as one member insisted, it would always be "up to labour to take the stand" against Asian immigration.[86]

Canadian labour's sense of isolation on this issue diminished somewhat in the 1930s, when there was widespread support to keep the gates to immigrants shut. But then sweeping changes in a different direction came in the 1940s, as the new industrial unions emerged in large part thanks to two forces that were also committed to fighting discrimination: the Communists and the CCF. Once again labour's relationship was hardly uncomplicated with either group. Since the Communist Party emerged in 1921, mainstream union leaders had been hostile toward its influence. Still, Communists not only performed much of the ground-level organizing work in establishing new unions, but also took some prominent positions in leadership, especially after the Soviet Union became an official ally in the war starting in late 1941.[87]

During the war, Communist-led community organizations—including many Eastern European organizations with heavy working-class memberships—were also vocal supporters of human rights laws. Ontario parliament member Joseph Salsberg, a long-time Communist and an activist in Jewish community organizations, played a key role in the passage of Ontario's first (albeit weak) human rights legislation in 1944. The onset of the Cold War put severe limits on the Communists' ability to influence unions' policies, let alone government legislation. It did not help that Communists also engaged in some xenophobia themselves, spreading fears about Eastern European fascist sympathizers in displaced persons camps coming to Canada instead of returning to the Soviet Bloc.[88] But the Communists' greatest influence was on unions' culture and broad approach to race. From the beginning of the new organizing wave in the United States, Communists were rigorously committed to treating all workers equally, regardless of their race or country of origin. Lichtenstein writes that in the United States "the Communists set the ideological standard by which American labor-liberalism would come to measure racial progress. . . . Formal equality between African Americans and whites would not be limited to the worksite or to the union membership roster. It must prevail at all levels of existence."[89]

The importance of the CCF to human rights campaigning in this period, including Kaplansky's dedication to the party, has been extensively documented.[90] I do not need to recount it in detail here, although it is important to highlight the role of the rise of the party—and the governing Liberals' determination to steal its thunder—in the enactment of legislation that granted unions key rights near the end of the war. The extent of the alliance between the CCF and Canadian unions should not be overstated. Although the bonds with the Canadian Congress of Labour were strong, much of the Trades and Labor Congress of Canada remained aloof, with many of its leaders remaining faithful to the American Federation of Labor tradition of political neutrality. There was also a solid contingent of labour leaders loyal to the Liberal Party, including TLC President Bengough.[91]

Nevertheless, the CCF was especially important in pushing for key pieces of human rights legislation and in espousing a more positive general view of the role of the state, including regarding human rights. The government's extensive powers in managing the war effort also gave weight to the CCF's social democratic approach, as did the popularity of new social welfare measures such as the Family Allowance.[92] But trusting the government on these matters was a remarkable leap for labour, which had spent decades attacking Ottawa for creating a corrupt immigration system that had duped people in the "Old Countries" into migrating and "ground down" Canadian workers through the "crushing competition" of immigrant workers.[93] It is no accident that they made the leap when there was major progress on key planks of a social democratic agenda, including in labour law and human rights legislation.

Conclusion

Labour leaders' decision to end their long-time isolation over immigration and race and join a broad and diverse range of interest groups in the human rights community highlights the extent of their shift in world view. Indeed, forging alliances with middle-class interests and well-established organizations in support of human rights in order to demand the striking down of discriminatory immigration policies would have been inconceivable a few years earlier. Labour leaders made this change in spite of skepticism—from both labour's traditionalists and leftists—that such cross-class alliances focused on human rights drew energy away from the fight for workers' interests.[94]

It required every one of the factors explored in this chapter for the change in labour's attitudes to go this far. It required both a transformation and a vast expansion of the union movement driven by an approach to organizing that saw the causes of labour rights and human rights as allied in important ways. It required a new set of activists to emerge from the ranks of labour—many of them Jewish—to lead human rights campaigns and urge unions to join them. It took a broad change in the social and political landscapes created by a new world war, which government propaganda insisted was a struggle for democracy and against racism. It required the revelation of the scale of Nazi atrocities to change the basic view of the potential implications and dangers of racist ideologies.

All of these factors helped to redraw the political landscape and convince labour leaders that there was a clear fault line between the united forces of reaction, racism, and anti-unionism, on the one side, and the forces of progress, human rights, and organized labour, on the other. Human rights activists such as Kaplansky were especially effective in convincing labour leaders about which side they needed to take in the 1940s. Yet it was also important that unions were in a position to tell their members credibly that rejecting discrimination would be in their interests because it would help the newly strengthened labour movement to deliver economic rewards.

Indeed, pragmatism and self-interest played important roles in labour's support for human rights, and there were clear limits to the extent of their conversion to the cause. It could not have happened if labour leaders remained alarmed about the possibility of large-scale influxes of immigrants in the 1930s and 1940s, unless they were assured that the new human rights campaigns were not demanding that the government take actions such as "open[ing] wide the doors to Chinese immigration."[95] The progress of human rights campaigns in these years was important in addressing deep inequities in Canadian society. But it comprised only the first steps.

In the introduction to the original *Taking Liberties* volume, Stephen Heathorn and I observed that "there was nothing inevitable about the emergence of human rights."[96] The process by which labour joined the human rights community in the 1940s is an especially good illustration of the point since it was full of surprises and paradoxes. A smooth and steady labour–human rights alliance going forward from the 1940s was even less inevitable. When new social movements arose in the 1960s, they would take a much different approach to human rights—and a much different view of organized labour. Although there were some important alliances, such as between the United Auto Workers and the civil rights movement in the United States in the early 1960s, labour (now often called "big labour") had already come to be seen as one of the establishment interests that left so many marginalized groups out of the state systems created in the postwar period.[97]

At least some of the roots of these tensions could be found in the developments of the 1940s explored here, such as labour's limited and uneven commitment to human rights or the self-interested aspects of union leaders' rhetoric. For many labour scholars, a more fundamental problem was Canadian unions' incorporation into the new legal regime in the social democratic moment of the 1940s: it might have given the unions more security and legitimacy than ever, but over the following decades unions became rule-bound and bureaucratic, unable to keep in touch with rank-and-file members, let alone engage with millions of marginalized workers who remained unorganized.[98] Nevertheless, in the 1940s, organized labour took a remarkable, positive step away from open racism and xenophobia and toward human rights. Labour's experience also shows that when new movements emerge—and when a wave of activism creates new possibilities—even the most entrenched hostilities can dissipate, and the unlikeliest of new allies in the fight for human rights can be found in a very short time.

Notes

1 Stephanie Bangarth, "'We Are not Asking You to Open Wide the Gates for Chinese Immigration': The Committee for the Repeal of the Chinese Immigration Act and Early Human Rights Activism in Canada," *Canadian Historical Review* 84, no. 3 (2003): 401.

2 See, for instance, James W.St.G. Walker, "The 'Jewish Phase' in the Movement for Racial Equality in Canada," *Canadian Ethnic Studies* 34, no. 1 (2002): 1–29; Ross Lambertson, "'The Dresden Story': Racism, Human Rights, and the Jewish Labour Committee of Canada," *Labour/Le Travail* 47 (2001): 43–82; and Ruth Frager and Carmela Patrias, "'This Is Our Country, These Are Our Rights': Minorities and the Origins of Ontario's Human Rights Campaigns," *Canadian Historical Review* 82, no. 3 (2001): 1–35.

3 Frager and Patrias, "'This Is Our Country,'" 1–4.

4 Lambertson, "'The Dresden Story,'" 50.

5 Lambertson, 51–53.

6 David Goutor, *Guarding the Gates: The Canadian Labour Movement and Immigration, 1872–1934* (Vancouver: UBC Press, 2007). See also Patricia Roy, *A White Man's Province: British Columbia Politicians and Japanese Immigrants, 1858–1914* (Vancouver: UBC Press, 1989), Chapter 2.

7 Frager and Patrias, "'This Is Our Country,'" 2.

8 Bangarth, "'We Are not Asking,'" 408–09; David Goutor, "Shifting Ground: Canadian Labour and Immigration in the 1940s," paper presented at the Canadian Historical Association Conference, 2008.

9 Percy Bengough, *Trades and Labor Congress Journal*, August 1946, 11–15.

10 Canadian Congress of Labour, *Canadian Unionist*, August 1946, 179; and Irving Abella and Harold Troper, *None Is Too Many: Canada and the Jews of Europe* (Toronto: Lester and Orpen Dennys, 1982), 233.

11 Goutor, "Shifting Ground," 11.

12 Frager and Patrias, "'This Is Our Country,'" 3.

13 Canadian Congress of Labour, *Canadian Unionist*, August 1946, 179.

14 Lambertson, "'The Dresden Story,'" 50.

15 Bangarth, "'We Are not Asking,'" 404.

16 This is a flashpoint in the international literature on human rights in general. See, for instance, Samuel Moyn, *The Last Utopia: Human Rights in History* (Cambridge, MA: Harvard University Press, 2010); and Dominique Clément, *Canada's Rights Revolution: Social Movements and Social Change, 1937–1982* (Vancouver: UBC Press, 2008), 19.

17 Wing Chung Ng, *The Chinese in Vancouver, 1945–1980: The Pursuit of Identity and Power* (Vancouver: UBC Press, 2008), 19–27.

18 James W.St.G. Walker, "Decoding the Rights Revolution: Lessons from the Canadian Experience," in *Taking Liberties: A History of Human Rights in Canada*, ed.

David Goutor and Stephen Heathorn (Toronto: Oxford University Press, 2013), 44.

19 Lambertson, "'The Dresden Story.'"

20 Walker, "The 'Jewish Phase,'" 15–16.

21 Ninette Kelley and Michael Trebilcock, *Making of the Mosaic: A History of Canadian Immigration Policy* (Toronto: University of Toronto Press, 1998), 152–53.

22 Donald Avery, *Reluctant Host: Canada's Response to Immigrant Workers, 1896–1994* (Toronto: McClelland and Stewart, 1995), 109–10; Kelley and Trebilcock, *Making of the Mosaic*, Chapters 5–8.

23 Barbara Roberts, *From Whence They Came: Deportation from Canada, 1900–1935* (Ottawa: University of Ottawa Press, 1988), Chapters 7 and 8.

24 Statistics Canada, "150 Years of Immigration in Canada," 29 June 2016, https://www150.statcan.gc.ca/n1/pub/11-630-x/11-630-x2016006-eng.htm.

25 Kelley and Trebilcock, *Making of the Mosaic*, 322.

26 *Proceedings of the Trades and Labor Congress* (henceforth *TLC Proceedings*), *1931*, 152–53, 158; and *Globe* [Toronto], 25 September 1931.

27 *TLC Proceedings, 1931*, 152–53.

28 See *Trades and Labor Congress Journal*, May 1932 and September 1933.

29 David Goutor, "Standing by Our Principles: The Trades and Labor Congress of Canada and Immigration, 1933–1939," *Just Labour: A Canadian Journal of Work and Society* 11 (2007): 55–65, http://www.justlabour.yorku.ca/volume11/pdfs/05_Goutor_Press.pdf.

30 Goutor, 58–59.

31 Irving Abella, *Nationalism, Communism and Canadian Labour* (Toronto: University of Toronto Press, 1973).

32 Nelson Lichtenstein, *State of the Union: A Century of American Labor* (Princeton, NJ: Princeton University Press, 2003), 54–97.

33 Bryan Palmer, *Working Class Experience: Rethinking the History of Canadian Labour* (Toronto: McClelland and Stewart, 1994), 285.

34 Eric Schickler, *Racial Realignment: The Transformation of American Liberalism* (Princeton, NJ: Princeton University Press, 2016), 58.

35 Bruce Nelson, *Divided We Stand: American Workers and the Struggle for Black Equality* (Princeton, NJ: Princeton University Press, 2002), xxxiii.

36 Schickler, *Racial Realignment*, 64; Nelson Lichtenstein, *A Contest of Ideas: Capital, Politics, and Labor* (Urbana: University of Illinois Press, 2013), 25.

37 Lichtenstein, *Contest of Ideas*, 19.

38 Nelson, *Divided We Stand*, xxxii.

39 Nelson Lichtenstein, *Walter Reuther: The Most Dangerous Man in Detroit* (Urbana: University of Illinois Press, 1995), 442; Nelson, *Divided We Stand*, xxxii–iii; Schickler, *Racial Realignment*, 59.

40 Wendy Cuthbertson, *Labour Goes to War: The CIO and the Construction of a New Social Order, 1939–45* (Vancouver: UBC Press), 88.

41 Cuthbertson, 90.

42 Cuthbertson, 87.
43 Lambertson, "'The Dresden Story,'" 48.
44 Lambertson.
45 Walker, "The 'Jewish Phase,'" 7.
46 Frager and Patrias, "'This Is Our Country,'" 12.
47 Lichtenstein, *State of the Union*, Chapter 3.
48 Ruth Frager and Carmela Patrias, "Transnational Links and Citizens' Rights: Canadian Jewish Human Rights Activists and Their American Allies in the 1940s and 1950s," in *Taking Liberties*, ed. David Goutor and Stephen Heathorn (Oxford: Oxford University Press, 2013), 154–56.
49 The war in Europe and the Allied "discovery" of the Holocaust were crucial in influencing this tone as well, as I discuss in the next section.
50 Frager and Patrias, "Transnational Links," 153.
51 Lambertson, "'The Dresden Story,'" 56; Sonya Kaufer (text) and Lee Levy (illustrations), *Discrimination Costs You Money*, International Union, United Automobile, Aircraft and Agricultural Implement Workers of America (UAW-CIO—Fair Practices and Anti-Discrimination Department), 1947, https://www.crmvet.org/docs/500000_uaw_discrim-r.pdf.
52 Cuthbertson, *Labour Goes to War*, 88.
53 Cuthbertson, 86.
54 Eric Arnesen, "The Specter of the Black Strikebreaker: Race, Employment and Activism in the Industrial Era," *Labor History* 44, no. 3 (2003): 319–35.
55 Schickler, *Racial Realignment*, 52–53.
56 David Roediger, *Working toward Whiteness: How America's Immigrants Became White* (New York: Basic Books, 2005), 211; Lichtenstein, *Walter Reuther*, 206–11.
57 Carmela Patrias, "Race, Employment Discrimination, and State Complicity in Wartime Canada, 1939–1945," *Labour/Le Travail* 59 (2007): 9–42.
58 Cuthbertson, *Labour Goes to War*, 87.
59 *Trades and Labor Congress Journal*, February 1947, 15.
60 Frager and Patrias, "Transnational Links," 151.
61 For examples of Kaplansky and the Jewish Labour Committee's rhetoric, see Walker, "The 'Jewish Phase,'" 7–8.
62 Cuthbertson, *Labour Goes to War*, 90.
63 Lambertson, "'The Dresden Story,'" 56; and Kaufer and Levy, *Discrimination Costs You Money*.
64 The neglect of the woman in the text is especially interesting since the pamphlet was written for the United Auto Workers by a woman, Sonya Kaufer. She was a human rights activist for several decades, mostly through the American Jewish Committee, and authored several other works on human rights. See Sonya Kaufer and Ethel Cohen Phillips, *You Hold the Key to Human Rights* (Cincinnati: Women's Division of Christian Service, Board of Missions and Church Extension, Methodist Church, 1953).
65 Kaufer and Levy, *Discrimination Costs You Money*, 2–3.

66 Kaufer and Levy, 13–14.
67 Kaufer and Levy, 19–24.
68 Editorial, *Trades and Labor Congress Journal*, September 1947, 11.
69 Walker, "Decoding the Rights Revolution," 42.
70 Ken Adachi, *The Enemy that Never Was* (Toronto: McClelland and Stewart, 1976); Patricia Roy, *The Oriental Question: Consolidating a White Man's Province, 1914–1941* (Vancouver: UBC Press, 2003).
71 Abella and Troper, *None Is Too Many*.
72 Franca Iacovetta, *Gatekeepers: The Politics of Citizenship in Cold War Canada* (Toronto: Between the Lines, 2006).
73 Ruth Roach Pierson, *They're Still Women after All: The Second World War and Canadian Womanhood* (Toronto: McClelland and Stewart, 1986).
74 David Goutor, "The Canadian Media and the 'Discovery' of the Holocaust," *Canadian Jewish Studies* 4–5 (1996–97): 87–116.
75 *Globe and Mail*, 17 September 1944.
76 Cuthbertson, *Labour Goes to War*, 109.
77 David Goutor, "Whose Fight for Freedom? Business and Labour's Nationalist Ideologies in World War II," paper presented at the Canadian Association for Work and Labour Studies Conference, 2015, 5–6.
78 Schickler, *Racial Realignment*, 59.
79 Cuthbertson, *Labour Goes to War*, 90.
80 Editorial, *Toronto Star*, 21 September 1944.
81 Goutor, "The Canadian Media," 108–11.
82 Jewish Labour Committee, "Report on Activities," 1947, Library and Archives Canada, Kalmen Kaplansky Fonds, MG30 A53, vol. 20.
83 Jewish Labour Committee.
84 Lambertson, "'The Dresden Story.'"
85 Roy, *A White Man's Province*, Chapters 5 and 6.
86 *BC Federationist*, 26 June 1914.
87 Palmer, *Working Class Experience*, 290–91; Desmond Morton, *Working People: An Illustrated History of the Canadian Labour Movement*, 5th ed. (Montreal and Kingston: McGill-Queen's University Press, 2007), 203–06.
88 Frager and Patrias, "'This Is Our Country,'" 8–10; Frager and Patrias, "Transnational Links," 148–49. There were indeed some fascist sympathizers in displaced persons' camps and some did come to Canada, but Communist propaganda was largely driven by hostility and distrust of anyone who did not want to return to Soviet-controlled territory.
89 Lichtenstein, *State of the Union*, 78.
90 Lambertson, "'The Dresden Story'"; Frager and Patrias, "'This Is Our Country'"; Stephanie Bangarth, "'Their Equality Is My Equality': F. Andrew Brewin and Human Rights Activism, 1940s–1970s," in *Taking Liberties*, ed. David Goutor and Stephen Heathorn (Oxford: Oxford University Press, 2013), 114–38.
91 Abella, *Nationalism*, 261; Morton, *Working People*, 198–203.

92 See, for example, Walter Young, *Anatomy of a Party: The National CCF, 1932–1960* (Toronto: University of Toronto Press, 1969), 102–25.

93 Goutor, *Guarding the Gates*, 115–44.

94 Frager and Patrias, "Transnational Links," 149–51.

95 Bangarth, "'We Are not Asking,'" 395.

96 David Goutor and Stephen Heathorn, "Introduction," in *Taking Liberties: A History of Human Rights in Canada*, ed. David Goutor and Stephen Heathorn (Oxford: Oxford University Press, 2013), 1.

97 See, for instance, Lichtenstein, *Contest of Ideas*, Chapters 8 and 9.

98 See, for instance, David Camfield, *Canadian Labour in Crisis—Reinventing the Workers' Movement* (Halifax: Fernwood Publishing, 2011).

CHAPTER 10

Universal Rights in Local Contexts: Postwar Human Rights Debates in Quebec (1940s–60s)

Paul-Etienne Rainville

ON 4 FEBRUARY 1963, a delegation representing thirty-nine Quebec civil society organizations appeared before the Quebec government to demand the adoption of laws prohibiting discrimination "based on race, nationality, religion or colour." Invoking the principles enshrined in the United Nations' 1948 Universal Declaration of Human Rights, these groups were calling for a fair employment practice law, together with a law prohibiting discrimination in public places (i.e., places where the public is generally admitted) as well as in housing.[1] Initiated by the Montreal Labour Committee for Human Rights, this delegation, which claimed to represent several hundred thousand citizens, was described at the time as "one of the largest and most widely representative delegations seen in the Provincial Legislature in recent years."[2] This was unprecedented in the history of Quebec: in addition to bringing together international and national unions, Protestant and Catholic organizations, associations of young anglophones and francophones, and a feminist group, it was composed, for the first time, of representatives of the Jewish, Italian, and Black communities. This coalition, made up of some of the most influential non-governmental organizations in the province, embodied not only the extent but also the limit of the social consensus in favour of human rights that was consolidated in Quebec in the postwar years.

In this chapter, I explore the genesis of this social movement by focusing on the group at the origin of this coalition: the Montreal Labour Committee for Human Rights (Comité ouvrier des droits de l'homme de Montréal), an inter-union committee formed in 1947 under the name of Montreal Labour Committee against Racial Intolerance (Comité du travail contre l'intolérance raciale). I analyze more broadly the discourses, strategies, demands, and networks of the activists involved in the "human rights committees" set up after the war by the provincial federations and the Montreal district councils of the "international unions" (affiliated with the American Federation of Labor [(AFL)] and the Congress of Industrial Organizations [CIO]) in Quebec. I pay particular attention to activists involved in industrial unions, which organized unskilled workers on the basis of their industry affiliation, as opposed to craft unions, and which were affiliated nationally, provincially, and locally respectively with the Canadian Congress of Labour (CCL), the Quebec Federation of Industrial Unions (Fédération des unions industrielles du Québec—FUIQ), and the Montreal Labour Council (Conseil du travail de Montréal).[3] By observing how these activists mobilized the paradigm of universal rights in their local struggles for the right to racial and religious equality, I shed light on some of the specificities of the debates on the recognition of these rights in the radically unique context of Quebec during the transition from the so-called Grande noirceur (Great Darkness) (1944–59) to the Révolution tranquille (Quiet Revolution) of the 1960s. In doing so, I demonstrate that Quebec, contrary to what some researchers have claimed, did not remain outside or at the margin of the international and Canadian postwar human rights movements, while highlighting specific elements of the province's local context that have received little attention so far from human rights historians in Canada.[4]

This case study sheds light on the transplantation, translation, and vernacularization of the universalist idiom of human rights, meaning the forms of appropriation, mobilization, adaptation, and redefinition of the discourse and norms of international human rights law by actors evolving in specific social, cultural, political, and legal contexts. Anthropologist Sally Merry indeed recalls that, if these rights find their most complete formulation in international law, then "human rights retain their fundamental meanings even as they become resources in local struggles."[5] I support Bonny Ibhahow's argument that the study of the human rights movement must consider "the multiple genealogies and the great variety of rights vernaculars that have shaped and continue to define modern human rights."[6] Building upon the theoretical approaches of the discursive, deliberative, and protest schools, my analysis finally focuses on the power relations that explain the discrepancies between, on the one hand, the affirmation on a global scale of legal and moral universalist standards and, on the other, their concrete implementation within the framework of militant action at the local level.[7] This critical approach is particularly relevant for studying a multicultural, plurinational society based on settler colonialism such as Quebec, where debates on human rights historically have been intertwined with complex identity issues related to language, religion, federalism, nation, and the collective rights of French Canadians.

The transnational character of the campaign led by the human rights committees of international trade unions, in Canada and the United States, reveals, with particular insight, the local factors that have influenced the debates on the recognition of these rights in the context of Quebec. At the end of the Second World War, these debates were first marked by the presence of the premier, Maurice Duplessis, as the head of a majority government from 1944 to his death in 1959. Conservative, autonomist, anti-unionist, anti-interventionist, closely tied to the Catholic hierarchy, and hostile to human rights, Duplessis embodied the main forces opposing the recognition of these rights in Quebec. These debates were also structured by the determining influence of the Catholic Church and culture, which appears—not without paradoxes—as both an obstacle to and a catalyst for the spread of human rights ideals in this province. Whereas many conservative Catholics considered human rights as a liberal, atheistic, individualistic, and materialistic ideal, other social, liberal, or progressive Catholics militated for a

Christian conception of these rights, based on the teachings of the Social Doctrine of the Church, the writings of personalist thinkers, and the precepts of Christian humanism.[8]

The linguistic, religious, and constitutional issues associated with the national question also structured postwar debates on racial and religious discrimination. Constantly articulated around issues related to the collective rights (linguistic, cultural, and constitutional) of French Canadians, these debates largely obscured the reality of systemic racism and its consequences for racialized people and communities in Quebec. Finally, the trajectories of the activists whom I follow demonstrate the persistent influence of the combined legacies of French, English, and then Canadian and Quebec colonialisms, which translated, among other things, into a denial of domestic colonialism (or "colonial agnosia"),[9] the marginalization of Indigenous rights issues, and the silencing of Indigenous voices and their demands for rights.

Particularly noticeable in debates on racism, discrimination, and minority rights, these local factors shed light on several ideological, regional, cultural, linguistic, ethnic, and national fault lines that shaped the evolution of the human rights movement in Canada in the postwar period and, to some extent, up to today.

International Unions and Human Rights in Quebec

Explicitly stated in the rallying speeches of the Allies during the war and in the global reconstruction project implemented by the United Nations, the human rights paradigm stood as a discursive and normative framework of first importance for actors from various sectors of Quebec society engaged in debates on the establishment of lasting peace and the reconstruction of a new world order. In the decade following the end of the Second World War, individuals and groups from different backgrounds embraced the principles enshrined in the Universal Declaration of Human Rights to give to their claims a seal of universality.[10] The anti-discrimination campaign initiated by activists from international unions is part of this context of growing mobilization of the discourse and norms of international human rights law in postwar Quebec. Like most of the actors who claimed to adhere to this legal-moral ideal, these activists situated their local struggle within the framework of a global movement for the defence of universal norms, although their discourses, demands, strategies, and networks remained largely dependent on their identities, interests, and confrontations with the local contexts in which they evolved.

From the creation of the Canadian Congress of Labour in 1940, its president, Aaron Mosher, affirmed—despite the sometimes contradictory attitudes of its members and affiliated unions—the doctrinal opposition of industrial unions to any form of racial or religious discrimination.[11] However, it was not until the end of the Second World War that the congress and its federations and local councils set up a sustained campaign to fight discrimination. This paradigm shift occurred in the context of the growing involvement of trade union leaders in Canada's first human rights campaign, which is analyzed in depth in David Goutor's chapter in this volume. As several historians have shown, these first commitments were largely the fruit of the lobbying and networking efforts of members of ethnic and racialized communities, especially those of some leaders of the Jewish community, including Kalmen Kaplansky, the national director of the Jewish Labour Committee of Canada.[12] Winning support from the senior leaders of the federations and councils of international unions in Canada, Kaplansky succeeded in convincing the national executives of the Canadian Congress of Labour and the Trades and Labor Congress of Canada (TLCC) to set up national committees to fight against racial and religious discrimination.[13] Beginning in January 1947, inter-union committees (CCL-TLCC) were also created in Winnipeg, Toronto, and Montreal, then in Windsor, Halifax, and Vancouver, on the model of the joint AFL-CIO committees formed in the United States.[14] In Quebec, human rights committees were also set up by the two provincial federations of international unions, the FUIQ and the Provincial Federation of Labor of Quebec (Fédération provinciale du travail du Québec—FPTQ), then by the Quebec Federation of Labour (Fédération des travailleurs du Québec—FTQ) when they merged in 1957.[15]

The Montreal Labour Committee against Racial Intolerance (Comité du travail contre l'intolérance raciale—renamed the Montreal Labour Committee for Human Rights or Comité ouvrier des droits de l'homme de Montréal in 1957) was set up during an imposing conference at the Mont-Royal Hotel on 12 May 1947. Bringing together more than 200 guests and delegates, it was described as "one of the most successful trade-union conferences ever held in Montreal."[16] At the time of its creation, the Montreal committee was made up of the leaders of the Jewish Labour Committee, including Kalmen Kaplansky, Michael Rubinstein, its president, Maurice Silcoff, its vice-president, and Bernard Shane, its treasurer. From its earliest years, the committee also attracted several francophones, including its co-presidents, Romuald Lamoureux (CCL) and Claude Jodoin (TLCC), as well as Paul Pichette (TLCC), Hector Marchand (TLCC), Léo M. Côté (TLCC), Roger Provost (TLCC), Jacques Victor Morin (CCL), Philippe Vaillancourt (CCL), Gérard Rancourt (CCL), Huguette Plamondon (CCL), Fernand Daoust (CCL), and Louis Laberge (CCL). These well-known personalities of the labour movement in Quebec then occupied influential positions as presidents, vice-presidents, or secretaries of federations (national and provincial) as well as district councils of international unions in Montreal.

Although its mandate was to fight against racial intolerance, the committee was composed almost exclusively of non-racialized people. It did not include any Indigenous people and had no ties with First Nations representatives. Apart from a workshop organized at the Chinese Catholic Mission of the Holy Spirit in 1949, the committee did not establish any relationship with members of Asian communities.[17] It was also not until the mid-1950s that union activists from Montreal's Black communities, Earl Swift and Arthur R. Blanchette, became involved—if sporadically—in its activities.[18]

The "Problems" of Quebec

The anti-discrimination campaign orchestrated by the activists of the Montreal committee—also members of the provincial human rights committees of the FUIQ and FPTQ—differed significantly from those of their counterparts in other provinces. In the early years in particular, their work was deeply influenced by what some called the "problems" of Quebec.[19] These problems concerned first and foremost the conflictual relations between representatives of international unions—especially industrial unions—and Maurice Duplessis, who headed a majority government from 1944 to his death in 1959.

As early as the late 1940s, the councils and federations of international unions in Quebec included in their annual memorandums to the provincial government demands for anti-discrimination laws and a provincial charter of rights.[20] These requests emanated from the resolutions presented by the influential members of the human rights committees and adopted unanimously during their annual conventions.[21] Throughout his four terms, Premier Duplessis adamantly refused to legislate in a matter, in his view, of individual moral conscience, not of the coercive power of the law and the state.[22] Described as "enemy no. 1 of the workers"[23] by the leaders of the Quebec Federation of Industrial Unions (FUIQ), Duplessis appeared to be the main obstacle to the recognition of the principles of international human rights norms in the domestic laws of Quebec. Following the February 1950 hearing with CCL representatives, he declared that a charter of rights was nothing more than "big words without meaning." He also reiterated an idea that he had previously stated: the "Rights of Man" were emphasized in the Gospel, the most perfect of all charters.[24] In several statements, Duplessis also pointed to Quebec as the place where minorities were best protected, comparing the treatment of Jewish and English-speaking minorities with that of French-speaking minorities in the rest of Canada.[25] His views represented more broadly the doctrinal opposition of several conservative Catholics, for whom human rights were a notion inherited from the French Revolution of 1789, which sacrificed the fundamental values of Catholicism on the altar of secularism, materialism, freedom, and individualism.[26]

This political deadlock, combined with the state of civil law jurisprudence on discrimination,[27] forced human rights committees in Quebec to turn to extrajudicial and parapolitical strategies based on awareness raising, popular education, moral persuasion, and the creation of networks and alliances.[28] However, this crucial aspect of their campaign was also marked by the problems of Quebec mentioned above. These problems concerned two other related issues: the adaptation of their work to the bilingual and predominantly French-speaking reality of Quebec and the anchoring of their fight against discrimination in debates about federalism, the national question, and respect for the cultural, linguistic, and constitutional rights of French Canadians.[29]

The language issue first appeared as a strictly material obstacle in the context of a transnational campaign conducted in English. The need to translate all material produced for English Canada or imported from the United States appeared at first glance to be an "enormous difficulty."[30] Until the early 1950s, for example, the journal published in French by the labour committees for human rights in Canada, *Rapports ouvriers canadiens* (*ROC—Canadian Labor Reports*), was only a compilation of imperfect translations of articles from the English editions of *Labor Reports* (United States) and *Canadian Labor Reports* (Canada).[31] This challenge of translation affected, in fact, all the public awareness and education materials (films, pamphlets, posters, drawings, etc.) produced in English for Canada or imported from the United States through the networks of international unions, the Jewish Labour Committee, and other Jewish organizations, notably based in Montreal.[32]

The issue of translation concerned not only language but also the adaptation of their campaign to the demographic, sociological, and cultural reality of Quebec. Until the early 1950s, the material translated into French by the CCL and TLCC human rights committees conveyed a discourse with a profoundly "Canadianist" and multiculturalist tone, which subsumed the issues related to the national question and the collective rights of French Canadians under the general issue of "minority rights." This view was part of the postwar debates on the construction of a Canadian citizenship distinct from the British imperial identity as well as the Canadianist movement for the development of civic belonging based on the sharing of national values and institutions that transcended subnational, ethnic, religious, cultural, linguistic, and provincial identities.[33]

The first press release published in French by the Montreal committee thus described Quebec as "the home of several religions and nationalities living in harmony."[34] Its first French leaflet, entitled *Vous appartenez à une minorité!* (You Belong to a Minority!), also insisted on the need to cultivate a sense of common belonging that transcended minority identities, emphasizing that French Canadians constituted a minority, among others, within the Canadian whole.[35] This idea found its most complete expression in an article entitled "La patrie des 'minorités,'" published by the committee and disseminated in several trade union newspapers in the province in 1953. Based on data from the 1951 census, this article was intended to remind Canadians in general, and French Canadians in particular, that, "although all groups are minorities, they all belong to one huge group—that all of their members are Canadians."[36]

Fundamentally colonialist in its denial of the anteriority of Indigenous presence and the valorization of settler colonialism, this discourse was also at odds with the bicultural (or even "biracial") conception of the Canadian nation held by a large segment of the French Canadian population and intelligentsia in the postwar period.[37] This division is all the more important in the context of the debates on racism in Quebec then marked by recurring conflicts between English Canadians—who often accused French Canadians of racism, intolerance, isolationism, and xenophobia—and French Canadians—who denounced the intolerance, racism, prejudice, and even imperialism of English Canadians (Protestants) toward francophones in Quebec and Franco-Catholic minorities in the rest of Canada.[38]

These ethnic divisions partly explain not only the scope but also the limit of the first alliances of labour human rights committees in Quebec. In the early years, their members were part of pan-Canadian networks made up of a nebula of private, public, or parapublic organizations whose objective was to promote Canadian unity. By co-opting its representatives into their decision-making bodies and establishing contacts with their leaders, notably they developed sustained ties with national and provincial sections of the Canadian Broadcasting Corporation, the National Film Board, the Citizenship Branch of the Secretary of State, the Canadian Citizenship Council, and the Canadian Association for Adult Education. Many of these groups, which historian Ryan Edwardson has called "nation builders" and "Canadianizers," had a mandate to strengthen Canadian unity through their work in the areas of immigrant integration, intercultural dialogue, and civic and popular education.[39] However, at the end of the war, these organizations encountered significant difficulties in penetrating French-speaking circles. In addition to the mistrust that arose regarding their federalist agenda, these groups (and their branches in Quebec) were often made up of a majority of English speakers.[40] Francophone allies of the Montreal committee thus complained about the "one-way bilingualism" that prevailed in these pan-Canadian organizations by which documents were rarely translated into French and francophones were often misunderstood when they expressed themselves in their mother tongue.[41]

It was not until the early 1950s that the labour human rights committees consolidated their support within French-speaking circles, thanks to the extensive networking undertaken by the successive secretaries of the Montreal committee with actors from the leftist, liberal, and progressive Catholic circles. As early as 1948, Secretary Roméo Girard made his first contacts with the national secretary of the French section of Catholic Action in Canada (Action catholique canadienne), Claude Ryan, founder of the Committee for Cultural Relations in Canada,[42] who regularly invited his committee to conduct educational and awareness-raising activities with young people from Catholic action movements across the province.[43]

The Montreal committee also established more sustained links with the Canadian and Catholic Confederation of Labour (CCCL), in the context of the first inter-union alliances against the repressive and anti-union policies of the Duplessis government. The committee's second secretary, Jacques-Victor Morin, undertook a close correspondence with the CCCL's main leaders, including Director of Education Fernand Jolicoeur, Secretary Jean Marchand, and President Gérard Picard. Thanks to his friendship with Jolicoeur, Morin organized conferences, educational activities, and film screenings in

CCCL-affiliated unions. He was also invited to present his committee and his material during the annual conventions of the organization.[44]

A former student of the Faculty of Social Sciences of the Université de Montréal, Morin also organized several popular and workers' educational activities within this Catholic educational institution, thanks in particular to the assistance of his friend Guy Beaugrand-Champagne, responsible for the Education Extension Service.[45] It was also under Morin's tenure as secretary that the committee established its first official partnerships with the Centre de recherches en relations humaines (Human Relations Research Centre), whose work, directed by Dominican Father Bernard Mailhiot, focused on psychocultural determinants of interethnic relations.[46] Since the founding of this centre in 1952, its members had sponsored and participated in the organization of the "conferences on human relations" organized each year by the committee in Montreal.[47] Just like Mailhiot, the founder of the Quebec section of the Canadian Council of Christians and Jews (1954), Jesuit Father Stéphane Valiquette, was one of the individuals most often invited to speak on the public activities of the committee.[48] In a context in which the fight against racism was largely thought of in terms of education for tolerance, Valiquette was called on to discuss the education of children against prejudice, ecumenical dialogue between Jews and Christians, and Christian foundations of the fight against racial and religious discrimination.[49]

The expansion of the Montreal committee's networks with French-speaking and Catholic groups was favoured during the 1950s by the growing adherence of several Catholic activists and intellectuals to personalism and by the creation of organizations, made up of clerics or laypeople, involved in intercultural relations, ecumenical dialogue, integration of immigrants, and promotion of "droits de la personne humaine" or rights of the human person.[50] That expansion was also favoured, as we will see, by the growing involvement of this committee in the promotion of the linguistic, cultural, and constitutional rights of French Canadians.

Race, Language, Religion, and the National Question

Active in the first pan-Canadian networks of human rights activists, the members of the labour rights committees in Quebec were also strongly influenced by the province's unique context and the specific conceptualization of the debates on racism that prevailed in the postwar period. Researchers such as David Austin, Sean Mills, and Corrie Scott have shown that representations associated with race in Quebec have been intertwined historically with discourses on the preservation of the French language and the Catholic religion as the basis for the survival of the French Canadian "race."[51] In the 1940s and 1950s, debates about racial discrimination continued to be structured around these enduring representations, which masked systemic inequalities based on racism and perpetuated what historian Constance Backhouse has called, in the Canadian case, a "mythology of racelessness."[52]

Thus, in the summer of 1946, as part of a visit to the offices of the Jewish Labour Committee in New York, Montrealers Claude Jodoin and Kalmen Kaplansky came to the conclusion that the posters, leaflets, caricatures, comic books, and films used by their counterparts in the United States did not fit well within the Canadian context and Quebec in particular. In addition to promoting the American way of life, they pointed out, the material essentially discussed the Black "problem," which in their view was not the fundamental issue of interethnic relations north of the forty-ninth parallel.[53] For many Jewish human rights activists at the time, the reality of racism in Quebec was strongly conceived through their own experience of social and doctrinal anti-Semitism that prevailed there, especially since the 1930s, as their community (non-Catholic and mainly non-francophone) appeared to be the main ethnic, religious, and racial figure of alterity.[54] This partly explains why the educational and awareness material translated into French, whether produced in Canada or imported from the United States, generally represented only non-racialized people. This was the case for leaflets, posters, cartoons, and films and documentaries used on a large scale by the committee in its popular and workers' educational activities.[55]

Figure 10.1. *Rapports Ouvriers Canadiens* 2, no. 9, September 1947, 8. Courtesy of Canadian Labour Congress.

Figure 10.2. *Rapports Ouvriers Canadiens* 3, no. 8, August 1948, 8. Courtesy of Canadian Labour Congress.

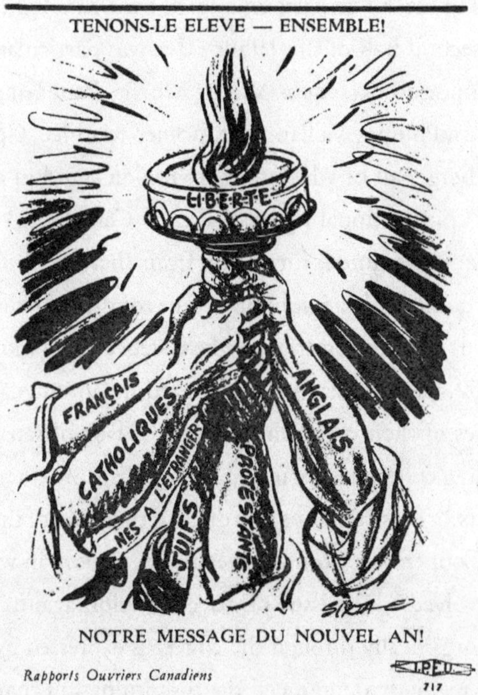

Figure 10.3. *Rapports Ouvriers Canadiens* 7, no. 12, December 1952, 8. Courtesy of Canadian Labour Congress.

This partial rendering of the invisibility of race was also fuelled by a widespread discourse in Quebec that French Canadians were among the main victims of racism, colonialism, intolerance, and discrimination in Canada. The image of the conquered or oppressed French Canadian (from which emerged that of the "colonized Quebecer" in the early 1960s)[56] increasingly occupied several French-speaking and bilingual members of the labour human rights committees, among whom there was a significant shift toward a discourse centred on the defence of biculturalism (and the colonial myth of "two founding peoples") and the collective rights of French Canadians. This intertwining of the fight for human rights and the rights of the French-speaking majority in Quebec manifested itself mainly in the field of discrimination in employment.

The paths of several activists embodied this "paradigm shift," consolidated in the second half of the 1950s. This was particularly the case for Huguette Plamondon, Jacques-Victor Morin, Paul King, Jean Philip, Fernand Daoust, Philippe Vaillancourt, Roméo Mathieu, Gérard Rancourt, and Louis Laberge, all of whom openly took a stand in defence of the linguistic and constitutional rights of French Canadians.[57] Their involvement in this area stemmed, for many, from their personal experiences within the predominantly anglophone bodies of the Canadian Congress of Labour. Indeed, since the creation of the Quebec Federation of Industrial Unions in 1952, its members had denounced the unilingual nature of the national bodies of their organization and the lack of sensitivity of their English-speaking colleagues regarding bilingualism and French Canadians' collective rights.[58] These tensions also divided the ranks of the federal socialist party, the Cooperative Commonwealth Federation, in which several of them were involved.[59] The issue of discrimination against francophones also emerged organically through the concerns expressed by rank-and-file workers, who regularly denounced the discrimination that they faced in industries that employed only English-speaking foremen.[60]

Beginning in the mid-1950s, the Montreal committee took an active part in the campaign to combat discrimination against francophones in employment. The two primary actions of its members in this area concerned the case of French-speaking nurses who were victims of discrimination in 1954 at the Queen Mary Veterans' Hospital in Montreal (under the authority of the Department of Veterans Affairs) and that of the Canadian mining company Iron Ore, which imposed in 1957 the exclusive use of English on employees working on its rail network in northern Quebec. Calling for the establishment of a royal inquiry on bilingualism in the federal service and Armed Forces,[61] committee members denounced the nurses' case as a matter of "racial intolerance," explicitly linking discrimination based on language and "race."[62] In the case of Iron Ore, they again intervened with the federal government, emphasizing "that such a policy is completely contrary to the bicultural character of this province and of Canada, as well as to all the principles which must govern the fair employment practices."[63]

These interventions were the first actions of the committee to be reported on the front pages of French-language newspapers in the province.[64] To publicize their anti-discrimination campaign, they also promoted closer ties between the committee and certain members of the nationalist intelligentsia, notably from the newspaper *Le Devoir* and the magazine *L'Action nationale*.[65] This media coverage encouraged the Montreal committee members to put the issue of bilingualism at the heart of their educational, networking, and political lobbying activities. In 1955 and 1958, for instance, they devoted their annual conferences on human relations to two themes that they considered to be closely related: bilingualism and racial discrimination.[66] At the conference in 1955, a session dealt explicitly for the first time with anti-Black racism through a discussion on the documentary *The Dresden Story*.[67] However, the issues related to the discrimination of francophones monopolized the bulk of conversation and media coverage. Denouncing the economic inferiority of French Canadians, the speakers pointed out that their "inferiority complex" and their "minority psychology" constituted obstacles to the establishment of harmonious relations among ethnocultural groups in Canada.[68] They also called on French Canadians to campaign more ardently for the respect of bilingualism in order to get rid of their victimhood reflexes and to engage more actively in the fight against racism and discrimination.[69]

At the turn of 1958 to 1959 and into the 1960s, members of the Montreal and provincial committees managed to put the issue of "economic discrimination" of French Canadians on the agenda of the national human rights committee of the Canadian Labour Congress.[70] In their annual briefs to the provincial government, representatives of the international unions also continued to call for laws to prohibit racial and religious discrimination while emphasizing that, "if we want French Canadians to defend the principles of tolerance and practice tolerance, they themselves must first be treated without prejudice."[71]

Human Rights and the Quiet Revolution

The brief presented to the Liberal provincial government of Jean Lesage by the coalition formed by the Montreal Labour Committee for Human Rights, in February 1963, bore witness to the growing connection between debates on the nation, language, and human rights, at the onset of the Quiet Revolution in Quebec in the 1960s. Presented by Gérard Rancourt of the Montreal committee, Roger Provost of the Quebec Federation of Labour, Louis Laberge of the Montreal Labour Council, and Jean Marchand of the Confederation of National Trade Unions (Conféderation des syndicats nationaux), the brief endorsed by thirty-nine civil society organizations referred extensively to the principles of international human rights law while situating their campaign in the unique context of early-1960s Quebec.

Faced with Lesage, the delegation insisted that the adoption of anti-discrimination laws seemed to be particularly relevant in a context in which French Canadians were campaigning to be recognized as equal partners in the Canadian federation.[72] The spokespersons also argued that the protection of universal rights was an extension of the struggles waged for centuries to defend the particular rights of French Canadians. Seeking to exonerate the latter from the traditional accusations of racism and xenophobia, they claimed that a tradition of tolerance existed in Quebec and that French Canadians, as a minority in North America, should be more sensitive to the protection of minority rights. The pressure exerted by the members of this coalition convinced Lesage and his government to adopt the first two anti-discrimination laws in the history of Quebec, which prohibited racial and religious discrimination in hotels and restaurants (1963) and in employment (1964).[73]

The scope and representativeness of this delegation, as well as the content of their brief, highlight both the advances and the limits of the social human rights movement consolidated in Quebec in the postwar period. Indeed, the concept of human rights referred to at the time remained essentially confined to civil liberties and the formal right to racial and religious equality. Although it was based on the text of the 1948 Universal Declaration of Human Rights, the brief said nothing about economic, social, and cultural rights. Its silence on discrimination linked to sex and gender also testifies to the fact that the rights of *man* continued to be thought of in terms of this generic marker, considered at best as universalist, at worst as exclusively male. It is more generally reflective of the broader exclusion of women's rights from human rights debates in Canada during this period, as highlighted in Ruth Frager's chapter in this volume.[74] Distinctions based on age, sexual orientation, social condition, disability, and other grounds were also excluded from the discriminatory criteria that the requested laws sought to combat.

What this coalition asked for, in short, was the recognition of formal equality for members of ethnic, religious, and racial minorities.[75] Thus, during the presentation of their brief and their subsequent interviews, the spokespersons never discussed systemic racism or colonialism while seeking to exonerate French Canadians of any accusation of intolerance.[76] Based on the abstract ideals of freedom, fraternity, tolerance, equal opportunity, and universality of rights, their arguments mentioned neither the structural foundations of systemic discrimination experienced by racialized people in Quebec nor the history and persistence of racist patterns inherited from slavery and its "afterlives."[77] The silence on Indigenous Peoples also contrasted with their status as second-class citizens in Quebec and Canada and with the rise in protests brought about by the Red Power movements in Canada and the United States beginning in the 1960s.[78]

The intertwining of the struggles for human rights and the collective rights of French Canadians was consolidated in this period, marked by the rise of nationalist movements in which several activists from the labour human rights committees played leading roles.[79] Characterized by a reappropriation, by white nationalist Quebecers, of postcolonial theories and, for some, of the discourse of *négritude blanche*, this period saw the reconstruction on new bases, and the perpetuation of enduring representations, of race, language, and nation partly at the source of the denial of systemic racism and domestic colonialism in Quebec. As in the postwar period, these systems of oppression, the existence of which many continue to deny in Quebec, perpetuate exclusions while contributing to fix the external boundaries of the human rights movement. As jurist Shelley Wright rightly points out, "too often . . . human rights discourse is constrained by boundaries which make the rights of the vast majority of human beings seem marginal, 'alternative' or irrelevant."[80]

Notes

1 Service des archives et de gestion des documents—UQAM (hereafter AUQAM), 100 P Fonds FTQ, 660:01/26, CODH, "Mémoire présenté au gouvernement provincial du Québec en la ville de Québec ce 4 février 1963."

2 Robert McKenzie, "Representation on Discrimination Draws 'Study' Pledge from Lesage," *Gazette* [Montreal], 5 February 1963, 1; Brief submitted "Mémoire présenté au gouvernement provincial du Québec en la ville de Québec ce 4 février 1963," 1.

3 Most often composed of unskilled, mobile, ethnically diverse, or immigrant workers, industrial unions were involved earlier in the fight against discrimination. Herbert Hill, *Black Labor and the American Legal System: Race, Work, and the Law* (Madison: University of Wisconsin Press, 1977), 22–23; Ross Lambertson, "'The Dresden Story': Racism, Human Rights, and the Jewish Labour Committee of Canada," *Labour/Le Travail* 47 (2001): 48.

4 Ross Lambertson, *Repression and Resistance: Canadian Human Rights Activists, 1930–1960* (Toronto: University of Toronto Press, 2005); Christopher MacLennan, *Toward the Charter: Canadians and the Demand for a National Bill of Rights, 1929–1960* (Montreal and Kingston: McGill-Queen's University Press, 2003).

5 Sally Merry, "Legal Transplants and Cultural Translation: Making Human Rights in the Vernacular," in *Human Rights: An Anthropological Reader*, ed. Mark Goodale (Malden, MA: Wiley-Blackwell, 2009), 268.

6 Bonny Ibhahow, *Human Rights in Africa* (New York: Cambridge University Press, 2018), 12.

7 Marie-Bénédicte Dembour, "What Are Human Rights? Four Schools of Thought," *Human Rights Quarterly* 32, no. 1 (2010): 1–20.

8 On these contradictory influences, see Xavier Gélinas, *La droite intellectuelle québécoise et la Révolution tranquille* (Québec: Presses de l'Université Laval, 2007), 286; and E.-Martin Meunier and Jean-Philippe Warren, *Sortir de la "grande noirceur": L'horizon "personnaliste" de la Révolution tranquille* (Sillery, QC: Septentrion, 2002), 207.

9 Catherine Larochelle, quoted in Kathleen Villeneuve, "Retour sur l'atelier 'Le colonialisme d'implantation au Québec: Un impensé de la recherche universitaire?' (25–26 November 2021)," *Histoire engagée*, 15 March 2022, https://histoireengagee.ca/retour-sur-latelier-le-colonialisme-dimplantation-au-quebec-un-impense-de-la-recherche-25-26-novembre-20211/.

10 For an analysis of the human rights movement in Quebec, from the 1940s to the 1960s, see Paul-Etienne Rainville, "De l'universel au particulier: Les luttes en faveur des droits humains au Québec, de l'après-guerre à la Révolution tranquille" (PhD diss., Université du Québec à Trois-Rivières, 2018), 596.

11 Aaron Mosher, "En garde! La haine raciale et religieuse tend à détruire l'unionisme ouvrier!," *ROC*, n.d. [1948], 4.

12 Carmela Patrias and Ruth A. Frager, "'This Is Our Country, These Are Our Rights': Minorities and the Origins of Ontario's Human Rights Campaigns," *Canadian Historical Review* 82, no. 1 (2001): 1–35; James W.St.G. Walker, "The 'Jewish Phase' in the Movement for Racial Equality in Canada," *Canadian Ethnic Studies* 34, no. 1 (2002): 1–29; Lambertson, "'The Dresden Story,'" 43–82.

13 To do this, he obtained financial support from the Canadian Jewish Congress and the B'nai Brith Anti-Defamation League. See Lambertson, "'The Dresden Story.'"

14 Library and Archives Canada (hereafter LAC), Jewish Labour Committee Fonds (hereafter JLCC), MG28 V75 29 1, Kalmen Kaplansky, "Activities in the United States and Recommendations for Work in Canada," 23 August 1946.

15 "Exposé du Programme syndical d'anti-discrimination et des droits de l'homme," *ROC*, November–December 1960, 2–3.

16 LAC, JLCC Fonds, MG28 V75 34 1, "Rapport de la conférence ouvrière pour combattre l'intolérance raciale et religieuse," 12 May 1947, 1; ZA 1947 11/127A, Kalmen Kaplansky, "Report of Activities for Improved Human Relations of the Jewish Labour Committee of Canada for the Year Ending July 31st, 1947," 12.

17 LAC, JLCC Fonds, MG28 V75 34 4, Comité du travail contre l'intolérance racial (CTCIR) activity report, June 1949.

18 A member of the CCL national human rights committee beginning in 1955, Blanchette was one of those who led the complaints of Black workers in the railway industry in Montreal. Involved in the FUIQ education committee, Earl Swift was also active in the FTQ human rights committee starting in 1957.

19 LAC, JLCC Fonds, MG28 V75 34 3, National Committee for Racial Tolerance, "Report of the National Committee for Racial Tolerance, Presented to the Eighth Annual Convention, Canadian Congress of Labour," Toronto, 11 October 1948.

20 See the memorandums of the CCL and FUIQ for the years 1948 to 1956, AUQAM, 85 P Fonds de la FUIQ, 660/6; 660/10,800: 02/51 and 640/28. For the FTQ, see AUQAM, 100 P Fonds FTQ, 660:01/11–12 and 13.

21 For the FUIQ and FTQ, see the series AUQAM, 85 P Fonds de la FUIQ, 160/1 and 640/13; 100 P FTQ Fonds, 640/45; 660:01/11 and 660:01/13; LAC /Archives nationales du Canada (ANC), JLCC Fonds, MG28 V75 34 16.

22 See, especially, "Les droits de l'homme dans la prov. de Québec," *Le Devoir*, 13 December 1948, 10; and "La dévotion à Marie est notre meilleure richesse," *La Presse*, 16 July 1951, 13.

23 "Duplessis rejette le mémoire du CCT," *Les nouvelles ouvrières*, February 1950, 1, 4.

24 "Des premiers ministres refusent des droits aux minorités," *ROC*, February 1950, 5.

25 LAC, JLCC Fonds, MG28 V75 34 7, Lettre de l'Hon. Maurice Duplessis à Claude Jodoin, 16 janvier 1952; "Une autre preuve de notre largeur de vues," *La Presse*, 24 October 1951, 20.

26 Gélinas, *La droite intellectuelle*, 198–99.

27 The jurisprudence affirmed the superiority of freedom of trade and enterprise over the right of individuals not to be victims of discrimination. Constance Backhouse, *De la couleur des lois: Une histoire juridique du racisme au Canada entre 1900 et 1950* (Ottawa: Presses de l'Université d'Ottawa, 2010), 327–31.

28 However, they could rely on the Canada Fair Employment Practices Act of 1953, which prohibited discrimination in Quebec companies operating in sectors under federal jurisdiction. LAC, JLCC Fonds, MG28 V75 35 3, Frank Hall, Chairman of the Human Rights Committee of the Canadian Labour Congress, "Juste méthodes d'emploi: Un bon commencement," n.d.

29 LAC, JLCC Fonds, MG28 V75 34 9, "Report by Mr. Bernard Shane to Meeting of January 11, 1953."

30 LAC, JLCC Fonds, MG28 V75 34 2, CTCIR, activity report to national staff conference, 17 January 1948.

31 Jacques-Victor Morin took over this newspaper in 1951. About 500 copies were published during the first years, and the circulation of the French-language edition increased to 1,100 copies in 1953.

32 On these transnational networks, see Ruth A. Frager and Carmela Patrias, "Transnational Links and Citizens' Rights: Canadian Jewish Human Rights Activists and Their American Allies in the 1940s and 1950s," in *Taking Liberties: A History of Human Rights in Canada*, ed. David Goutor and Stephen Heathorn (Toronto: Oxford University Press, 2013), 139–65.

33 Janine Brodie, "Three Stories of Canadian Citizenship," in *Contesting Canadian Citizenship: Historical Readings*, ed. Dorothy E. Chunn, Robert Adamoski, and Robert Menzies (Peterborough: Broadview Press, 2002), 43–66.

34 LAC, JLCC Fonds, MG28 V75 34 2, "Le mouvement ouvrier unit les citoyens de Québec," 1948 (translated from French).

35 LAC, JLCC Fonds, MG28 V75 34 3, "Vous appartenez à une minorité!," *ROC*, n.d., 1.

36 *ROC*, "La patrie des 'minorités,'" *Les nouvelles ouvrières*, September 1953, 3.

37 Valerie Lapointe-Gagnon, "Les origines intellectuelles de la commission Laurendeau-Dunton: De la présence d'une volonté de dialogue entre les deux peuples fondateurs du Canada au lendemain de la Seconde guerre mondiale, 1945–1965," *Mens* 14–15, nos. 1–2 (2014): 131–73.

38 These tensions divided Catholic and international unions in Quebec. See "L'internationale insulte les ouvriers can.-français," *Le Travail*, July 1948, 2–7; and "Une mise au point de Gérard Picard," *Le Travail*, 16 October 1953, 1.

39 Ryan Edwardson, *Canadian Content: Culture and the Quest for Nationhood* (Toronto: University of Toronto Press, 2008), 360.

40 Loris Racine, "La situation des Canadiens français à l'Office du film," *L'Action nationale*, January 1955, 411–19. See also Mélanie Chabot, "À la découverte de l'"autre': Le mouvement de l'éducation des adultes au Québec et les questions des relations interculturelles (1945–1960)," in *Vers la construction d'une citoyenneté canadienne*, ed. Jean-Michel Lacroix and Paul-André Lintel (Paris: Presses Sorbonne Nouvelle, 2006), 171–86.

41 Confédération des syndicats nationaux archives, Service d'éducation fonds, 1297, Fernand Jolicoeur à M. Pierre de Bellefeuille, 24 April 1962; LAC, JLCC Fonds, MG28 V75 34 6, Romain Desbois à J.-V. Morin, 16 November 1951, 1.

42 Bringing together members of the Canadian Association for Adult Education and the Société canadienne d'enseignement postscolaire, this committee aimed to "improve inter-group relations in Canada." Ruby Kidd, *Adult Education in Canada* (Toronto: Garden City Press, 1950), 83.

43 LAC, JLCC Fonds, MG28 V75 34 3, CTCIR, activity report, 1 July–12 November 1948; LAC, JLCC Fonds, MG28 V75 34 4, "Report of the Activities of the Montreal Labour Committee . . . for the Period Starting November 4th 1949 ending October 19th 1950."

44 See, for instance, the correspondence between Jolicoeur and Morin during 1952 in LAC, JLCC Fonds, MG28 V75 34 6 and 7.

45 See LAC, JLCC Fonds, MG28 V75 34 11, "Labor Committee against Racial Intolerance, Monthly Report," April 1954.

46 Bernard Mailhiot, "Le Centre de recherches en relations humaines de Montréal," *Recherches sociographiques* 2, no. 1 (1961): 101–03.

47 See, for example, "Conférence annuelle sur les relations humaines," *ROC*, March–April–May 1954, 1–2; and LAC, JLCC Fonds, MG28 V75 34 16, CTCIR, "Conférence ouvrière en relations humaines, les 26 et 27 janvier 1957."

48 For an overview of the role and mission of the CCCJ, see Alex Dworkin Canadian Jewish Archives, Canadian Jewish fund, ZA 1948 6/81, "Qu'est-ce que l'Amitié judéo-chrétienne?" AUQAM, 85 P—FUIQ Fonds, 800:02/9, "Le Conseil canadien des Chrétiens et des Juifs," n.d. [1954], 2.

49 On the first contacts between Morin and Valiquette, see LAC, JLCC Fonds, MG28 V75 34 7, "Lettres de S. Valiquette à J.-V. Morin," 15 and 25 February 1952.

50 Paul-Etienne Rainville, "'Un programme unique dans le monde entier': Le Congrès juif canadien et la lutte pour le droit à l'égalité 'raciale' et religieuse au Québec (1945–1950)," *Histoire sociale* 53, no. 109 (2020): 597–624; Meunier and Warren, *Sortir de la "grande noirceur."*

51 David Austin, *Fear of a Black Nation: Race, Sex, and Security in Sixties Montreal* (Toronto: Between the Lines, 2013); Sean Mills, *A Place in the Sun: Haiti, Haitians, and the Remaking of Quebec* (Montreal and Kingston: McGill-Queen's University Press,

2016); and Corrie Scott, "How French Canadians Became White Folks: Or, Doing Things with Race in Quebec," *Ethnic and Racial Studies* 39, no. 7 (2016): 1280–97.

52 Backhouse, *De la couleur des lois*, 16–18.

53 Kaplansky, *Activities in the Field*, 1.

54 Pierre Anctil, "Interlude of Hostility: Judeo-Christian Relations in Quebec in the Interwar Period, 1919–1939," in *Antisemitism in Canada: History and Interpretation*, ed. Alan Davies (Waterloo: Wilfrid Laurier University Press, 1992), 147; Pierre Anctil and Ira Robinson, "Introduction: L'antisémitisme au Québec," *Globe* 18, no. 1 (2015): 13–17.

55 For example, the French films available to the committee—whether produced by the National Film Board (*Compagnons d'une même destinée*), translated from American productions (*La famille des hommes*), or imported from France (*Maître après Dieu*)—primarily discussed anti-Semitism and the role of European immigrants in building Canada. LAC, JLCC Fonds, MG28 V75 34 12, CTCIR, "Films que nous avons en main," 1954.

56 For a recent analysis of this mythology and its persistence, see Villeneuve, "Retour sur l'atelier."

57 Morin confirms this profound transformation of his position, and that of several of his trade union colleagues, during the 1950s. See Mathieu Denis, *Jacques-Victor Morin, syndicaliste et éducateur populaire* (Montréal: VLB Éditeur, 2003).

58 See the resolutions adopted by the annual congresses of the FUIQ in 1952 and 1954. SAGD (AUQAM), 85 P FUIQ Collection, 160/1 and 640/13.

59 On the splits in the CCF-PSD (Parti social démocratique) "Quebec wing" over issues related to bilingualism and the national question, see André Lamoureux, *Le NPD et le Québec: 1958–1985* (Montréal: Éditions du Parc, 1985), 52–58.

60 "Cercles d'études sur la tolérance," *ROC*, January 1953, 5; "Succès de la conférence sur les relations humaines," *ROC*, April–May 1953, 2.

61 "Un comité syndical proteste," *Le Devoir*, 3 December 1954, 1; LAC, JLCC Fonds, MG28 V75 34 12, "Fédération des unions industrielles du Québec au Très Honorable Louis Saint-Laurent," 15 December 1954.

62 "Un cas d'intolérance raciale à l'hôpital des vétérans," *ROC*, December 1954, 3.

63 With reference to the Fair Employment Practices Act adopted by the federal government in 1953 (my translation). "L'Iron ore interdit l'usage du français," *Le Devoir*, 12 December 1957, 1; "Le Comité du travail contre l'intolérance fera enquête," *Le Devoir*, 13 December 1957, 2.

64 This is particularly the case for *Le Devoir* in "Un comité syndical proteste"; and "On exige le renvoi de Mlle Anderson," *Le Devoir*, 3 December 1954, 1. On the publicity given to the committee's interventions in the Iron Ore case, see LAC, JLCC Fonds, MG28 V75 34 16, "Report of the Montreal Secretary Dec. 1957," 1.

65 See LAC, JLCC Fonds, MG28 V75 34 13.

66 "Études en relations humaines," *La Presse*, 15 February 1958, 15.

67 Julian Biggs, *Dresden Story*, National Film Board, 1954, 30 min.

68 "Les conditions d'un véritable bilinguisme," *La Presse*, 14 November 1955, 22.

69 AUQAM, 85 P—FUIQ Fonds, 160/6, "Une conférence ouvrière traite du bilinguisme et de la discrimination," 14 November 1955; "Les syndiqués doivent se libérer de tout préjugé," *La Presse*, 3 March 1958, 13.

70 "Exposé du Programme syndical d'anti-discrimination et des droits de l'homme," *ROC*, November–December 1960, 2–3.

71 AUQAM, 100 P—FTQ Fonds, 640/105, "Rapport du Comité des droits de l'homme au 7ième Congrès de la FTQ," 22 November 1962 (my translation).

72 McKenzie, "Representation on Discrimination."

73 Loi sur l'hôtellerie, SQ 1963, c. 40, art. 8; Loi sur la discrimination dans l'emploi, SQ 1964, c. 46.

74 See also Dominique Clément, *Equality Deferred: Sex Discrimination and British Columbia's Human Rights State, 1953–1984* (Vancouver: UBC Press, 2015); and Shirley Tillotson, "Human Rights Law as Prism: Women's Organizations, Unions, and Ontario's Female Employees Fair Remuneration Act, 1951," *Canadian Historical Review* 72, no. 4 (1991): 532–57.

75 Their strategies are part of the second phase of the equality rights movement identified by Walker that aims to outlaw discrimination by citizens against each other. Walker, "The 'Jewish Phase.'"

76 "Les prises de positions contre la discrimination raciale se multiplient," *La Presse*, 15 March 1963, 16; "40 organismes présentent à M. Lesage un 2e mémoire contre la discrimination," *Le Devoir*, 3 April 1963, 3.

77 Austin, *Fear of a Black Nation*.

78 Brian Palmer, "'Indians of All Tribes': The Birth of Red Power," in *Debating Dissent: Canada and the Sixties*, ed. Lara Campbell, Dominique Clément, and Gregory S. Kealey (Toronto: University of Toronto Press, 2012), 193–210.

79 Rainville, "De l'universel au particulier," 336–39.

80 Shelley Wright, *International Human Rights, Decolonisation and Globalisation: Becoming Human* (London: Routledge, 2001), 12.

CHAPTER 11

Native Non-Governmental Organizations: Grassroots Constructions of Aboriginal Human Rights in Canada

María Cristina Manzano-Munguía, Dan Smoke, and Mary Lou Smoke

In memory of our beloved Dr. Dan Smoke (28 April 1954, Seneca Nation–4 November 2024, London, Ontario). We will always honour and remember his legacy, teachings, activism, and knowledge. Our chapter is a tribute to his work among and between our Indigenous communities across and beyond Canada.

"If you are Indigenous, you don't have any rights; . . . you are considered second-class citizens, . . . but if you are white then you have human rights and respect in Canada."

Dan Smoke, Seneca Nation
(interview with Manzano-Munguía, 2022).

IN 1948, the United Nations became the internationally recognized promoter of human rights norms and privileges. Since then, human rights have been reaffirmed and expanded across the world. A major development of human rights in Canada was the recognition of Aboriginal rights in the 1982 Canadian Constitution, as stated in the newly established Charter of Rights and Freedoms. There Aboriginal rights were "protected" by provisions of the Charter, in particular Sections 1 through 15 and 25, which state that "every individual is equal before and under the law and has the right to the equal protection and equal benefit of the law without discrimination and, in particular, without discrimination based on race, national or ethnic origin, colour, religion, sex, age or mental or physical disability."[1] It was precisely this recognition in the Canadian Constitution that set the introduction for Bill C-31, a Bill to Amend the Indian Act, adopted in April 1985. Bill C-31 was designed to address gender inequities in the Indian Act. The Act stated that Indian women who married non-Indian men, and the children of such unions, lost their Indian status, band membership, and entitlements as registered Indians, including tax exemptions, health benefits, the right to hold property, and the right to live on Indian reserves.[2] This discrimination against women continued in subsequent Indian Acts, and Bill C-31 worked not only to bring this legislation in line with the Charter's gender equality provisions but also to restore Indian status to others who had been disenfranchised because of discriminatory provisions.[3]

In this example, recognition of Aboriginal rights in the Charter limited the extent to which the Indian Act could discriminate against "Indians,"[4] specifically women. Nevertheless, Indigenous Peoples in Canada continue to face, resist, and negotiate multiple experiences of genocide, poverty, violence, racism, political isolation, and economic inequality. As a result, across Canada, Indigenous populations have various perspectives on the Aboriginal rights outlined in the Charter, on human rights more broadly, and on the claims of universality associated with these human rights. In this chapter, we want to explore urban Indigenous populations specifically, how Native non-governmental organizations (NGOs) advocate and honour human rights for Indigenous Peoples in Canada, and how the language of "universal human rights" works at the local level through Native organizations, which in turn mediate grassroots constructions of human rights. Our chapter emphasizes the need for a multinational and multicultural human rights policy in government programs and projects as well as the honouring of grassroots constructions of Aboriginal human rights.

To do so, first we provide a brief overview of Aboriginal rights in Canada. Then we illustrate how Native NGOs have advocated for Indigenous Peoples' human rights in Canada at the local level. Using examples from London, Ontario, we emphasize how these organizations represent the locale for grassroots constructions of Aboriginal human rights. This is an ongoing process of grassroots constructions of Indigenous human rights epistemologies in Canada, which in turn represent changes to the social relations and practices of human rights as constructed by and from the West.[5]

Aboriginal Rights in Canada

There is a growing literature, as discussed in the introduction and first chapter of this edited volume, tracing the evolution of human rights movements in Canada, beginning in the 1930s and strengthening during and after the Second World War.[6] Although, as Asa McKercher's chapter makes clear, the Canadian government continued to resist international human rights developments, by the 1950s most jurisdictions in Canada had adopted basic laws to prohibit discrimination based on grounds such as race, ethnic origin, and religion.[7] In the same period, Indigenous leaders and Native organizations such as the North American Indian Brotherhood and the Indian Association of Alberta resisted and contested discriminatory Indian policy and legislation. For instance, "Indians" were not entitled to the privileges of full citizenship such as voting, holding property, selling the products of their labour, or investing. Moreover, as stated above, women lost their Indian status, band membership, and entitlements as registered Indians.[8] Combined with the longer history of Indigenous resistance to colonial policy—pressuring Parliament to establish a Special Joint Committee of the Senate and House of Commons from 1946 to 1948—anti-discrimination activism focused on amending the Indian Act.

The 1951 version of the Act included the removal of the most odious aspects of the law. The government dropped cultural bans and pass system laws,[9] some of the prohibitions against alcohol were lifted, and Status Indians were allowed to raise money in order to pursue land claims against the government.[10] In addition, women were now allowed to vote, and secret ballots became the norm in band elections.[11] Nonetheless, the Indian Act continued to focus on assimilation through education and enfranchisement.[12] John Leslie and Robert Maguire argue that, although the government ended aggressive policies of assimilation, most Indigenous Peoples "refused to surrender their separate legal status, treaty rights, and privileges."[13]

In 1965, the Department of Indian Affairs moved to the Department of Northern Affairs and National Resources, culminating in the establishment of the Department of Indian Affairs and Northern Development (DIAND) by 1966.[14]

In 1969, Pierre Elliott Trudeau's government released its *Statement of the Government on Indian Policy*, better known as the White Paper, triggering a new phase in its legislative approach to Indigenous populations.[15] Historically, the British Parliament used "white papers" for public discussion on drafted legislation. The Canadian state, however, used the white paper format for government reports and information until 1969, when it metamorphosed into a policy instrument.[16] Restated, the Canadian White Paper was co-opted into a formal policy document rather than being used as a tool by the government for obtaining public consensus on drafted policy or legislation. In principle, consultations with Indigenous communities were a part of drafting the White Paper, including meetings with Indigenous leaders and their organizations at the national level. However, Alison DuBois and A.D. Doerr argue that Indigenous participation in the process was null and in direct contradiction to Trudeau's 1968 election campaign promise of a "participatory" policy-making process.[17]

The proposal of the White Paper to change fundamentally the legislative relationship between the state and Indigenous Peoples, including the removal of Indians' special status and the dismantling of the reserve system, without meaningful consultation, led to widespread Indigenous resistance to the plan. This resistance strengthened the growth of Native NGOs' networking and activism across Canada.[18] The White Paper served "as a catalyst in promoting Aboriginal people's participation in the policy-making process of the federal government."[19] Publicly demonstrated in the aftermath of the White Paper was the "ability of Canadian Aboriginal people to articulate their interests directly and most effectively to politicians and to members of the public" through their lobbying in Ottawa and stand-up demonstrations across Canada.[20] The aforementioned actions set the stage for the 1982 Constitution, including Section 35, which recognized and affirmed the existing Aboriginal and treaty rights of Aboriginal people.

Yet discrimination against Indigenous Peoples, and women specifically, continued after the adoption of the Charter of Rights and Freedoms in 1982. The last major revisions to the Indian Act took place in 1985, when the Act returned to the philosophy of encouraging "civilization" rather than directing or forcing it on Indians.[21] However, the Charter did provide a legal language with which Indigenous activists and organizations could fight this discrimination. *Sandra Lovelace v. Canada* (1981) was an example of how a non-Status Indian utilized this legal discourse to contest the Indian Act definition of Indian Status.[22] Nevertheless, the Supreme Court of Canada failed to recognize that Section 12 (1) (b) of the Indian Act[23] discriminated against Indian women who married non-Indian men and their descendants in light of the Canadian Bill of Rights enactment (1960, c. 44). Sandra Lovelace decided to appeal that decision in an international forum: the United Nations Human Rights Commission.[24] By July 1981, that commission found Section 12 (1) (b) of the Indian Act to be discriminatory and in contradiction to the International Covenant on Civil and Political Rights (United Nations General Assembly Resolution 1976). After gaining international recognition, Parliament passed Bill C-31 in 1985, and Section

12 and other sections were repealed in order to reinstate Indian status to non-Status female Indians who married non-Indian men.[25]

Here the universal claim of human rights norms and privileges across countries proved to be useful for Lovelace while rallying and advocating for her Indian status and the withdrawal of discriminatory sections of the Indian Act. Furthermore, Bill C-31 included the Euro-Canadian preference for male lineage applied to Indian status, challenged by Sharon McIvor, a member of the Lower Nicola First Nation in British Columbia, at the British Columbia Supreme Court.[26] As a professor of Aboriginal law, she challenged the oppressive legislation for sixteen years, and in 2006 she received her Indian status. Moreover, the voices of Indigenous people and the construction of their rights from below, as Dan Smoke stated, has been a challenge for countries such as Canada to recognize:

> We had our clan mothers, our storytellers, gatekeepers, hereditary Chiefs (governing system), our ceremonial protocols; . . . we governed ourselves. Colonization divided and conquered us: our culture and traditions were forbidden, we were not able to practise our ceremonies, our children were stolen from their parents [referring to residential schools], families separated, the Indian Act imposed to our people a huge violation of human rights. Human rights for whom? . . . For us only if we voiced our needs, asserted ourselves, united; we had the right to be here, the right to represent Indigenous people and make our claims as sovereign nations, and our right to be Indigenous people. . . . We intervened in the United Nations Declaration on the Rights of Indigenous People (UNDRIP) in 2007, . . . [and] one by one all the countries voted in favour, except Canada, the United States, Australia, and New Zealand voted against it. Why was that? Because they [the aforementioned countries] want to keep control and power over Indigenous people. They don't want Indigenous people to take back what has been stolen from us; . . . they want to keep us down and controlled. Those four countries

> who voted against the declaration did not stop us, [and] we had a sit-in [at] the United Nations, including the other nations who voted against it: New Zealand, Australia, and the United States.[27]

Consequently, we deem it necessary to look at Native NGOs that advocate for the human rights and well-being of their communities in urban centres.

Non-Governmental Organizations: An Overview

In 1945, the United Nations coined the term "non-governmental organization" and stipulated in Fourth Geneva Convention Article 47 these organizations as international bodies for consulting purposes.[28] Over the following decades, NGOs proliferated beyond the UN framework in local, regional, and national contexts in both northern and southern countries. Despite earlier attempts by scholars to consolidate NGOs, this category remained unclear and ambivalent. As Kerstin Martens states, "many studies fail(ed) to offer any definition of the term NGO as if the components and the understanding of the phrase [were] common knowledge."[29]

Since the 1980s, NGOs have proliferated around the world and engaged in community-based initiatives, funded largely through government aid agencies. Michael Edwards and David Hulme argued about the rise and spread of these organizations, which was neither an accident nor a response to local initiatives and/or voluntary actions.[30] Rather, these organizations represented a series of calculated actions from governments and their official aid agencies honing new neo-liberal state projects. For instance, some NGOs worked as counterweights to state power, promoters of good government, and conductors of democracy due to the lack of knowledge of "what NGOs are and perhaps even less about what they should be called."[31] In other cases, the funding promoted by official aid agencies, including the United States Agency for International Development and the Canadian International Development Agency, linked NGO projects to governments' political and economic interests.[32] In other words, industrialized countries funded NGO projects through aid agencies while seeking their own benefits.[33]

As Paul Barnsley notes, these government-funded advocacy groups "serve[d] two masters": that is, "their founders and their membership."[34] Yet the issue of NGOs serving "two masters" remains poorly explored.[35] Accountability, or "holding individuals and organizations responsible for their actions and performance,"[36] represents another gap within NGO literature, although Patrick Kilby introduces "downward accountability" or accountability to constituents as desirable in future research on NGOs.[37] Using the Canadian example, we illustrate the need for downward accountability, specifically in the design of grassroots projects for Indigenous Peoples.

Bruno Barras and Mario Blaser demonstrate how governmental organizations and NGOs hindered Indigenous life projects among the Yshiro Indians in Paraguay.[38] Barras, an Indigenous leader, states that "we (Yshiro Indians) are proposing what I call life projects. I call it that because our plans and projects are oriented to achieving autonomy in deciding our own future."[39] In El Chaco, Paraguay, both government organizations and NGOs have provided, in principle, a variety of "expert knowledge" on Indigenous needs, lobbying for funding from both governmental and transnational agencies. However, these NGOs are neither organic nor Native per se, since most of the time they are run and administered by non-Indigenous personnel. For instance, NGOs have claimed legitimate representation of Indigenous Peoples in Paraguay since their life projects bear the interests and needs of Yshiros, but Barras argues quite the opposite: "NGOs treat us as if we are babies. . . . They speak for us and design projects for us. Most of the time, they are the main beneficiaries of the projects for the communities."[40] The aftermath of confrontations between Indigenous Peoples' projects and government-driven agencies has included the creation of Native NGOs, envisioned as community-driven organizations led by Indigenous community leaders. In this case, the major differences are the design and implementation of community projects linked to community needs, similar to intercultural education programs and curricula in other developing countries.[41] For instance, in El Chaco, five Yshiro community leaders founded La Unión de las Comunidades Indígenas de la Nación Yshir in 1999.[42] Through this Native NGO, the Yshir pursued their interests as well as reduced the power and misrepresentation enforced by multiple governmental and non-governmental Paraguayan organizations.[43] Therefore, though some NGOs might engage politically with and rally against state policies, programs, and projects, they might marginalize Indigenous Peoples, whereas Native NGOs centre Indigenous needs, interests, and rights. Thus, we deem it necessary to explore such organizations in Canada.

Native NGOs in Canada

Despite the Indian Act of 1927, which banned Indigenous populations from organizing or raising money for political purposes, Native political organizations proliferated in Canada in the last quarter of the twentieth century.[44] Brian Titley noted that Native organizations deliberately started at local and regional levels as early as the 1870s in order to subvert contentious policies emanating from the federal Department of Indian Affairs.[45] Harold Cardinal also looked at how the Indian Act hindered the establishment and effectiveness of Native organizations across Canada, arguing that, "at the time our founders were attempting to create Indian organizations, it had to be an underground task. . . . In many ways, the stories of early Indian organizations would parallel the problems labour had in getting organized in the late 1800s."[46]

In a similar vein, Titley examined the political threat that Native organizations posed to the Department of Indian Affairs on a national scale.[47] Organizations such as the Grand Indian Council of Ontario and Quebec, the League of Indians of Canada, the Manitoba Indian Brotherhood, the Union of Ontario, and the Indian Association of Alberta faced constraints and challenges endured by their leaders from the last third of the nineteenth century through the first half of the twentieth century. For instance, Duncan Campbell Scott, the deputy superintendent general of the Department of Indian Affairs from 1913 to 1932, obstructed Frederick Ogilvie Loft's attempts to establish a national organization called the League of Indians of Canada. As Titley states, "D.C. Scott initially greeted the existence of the league (of Indians) with annoyance and irritation. Here was another unwelcome impediment to efficient administration. What Loft and his organization were proposing was often in direct opposition to established department policy [e.g., Indians' right to vote without losing their status, greater control of their lands, funds, and resources]."[48] This fragmentation and the complexity of the social relations between state agents and Indigenous leaders are well illustrated by Loft and the League of Indians. By 1916, the Department of Indian Affairs recognized his organization as an imminent threat because it was attempting to unite Indigenous Peoples against long-festering grievances, including but not limited to "the gradual alienation of reserve lands, restrictions of traditional hunting and fishing rights, the suppression of native customs, the debilitating effects of boarding school education, the inadequacy of health services, [the] lack of economic opportunities, and the paternalistic overlordship of Indian Affairs."[49]

Despite Loft's limited success in uniting Indigenous Peoples and communities against Indian Affairs policies through Native organization, his leadership was undermined by the actions of the deputy superintendent general. Scott refused to cooperate, and "this was the advice he transmitted to the department's agents as they began to complain of the organization's activities."[50] Moreover, Cardinal describes how, under Loft's leadership, the Indian Association of Alberta complied with federal government requirements in order to qualify for the funding available under the Agricultural Rehabilitation Development Act.[51]

Nevertheless, Indigenous leaders and community members, especially activists, contested political spaces and lobbied against the Crown, the state, and its institutions.[52] By the late 1960s, the Liberal government was conducting meetings across Canada with Native leaders, which gave them "the first stimulus to organize" more formally.[53] It was the White Paper, however, the government Indian policy initiative in 1969, that boosted the process of establishing off-reserve provincial and national Native organizations.[54]

Sally Weaver notes that the level of leadership among provincial Native organizations varied. For instance, the prairie provinces were the most politically engaged, whereas Ontario, Quebec, and the Maritimes remained less organized. British Columbia, the Yukon, the Northwest Territories, and Newfoundland had no participation in this period.[55] Weaver also outlines eight challenges facing national and provincial Native organizations:

1. the cost and time involved in contacting the widely dispersed Indian communities
2. the extensive cultural heterogeneity among Indians
3. the historic inter-tribal distrust among certain groups
4. language diversity
5. various degrees of acculturation within and between communities
6. poverty
7. limited education
8. the lack of funding to organize or to maintain the organizations.[56]

In addition, state agents played a decisive role in precluding the earlier formation of Native national and local organizations in Canada. Despite the aforementioned challenges faced by Indigenous people, the Department of Indian Affairs funded provincial and territorial organizations (PTOs) and national Aboriginal organizations (NAOs) to deliver and implement social services, education, health, employment, and child and youth programs for Aboriginal people during the second quarter of the twentieth century. These initiatives greatly empowered Native organizations to work closely with federal, provincial, and local governments on Indian policy and program design.[57]

One such national organization was the National Indian Brotherhood (NIB), which represented by 1968 the interests of registered Indians and took the lead on issues affecting their housing, poverty, treaty rights, Aboriginal rights, and land settlements. The following Native organizations were members of the NIB: the Union of New Brunswick Indians, the Union of Nova Scotia Indians, the Union of British Columbia Indian Chiefs, the Manitoba Indian Brotherhood, the Indian Association of Alberta, the Yukon Native Brotherhood, the Lennox Island Development Corporation, the Federation of Saskatchewan Indians, the Indians of Quebec Association, the

Union of Ontario Indians, and the Indian Brotherhood of the Northwest Territories.[58] The NIB needed better representation of and accountability to its constituents, and by 1982 it had evolved to become the Assembly of First Nations (AFN). The AFN took the mandate of representing the interests of registered Indians and Native organizations and became one of five NAOs recognized and funded by the federal government across Canada.[59] The other four NAOs were the Congress of Aboriginal Peoples (CAP), the Inuit Tapiriit Kanatami (ITK known before 2001 as the Inuit Tapirisat of Canada), the Native Women's Association of Canada (NWAC), and the Métis National Council (MNC).

In principle, NAOs and PTOs assumed the role of directly representing Aboriginal people's interests, values, and rights.[60] In 2005, AFN National Chief Phil Fontaine announced $150 million from the federal government for Aboriginal political organizations, "approximately 100 tribal councils, PTOs and other funded bodies."[61] Currently Native organizations face an accountability conundrum: increasing their dependence on federal, provincial, and municipal funds might hinder their political pleas, needs, and interests.[62] This conundrum opens up space for local urban Native organizations, with an emphasis on their human rights claims, to play a greater role in representing the interests and needs of Indigenous populations in Canada.

Native NGOs and Grassroots Constructions of Aboriginal Human Rights

María Cristina Manzano-Munguía has argued elsewhere how and why Indigenous people in urban centres in Canada have perceived local and urban Native organizations as non-governmental.[63] The "storied experience"[64] gives force to the construction of Native organizations as non-governmental based on multiple conversations with Indigenous individuals in London, Ontario. Here we examine local and urban stories of particular Native NGOs, specifically those related to human rights for Indigenous people in London, to demonstrate how, at the local level, the establishment of these organizations was often the result of the challenges faced by Indigenous people while living in the city.[65]

The vast majority of Native NGOs were founded through the work of one or more concerned Indigenous community members in urban areas. They worked or volunteered for a governmental or non-governmental organization on issues pertaining to the improvement and well-being of Indigenous Peoples.[66] In addition, most of them had experience coordinating and conducting social, recreational, and cultural activities; accessing information on Indigenous people's eligibility criteria for economic programs; obtaining knowledge about Indigenous social justice; and organizing health and well-being programs. The activities with which these founders had experience related to, but were not limited to, volunteering for and organizing social gatherings, traditional teaching workshops, language courses, and feasts. They might also have had some experience in employment and educational services, Native housing co-ops, and income support programs. Finally, some founders provided advocacy services on human rights issues, violence against Indigenous women, land claims, and addiction recovery programs.

Funding for these organizations came from a variety of sources. The granting agencies for Native NGOs included Canadian Heritage (Aboriginal friendship centres, national Aboriginal women's organizations, northern Aboriginal broadcasting), Industry Canada, the City of London, the federal and provincial Ministries of Health (Aboriginal Healing Foundation), Human Resources and Social Development Canada (Aboriginal Human Resources Development Strategy), and the Ontario Trillium Foundation.

Specific examples of Native NGOs in London include Nokee Kwe Occupational Skills and Development Incorporated, Atlohsa Native Family Healing Services Incorporated, and N'Amerind Friendship Centre. Nokee Kwe is Anishinaabemowin/Ojibwa for "working woman," and, through a Native Women's Workshop held in 1977, a program to serve Native women was established in London. According to its website, Nokee Kwe, founded on Aboriginal principles, is a community-based and client-focused charitable organization that encourages and supports self-determination and personal development through individual workplace preparation, life skills, and vocational training.[67] Incorporated as Nokee Kwe Occupational Skill Development in 1983 to sponsor a funded employment readiness training program, the organization presents itself as "at the forefront of providing services to unemployed and underemployed Native and Non Native individuals."[68] Nokee Kwe identifies itself as "a leader in the provision of holistic and comprehensive services to Aboriginal and Non-Aboriginal individuals, assisting them in making meaningful life choices."[69]

Atlohsa is a word from the On^yota'a:ka Oneida language that stems from the root word Atunhetsla, referring to the spiritual seed inside each of us. Atlohsa is a place where people can go to feel safe, to heal, and to nurture their spiritual needs. They can find comfort in knowing that they are being taken care of in a good way, as friends take care of friends. Atlohsa offers help when someone is in need. It was founded in 1986 in response to the results of a needs assessment survey and was incorporated in 1989. Survey findings provided the mandate for the development of Native family healing services designed to meet the health needs of our women, men, and children. Atlohsa helps First Nations people to discover a healing path. We promote a sense of balance among our four states of being: physical, mental, emotional, and spiritual.[70]

The N'Amerind Friendship Centre is a charitable, non-profit organization that has been serving the needs of Aboriginal people throughout southwestern Ontario for over forty years. N'Amerind was incorporated on 20 April 1967 and is an established member of the Ontario Federation of Indian Friendship Centres and the National Association of Friendship Centres.[71]

For the purpose of this chapter, we will focus on Nokee Kwe because of the availability and accessibility of its archival record and consent to conduct research while Manzano-Munguía was completing her fieldwork in 2006–08.[72] The documents described in a limited manner the establishment of this Native NGO and the work of its founders.

During the second half of the twentieth century, there was major interest from the state (specifically the Department of the Secretary of State) to support and work with Native people. Most were girls and women who migrated from reserves to urban areas to escape sexual and physical abuse, leave oppression and discrimination experienced on the reserves, and access social and health services.[73] In 1977, a group of women voluntarily formed an ad hoc committee that recognized the need to work for the well-being of Native women and their families: Joyce Albert from the Chippewa of the Thames, Barbara Antone from the Oneida of the Thames, Carole Aziz representing the Department of the Secretary of State, and Donna Phillips from London. They successfully applied to the Secretary of State for funding and sponsoring their Native Women's Gathering. It included guest speakers, seminars, and workshops. This initial workshop led to the formation of the Native Women's Workshop, a non-profit organization incorporated on 14 January 1983. This Native NGO had the following objectives: to develop programs and resources unique to Native women while meeting their socio-economic needs, promoting better understanding and cooperation between Native and non-Native people, and supporting and encouraging Native women's participation in the development of their community.[74]

Beginning in 1977, the Native Women's Workshop organized a series of workshops and gatherings that supported Native women's well-being and socio-economic development and the teachings and revival of their Native identity. The following examples of gatherings and workshops are illustrative. In April 1978, the Native Women Speaking Together workshop, funded by the Department of the Secretary of State, had 100 participants from southwestern Ontario who voiced their concerns about their health, nutrition, substance abuse, effective parenting, rights as Native women, and traditions. By 1979, the Secretary of State sponsored the Native Youth Gathering with 150 participants, including elders and youth; the gathering emphasized Native culture, identity, and education. In 1980, the same sponsor supported the Elders' Gathering and the Teaching of Our Elders.[75] Both events emphasized the importance of elders and the need to preserve their knowledge for future generations.

As early as 1981, there was an employment project that provided contact, support, and liaison from fieldworkers and two facilitators to work with Native women who lived in rural and urban areas and to target their social and economic needs. This project was called Native Women Working for

Tomorrow and funded by the local Employment Assistance Program. It sought to develop resource materials and kits with information about Native women's needs and to build the resources for their future. In the same year, this Native NGO conducted a Child Care Research Project funded by the Canada Community Development Project; it documented the need for daycare within the London Native community. A survey evaluated the feasibility of establishing a Native daycare centre. It was not until 1983, however, that The Four Winds Day Care was incorporated and housed other projects for children and their mothers.

In May 1982 and April 1983, the Nokee Kwe Native Women's Employment and Skills Program established training programs for Native women who, after completion of the programs, would be able to obtain meaningful employment. The funds came from the local Employment Assistance Program. In May 1983, Nokee Kwe Occupational Skills Development was incorporated and left the Native Women's Workshop. The comments offered by Bryan Loucks, an Anishinaabe leader from Walpole Island, further illustrate the birth of this Native NGO:

> I was brought up in that kind of an environment of community development and community activism and so on. And one of the natural evolutions that happen[ed] [in London] was that we were able to evolve a women focus within the Native people in the multicultural centre, which very quickly took leadership and direction from women such as Barbara Antone . . . , Colleen Nadjiwon-Johnson, [and] Donna Phillips, . . . so there were a number of them who started to work on women issues. . . [T]hey had a joint office to the Native Peoples Resource Centre that was called [the] Native Women Workshop. They started to plan and separate, and it was really I believe out of their work with the London community. This is where Nokee Kwe found its way, . . . and Nokee Kwe was then officially established.[76]

Indeed, Nokee Kwe is one of the major Native agencies providing services and programs to Aboriginal people in urban areas, and here we want to make the connection with Aboriginal human rights grassroots constructions and advocacy for community members.

Aboriginal Human Rights from Below

> "I lived with my auntie. I took the bus and g[o]t off [at] Dundas. I walked . . . [and found] Nokee Kwe."[77]

The rise of participatory democracy triggered the funding of Native organizations across Canada during the last quarter of the twentieth century.[78] The ongoing political stand and negotiating power of Aboriginal leaders have been documented through the work of scholars and community initiatives.[79] The creation of Native NGOs such as Nokee Kwe should be seen as a project promoting both state and Aboriginal people's interests. This process has been referred to in the governmentality literature as the alignment of interests.[80] Some of these intersections pertained to employment; training; economic programs; health promotion and services; educational programs for adults, youth, and children; Aboriginal rights; youth leadership; the practice of traditional feasts, socials, and spiritual ceremonies; as well as development programs.

Here our emphasis is on the grassroots constructions of Aboriginal human rights. Dan Smoke Asayenes (Seneca) and his wife, Mary Lou Smoke-Kwe (Ojibwe), carried out educational and awareness work on issues pertaining but not limited to Aboriginal human rights and well-being as well as traditional knowledge. Beginning in 1991, every Sunday evening they hosted the radio program known as *Smoke Signals First Nations Radio* (CHRW Radio Western, 94.9 FM). They were also community commentators on Native issues starting in 2003 on the New PL and London A Channel News, both CITY TV-owned news programs, and elders in the southwestern area of Ontario.[81] In 2000, London's mayor honoured them for their work in humanitarianism. Moreover, their advocacy work centred on the resolution of the challenges and needs faced by Aboriginal people in this country with an emphasis on human rights issues in London.

In 2001, Dan and Mary Lou Smoke envisioned an Aboriginal cultural and social "gathering" at which non-Native people could learn about and respect Aboriginal people. It was called The Gathering of the Good Minds, which marked the beginning of a long journey dedicated to building a respectful, non-racist relationship to honour Aboriginal human rights within and beyond London. Nokee Kwe became the agency responsible for housing the steering committee meetings and the legal entity accredited to receive funds and donations. Some of the donors included, but were not limited to, the Museum of Ontario Archaeology, Dream Catcher fund (Casino Rama), Museum of London, Ontario Arts Council, Trillium Foundation, N'Amerind Friendship Centre, Western University (Centre for Research and Teaching of Canadian Native Languages and First Nations Studies program), Atlohsa Native Family Healing Services, A-Channel, Sterling Marking Products, CHRW Radio Western, National Aboriginal Achievement Foundation, and London Community Foundation. Consequently, the Gathering of the Good Minds represented

> a celebration of First Nations Arts and Wisdom [a]s a bi-annual event organized by a London group of First Nations and non-First Nations volunteers called "Wiiche Ke Yig" [Ojibway for Friends Who Walk with Us]. We organize the First Nations festival that is unique for London and the South-western Ontario area. Our endeavour is to promote in the non-Native community a better understanding of, and hence, co-operation with First Nations people. We believe that increased knowledge will help to bring peace and just relationships between First Nations and non-Native individuals. Moreover, we feature First Nations artists and cultural performances such as, visual artists, dancers, singers, stone carvers, story-tellers, film makers, writers, and Elders who speak about First Nations traditions. Our vision is to bring together participants from First Nations and non-natives

> from London and across S.W. Ontario to share in a feast of First Nations' cultures. The major outcome of this "Good Mind" experience will be a greater understanding [of] and respect for First Nations people.[82]

This "understanding and respect" included constructions from below of Aboriginal human rights such as seeking respect for cultural practices (e.g., feasts, celebrations, ceremonies such as the pipe ceremony and drumming) and traditions. There was a call to embrace diversity, respect cultural differences and social practices, and revive Indigenous identities. For instance, the smudging ceremony (sweetgrass or cedar) is mostly related to the Creator, but it also represents an opportunity to respect and learn about Aboriginal traditions and knowledge constructions with reference to community experiences.

As Helen, in her interview with Manzano-Munguía, clearly stated, Native NGOs carried on with traditional activities and ceremonies; they represented a solid foundation for reconstructing Aboriginal worldviews and identities.[83] In addition, these organizations represented the freedom to construct human rights related to cultural practices, banned for many years (e.g., Sundance, Potlatch). Amber vividly expressed the freedom that she felt at Nokee Kwe, her workplace: "I was able to practise smudging at any time of the day and without being punished or fired by my boss."[84] Her ad hoc statement is appropriate in terms of the ongoing recognition of Aboriginal rights, and we should expect such "freedom" at work, school, and public and social gatherings. This is still one of the major challenges: recognition of Aboriginal human rights beyond the comfort zones and the appropriate locales for exercising their rights and freedoms.

Chief Stephen Keptin Augustine clearly illustrates the latter while noting that "we [referring to Aboriginal people] have to reconstruct our world for the rest of the Canadians to show them what we have lost. . . . We have to argue on the premise of our priorities and concerns in relation to our own governance structures and knowledge systems, and according to our own collective experience and relationships with the land and what it has provided for us (our culture and language, our identity)."[85] Indeed,

Aboriginal people have reconstructed not only their "world" but also their Aboriginal human rights from the ground up while seeking respect for and inclusion of their cultural practices and worldviews. In other words, their epistemological constructions of Aboriginal human rights are paving the way through the work of Native NGOs and their leaders.

Conclusion

Native non-governmental organizations continue to serve urban Aboriginal communities. Their advocacy work to reduce or eliminate racism and violence, protect human rights, and ensure accessible and affordable housing, employment, daycare, education, health, and so forth represent a milestone in many Canadian cities.

Nokee Kwe is a good example of the services and advocacy work for and embraced by the Aboriginal community in London. For instance, the Native Learning Centre provides basic skills and literacy services to Aboriginal people. Its mandate is "to learn and understand the needs of Native learners, thereby responding to their needs and respecting their heritage and culture, as well as developing their literacy and numeracy needs, all within one holistic environment."[86] Respect for Aboriginal people's cultural heritage is a major recognition of their right to cultural diversity rather than assimilation, Christianization, and civilization.

Under our lens, Native NGOs, to a greater extent, are the locales for grassroots constructions of Aboriginal human rights. This ongoing process has made great progress in the past two decades. This process is paving the way for understanding the changes in social relations and practices of human rights as contracted by and from a Western paradigm to grassroots Indigenous epistemologies of human rights from and for Aboriginal people in Canada.

We express a very special thank you to First Nations communities across Canada; without their courage and wisdom our human rights understandings are, indeed, incomplete. We also acknowledge and thank Stephanie Bangarth and Jennifer Tunnicliffe's hard work in editing this collection. Needless to say, we are responsible for the views and the content provided in this chapter.

Notes

1 Canadian Charter of Rights and Freedoms, Part I of the Constitution Act, 1982, being Schedule B to the Canada Act 1982 (UK), 1982, c. 11, ss.1–15, 25.

2 Act for the Gradual Enfranchisement of Indians, for the Better Management of Indian Affairs 1869, c. 6, s. 6. Act for the gradual enfranchisement of Indians, the better management of Indian affairs, and to extend the provisions of the Act 31st Victoria, Chapter 42 S.C.1869, c.6. s. 111. Victoria, *Indian Acts and Amendments 1868–1975: An Indexed Collection*, edited by Sharon Venne, 11–15 (Saskatchewan: Native Law Centre, 1981).

3 Act to Amend the Indian Act. 1985. c. 31 (Bill C-31). *The Indian Acts and Amendments 1970–1993: An Indexed Collection*, edited by Zandra Wilson, 59–111 (Saskatchewan: Native Law Centre, 1993); *Lovelace v. Canada*, Human Rights Legal Jurisdiction 158 (United Nations Human Rights Commission, 1981); and Thomas Isaac, *Aboriginal Law Commentary: Cases and Material* (Saskatoon: Purich Publishing, 1981).

4 Throughout this chapter, we use the following terms: "Indians," "Aboriginal people," "Natives," and "Indigenous Peoples." The first relates to registered band member Indians, as outlined in the Indian Act 1985, ss. 5 (1) and 10s. 5(1). The second refers to First Nations, Inuit, and Métis as defined by the Constitution Act 1982, s. 35. The third addresses Indigenous people's services and programs offered by mainstream society, Indigenous organizations, government institutions, and other non-governmental organizations. This is also a term used in the period under study by Indigenous people themselves to self-identify. Finally, the fourth refers broadly to First Nations, Métis, and Inuit Peoples in Canada.

5 Following Édouard Glissant, we use the term "West" as a state project rather than a locale. See Édouard Glissant, *Poetics of Relation* (Ann Arbor: The University of Michigan Press, 2010).

6 See, for instance, Thomas Buergenthal, "The Evolving International Human Rights System," *The American Journal of International Law* 100, no. 4 (2017): 783–807; and Jack Donnelly, *Universal Human Rights in Theory and Practice* (Ithaca: Cornell University Press, 1989) for international human rights studies.

7 See Andrew Clapham, *Human Rights: A Very Short Introduction* (London: Oxford University Press, 2007); Debra DeLaet, *The Global Struggle for Human Rights: Universal Principles in World Politics* (Belmont, CA: Wadsworth Publishers, 2005).

8 James Rodger Miller, *Reflections on Native-Newcomer Relations: Selected Essays* (Toronto: University of Toronto Press, 2004).

9 Canada had a pass system in treaty areas from 1886 to 1930. It served to prevent Indians from participating in any uprising and to remain in a reserve. See Donald Purich, *Our Land: Native Rights in Canada* (Toronto: James Lorimer, 1986).

10 John Leslie and Robert Maguire, eds., *The Historical Development of the Indian Act* (Ottawa: Indian and Northern Affairs, 1978), 151; Miller, *Reflections on Native-Newcomer Relations*, 189.

11 John Tobias, "Protection, Civilization, Assimilation: An Outline History of Canada's Indian Policy," in *As Long as the Sun Shines and Water Flows: A Reader in Canadian Native Studies*, ed. Ian Getty and Antoine Lussier (Vancouver: UBC Press, 1983), 55.

12 See Indian Act, SC 1951, c. 29 ss. 113–22 and 108–12 respectively.

13 Leslie and Maguire, *Historical Development of the Indian Act*, 151. Their "special" legal status refers to the fiduciary and fiscal responsibilities that the federal government honours regarding treaty Indians, such as the transfer of funds to reserves, health, education, and tax relief.

14 Leslie and Maguire, *Historical Development of the Indian Act*.

15 See Alison DuBois, "Instruments of Policy-Making: Canadian 'Indian' and 'Aboriginal' Policy," in *Native Voices in Research*, ed. Jill Oakes et al. (Winnipeg: Aboriginal Issues Press, 2003), 233–42; Alain Cunningham, *Canadian Indian Policy and Development Planning Theory* (New York: Garland, 1999); Noel Dyck and James Waldram, "Anthropology, Public Policy, and Native Peoples: An Introduction to the Issues," in *Anthropology, Public Policy and Native Peoples in Canada*, ed. Noel Dyck and James Waldram (Montreal and Kingston: McGill-Queen's University Press, 1993), 3–38; and Roger Nichols, *Indians in the United States and Canada: A Comparative History* (Lincoln: University of Nebraska Press, 1998).

16 A.D. Doerr, "Indian Policy," in *Issues in Canadian Public Policy*, ed. G. Bruce Doern and V. Seymour Wilson (Toronto: Macmillan, 1974); DuBois, "Instruments of Policy-Making."

17 DuBois, "Instruments of Policy-Making"; A.D. Doerr, *Participative Policy-Making and the White Paper Process: A Critical Analysis of the White Paper on Indian Policy* (Montreal: Canadian Political Science Association, 1972).

18 See Cunningham, *Canadian Indian Policy*; DuBois, "Instruments of Policy-Making"; María Cristina Manzano-Munguía, "Mediating Aboriginal-State Relations through Native Non-Governmental Organizations and Aboriginal Leaders: An Alternative Model" (PhD diss., University of Western Ontario, 2009); Sally Weaver, *Making Canadian Indian Policy: The Hidden Agenda 1968–1970* (Toronto: University of Toronto Press, 1981); and Sally Weaver, "Indian Policy in the New Conservative Government, Part 1. The Nielsen Task Force of 1985," *Native Studies Review* 2, no. 1 (1986): 1–43.

19 Doerr, *Participative Policy-Making*, 25.

20 Dyck and Waldram, "Anthropology, Public Policy, and Native Peoples," 10.

21 Tobias, "Protection, Civilization, Assimilation," 39–55; Act to Amend the Indian Act, 1985, c. 31 (Bill C-31), in *The Indian Acts and Amendments 1970–1993: An Indexed Collection*, ed. Zandra Wilson (Saskatoon: Native Law Centre, 1993), 59–111.

22 *Sandra Lovelace v. Canada*, Views of the United Nations Human Rights Committee, Communication, 1970, https://digitallibrary.un.org/record/788677.

23 See *Indian Acts and Amendments: An Indexed Collection*, ed. Sharon Venne (Saskatoon: Native Law Centre, 1981).

24 *Lovelace v. Canada*, Human Rights Legal Jurisdiction 158 (United Nations Human Rights Commission, 1981); Isaac, *Aboriginal Law Commentary*.

25 Act to Amend the Indian Act, 1985, c. 31 (Bill C-31).

26 Barbara Barker and Tyler McCreary, "Sharon McIvor's Fight for Gender Equality in the Indian Act," *Briarpatch Magazine*, 1 March 2008, https://epe.lac-bac.gc.ca/100/201/300/briarpatch/2004-2011/2008/03/01/sharon-mcivor/default.htm.

27 Dan Smoke, Seneca Nation, interview with María C. Manzano-Munguía, 2022.

28 Kerstin Martens, "Mission Impossible? Defining Nongovernmental Organizations," *Voluntas: International Journal of Voluntary and Nonprofit Organizations* 13 (2002): 271.

29 Martens, "Mission Impossible?," 272.

30 Michael Edwards and David Hulme, "NGO Performance and Accountability: Introduction and Overview," in *Changing Challenges for NGO Management*, ed. Michael Edwards and Alan Fowler (London: Earthscan, 2002), 187–203.

31 Andrew Clayton, ed., *Governance, Democracy and Conditionality: What Role for NGOs?* (Oxford, UK: INTRAC, 1994); Cunningham, *Canadian Indian Policy*; Michael Robinson, "Governance, Democracy and Conditionality: NGOs and the New Policy Agenda," in Clayton, *Governance*, 35–51.

32 William Fisher, "Doing Good? The Politics and Antipolitics of NGOs Practices," *Annual Review of Anthropology* 26 (1997): 440.

33 Robinson, "Governance, Democracy and Conditionality"; Edwards and Hulme, "NGO Performance and Accountability."

34 Paul Barnsley, "National Aboriginal Organization (NAOs): Funding Review Complete," *Windspeaker Canada Aboriginal News Source* 22, no. 12 (2005), https://www.mail-archive.com/natnews-north@yahoogroups.com/msg00746.html.

35 Robinson, "Governance, Democracy and Conditionality"; Edwards and Hulme, "NGO Performance and Accountability"; Susan MacDonic, "Giving until It Hurts: The Child Sponsorship Paradox," manuscript, University of Western Ontario, 2005; Raymond Bryant, "False Prophets? Mutant NGOs and Philippine Environmentalism," *Society and Natural Resources* 15 (2002): 629–39.

36 Barnsley, "National Aboriginal Organization."

37 Patrick Kilby, "Accountability for Empowerment: Dilemmas Facing Non-Government Organizations," *World Development* 34 (2006): 951–63.

38 Bruno Barras, "Life Projects: Development Our Way," in *In the Way of Development: Indigenous Peoples, Life Projects and Globalization*, ed. Mario Blaser, Harvey A. Feit, and Glenn McRae (London: Zed Books, 2004), 47–52; Mario Blaser, "'Way of Life' or 'Who Decides': Development, Paraguayan Indigenism and the Yshiro People's Life Projects," in Blaser, Feit, and McRae, 52–71.

39 Barras, "Life Projects," 47–52.

40 Barras, 51.

41 See, for instance, María Cristina Manzano-Munguía, Iliana Viridiana Roa González, and Iván Romero Serrano, "Xra Nche'e Ni Kunixin Rajna: Prácticas de Vinculación Comunitaria en la Universidad Intercultural del Estado de Puebla, San Marcos Tlacoyalco," *Mirada Antropológica* 18, no. 24 (2023): 58–77; and Guillermo López Varela and María Cristina Manzano-Munguía, "Governance, De-Commoditization and Communality: The Ngiguas of San Marcos Tlacoyalco in Puebla, Mexico,"

Indigenous Governance and Development: How Do Community Members Respond?, special issue of *Ethnologies: Journal of the Folklore Studies Association of Canada* 43 (2021): 145–64.

42 The Yshir Nation Union of Indigenous Communities.

43 Barras, "Life Projects," 49; Blaser, "'Way of Life.'"

44 Indian Act, RSC 1927, c. 98, in Venne, *An Indexed Collection*, 244–314.

45 Brian Titley, *A Narrow Vision: Duncan Campbell Scott and the Administration of Indian Affairs in Canada* (Vancouver: UBC Press, 1986).

46 Harold Cardinal, *The Rebirth of Canada's Indians* (Edmonton: Hurtig, 1977), 169–70.

47 Titley, *A Narrow Vision*.

48 Titley, 104.

49 Titley, 102.

50 Shelagh Grant, "Indian Affairs under Duncan Campbell Scott: The Plains Cree of Saskatchewan, 1913–1931," *Journal of Canadian Studies* 18 (1983): 21–39.

51 By the end of the 1920s, the League of Indians of Canada ceased to attract members throughout Canada. In 1933, Indian leaders divided the League of Indians into the Indians of Alberta and the Indians of Saskatchewan, later transformed respectively, into the Indian Association of Alberta and the Federation of Saskatchewan Indians. Cardinal, *The Rebirth of Canada's Indians*, 166–77.

52 Harold Cardinal, "Canadian Indians and the Federal Government," *Western Canadian Journal of Anthropology* 1 (1969): 90–97.

53 Weaver, *Making Canadian Indian Policy*.

54 Doerr, *Participative Policy-Making*, 36–54; George Manuel and Michael Posluns, *The Fourth World: An Indian Reality* (Don Mills, ON: Collier-Macmillan Canada, 1974), 210; Weaver, *Making Canadian Indian Policy*, 41.

55 Weaver, *Making Canadian Indian Policy*.

56 Weaver, 42.

57 Michael Prince, "Aboriginals Are Securing a Role," *Policy Options* 21, no. 3 (2000): 45–46; "Putting the New Governance Act into Context: The Long History of Opposition to Government Assimilation Policies. Understanding Why First Nations Oppose Minister Nault's Governance Bills," unpublished document adapted from the Atlantic Policy Congress of First Nations Chiefs, 2000.

58 Manuel and Posluns, *The Fourth World*, 210; Weaver, *Making Canadian Indian Policy*.

59 *Assembly of First Nations*, http://www.afn.ca.

60 Barnsley, "National Aboriginal Organization."

61 Paul Barnsley, "Fontaine Wants Pressure Kept on PM," *Windspeaker Canada Aboriginal News Source* 23 (2005): 10.

62 Gerald Alfred, *Heeding the Voices of Our Ancestors: Kahnawake Mohawk Politics and the Rise of Native Nationalism* (Don Mills, ON: Oxford University Press, 1995).

63 María Cristina Manzano-Munguía, "Conceptualizing Native Non-Government Organizations in Canada: An Ethnographic Approach," *International Journal of Interdisciplinary Social Sciences* 2 (2007): 449–59.

64 Regna Darnell, "Qualitative Demographics of Aboriginal Urban-Rural Migration: The Persistence of Nomadic Habits," paper presented at the Canadian Anthropology Society, Halifax, 2003, 24–25.

65 There has been some research conducted on Aboriginal-run programs by Native organizations in urban areas such as the insightful work of Craig Proulx in Toronto. Craig Proulx, *Reclaiming Aboriginal Justice, Identity, and Community* (Saskatoon: Purich Publishing, 2003).

66 Ginette Lafreniere, Papa Lamine Diallo, Donna Dubie, and Lou Henry, "Can University/Community Collaboration Create Spaces for Aboriginal Reconciliation? Case Study of the Healing of the Seven Generations and Four Directions Community Projects and Wilfrid Laurier University," *First Peoples Child and Family Review* 2 (2005): 53.

67 See the Nokee Kwe website at http://nokeekwe.ca/.

68 Nokee Kwe.

69 Nokee Kwe.

70 See Atlohsa, https://atlohsa.com/pages/our-story?srsltid=AfmBOoqtpVir0WZg-QGgVXFaxCPsFoJbdeK7b7PwLYMDlXfkRavxN3FUC.

71 See the N'Amerind Friendship Centre website at http://www.namerind.on.ca/.

72 Manzano-Munguía, "Mediating Aboriginal-State Relations."

73 Sylvia Maracle, "The Eagle has Landed: Native Women, Leadership and Community Development," in *Strong Women Stories: Native Vision and Community Survival*, ed. Kim Anderson and Bonita Lawrence (Toronto: Sumach Press, 2003), 70–80.

74 Workshop documents from the Nokee Kwe archive.

75 Weaver, *Making Canadian Indian Policy*.

76 Bryan Loucks, interview with María Cristina Manzano-Munguía, 2007.

77 Carol, interview with María Cristina Manzano-Munguía, November 2005.

78 Noel Dyck, "'Telling It Like It Is': Some Dilemmas of Fourth World Ethnography and Advocacy," in *Anthropology, Public Policy and Native Peoples in Canada*, ed. Noel Dyck and James Waldram (Montreal and Kingston: McGill-Queen's University Press, 1993), 192–211.

79 Miller, *Reflections on Native-Newcomer Relations*.

80 Peter Miller and Nikolas Rose, "Governing Economic Life," *Economy and Society* 19 (1990): 31.

81 Smoke Signals Radio Station, https://archive.fims.uwo.ca/smokesignals/about-the-smokes.

82 See The Gathering of Good Minds, https://www.pastforward.ca/perspectives/columns/oct_172003.htm.

83 Helen, interview with María Cristina Manzano-Munguía, June 2008.

84 Amber, interview with María Cristina Manzano-Munguía, November 2007.

85 Stephen Keptin Augustine, Hereditary Chief of Sigenitog, Nova Scotia, "Keynote Address at the Mi'kmaq Grand Council Mi'gmawei Mawiomi Secretariat," 2005, 6.

86 Nokee Kwe.

PART IV

Canada, Foreign Policy, and Transnational Human Rights Approaches

CHAPTER 12

Inside Out: The Rights Revolution and Canadian Foreign Policy since 1948

Asa McKercher

IN 2021, as Canadian diplomats spearheaded a United Nations effort to investigate China's acts of genocide against its Uighur population, Chinese delegates responded by demanding an investigation of Canada's treatment of Indigenous Peoples. Although Prime Minister Justin Trudeau struck back, noting both Canada's commitment to reconciliation and the lack of such a policy regarding the Uighurs, China's charge stung.[1] Nor was it unprecedented. In November 1938, amid an outcry in Canada over the Kristallnacht pogrom, the Nazi Party's *Völkischer Beobachter* warned Canadians to "cease messing in the affairs of other countries" and pointed journalists to the "real atrocities" taking place on reservations.[2] Indigenous Peoples themselves have highlighted the hypocrisy of Canada's stand on human rights issues. In 1980, Marie Smallface-Marule, administrator of the World Council of Indigenous Peoples, decried that, while Canada's foreign minister was condemning Soviet discrimination of Jews, Ottawa was "quietly violating the right of self determination for Aboriginal Peoples in Canada."[3]

These varied examples are indicative of what scholars Whitney Lackenbauer and Andrew Cooper have referred to as the "'Achilles heel' of Canada's international image."[4] As they contend, Canadians' perception of their country as a good international citizen is undermined by the reality of the state's relations with Indigenous Nations. The same is true with immigration policy, where, for decades, race-based restrictions were a source of discontent in Canadian dealings with countries in the Global South. Both issues call into question the Canadian government's past and ongoing commitment to human rights, often traced to the 1948 Universal Declaration of Human Rights (UDHR). As the Global Affairs Canada website boasts, "Canada has been a consistently strong voice for the protection of human rights and the advancement of democratic values," which "started with our central role in the drafting" of the UDHR.[5] This statement is false. In reality, John Humphrey, the UDHR's Canadian author, worked independently of Ottawa, and the Canadian government at first opposed the document and then reluctantly voted for its eventual passage. As Humphrey had complained, "the international promotion of human rights had no priority in Canadian foreign policy."[6] In subsequent decades, the situation changed little.

As interest in Canada's human rights history has grown, historians have demonstrated that Canadian foreign policy makers paid fleeting attention to international human rights, subordinating such concerns to economic and strategic interests and to a strict adherence to state sovereignty.[7] As I emphasize below, the Achilles heel was another source of Canada's caution in promoting human rights internationally. Since the rights revolution began in the 1940s, Canadian government officials have been concerned that foreign governments could call Canada to account for maintaining racial barriers to immigration and citizenship and because, as a settler-colonial state, Canada has denied Indigenous Peoples the right to self-determination while instituting assimilationist policies. Ottawa's desire to avoid embarrassment—the preferred bureaucratic euphemism—demonstrates that policy makers have been mindful of the salience of human rights. At the same time, it has also provided a tool to activists and other interested parties who have utilized Canada's Achilles heel to force government action. As we rethink Canada's human rights history, it is clear that foreign opprobrium, real or imagined, has been an important factor in the Canadian rights revolution and that domestic activism and foreign policy are much more intertwined than often recognized.

As the Cold War unfolded in the late 1940s, Canadian diplomat Escott Reid took stock of the world and the emerging struggle against communism. In a draft study of Soviet intentions concerned largely with military issues, he noted Moscow's success in currying global influence by casting itself as the "defender of the rights of coloured and colonial peoples." For Reid, this issue was important given the looming spectre of decolonization, and it was likely, he wrote, that inaction "to remove racial discriminations rapidly and to satisfy the demands of colonial peoples for self-government" would create immense hostility toward the West.[8] Reiterating this message in a subsequent report, Reid stressed the importance of "rapid progress . . . particularly in the English-speaking countries . . . in the removal of racial discriminations." Since two-thirds of the global population were non-white, he contended that racism and colonialism were major handicaps for Canada and its allies. "In order to save itself from Soviet domination," he concluded, "the Western section of the white race" had to tackle discrimination.[9] Reid was perhaps the most progressive minded of Canada's senior diplomats, and, though his recommendation was ignored in favour of a focus on the militarized containment of the USSR, it showcased awareness of discrimination's international resonance.

On the day that Reid offered his first warning regarding the racial handicap, Prime Minister William Lyon Mackenzie King confided to his diary that the United Nations' interest in racial discrimination posed a "great danger" to Canada.[10] Several months later King rose in the House of Commons to announce a new immigration policy. A huge influx of immigrants soon arrived, helping to fuel the booming postwar economy. Yet Ottawa preferred immigrants from northern Europe, restricting non-white immigration.

As King famously put it, the goal was to avoid altering the "fundamental composition of the Canadian population." Importantly, he added that it was "not a 'fundamental human right' of any alien to enter Canada."[11] This reference to human rights was no off-hand comment. Rather, it reflected King's deep skepticism of the emerging UDHR as well as a need to silo immigration as a domestic issue.

King's statement on immigration followed several policy changes stemming from international pressure. In late 1946, Indian diplomats protested the denial of voting rights to Indians in British Columbia as "a humiliation to India."[12] Since the offending laws were provincial, Ottawa demurred. Facing domestic criticism, too, in early 1947 British Columbia relented, allowing Indian, Chinese, and Japanese residents to vote, a move applauded by Jawaharlal Nehru, India's foreign minister.[13] Despite Ottawa's inaction, Louis St. Laurent, the secretary of state for External Affairs and Nehru's Canadian counterpart, concluded that this development was bound to have "an excellent effect" on Canada's relations with newly independent India and Pakistan.[14] A similar situation played out with Ottawa's repeal of the exclusionary Chinese Immigration Act. Made in response to pressure from China's government and domestic activists, this step also reflected federal officials' fears that Canada would be called to account before the United Nations.[15] Still, immigration from China remained limited.[16]

Beyond these small reforms was the enactment in 1947 of the Canadian Citizenship Act, granting citizenship to all residents regardless of race. There were two exceptions: "Status Indians" and Japanese Canadians. The latter had been interned during the Second World War; subsequently, Ottawa sought to deport them to Japan. An advocate of deportation, St. Laurent emphasized that, if Japanese Canadians remained in Canada, then Tokyo would demand that they be "given the same rights as the white population." As King recorded in his diary, St. Laurent worried about "the issue being raised at the United Nations."[17] St. Laurent's stance is interesting because, a week earlier, he had delivered his famous Gray Lecture touting a new, internationally engaged foreign policy. It also doubled as a sales pitch for the Citizenship Act.[18] Clearly, when it came to Japanese Canadians—for whom voting rights and naturalization came in 1948—St. Laurent judged that citizenship had its limits.

The Gray Lecture listed five principles upon which Canadian foreign policy rested. Among them was what St. Laurent referred to as "human values": that is, "the importance of the individual, on the place of moral principles in the conduct of human relations, on standards of judgment which transcend mere material well-being."[19] Here Canada's foreign minister outlined the importance of human rights as a guide to global affairs. But a stark disconnect between rhetoric and policy emerged. In the year that followed St. Laurent's speech, Ottawa adopted a reluctant, if not obstructionist, stance toward the drafting and adoption of the UDHR. Jealous of sovereignty, Ottawa was also concerned that the UDHR could become "a source of embarrassment," as St. Laurent put it, and might "merely serve to provoke contentious even if unfair criticism" of government policies.[20] These twin concerns came to influence Canada's stance on human rights more broadly. As for the UDHR, Ottawa supported it to avoid being placed "in a rather undesirable minority,"—mainly with the Soviet bloc.[21] Reluctant backing of the UDHR was among St. Laurent's first acts after becoming prime minister in November 1948.

Canada's position on the UDHR showed officials' sense that discrimination damaged relations with foreign governments. For example, amid final negotiations over the UDHR, now-independent India criticized Canada's immigration laws barring Indians in Canada from bringing relatives into the country. In Delhi, Canadian High Commissioner John Kearney suggested admitting "a 'token' quota" of 100 Indian immigrants annually as a means of appeasing "Indian pride and sensibility."[22] At first, Kearney's suggestion was mooted, but under repeated Indian government pressure, in 1950, Secretary of State for External Affairs Lester Pearson concluded that a quota was the only way to avoid "embarrassing our relations with India . . . and at the same time ensure that no substantial Indian immigration" occurred.[23] In January 1951, Canada concluded a treaty with India to admit 150 immigrants annually; concurrent agreements with Pakistan and Ceylon saw annual quotas of 100 persons and 50 persons respectively. The quota option negated opening up Canada's immigration regulations, thereby allowing discriminatory provisions to remain. An incremental step, it was hardly a shining moment for racial equality. Indeed, that December the cabinet voted to continue barring Black Caribbean migrants.[24]

These incidents showcase Canadian officials' recognition that restrictive policies damaged Canada's image abroad. They show, too, the disconnect between international commitments and government policy. A Department of External Affairs (DEA) briefing note on immigration identified a "twofold" problem in dealing with Asian immigration: the domestic problem of assimilation and the "international problem of avoiding the charge of racial discrimination." On the latter point, the brief observed that UN membership imposed on Canada an "unqualified obligation to eliminate racial discrimination in its legislation."[25] Conversely, Canadian policy was premised on denying entry based on race. Echoing King, in 1955, Minister of Citizenship and Immigration Jack Pickersgill affirmed that "immigration isn't a matter of right at all."[26]

Ottawa's reluctance to back the UDHR was matched by skepticism about the subsequent effort to conclude rights covenants as a means of fleshing out an International Bill of Rights. One diplomat dismissed the "misbegotten" notion that a covenant "actually 'gives' human rights in some obscure way."[27] In more practical terms, Canadian policy makers sensed that adherence to the covenants would undermine the country's immigration restrictions. Ottawa also opposed the 1951 Convention Relating to the Status of Refugees because it would apply universally.[28] The St. Laurent government did welcome refugees—165,000 displaced persons and 37,000 Hungarians in 1956—but only those from Europe. Although credited for establishing the main lines of Canadian internationalism, St. Laurent's government remained opposed to international human rights.

Immigration was one reason for Canadian opposition to an International Bill of Rights; Canada's treatment of Indigenous Peoples was another. From the paternalistic Indian Act of 1876 to the cultural genocide undergirding the residential schools program, Canadian policy aimed to eliminate Indigenous Nations as independent polities in North America by forcibly assimilating

Indigenous Peoples into Canadian society. The discrimination directed at Indigenous Peoples and the destitution of many of their communities through government neglect were apparent. "The sight of these wretched people," wrote a contributor to *Canadian Forum* in 1946, "is a denial of all our high-sounding pronouncements, our Atlantic charters, our San Francisco agreements."[29] That year saw the appointment of a joint Senate–House of Commons committee to review policy on Indigenous Peoples. After two years of testimony, the need for reform was clear. "Parliament and the country," stated committee member and MP John Blackmore, were "'human rights' conscious."[30]

In 1949, the St. Laurent government moved oversight of the Department of Indian Affairs from the Ministry of Mines and Resources to the new Department of Citizenship and Immigration, signifying a federal effort to turn Indigenous people into citizens.[31] Two years later the Indian Act was overhauled, removing some of its most discriminatory provisions, such as banning Indigenous cultural practices. Even so, assimilation remained Ottawa's core approach. Canadian policy sought to subordinate Indigenous Peoples to the Canadian state by denying Indigenous forms of self-governance and sovereignty. In this regard, Ottawa had long restricted Indigenous Nations' international activities.[32] Canadian efforts to keep Indigenous issues under a domestic umbrella and prevent international scrutiny included blocking a 1949 Bolivian proposal to create a sub-commission of the UN Economic and Social Council (ECOSOC) to study problems facing the Indigenous Peoples in the Americas.[33] Additionally, Canada's delegation to the International Labour Organization worked to undermine that body's adoption of Convention 107 (1957), an instrument designed to protect Indigenous rights and that, theoretically, would recognize Indigenous Nations internationally. Unsuccessful in its attempts to undermine the convention, Ottawa neither endorsed nor ratified it.[34]

This opposition reflected extreme doubts about the applicability of international human rights to Indigenous Peoples in Canada. In 1957, the deputy minister of Northern Affairs and Natural Resources—responsible for state dealings with the Inuit—warned that adherence to the international rights covenants "might well leave us vulnerable to outside criticism from those who do not, or who will not, understand the peculiar conditions of the north at this stage of human history."[35] A special concern was that the covenants might recognize the right of self-determination—a danger for Canada and its imperial allies. In UN forums in 1955, Canadian delegates made the case that self-determination was both "too vague to be defined with the desirable accuracy" and "more of a goal than a right."[36]

Awareness of Canada's Achilles heel prompted reforms under Prime Minister John Diefenbaker. A long-time civil libertarian, he undertook several rights initiatives, most notably passage of the Bill of Rights in 1960, the same year that his government granted the right to vote to First Nations and Inuit. To Diefenbaker, these developments had a global resonance; he told radio and television audiences that the Bill of Rights affirmed "the principle that every individual, whatever his colour, race or religion, shall be free from discrimination and will have guaranteed equality under the law."[37] Internationally, although the Tories continued to oppose the international covenants, in December 1960, despite opposition from most NATO members, Canada supported Resolution 1514 (the declaration on the granting of independence to colonial countries and peoples), a landmark in affirming the right to self-determination. Over the next two years, the Canadian delegation supported several other anti-colonial measures as part of an outreach effort to the Global South.[38] Importantly, these measures applied to what contemporaries called "salt-water colonialism," not settler colonialism, a concept that emerged slowly in this period.[39]

Diefenbaker's domestic initiatives were important given his effort to make human rights promotion a firmer aspect of Canadian foreign policy.[40] Beyond the anti-colonial resolutions at the United Nations, Diefenbaker helped to engineer apartheid South Africa's exit from the Commonwealth in 1961. Still, he had been reluctant to do so. "What would be our reaction," he wondered, "if some other part of the Commonwealth were to criticize us?"[41] Indeed, shortly after South Africa quit the Commonwealth, its foreign minister, Eric Louw, publicly criticized Canada's dealings with Indigenous Peoples.[42] When Diefenbaker sought to channel anti-colonial attention at the United Nations to Soviet control of Eastern Europe, Moscow's emissaries warned their Canadian counterparts that they were prepared to launch a complaint through the UN Human Rights Commission highlighting discrimination faced by Black Canadians and Indigenous Peoples.[43] Domestic critics made similar points. Decrying Canadians' "self-congratulation" over Diefenbaker's stand on South Africa, one journalist contended that Ottawa's own apartheid-like treatment of Indigenous Peoples was worthy of "kicking Canada out of the Commonwealth."[44] Recognizing that Canada's record undermined its position abroad, Diefenbaker made a conscientious attempt at reform.

Concern about Canada's international image perhaps had its greatest policy impact on immigration. Shortly after South Africa's exit from the Commonwealth, cabinet ministers worried that Pretoria might respond to Diefenbaker's actions by sending "a group of Bantu emigrants" to test Canadian attitudes and policies.[45] Several months earlier Canada's high commissioner in Trinidad warned that the prime minister's anti-apartheid stance gave the impression to West Indians that "Canadian immigration policy vis-à-vis coloured migrants" was changing. Given West Indian criticism of Canadian restrictions, a possible crisis loomed.[46] As she contemplated reforms Ellen Fairclough, the minister of Citizenship and Immigration, was mindful of these problems. In late 1961, Fairclough secured cabinet approval of a new immigration policy that removed "racial or colour discrimination," which she determined was at the "heart of Canada's immigration laws" and "the main source" of international and domestic criticism.[47] Announcing the new immigration policy in early 1962, Fairclough proclaimed that countries in the Global South would be "watching with interest" to gauge Canada's sincerity.[48]

Despite immigration reform, restrictions remained via bureaucratic recalcitrance. As the director of immigration admitted privately, "we shall still give preference in our selection of immigrants to those countries which have traditionally supplied our immigrants." A means of continuing the status quo was a refusal to open new immigration offices.[49] When Lester Pearson's Liberals formed government in 1963, they inherited a sclerotic policy. The new prime minister planned to take "a special interest" in the Caribbean, but he soon found that immigration was a roadblock, with his Caribbean counterparts complaining about ongoing restrictions.[50] So, when visiting Jamaica in 1965, Pearson promised reform "in fact as well as in theory."[51] A 1966 White Paper on Immigration outlined a policy free from discrimination, the source of "strong resentments in international relations."[52] The resulting points system implemented the following year removed racial biases from immigrant selection—a move followed by the opening of new immigration offices in the Global South. It is important to note that racial discrimination continued to mar Canada's reputation—witness the 1969 Sir George Williams affair that saw protests in the Caribbean against racism encountered by Black students at the Montreal university.[53] Still, the Pearson government's reforms were hugely significant.

The 1966 White Paper also signalled a willingness to take in additional refugees, a sign of growing attention to this issue in government circles. In 1963, Norman Robertson, the undersecretary of state, pressed immigration officials by underscoring that adherence to the 1951 Convention Relating to the Status of Refugees was "desirable in the broad context of Canadian international relations."[54] Caution prevailed among immigration officials, ending only in 1969, when Canada signed the refugee convention. Seven years later Canada's Immigration Act was amended to include refugees as an official immigration category. Beyond immigration, under Pearson Canada supported the two international rights covenants during their passage at the United Nations in 1966. As with the UDHR, diplomatic advisers stressed that it would "be embarrassing—or worse" for Canada not to support the covenants.[55] Ratifying the covenants took a decade.

In addition to the immigration White Paper and the covenants, in 1966 *A Survey of the Contemporary Indians of Canada*, the so-called Hawthorn Report, was published. Commissioned by Indian Affairs, anthropologist H.B. Hawthorn recommended wholesale reforms to Canada's Indian Act. Change was important, he wrote, given the "national and international interest in the relations between different racial groups within industrialized nation states," and he noted parallels "drawn between the position of

Indians and the struggle of American Negroes for full participatory rights in American society, the apartheid policies of the South African government, or the general development needs of the emerging nations."[56] In 1967, the Canadian government initiated a review of the Indian Act. In interdepartmental talks, DEA officials stressed that Canada's adherence to the covenants established policy benchmarks, creating a need "to remove, as quickly as feasible, inequalities" between Indigenous Peoples and non-Indigenous peoples. At the same time, they were insistent that "many of the human rights standards elaborated in United Nations international instruments were really goals, and not always capable of immediate achievement."[57] The impetus to make reforms increased in 1968 when Pierre Trudeau became prime minister on a pledge to build a just society. His government soon issued a White Paper proposing to eliminate the special status of Indigenous Peoples within the federation and to grant them instead "full and equal participation in the cultural, social, economic and political life of Canada."[58] In the view of DEA officials who had commented on it, the proposed policy "would constitute compliance in a real and practical way" with the covenants and the International Convention on the Elimination of All Forms of Racial Discrimination, which Canada had signed but not yet ratified.[59]

Whatever the positive intentions of the White Paper, many Indigenous Peoples across Canada viewed it as another attempt at assimilation and a denial both of Canada's ongoing treaty obligations and of Indigenous Peoples' right to self-governance and their unique land title. Opposition was swift and firm. In a letter to the UN secretary general, the Six Nations of the Haudenosaunee Confederacy protested that the proposed policy was a violation of the Atlantic Charter's affirmation of their right to self-determination, and they demanded respect for "the right and responsibility of our authority for our lands, our laws and our people."[60] Harold Cardinal, a Cree lawyer from Treaty 8 territory, delivered a blistering attack on the federal government's "programme of extermination through assimilation" and on Canadians who "have walked blisters on their feet and fat off their rumps to raise money for underdeveloped countries" but did not "give a damn" about Indigenous Peoples.[61] Faced with this backlash to the notion that Indigenous

Peoples were just another minority group, the Trudeau government withdrew the White Paper, which succeeded only in galvanizing Indigenous activism.

Perhaps the most prominent activists to emerge at this time were George Manuel, president of the National Indian Brotherhood (NIB), and Marie Smallface-Marule, the NIB's executive director. Announcing the NIB's creation in 1970, Manuel affirmed the need for an organization "reacting to the bureaucratic machine that has directed [Indigenous lives] for the past 100 years," adding a call for the right to self-determination for Indigenous Peoples.[62] The latter comment marked an important element in Manuel and Smallface-Marule's advocacy efforts: securing Canadian and international recognition that Indigenous Peoples in Canada were colonized peoples.[63] "Aboriginal people in Canada," the NIB stated in 1973, "have borne the brunt of imperialism that has emanated successfully from Paris, London and the St. Lawrence–Ottawa Valley."[64] In the early 1980s, Indigenous activists sought the protection of their rights amid the Trudeau government's patriation of the Canadian Constitution. As part of this campaign, Smallface-Marule petitioned the United Nations' Special Committee on Decolonization (C-24), which dealt with the recognition of Indigenous Peoples' right to self-determination globally.[65]

Manuel and Smallface-Marule did much to bring international and domestic attention to the colonial situation within Canada. When Alexei Kosygin visited Canada in 1971, the Soviet premier was met with protests by Jewish and Eastern European groups highlighting rights abuses behind the Iron Curtain. In an effort to embarrass the Canadian government, Manuel wrote to Kosygin to point out the Canadian state's "policies of colonialism and paternalism."[66] Shortly thereafter, Manuel travelled to Tanzania, where, much to the regret of local Canadian diplomats, he drew unfavourable parallels between British imperialism and Canadian settler colonialism.[67] Speaking to a Danish magazine in 1972, Manuel highlighted that "environmental and human rights are trampled underfoot in Canada when we Indians are concerned."[68] Likewise, Smallface-Marule engaged in international lobbying while also meeting with Canadian state authorities. For instance, in 1974, she told Canadian diplomats of the NIB's interest in the

UDHR's "applicability to native peoples," a comment passed along as a warning to Canada's foreign minister.[69]

Smallface-Marule and Manuel's activities went far beyond critical statements about the Canadian state. The two built solidarity networks with international organizations and other Indigenous Nations beyond North America—what Manuel called the "Fourth World." Critically, the two spearheaded the creation of the World Council of Indigenous Peoples in 1974, the same year that the NIB secured consultative status at ECOSOC. These actions were critical in advancing Indigenous rights internationally, an achievement that Sheryl Lightfoot called a "subtle revolution" in global politics.[70]

Smallface-Marule and Manuel's pursuits brought the attention of Canadian officials, who took a dim view of the internationalization of issues facing Indigenous Peoples. In a brief for the Department of External Affairs on the topic, Indian Affairs complained that, by pursuing an international route, the NIB and other groups were opting for "confrontation politics rather than serious dialogue," a comment signifying officials' preference for keeping matters away from the spotlight, under which undue attention would embarrass Canada. For example, the report cautioned that UN members might view reserves "as a form of apartheid."[71] Given the potential scrutiny that Canada might face, Canadian diplomats greeted with little enthusiasm the news that the NIB gained consultative status at ECOSOC.[72] Importantly, from 1970 to 1974, H. Basil Robinson, a career foreign service officer well aware of the international context, took the position of deputy minister in the Department of Indian Affairs and Northern Development. In a memorandum to his counterpart at External Affairs, Robinson complained that Manuel's travel abroad was leaving "the impression that there is a very serious racial conflict in Canada," necessitating the need for an information campaign to counteract this "badly distorted picture."[73] Officials chose not to confront the NIB or block its activities—a change from past policy—in part because of outside scrutiny. At an interdepartmental meeting to review potential responses to the internationalization of issues facing Indigenous Peoples, DEA and Indian Affairs authorities agreed to approach "the problem with great circumspection" and to avoid either disrupting groups or supporting them with additional funding, a decision accepted by their respective ministers even with the likelihood of "possible embarrassment" in international forums.[74]

Increased international activism did lead to growing attention to Canada's treatment of Indigenous Peoples. Whereas criticism of Canada from South Africa and Soviet Bloc countries was typical and expected, Canadian diplomats found recriminations from friendlier countries more troubling. In 1970, for instance, Swedes protested in front of Canada's embassy in Stockholm, where Haudenosaunee Chief Emerson Hill told the crowd that Canadian policy amounted to "genocide" and differed little from the Nigerian government's treatment of the Biafran population—a reference to the leading humanitarian crisis at that time.[75] Condemnatory stories in several African newspapers in 1974 were another cause of concern since they likened Canadian conduct to South African apartheid. External Affairs counselled that a response was needed, even at the risk of giving "the impression that we are inordinately sensitive on this issue."[76] When a letter from a Canadian embassy official to the editor of the *Nairobi Daily Nation* was printed, Canada's mission in Kenya reported that by an "unfortunate coincidence" it appeared alongside a report on police breaking up a protest by Indigenous activists on Parliament Hill.[77] A variety of international human rights organizations made representations on Indigenous issues to External Affairs and local Canadian missions, including the London-based Anti-Slavery and Aborigines Protection Society.[78] Canada was also mentioned critically at the NGO Conference on Discrimination against Indigenous Populations in the Americas held in Geneva in 1977. This meeting was particularly troubling for Canadian authorities, who judged that, by addressing a large organization and gaining global press attention, the "Indians have won this public relations exercise." Soviet Bloc regimes, Canada's UN mission in Geneva complained, now had a "heavy stick to use" when Canadians raised the fate of dissidents.[79]

As Indigenous rights activism increased, the United Nations became a fraught arena for Canadian diplomats. At the UN Human Rights

Commission (HRC), there were constant complaints and inquiries regarding Indigenous issues. The flow of attention, Canadian diplomats worried, could create the public perception that gross violations of human rights were occurring in Canada, in turn proving "extremely embarrassing" and possibly putting "sorely to the test Canadian support for UN human rights procedures."[80] In 1981, the HRC concluded in favour of Sandra Lovelace, who objected to a clause in the Indian Act denying her Indian Status after she married a non-Indigenous man; no such restriction applied to Indigenous men who married non-Indigenous women. The HRC determined that the Indian Act violated the International Covenant on Civil and Political Rights (1966) by denying Lovelace the right to live in her own community. Responding with legislation to amend the Indian Act in 1985, Ottawa emphasized that this move complied with the covenants as well as the Convention on the Elimination of All Forms of Discrimination against Women.[81] Given this new reality—in which Canada was on the backfoot—Canadian officials sought to limit the damage done to the country's reputation. In 1983, diplomats saw a proposed skills and employment program from Indian Affairs as a means of helping "to avoid criticism of Canada in the United Nations and other international fora where the voice of indigenous peoples is being increasingly heard."[82] A Canadian goal was to muffle that voice—a difficult task.

Scrutiny of Canada only increased when, in 1982, the HRC formed a Working Group on the Rights of Indigenous Populations (WGRIP).[83] By this point, the Canadian government had itself formed a Working Group on International Questions Relating to Indigenous Peoples to respond to Indigenous issues at the United Nations, though much of its early activity was directed toward dealing with activists' successful efforts to see Canada's patriated Constitution recognize Indigenous and treaty rights. A key element of Canadian diplomatic efforts through the WGRIP was to ensure that "the traditional concept of self-determination" was not "used to attack the territorial integrity of a sovereign, non-colonial state" or deemed "applicable to Indigenous Populations within Canada."[84] There were also attempts to deflect criticism. In 1984, after Canadian delegates raised the plight of jailed dissident Andrei Sakharov, the Soviet delegation responded with a resolution citing Canada's "cultural and physical extinction" of Indigenous Peoples.[85] The Canadian record with WGRIP was reactive and negative, revealing "a side of Canada at odds with its reputation as a defender of both human rights and the UN human rights system."[86] That reputation was not earned, and Canadian actions via the WGRIP to limit Indigenous Peoples as distinct rights claimants were more in keeping with Canada's wider record on international human rights.

The apogee—or nadir—of Canada's Achilles heel was perhaps reached in the late 1980s and early 1990s as Prime Minister Brian Mulroney's government undertook a concerted campaign against apartheid South Africa. As Daniel Manulak demonstrates in his chapter, there were new sanctions and coordinated diplomatic efforts at the United Nations and through the Commonwealth as Canadian diplomats on the ground supported grassroots resistance. South Africa's foreign minister complained that the Canadian government was "in the forefront of the anti–South African campaign."[87] As in the past, Pretoria responded by highlighting Canada's treatment of Indigenous Peoples. In a controversial move, in 1987, Chief Louis Stevenson of the Peguis First Nation hosted South African Ambassador Glenn Babb, who relished the opportunity to embarrass Ottawa by accepting an aid request. Stevenson, meanwhile, reminded accompanying reporters that "Canada's treatment of its aboriginal people makes a mockery of the image it portrays to the rest of the world."[88] Similarly, when Joe Clark, Canada's foreign minister, undertook a fact-finding mission to South Africa later that year, his apartheid regime counterpart, Roelof Botha, hosted a group of Nēhiyaw elders and suggested that Canada should "clean up its own backyard."[89] Even anti-apartheid campaigners were aware of Canada's faults, which they used to criticize the hypocrisy of Canadian policy. Visiting Canada in 1990, Archbishop Desmond Tutu spent two days on a Mishkeegogamang First Nation reserve in northern Ontario in the company of National Chief of the Assembly of First Nations Georges Erasmus, who pointed out that many of South Africa's apartheid laws had their basis in Canadian examples.[90]

Tutu's Canadian visit occurred amid the Oka crisis, a standoff that began in Kanesatà:ke territory near Montreal over disputed land between Mohawk land defenders and Quebec provincial police and quickly escalated when the Canadian military arrived. "Canada pretends to the world that armed confrontations such as the present crisis have never occurred in the 'unblemished' history of Canada," the besieged Mohawk proclaimed, adding an appeal for international assistance "to stop these crimes against humanity."[91] Seeking international attention, Kahnawà:ke Grand Chief Joseph Norton implored the United Nations to invoke sanctions against Canada, which was "dealing with natives in the same way as the South African white government is dealing with its black people."[92] Similarly, drawing comparisons between Canadian policy and "the South African apartheid system" in a speech to the European Parliament, Manitoba MLA Elijah Harper observed that, if "Oka could happen in Canada, one of the most humane and peaceful countries in the world, [it] shows that racism and the denial of basic political rights can erupt in violence."[93] For Ottawa, this attention was unwelcome. Despite two deaths—one on each side of the conflict—negotiations eventually defused the months-long confrontation. The federal government subsequently formed a Royal Commission on Aboriginal Peoples. Among its many recommendations, the commission advised Canada to build "nation-to-nation relationships" with Indigenous Peoples.[94]

The Royal Commission was an important marker in asserting the need for Indigenous self-government and in recognizing de facto colonialism. It was neither a panacea nor an end to the embarrassment suffered by the Canadian government when it came to its relations with Indigenous Peoples. Indeed, the decades since the 1990s only saw increased international attention to Canadian settler colonialism. At the 2001 World Conference against Racism, Racial Discrimination, Xenophobia and Related Intolerance in Durban, South Africa, Matthew Coon Come, the national chief of the Assembly of First Nations, compared the Canadian "racist and colonial syndrome of dispossession and discrimination" with apartheid in South Africa. Demanding an apology, Minister of Indian Affairs Bob Nault stated that there was "no proof . . . in modern times that the Canadian government and the general population are racist towards aboriginal people," and Prime Minister Jean Chrétien dismissed Coon Come's "dumping on Canada" as "not very useful."[95] Coon Come's use of an international forum to embarrass the Canadian government stung.

Six years later Canada was one of four countries—all settler-colonial states—to oppose the 2007 UN Declaration on the Rights of Indigenous Peoples (UNDRIP), a pivotal affirmation of Indigenous rights. In negotiations on what would become the resolution, Canada and Australia had worked together to have the draft remove language about land rights and heavily qualify the use of the term "self-determination."[96] The Canadian government eventually reversed course, giving qualified support to UNDRIP as "an aspirational document" that did not "reflect customary international law nor change Canadian laws."[97] This reversal—a partial one, in keeping with Canada's decades-long reluctance to recognize Indigenous rights—followed activism at home and abroad that highlighted the embarrassing position in which Canada found itself as one of the few holdouts. And for Canadian officials, preserving Canada's international "brand" was important.[98]

In this regard, revelations about Indian residential schools and the Canadian government's assimilationist actions toward Indigenous Peoples have been damaging in the extreme, a reminder of the ongoing problems that Canada faces with its Achilles heel.[99] As we reconsider the history of human rights in Canada, it is worth remembering the power of shame. Since the dawn of the modern human rights era in 1948, Canadian government officials have feared being called to account for Canada's shameful conduct, whether racially based immigration restrictions or the treatment of Indigenous Peoples—or, no doubt, other issues not covered above. In turn, efforts to expand rights at home have been aimed, in part, at improving Canada's standing globally.[100] For human rights activists, the ability to embarrass Canada has been an important tool in the drive for change at home, one that draws its power from Canadian rhetoric about its shining role abroad.

Notes

1 Brennan MacDonald, "China Hits Back at Canada," CBC News, 22 June 2021, https://www.cbc.ca/news/politics/china-canada-un-calls-investigation-crimes-indigenous-uyghurs-1.6075025.

2 "Hitler Finds Us Out!," *Vancouver Sun*, 21 November 1938.

3 World Council of Indigenous Peoples, press release, 19 November 1980, Library and Archives Canada (hereafter LAC), RG 25, file 45-CDA-13-3-1-pt.7.

4 Whitney Lackenbauer and Andrew Cooper, "The Achilles Heel of Canadian International Citizenship: Indigenous Diplomacies and State Responses," *Canadian Foreign Policy* 13 (2007): 99.

5 Government of Canada, "Canada's Approach to Advancing Human Rights," 9 January 2020, https://www.international.gc.ca/world-monde/issues_development-enjeux_developpement/human_rights-droits_homme/advancing_rights-promouvoir_droits.aspx?lang=eng.

6 Quoted in William Schabas, "Canada and the Adoption of the Universal Declaration of Human Rights," *McGill Law Journal* 43 (1998): 424. See also Jennifer Tunnicliffe, *Resisting Rights: Canada and the International Bill of Rights, 1947–76* (Vancouver: UBC Press, 2019).

7 See, for example, Richard Pilkington, "In the National Interest? Canada and the East Pakistan Crisis of 1971," *Journal of Genocide Research* 13 (2011): 451–74; Stephanie Bangarth, "'Vocal but not Particularly Strong'? Air Canada's Ill-Fated Vacation Package to Rhodesia and South Africa and the Anti-Apartheid Movement in Canada," *International Journal* 71 (2016): 488–97; David Webster, *Challenge the Strong Wind: Canada and East Timor, 1975–99* (Vancouver: UBC Press, 2020); and Laura Madokoro, "'Nothing to Offer in Return': Refugees, Human Rights and Genocide in Cambodia, 1975–1978," *International Journal* 75 (2020): 220–36.

8 Escott Reid, "Political Appreciation of the Prospects of Soviet Aggression against North America," 13 February 1947, LAC, MG 31 E46, vol. 5, file 4.

9 Escott Reid, "The United States and the Soviet Union: A Study of the Possibility of War and Some of the Implications for Canadian Policy," 30 August 1947, LAC, RG 25, vol. 5750, file 52-F-pt.1.

10 William Lyon Mackenzie King, Diary (hereafter King Diary), 13 February 1947, online at Library and Archives Canada, https://library-archives.canada.ca/eng/collection/research-help/politics-government-law/Pages/diaries-william-lyon-mackenzie-king.aspx.

11 *House of Commons Debates*, (1 May 1947), 2645.

12 Pai to St. Laurent, 6 December 1946, LAC, RG 25, vol. 3706, file 5550-40; J.F. Hilliker, "The British Columbia Franchise and Canadian Relations with India in Wartime, 1939–1945," *BC Studies* 46 (1980): 40–60.

13 Nehru to St. Laurent, 17 April 1947, LAC, RG 25, vol. 3706, file 5550-40.

14 St. Laurent to Hart, 12 November 1947, LAC, RG 25, vol. 3706, file 5550-40.

15 F.J. McEvoy, "'A Symbol of Racial Discrimination': The Chinese Immigration Act and Canada's Relations with China, 1942–1947," *Canadian Ethnic Studies* 14 (1982): 24–42; Stephanie Bangarth, "'We Are Not Asking You to Open Wide the Gates for Chinese Immigration': The Committee for the Repeal of the Chinese Immigration Act and Early Human Rights Activism in Canada," *Canadian Historical Review* 84 (2003): 395–422.

16 Laura Madokoro, "'Slotting' Chinese Families and Refugees, 1947–1967," *Canadian Historical Review* 93 (2012): 25–56.

17 King Diary, 22 January 1947. Also see Stephanie Bangarth, *Voices Raised in Protest: Defending North American Citizens of Japanese Ancestry, 1942–49* (Vancouver: UBC Press, 2008).

18 Adam Chapnick, "The Gray Lecture and Canadian Citizenship in History," *American Review of Canadian Studies* 37 (2007): 443–57.

19 Louis St. Laurent, *The Foundations of Canadian Policy in World Affairs* (Toronto: University of Toronto Press, 1947), 33.

20 DEA to UN Delegation, tel. 117, 8 October 1948, LAC, RG 25, vol. 3701, file 5475-DP-40-pt.1; Schabas, "Canada and the Adoption of the Universal Declaration of Human Rights."

21 UN Delegation to DEA, tel. 461, 23 November 1948, LAC, RG 25, vol. 3701, file 5475-DP-40-pt.1.

22 Kearney to Reid, 26 October 1948, LAC, RG 25, vol. 4479, file 50017-40-pt.1.

23 Pearson to Harris, 11 September 1950, LAC, RG 25, vol. 6178, file 232-AH-40-pt.1.1.

24 Cabinet Conclusions, 20 December 1951, LAC, RG 2, vol. 2649.

25 "Asiatic Immigration into Canada," briefing note, n.d. [1951], LAC, RG 76, vol. 854, file 554-5-pt.1.

26 Fred Bodsworth, "What's Behind the Immigration Wrangle?," *Maclean's*, 14 May 1955, 12.

27 Quoted in Tunnicliffe, *Resisting Rights*, 60.

28 Laura Madokoro, "'Belated Signing': Race-Thinking and Canada's Approach to the 1951 Convention Relating to the Status of Refugees," in *Dominion of Race: Rethinking Canada's International History*, ed. Laura Madokoro, Francine McKenzie, and David Meren (Vancouver: UBC Press, 2017), 160–82.

29 Hazel Robinson, "Blueprint for the Redman," *Canadian Forum*, January 1946, 233–34.

30 Special Joint Committee of the Senate and of the House of Commons Appointed to Consider the Indian Act, *Minutes and Proceedings*, 10 June 1947, 1673, https://parl.canadiana.ca/view/oop.com_SOCHOC_2004_2_1/1.

31 Heidi Bohaker and Franca Iacovetta, "Making Aboriginal People 'Immigrants Too': A Comparison of Citizenship Programs for Newcomers and Indigenous Peoples in Postwar Canada, 1940s–1960s," *Canadian Historical Review* 90 (2009): 427–62.

32 Yale Belanger, "The Six Nations of Grand River Territory's Attempts at Renewing International Political Relationships, 1921–1924," *Canadian Foreign Policy Journal* 13 (2007): 29–43; David Webster, "'Red Indians' in Geneva, 'Papuan Headhunters' in

New York: Race, Mental Maps, and Two Global Appeals in the 1920s and 1960s," in Madokoro, McKenzie, and Meren, *Dominion of Race*, 254–83.

33 David Meren, "Safeguarding Settler Colonialism in Geneva: Canada, Indigenous Rights, and ILO Convention No. 107 on the Protection and Integration of Indigenous Peoples (1957)," *Canadian Historical Review* 102 (2021): 212.

34 Meren, 212.

35 Robertson to Léger, 12 March 1957, LAC, RG 25, vol. 6950, file 5475-DP-3-40-pt.1.1.

36 Final Report on the 10th Session of the General Assembly re: Human Rights, 1955, and Final Report on Item No. 28: Draft International Covenants on Human Rights, 1955, LAC, RG 25, vol. 6923, file 5475-W-40-pt.1.2.

37 John Diefenbaker, notes for an address on the "Nation's Business," 30 June 1960, LAC, MG 31 E83, vol. 7, file 6.

38 Asa McKercher, "The Centre Cannot Hold: Canada, Colonialism, and the 'Afro-Asian Bloc' at the United Nations, 1960–1962," *Journal of Imperial and Commonwealth History* 42 (2014): 329–49.

39 Lorenzo Veracini, "'Settler Colonialism': Career of a Concept," *Journal of Imperial and Commonwealth History* 41 (2013): 313–33.

40 Asa McKercher, "Sound and Fury: Diefenbaker, Human Rights, and Canadian Foreign Policy," *Canadian Historical Review* 97 (2016): 165–94.

41 Quoted in Douglas Anglin, "Canada and Apartheid," *International Journal* 15 (1960): 126.

42 Republic of South Africa, Senate, *Debates*, 7 June 1961, 4884.

43 Asa McKercher, "The Trouble with Self-Determination: Canada, Soviet Colonialism, and the United Nations, 1960–1963," *International Journal of Human Rights* 20 (2016): 343–64.

44 Kildare Dobbs, "The Case for Kicking Canada out of the Commonwealth," *Maclean's*, 6 May 1961, 6.

45 Cabinet Conclusions, 30 May 1961, LAC, RG 2, vol. 6176.

46 Port of Spain to DEA, tel. 20, 20 March 1961, LAC, RG 25, vol. 5009, file 232-AM-40-pt.4.

47 Cabinet Conclusions, 18 October 1961, LAC, RG 2, vol. 6177.

48 Quoted in David Corbett, "Canada's Immigration Policy, 1957–1962," *International Journal* 18 (1963): 179–80.

49 Baskerville to Davidson, 10 November 1961, LAC, RG 26, vol. 100, file 3-15-1-pt.8; Vic Satzewich, "Racism and Canadian Immigration Policy: The Government's View of Caribbean Migration, 1962–1966," *Canadian Ethnic Studies* 21 (1989): 77–97.

50 Escott Reid, "L.B. Pearson—Lunch—Ottawa," 28 May 1963, LAC, MG 31 E46, vol. 35, file "Pearson, Lester."

51 Prime Minister's Press Conference, Jamaica, 30 November 1965, LAC, RG 76, vol. 824, file 552-1-577.

52 Department of Manpower and Immigration, *White Paper on Immigration* (Ottawa: Queen's Printer, 1966), 6–7, 17.

53 Dennis Forsythe, *Let the Niggers Burn: The Sir George Williams University Affair and Its Caribbean Aftermath* (Toronto: Black Rose Books, 1971); Adaeze Greenidge and Levi Gahman, "Roots, Rhizomes and Resistance: Remembering the Sir George Williams Student Uprising," *Race and Class* 61 (2019): 27–42.

54 Madokoro, "'Belated Signing,'" 176.

55 Wershof to UN Division, "Re: Canada's Position on the Human Rights Covenants," 17 December 1963, LAC, RG 25, vol. 13112, file 45-13-2-3-pt.1.

56 H.B. Hawthorn, *A Survey of the Contemporary Indians of Canada* (Ottawa: Indian Affairs Branch, 1966), 362.

57 Shortliffe to file, "Covenants on Human Rights: Discussion with Indian Affairs Branch," 2 June 1967; "The Indian Act," memorandum for the prime minister, 29 November 1967; Cole to file, "Amendment of the Indian Act and Human Rights," 27 December 1967, LAC, RG 25, file 45-CDA-13-3-1-pt.1.

58 Department of Indian Affairs and Northern Development, *Statement of the Government of Canada on Indian Policy* (Ottawa: Queen's Printer, 1969).

59 Bissonnette to Strayer, draft "Re: Constitutional Provisions Relating to Indians," April 1969, LAC, RG 25, file 45-CDA-13-3-1-pt.2.

60 Six Nations Confederacy to U Thant, 13 November 1969, LAC, RG 25, file 45-CDA-13-3-1-pt.3.

61 Harold Cardinal, *The Unjust Society: The Tragedy of Canada's Indians* (Edmonton: Hurtig, 1969), 3.

62 George Manuel, "Statement," in *The Only Good Indian*, ed. Waubageshig (Toronto: New Press, 1970), 2.

63 Jonathan Crossen, "Marie Smallface-Marule: An Indigenous Internationalist," in *Breaking Barriers, Shaping Worlds: Canadian Women and the Search for Global Order*, ed. Jill Campbell-Miller, Greg Donaghy, and Stacey Barker (Vancouver: UBC Press, 2021), 140–41.

64 National Indian Brotherhood, *Aboriginal People of Canada and Their Environment* (Ottawa: NIB, 1973), 1.

65 New York to DEA, tel. 2608, 10 December 1980, LAC, RG 25, file 45-CDA-13-3-1-pt.7.

66 Manuel to Kosygin, 22 October 1971, LAC, RG 25, file 45-CDA-13-3-1-pt.3.

67 Dar Es Salaam to DEA, no. 965, 31 December 1971, LAC, RG 25, file 45-CDA-13-3-1-pt.3.

68 George Manuel, "Canadian Indians," *Politiken*, 17 June 1972, LAC, RG 25, file 45-CDA-13-3-1-pt.3.

69 Ritchie to Sharp, "National Indian Brotherhood," 4 February 1974, LAC, RG 25, file 45-CDA-13-3-1-pt.4.

70 Sheryl Lightfoot, *Global Indigenous Politics: A Subtle Revolution* (New York: Routledge, 2016).

71 Robinson to Tremblay, 18 September 1972, and attached brief, "International Activities of Canadian Indian Associations," 7 September 1972, LAC, RG 25, file 45-CDA-13-3-1-pt.3.

72 Thibault to Buick, "The Canadian Indian Brotherhood," 6 December 1973, LAC, RG 25, file 45-CDA-13-3-1-pt.3.

73 Robinson to Ritchie, 29 February 1972, LAC, RG 25, file 45-CDA-13-3-1-pt.3.

74 Lessard, "Activités international des associations indigènes," 25 March 1974; Robinson to Chrétien, "International Activities of Canadian Native Associations," 27 April 1974; and Ritchie to Sharp, "International Activities of Canadian Native Associations," 29 April 1974, LAC, RG 25, file 45-CDA-13-3-1-pt.4.

75 Stockholm to DEA, no. 317, 28 May 1970, LAC, RG 25, file 45-CDA-13-3-1-pt.3.

76 DEA to Lusaka, no. GAA-369, 29 October 1974, LAC, RG 25, file 45-CDA-13-3-1-pt.4.

77 Nairobi to DEA, no. 1722, 11 October 1974, LAC, RG 25, file 45-CDA-13-3-1-pt.4.

78 London to DEA, no. 167, 28 January 1975, LAC, RG 25, file 45-CDA-13-3-1-pt.4.

79 Rowe to Voisin, 13 October 1977, LAC, RG 25, file 45-CDA-13-3-1-pt.5.

80 Crowe to Edelstein, "1503 Procedures with Respect to Canada," 8 July 1980, LAC, RG 25, file 45-CDA-13-3-1-pt.7.

81 "Minister Introduces Legislation to Eliminate Discrimination," news release, 18 June 1984, LAC, RG 25, file 45-CDA-13-3-1-pt.10.

82 Dupuis to MacEachen, Briefing Note—Cabinet Committee on Social Development, 25 October 1983, LAC, RG 25, file 45-CDA-13-3-1-pt.9.

83 Andrew Thompson, *On the Side of the Angels: Canada and the United Nations Commission on Human Rights* (Vancouver: UBC Press, 2017), 77–87.

84 Department of Indian and Northern Affairs, "Working Group on Indigenous Peoples," briefing for statement, 2 August 1982, LAC, RG 25, vol. 15908, file 45-13-1-1-pt.14.

85 Draft Soviet Resolution on Discrimination against Indigenous Populations in Canada, 28 August 1984, LAC, RG 25, vol. 15908, file 45-13-1-1-pt.20.

86 Thompson, *On the Side*, 87.

87 Daniel Manulak, "'A Marathon, not a Sprint': Canada and South African Apartheid, 1987–1990," *International Journal* 75 (2020): 90.

88 Doug Smith, "An Awkward Visit," *Maclean's*, 23 March 1987; "Indian Blanket, Aid Request Greet Babb at Peguis Reserve," *Globe and Mail*, 11 March 1987; "Ottawa Caught with a Weak Hand as South African Plays Indian Ace," *Globe and Mail*, 14 March 1987.

89 "Indians Present Botha with Headdress," *Globe and Mail*, 19 August 1987; "Clark, Botha Stay at Odds over Release of Mandela," *Globe and Mail*, 15 August 1987; "Visiting Clark Told to 'Get Lost,'" *Globe and Mail*, 14 August 1987.

90 "Tutu Likens Native Fight to Blacks of South Africa," *Winnipeg Free Press*, 14 August 1990; "Tutu Makes Common Cause with Aboriginal Canadians," *Anglican News Service*, 14 August 1990.

91 Haudenosaunee Mohawk Nation of Kanesatake, press release, 20 October 1990, LAC, RG 25, file 45-CDA-13-3-1-pt.5.

92 "Chiefs Urge Swift Recall of Parliament," *Globe and Mail*, 21 July 1990.

93 Speaking notes for Elijah Harper, address to European Parliament, 24 October 1990, LAC, RG 25, file 45-CDA-13-3-1-pt.5.

94 Royal Commission on Aboriginal Peoples, *Looking Forward, Looking Back*, vol. 1 of *Report* (Ottawa: Minister of Supply and Services, 1996), 610.

95 "Canadian Apartheid Grabs Local Headlines," *National Post*, 31 August 2001; "Minister Demands Native Leader Apologize," *Toronto Star*, 1 September 2001; "Summit 'Not Very Useful,' Chrétien Says," *Toronto Star*, 7 September 2001.

96 "Draft Declaration on the Rights of Indigenous Peoples," Cabinet Memorandum JH02/0267, 26 August 2002, National Archives of Australia, JH02/0267/CAB.

97 Indian and Northern Affairs Canada, "Canada's Statement of Support on the United Nations Declaration on the Rights of Indigenous Peoples," 12 November 2010, https://www.rcaanc-cirnac.gc.ca/eng/1309374239861/1621701138904.

98 Terry Mitchell, ed., *The Internationalization of Indigenous Rights: UNDRIP in the Canadian Context* (Waterloo, ON: Centre for International Governance Innovation, 2014); Heather Exner-Pirot, "Friend or Faux? Trudeau, Indigenous Issues and Canada's Brand," *Canadian Foreign Policy Journal* 24, no. 2 (2018): 165–81.

99 Kristy Kirkup, "Kamloops Residential School Has Woken Up World to 'Genocide' in Canada, Bellegarde Says," *Globe and Mail*, 20 June 2021, https://www.theglobeandmail.com/politics/article-kamloops-residential-school-has-woken-up-world-to-genocide-in-canada/; Maan Alhmidi, "Unmarked Burial Site at Residential School Damages Canada's Human Rights Reputation, Advocate Says," *Globe and Mail*, 2 June 2021, https://www.theglobeandmail.com/canada/article-un-seeks-probe-into-deaths-of-indigenous-students-at-residential/.

100 A development also seen with the United States; see Azza Salama Layton, *International Politics and Civil Rights Policies in the United States, 1941–1960* (Cambridge, UK: Cambridge University Press, 2000); and Mary Dudziak, *Cold War Civil Rights* (Princeton, NJ: Princeton University Press, 2001).

CHAPTER 13

"Eyes on the Prize": Canada, Human Rights, and South African Apartheid in the Transition Years

Daniel Manulak

ON 2 FEBRUARY 1990, President of South Africa F.W. de Klerk made a series of pronouncements that would presage the end of apartheid four years later. The world's most famous political prisoner, Nelson Mandela, was to be released after nearly three decades, liberation movements unbanned, and some apartheid legislation repealed. Although these announcements did not represent an end to South Africa's system of racial oppression, most observers acknowledged that this was an opportunity that needed to be grasped lest an opening for peaceful change close forever. Nevertheless, the "transition" years in South Africa were the bloodiest in apartheid's history, with more political murders, human rights abuses, and twists and turns than at any other time during the previous four decades.[1]

Scholars have contended that, into the early 1990s, Prime Minister of Canada Brian Mulroney and his Progressive Conservative government had retreated from its commitment to fighting apartheid.[2] From this vantage point, Ottawa was uncomfortable being at odds with its major Western partners on a significant global issue and increasingly under pressure from an assertive business community looking to find lucrative gains in a "new"

South Africa. This interpretation fits with a broader narrative of Canadian foreign policy, positing that, when push has come to shove, Ottawa has had a less principled track record on human rights than its rhetoric suggests, prioritizing economic gains and national interests over morality.[3] As the chapters in this volume demonstrate, at times Canada has obstructed rather than advanced the spread of human rights norms, both at home and abroad.

The case of Canada and South African apartheid in the transition years nuances this record. Ottawa experienced pressure from its major Western partners, Pretoria, and the business community to adjust course and lift economic sanctions, but it would not do so until September 1993—over two years after the United States, Britain, and the European Community. This was not because Canada was more benign than its Western partners or more committed to international human rights per se. Canadian policy makers, as well as many anti-apartheid activists, believed that Canada had an ideal model for organizing modern industrial society that South Africans would do well to follow in their transition to a post-apartheid state. Yet to effectively influence the direction of a post-apartheid South Africa required that Canada preserve its reputation as a trusted and committed friend of the anti-apartheid movement and support leading pragmatists within the African National Congress (ANC).

Maintaining this reputation was a critical element shaping Canada's approach to South African apartheid during the 1990s. Canadian policy makers and officials felt that they belonged to a global community lest they experience social costs in violating its norms and rules. Time and again the Mulroney government's response to apartheid was informed by concerns about losing face and influence with the ANC and its African Commonwealth partners, regardless of their preferred policy. Consequently, although historians of Canada's foreign relations have contended that Ottawa's approach to international human rights has been motivated primarily by geopolitical and economic interests, in this chapter I posit that social and emotional dynamics, such as reputation, need to be given greater attention to appreciate how such interests are formulated and negotiated in the first place. If reputation can be used to influence others to behave in ways that they might not have otherwise, then it also places social pressure on its beneficiaries to maintain their status and thus act as constraints on policy makers.

Early Canadian Assessments of the Transition in South Africa

Major developments in South Africa were promised in 1989. Notably, South Africa's combative president, P.W. Botha, resigned and was replaced by F.W. de Klerk—a change indicating that hardliners had lost to reform-minded figures within the regime. De Klerk promptly announced that several political prisoners would be released, and it was hinted that Nelson Mandela might follow shortly thereafter. In Ottawa, officials scrambled to decipher what it all meant and whether a window had truly opened to bring about a peaceful transition to a non-racial, democratic South Africa. They had reason to be skeptical: the South African government had burned them before, as recently as 1985, when fundamental reform was promised but amounted to little more than window dressing. So, when de Klerk announced that Mandela would be released from prison and that some apartheid legislation would be lifted, the Canadian government was cautious, suggesting that, though this represented a welcome "beginning," it was not an end to apartheid itself.[4] Canada's measures would be maintained to encourage Pretoria to follow through with concrete movement toward ending apartheid. For Canada, sanctions were a tool to influence political change in South Africa, and this included the question of when to lift them.

Here Ottawa faced a dilemma. The messages that it received from Pretoria and its major Western partners were that now was the time to re-establish ties with South Africa lest Canada be left out in the cold once apartheid ended.[5] As South African officials conveyed, Ottawa's views had not been taken seriously since they had been perceived as biased in favour of the ANC, but a more constructive relationship was possible in which Canadians could play a key role in shaping a new South Africa.[6] These arguments registered with the Mulroney government. During Mandela's first trip to Canada in June 1990, Secretary of State for External Affairs Joe Clark privately urged the ANC to develop a plan for lifting sanctions and to begin negotiations or risk losing credibility when the international sanctions campaign began to dissipate. To some extent, Clark was providing a realistic assessment of the political landscape: Britain was lobbying its allies to rescind sanctions, and it would not be long before they followed suit. After all, de Klerk had undertaken a successful tour of Europe in the summer of 1990, and Western European policy makers found his perspective on sanctions persuasive. As Clark told Mandela, "the absence of a formula runs the risk of giving leadership to anti-sanctions forces in the West."[7]

Although leading members of the ANC agreed in principle, they were committed to sanctions and believed that the international community needed to maintain, if not intensify, pressure on the South African government. Clearly, sanctions had contributed to Pretoria's willingness at least to appear more internationally acceptable and make some concessions, so to lift them before the process of ending apartheid was irreversible was ill advised—an argument with which Ottawa agreed.[8] In conversation with Clark and Mulroney, Mandela and the head of the ANC's Department of International Affairs, Thabo Mbeki, intimated that, while they could not count on most Western governments, true friends would not waver when it mattered.[9] These messages worked on two levels. First, they placed social pressure on Canadian policy makers to maintain their support for the ANC's position. Mulroney and Clark both privately and publicly had committed to supporting the ANC—developing friendships with leading personalities in the process—and they felt compelled to continue to do so, regardless of their attitude toward sanctions. Second, the messages gestured toward what awaited Canada when the ANC came to power as well as a subtle threat of lost opportunities if Ottawa were to join its Western partners in dismantling sanctions at this stage.

These efforts shaped Ottawa's assessment of developments in South Africa. Although the Mulroney government pushed the ANC to rethink its position on sanctions, policy makers decided that they should have Mandela's explicit approval before they lifted their own. This was partly because Ottawa concluded that it had a unique contribution to make in bringing about a non-racial, democratic, post-apartheid South Africa, and to play this role Canada needed to maintain its credibility with the ANC. Motivating Ottawa was not just the promise of a new South Africa but also the catastrophe that would ensue if a peaceful transition failed. It was readily apparent to Canadian officials that, sooner or later, the ANC would be the governing party in South Africa when apartheid collapsed. How this outcome occurred—whether it was violent or peaceful—and what kind of post-apartheid South Africa would emerge remained undetermined. At the end of the struggle, Ottawa concluded, the opponents of apartheid would ask where the West stood on the matter. As such, the struggle against apartheid was a test case of the West's sincerity in living up to its proclaimed values. At the same time, Canada worked to "moderate" Black South Africans, believing that their special relationship relative to other Western countries afforded them the requisite influence to shape the ANC's thinking on major issues, such as armed struggle and nationalization. As Clark proclaimed, without Canada's leadership, there would be more "violence, murder, and disorder" in South Africa.[10]

Sanctions, Reform, and the Commonwealth

In December 1990, the South African government, the ANC, and others agreed to a process for negotiations called the Convention for a Democratic South Africa (CODESA). CODESA was not a perfect instrument, but it did offer the promise of an eventual peaceful end to apartheid. For Ottawa, it provided a tangible development by which the government could begin shifting its approach from applying punitive measures to laying the groundwork through which a new South Africa would emerge. Sticking points, for Canada, remained its African Commonwealth colleagues and the ANC. Since much of the Mulroney government's efforts on the South Africa issue had been organized collectively through the Commonwealth, this also meant that the question of whether and when to lift sanctions was to be coordinated through the association. Consequently, even if Ottawa was inclined to move ahead with its Western partners in forming a more "constructive" relationship with Pretoria, it was constrained by its Commonwealth commitments.

Canada had become the de facto leader of the Commonwealth on the South Africa issue since Britain abdicated its responsibility, but the association also became as much an avenue through which African Commonwealth countries could lobby Canada to maintain a forward position against apartheid.

In 1991, the Commonwealth was scheduled to have three meetings: two of the Commonwealth Committee of Foreign Ministers on Southern Africa (CFMSA) and a Commonwealth Heads of Government Meeting in Harare in October.[11] All three meetings promised to be dominated by discussion of South Africa, and its outcome would be contingent on whether de Klerk made notable advances in reversing white minority rule. Britain had refused to join the CFMSA, viewing it as a pro-sanctions lobby group, but it remained a member of the Commonwealth and hoped that the issue could be dispensed with before the Harare summit. Accordingly, in the lead-up to the CFMSA meeting in February, Britain worked to persuade Canada to push for an early lifting of sanctions within the Commonwealth. One element of its approach emphasized that a political settlement in South Africa required a firm economic underpinning, and sanctions only disrupted this process. If Canada delayed lifting sanctions, then not only would it lose out on business opportunities, but also it would be even further outside the Western "mainstream." Sanctions were on the way out, and for the Commonwealth to be the only holdout risked making the association irrelevant.

As it happened, Ottawa's enthusiasm for sanctions was beginning to wane, and the government was eager for movement at the CFMSA. A report from the Department of External Affairs noted that public opinion was evenly split on sanctions for the first time in six years, such that Canada could begin easing restrictive measures without a significant political fallout. This last part was especially important to the Mulroney government, whose approval ratings had cratered to 12 percent following an economic recession and a constitutional crisis. Ottawa was also facing considerable pressure from other constituencies, such as the business community and caucus, anxious to normalize relations with South Africa as European competitors re-established corporate partnerships.[12] Following Mandela's release from prison and de Klerk's speeches promising fundamental reform, many

Canadians believed that the fight against apartheid was, for all intents and purposes, over.[13]

Nevertheless, the Canadian government would not shift its sanctions policy without Mandela's approval or act unilaterally outside a Commonwealth context. Clark presented a diplomatic strategy that could circumvent this thorny problem: Canada would use its influence to push for an early lifting of sanctions within the Commonwealth in response to meaningful advances toward irreversible change by the de Klerk regime. In so doing, it would maintain its reputation as a committed friend of the anti-apartheid movement by acting in tandem with its African Commonwealth colleagues, even while restoring its ties to South Africa. In practice, this required that the ANC and the African Commonwealth countries support the lifting of sanctions. The African Commonwealth countries refused to do so without the ANC's express permission. As a British memorandum noted, without firm steering from the ANC, the CFMSA would be unable to agree to a response to de Klerk's initiatives.[14] In other words, even though Ottawa chaired the CFMSA, it had become an instrument through which the Global South could shape and constrain Canadian policy and, through it, the West's approach to apartheid.

From Canada's perspective, the ANC was sending mixed signals about its policy on sanctions. The Mulroney government was in close contact with the ANC's Department of International Affairs, which tended to be receptive to moving ahead with negotiations and sensitive to global currents. Indeed, Mbeki directly intervened at the February CFMSA meeting to bridge the difference between Ottawa and the African Commonwealth members, encouraging the group to accept a phased lifting of sanctions in response to specific reforms from the South African government.[15] The ANC's former chief representative to Canada and a senior official in International Affairs, Yusuf Saloojee, had also informed Ottawa that it should expect a softened attitude regarding sanctions and that it was the ANC's job to educate younger cadres to accept this eventuality and abandon their revolutionary rhetoric.[16] Consequently, when the ANC presented a less flexible position on sanctions—a policy that shaped the African Commonwealth's responses—it left Ottawa exposed and subject to criticism from anti-apartheid circles. Canadian officials would complain about what they regarded as the ANC's "incoherence."[17] All of this indicated that, although Ottawa would have preferred to abandon sanctions, it felt compelled to follow the ANC's lead.

The fact that Ottawa was willing to move out of step with its Western partners on sanctions was a major departure in Canadian foreign policy. It would continue to do so at the Group of Seven (G7) summit in July 1991. The summit was convened a month after the South African government repealed two of the remaining three legislative pillars of apartheid, and Britain was adamant that de Klerk be rewarded, arguing that now was the time to put the country on a firm economic footing. For the government of John Major, its primary political objective at the G7 summit was to erode the global sanctions movement by restoring South Africa's access to international financial institutions. Mulroney and American President George H.W. Bush disagreed, revising the language of the G7's final communiqué. Ottawa had committed to the Commonwealth's position that economic sanctions would remain in place until constitutional negotiations were under way in South Africa and would not budge. Canada's rationale was predicated on its assessment of the costs to its global reputation: "If we were to agree to the suggested language in the London summit, it would be seen as a volte face and could incur severe criticism in the media and from the opposition members in the House, both of which had received the Commonwealth position very positively."[18] Other than this "consistency problem," Ottawa concluded that international investment would not return to South Africa until violence subsided, so there was not any urgency to remove financial restrictions.

Difficult as the G7 summit was politically for Canada, the situation became more fraught once the American government lifted its sanctions in July 1991. For the past year, the Canadian government had cautioned the ANC and its African Commonwealth colleagues that pressure from the business community to follow the Americans would intensify and might become "irresistible."[19] A forward-looking and "realistic" strategy needed to be agreed to by the Commonwealth but, in the meantime, Mulroney publicly stated that Canada would "not break ranks" and that Washington's decision was "premature." Even more to the point, the Canadian prime minister added that "we've had a disagreement with the American administration going back to the days when the President was the Vice-President."[20] Since Mulroney had imposed sanctions to help Mandela, he was "tempted to look at his [Mandela's] assessment of the situation rather than somebody else's."[21]

But Ottawa did have grave reservations about the ANC's approach to sanctions and the state of negotiations more broadly. Negotiations in South Africa had broken down as reports surfaced documenting Pretoria's responsibility in covertly funding and supplying weapons to the Inkatha Freedom Party, which in turn carried out attacks against the ANC.[22] In this context, Mulroney considered making an official trip to South Africa to encourage de Klerk to move forward with reforms and bring the two parties together in a "rainbow coalition."[23] Canada's ambassador to South Africa, Chris Westdal, spoke plainly against the trip: "The prospect of a visit in which the prime minister brought them together is a mirage. . . . [T]he very fact of the visit taking place would be regarded by some in the ANC as an unfathomable volte-face and by others as a straightforward betrayal."[24] The ANC's chief representative in Canada, Victor Moche, confirmed Westdal's interpretation, informing the media that such a visit would "diminish his [Mulroney's] role as a leader on the Southern Africa issue in the Commonwealth."[25] Ultimately, Mulroney decided against the visit because Mandela personally urged him not to go since it would upset the delicate balance of negotiations between Pretoria and the ANC.[26]

In the lead-up to the October 1991 Commonwealth meeting in Harare, Canada would work behind the scenes to ensure movement on sanctions. Although its CFMSA partners had agreed, in principle, to a phased lifting of sanctions, Canada was skeptical that the African Commonwealth members would follow through when push came to shove. As the conference inched closer, Ottawa reminded its Zambian and Zimbabwean colleagues that they had committed to such an approach and that this represented the best way to move forward. Even as Canadian policy was shaped by reputational concerns, they also leveraged social pressure in their diplomatic strategies. In this case, Canada relied on a psychological propensity to appear consistent in social interactions to compel its African partners to abide by their promises. Canada was working against the fact that these leaders were more committed to the ANC and preserving their credibility in postcolonial organizations such as the Organization of African Unity, which met prior to the Commonwealth summit. In the end, the Commonwealth did agree to lift restrictions against people-to-people exchanges with South Africa at the Harare Commonwealth Heads of Government Meeting—largely through Canada's insistence—but trade and investment sanctions remained until an "appropriate transitional mechanism" was agreed to by South Africans.

Political Violence, Democracy Promotion, and the Ending of Apartheid

In 1991–92, Canada began actively, if quietly, shifting its policy on South Africa. Instead of focusing primarily on fighting apartheid, it would take a more regional approach that emphasized democracy promotion and economic development. To some extent, Canada's South Africa policy was a victim of economic recession and consequent budgetary cuts. Within Canada's foreign ministry, Africa had traditionally been deemed of low priority, marginalized relative to events in Europe and North America. Clark had vigorously resisted this trend, but by April 1991 he was replaced by Barbara McDougall—a politician allegedly more interested in developments in Eastern Europe than South Africa. As the Australian high commissioner to Canada reported, "in assessing Ottawa's intentions, the impression we have gained from Canadian colleagues is that Foreign Minister McDougall does not have a bent for South African issues or the CFMSA (which she sees as having been Clark's pet) and wants to be rid of the business."[27] Accordingly, the Southern Africa Taskforce—the nerve centre of Canada's efforts against apartheid since 1985—was closed in January 1992.

Former stalwarts also began arguing that Canada needed to adjust course lest it suffer economic and reputational costs. Writing to Ottawa, Ambassador Westdal contended that it was time to lift trade and investment sanctions on South Africa since most of the preconditions established through the Commonwealth had been met. CODESA, he argued, represented the "appropriate transitional mechanism" that the Harare communiqué outlined, so Ottawa was now "forced to choose between respecting the decisions that Canada led the Commonwealth to make at New Delhi and Harare" and "continuing to take their lead from Mandela." Directly contradicting Mandela posed serious political risks, Westdal admitted, but they needed to persuade him to call off "the dogs of sanctions."[28] Others within the foreign ministry also made the case for South Africa as the most important market for Canada in Africa and that Canada should move ahead, with or without the Commonwealth. As one assessment concluded, "a failure to move quickly will place our exporters at a serious disadvantage to competitors who are already well established yet continue to pursue this market actively and vigorously."[29] In the House of Commons, members of Mulroney's caucus publicly interceded, suggesting that "a window of opportunity had opened for new economic relations" and that Canada needed to act "before the window is shut."[30]

Ottawa did not disagree with these assessments per se, but it did push back, primarily because of the potential loss to its credibility—and, with it, its ability to shape a post-apartheid South Africa. Replying to Westdal, officials wrote that "we don't agree with the recommendation on timing for lifting Canadian sanctions. We believe there would be little immediate benefit in terms of Cdn econ interests and some risks in terms of Cdn reputation in Comwel and public opinion."[31] This was not idle talk. The ANC made its position clear to Canadian officials, reiterating that it did not want to see sanctions lifted. It was Canada's prerogative whether or not to remove sanctions unilaterally, but such an action would be perceived as a shift in Canadian policy toward supporting Pretoria. Canada should take into account any "fallout" from a unilateral decision to remove economic sanctions.[32] Ottawa had reasons for dropping economic sanctions that conformed to national interests such as trade and not deviating from its Western partners, but a more important priority was maintaining its image and credibility with the ANC and the Commonwealth.

Maintaining its reputation mattered for several reasons, but most proximately it provided Canada with some leverage to facilitate a peaceful transition to a non-racial, democratic South Africa. This objective was contingent on successful negotiations between the ANC and the South African government. Negotiations proceeded in fits and starts, stalling because of ongoing violence among the ANC, the Inkatha Freedom Party, and a third force composed of ex-military and police from the apartheid regime. Talks were nearly suspended in March 1992 when de Klerk announced a "whites-only" referendum to determine whether the National Party had the requisite support to continue along the path of reform. Western countries made it clear that the only viable decision was a "yes" vote, and, though they expected de Klerk's mandate to be approved, they held their breath. "In the event of the apocalypse," an Australian official wrote, there was international consensus that sanctions would be reimposed and South Africa isolated.[33] If the reverse occurred, then there would be substantial pressure to remove trade and investment sanctions since it appeared that ending apartheid was irreversible.

De Klerk won the referendum handily, temporarily alleviating international concerns about a return to the 1980s. Mulroney approved, writing personally to de Klerk to congratulate him on his "courageous leadership" and asking the South African president to receive McDougall on an official visit in April.[34] Ostensibly, McDougall's trip was cast as helping to revitalize negotiations after the referendum, but it was also intended as a tangible sign of support for de Klerk. During the visit, the Canadian foreign minister emphasized that ending political violence was the key for South Africa "to assume its rightful place among the nations of the world," yet she also signalled that Ottawa was looking ahead to lifting sanctions.[35] It would be "a matter of weeks rather than months" until South Africa could expect major changes in Canadian policy, McDougall commented. Upon her return to Canada, she told Parliament that the government did not want to "maintain sanctions any longer than necessary." For Canada, the next CODESA plenary the following month seemed to be an opportune time when it might consider removing its sanctions if sufficient progress had been made.[36]

Any post-referendum enthusiasm proved to be overly optimistic. The CODESA talks ended in abject failure, and in June reports surfaced of an Inkatha attack on ANC supporters in the Boipatong township.[37] Thirty-nine people were murdered. In response, the ANC suspended negotiations with the South African government given the latter's documented role in arming Inkatha. Ottawa's response to the massacre was revealing. Although the government urged de Klerk to establish an independent inquiry and prosecute the perpetrators, officials emphasized that all sides should accept responsibility for crimes, stop blaming each other, and return to the negotiating table. In the Canadian media, McDougall pointed out, the ANC's objectives were portrayed as attaining power rather than democracy. Any direct confrontation in South Africa would lead to a loss of the ANC's "moral high ground" within the international community.[38] In short, Ottawa downplayed human rights atrocities that could upset the apple cart. Officials were concerned about the humanitarian costs of violence, but above all Canada had a vested interest in an orderly political transition in South Africa. As a senior official in External Affairs later explained, "we kept our eyes on the prize."[39]

The South African drama would continue to unfold for over another year, culminating in a Transitional Executive Council that facilitated South Africa's first non-racial, democratic elections scheduled for April 1994. There continued to be diplomatic manoeuvring in private, but Ottawa argued that this development satisfied the criteria for lifting trade and investment sanctions established at the 1991 Harare Commonwealth meeting.[40] With the ANC's acceptance, if not its endorsement, Canada, along with Australia and Sweden, announced the restoration of trade with and investment in South Africa in September 1993.[41] They would be the final Western countries to do so.

Conclusion

The case of Canada and South African apartheid in the 1990s complicates the narrative of a clear distinction between the pursuit of national interests and human rights in Canadian foreign relations history. A conventional view of statecraft would suggest that Canada's national interests were better served by lifting sanctions, with or without the Commonwealth. Canada's approach to apartheid left the country isolated from its closest allies in the G7 and a target of Britain's campaign to undermine the global sanctions program. The Canadian business community also aggressively lobbied Ottawa, making the case that Canadian businesses were at a major disadvantage relative to their American, European, and Asian competitors. By the 1990s, the Canadian public was less interested in happenings in South Africa, and the anti-apartheid movement was in disarray, struggling to respond to a rapidly changing political landscape. On top of this, Ottawa wanted to lift sanctions and re-establish ties with the South African government.

Yet, as South Africa began its uneasy transition to non-racial majority rule, the Mulroney government believed that they needed to keep their commitment to the ANC and retain their reputation as a leading Western opponent of apartheid. In practice, this meant maintaining sanctions against South Africa until the ANC explicitly gave its seal of approval to remove them in September 1993—over two years after Canada's Western partners had restored trade with and investment in the country. Canadian policy makers expressed the hope that the victims and opponents of apartheid would remember their friends when a non-racial democracy emerged—a sentiment implying that they anticipated a reward in due course for their engagement. At the same time, if apartheid was allowed to persist, then officials feared that it was only a matter of time before the situation exploded into a "race war."

Even so, policy makers concluded that maintaining sanctions damaged Canada as well as the Commonwealth as a viable international association. They also believed that doing so hindered South Africa's prospects for a stable, non-racial democracy. Ottawa unsuccessfully tried to square the circle by using its influence within the organization and its credibility as a leading Western opponent of apartheid to remove sanctions within a Commonwealth context. However, rather than acting unilaterally, Canada opted to stay the course. The ANC and the African Commonwealth leaders held Ottawa accountable for its policies and were not shy about detailing the reputational costs that it would incur in moving without them, both at home and abroad. Canadian policy was therefore shaped less by national interests than by social politics. Much of the Mulroney government's accolades and identity on the world stage stemmed directly from its engaged role against apartheid during the mid-to-late 1980s. Moreover, policy makers had developed close friendships with and made promises to leading Global South actors, such as Mandela and Mbeki. These were commitments that they felt compelled to honour, even if they had grave misgivings. After all, try as they might to distance themselves from emotions and to behave "rationally," policy makers are still people.

Notes

1 Saul Dubow, *Apartheid: 1948–1994* (Oxford: Oxford University Press, 2012), 68.

2 Rhoda E. Howard, "Black Africa and South Africa," in *Human Rights in Canadian Foreign Policy*, ed. Robert O. Matthews and Cranford Pratt (Montreal and Kingston: McGill-Queen's University Press, 1988), 265–84; Linda Freeman, *The Ambiguous Champion: Canada and South Africa in the Trudeau and Mulroney Years* (Toronto: University of Toronto Press, 1997); and Renate Pratt, *In Good Faith: Canadian Churches Against Apartheid* (Waterloo, ON: Wilfrid Laurier University Press, 1997).

3 Stephanie Bangarth, "The Politics of African Intervention: Canada and Biafra, 1967–1990," in *From Kinshasa to Kandahar: Canada and Fragile States in Historical Perspective*, ed. Michael K. Carroll and Greg Donaghy (Calgary: University of Calgary Press, 2016), 53–72; Asa McKercher, "Reason over Passion: Pierre Trudeau, Human Rights, and Canadian Foreign Policy," *International Journal* 73, no. 1 (2018): 129–45; Jennifer Tunnicliffe, *Resisting Rights: Canada and the International Bill of Rights, 1947–76* (Vancouver: UBC Press, 2019); David Webster, *Challenge the Strong Wind: Canada and East Timor, 1975–79* (Vancouver: UBC Press, 2020); and David Webster, "The Myth of Canada as a Voice for Human Rights," *Policy Options*, 4 March 2020.

4 "Clark Applauds South African President's Speech," Department of External Affairs news release, Communiqué No. 121, 2 February 1990, Library and Archives Canada (hereafter LAC), Joe Clark Papers (hereafter JCP), MG 26 R5-11, vol. 5, folder 1.

5 "Secretary of State's Meeting with the Canadian Foreign Minister," 12 February 1990, National Archives (hereafter NA), Kew, UK, FCO 105/3803.

6 "Canada and South Africa: Towards a More Influential Relationship," 30 November 1989, LAC, JCP, MG 26 R5-11, vol. 5, folder 2.
7 "Discussion between SSEA and Nelson Mandela, June 20, 1990," 22 June 1990, LAC, JCP, MG 26 R5-11, vol. 6, folder 1.
8 "The Impact of Sanctions," 10 October 1989, LAC, JCP, MG 26 R5-11, vol. 5, folder 2.
9 "Observations from Visit of Nelson Mandela," 12 July 1990, LAC, JCP, MG 26 R5-11, vol. 6, folder 1.
10 "South Africa," n.d., LAC, JCP, MG 26 R5-9, box 15, file 15.
11 The CFMSA was composed of eight Commonwealth member states—Australia, Canada, Guyana, India, Malaysia, Tanzania, Zambia, and Zimbabwe—and would meet biannually from 1988 to 1991. Its objective was to maintain international pressure on apartheid during the two-year gap between Commonwealth Heads of Government Meetings.
12 "L. James Taylor to Joe Clark," 3 April 1991, South African Department of Foreign Affairs Archives, Pretoria, 1/28/3.
13 "Minutes of Unit Meeting 7 November 1990," University of Fort Hare, Alice, African National Congress Canada Mission Papers, box 54, folder 26.
14 "Canada/South Africa: Secretary of State's Bilateral with Mr. Clark at CSCE Meeting, 20 November," 14 November 1990, NA, FCO 105/3803.
15 Although no sanctions were recommended to be lifted at the February 1991 London CFMSA, members did sign on to a phased lifting in response to specific triggers.
16 "ANC Thinking," 30 January 1991, National Archives of Australia (hereafter NAA), Canberra, A9737, file 91/3175 (part 3).
17 "Canada/South Africa."
18 "London Summit Draft Political Declaration," 19 June 1991, LAC, RG 25, 20-1-2-RSA, vol. 70.
19 "Consults on SAfrica with Zambian Foreign Minister," 11 June 1991, LAC, RG 25, 20-1-2-RSA, vol. 70.
20 "Prime Minister Mulroney, President Bush at Baseball Summit," press conference, 9 July 1991, LAC, RG 25, 20-1-2-RSA, vol. 70.
21 Brian Mulroney, interview with the author, 15 August 2013; "South Africa Sanctions: Canadian Response to U.S. Decision," 15 July 1991, NAA, A9737, file 91/3175 (part 3).
22 The Inkatha Freedom Party was based in the KwaZulu-Natal "homeland." This episode was referred to as "Inkathagate." "Inkatha-gate—South African Government's Secret Funding of Chief Buthelezi's Inkatha Freedom Party," 25 July 1991, LAC, RG 25, vol. 80017, file 20-18-9-2 (part 17).
23 "SAfrica Prime Ministerial Visit," 30 August 1991, LAC, RG 25, 20-1-2-RSA, vol. 77.
24 "SAfrica Prime Ministerial Visit."
25 "Canada: Possible Visit to South Africa by Prime Minister Mulroney," 25 July 1991, NAA, A9737, file 91/3175 (part 3).

26 "South Africa," 13 September 1991, record of a telephone conversation between Australian Prime Minister Bob Hawke and Canadian Prime Minister Brian Mulroney," NAA, A9737, file 91/3175 (part 3).
27 "South Africa: What to Do?," 16 March 1992, NAA, A9737, file 91/3175 (part 3).
28 "SAfrica: Cdn Trade and Financial Sanctions: Time to Move," 11 February 1992, LAC, RG 25, 20-1-2-RSA, vol. 76.
29 "Opening of a Trade Office in Johannesburg/Pretoria, RSA," 24 August 1992, LAC, RG 25, 20-1-2-RSA, vol. 80.
30 "Canada May Urge Commonwealth to Lift Sanctions," *Globe and Mail*, 19 March 1992.
31 "SAfrica: Cdn Trade and Financial Sanctions," 12 February 1992, LAC, RG 25, 20-1-2-RSA, vol. 76.
32 "SAfrica: CODESA II, ANC and Sanctions," 14 May 1992, LAC, RG 25, 20-1-2-RSA, vol. 78.
33 12 March 1992, "Letter from Gareth Evans to Barbara McDougall," NAA, A9737, file 1991/3175 (part 3).
34 "Letter from Brian Mulroney to F.W. de Klerk," 19 March 1992, South African Department of Foreign Affairs Archives, 1/28/3.
35 "Letter from Barbara McDougall to F.W. de Klerk," May 1992, South African Department of Foreign Affairs Archives, 1/28/3.
36 "South Africa: Canadian Views," 22 January 1992, NAA, A9737, file 91/3175 (part 3).
37 "African National Congress (Toronto) Special Meeting with Chief Rep, Victor Moche, June 17, 1992," University of Fort Hare, Alice, ANC Canada Mission Papers, box 35, folder 56.
38 "SAfrica: Bisho Massacre—SSEA Phone Call to ANC," 9 September 1992, LAC, RG 25, 20-1-2-RSA, vol. 81.
39 Lucie Edwards, interview with the author, 21 April 2022.
40 "South Africa: Sanctions," 3 September 1993, NAA, A9737, file 91/001653.
41 "SAfrica: ANC and Lifting of Sanctions," 13 September 1993, LAC, RG 25, vol. 80016, file 20-18-9-2 (part 20).

CHAPTER 14

Pacific Flows: Asia, Canada, and Human Rights Norms Diffusion

David Webster

THE GENEALOGY OF human rights too often simply assumes that the story was written by Europeans, flowing like a river from "natural rights" through the French Revolution to the sea of twentieth-century human rights law.[1] Whole books debate the question of precisely when the natural rights idea was born in Europe.[2] Then there are those who assign a birth date in the 1940s and, even more extreme, those who insist that human rights were "stillborn and then somehow resurrected" as a script written on an almost blank slate in the 1970s—but still in what we are pleased to call "the West."[3]

The history of human rights in Canada cannot be considered solely within a national frame. Although there might be a "Canadian rights tradition," it was obviously inspired by traditions from other parts of the world.[4] The influences were not simply European, a Canadian adaptation of European ideas or even simply of "British liberties." In this chapter, I argue that Canadian ideas of human rights not only flowed from Europe but also emerged in the encounter with Asia.[5]

"Natural rights" can hardly be said to be a uniquely Western idea. They lie just a stone's throw from the Confucian ideal of justice, for instance.

"He who is cruel to the last degree to the people will himself be killed, and his kingdom will perish," Mencius wrote about the right (and duty) to rebel against an unjust ruler. Confucian views on rights were shared as the Universal Declaration of Human Rights (UDHR) was being drafted.[6]

It is important to conceive of rights less as a script written in one place and transmitted to another and more as a multidirectional series of transmissions in which people in different lands rewrite each other's scripts. Think of the process not as a handbook but as a Google document.

This multidirectional transmission has allowed a wider popular embrace of human rights norms, and of the idea that human rights should be respected, than would have been possible if there was simply one-way transmission. Priyamvada Gopal's *Insurgent Empire: Anticolonial Resistance and British Dissent* shows how colonial resistance encounters and resistance movements, framed in the language of rights claims, also shaped "rights talk" back in the imperial centres.[7]

"Human rights only become meaningful as they gain political context," as Lynn Hunt reminds us.[8] Human rights are a process, not a project, a notion borrowed from Timorese thinker Jovito de Araújo.[9] Thus, I side with those who include decolonization as an integral aspect of human rights, pointing out, for instance, that access to the form of the nation-state has been vital to having one's rights respected, and against those who see struggles for national independence as incidental to human rights.[10]

Asian thinkers, activists, and policy makers framed decolonization as a right, and it would be bizarre to write about them in ways that ignore their own rights thinking and talk. It seems to be indisputable (though it is disputed) that, in Eric Weitz's words, "other, non-Western ideas and traditions contributed to the broadening and the deepening of rights." We need to concede that "rights regimes are never stable: account must be taken of the way rights change and evolve."[11]

Rather than assuming stable meanings of rights, we should see how different rights languages intersected with and shaped each other, how they were read into and transformed by policy makers and activists, and how they were globalized rather than diffused from the Global North to the

Global South. Southern actors did not marginalize rights as they brought decolonization to the centre of global politics: they expanded rights as part of a dynamic conversation, permitting "a much more radical vision of rights."[12] Steven Jensen terms this "negotiating universality" and thereby challenges the Cold War line often drawn between civil-political rights and economic-social-cultural rights.[13]

To examine this mutual writing and rewriting of human rights scripts, I explore Canada-Korea missionary interactions, Asian constitution writing in the 1950s alongside the development of the international human rights system, and finally the role of Asian Canadians in building Canada's rights culture.

Before the Creation? Missionary Exchange and Korean Nationalism

Early European and North American interest in Asia was dominated by merchants seeking profits and missionaries seeking converts. Missionaries were not simply spreading Christianity but also seeking to reinvent Asian societies in ways that would make them, to the minds of the missionaries, more humanitarian. Here was an impulse to centre and civilize individuals, giving them equality within the people of God. Missionaries and Chinese converts crusaded against foot binding and infanticide and for education and health care. Their efforts "to change China" were driven by an overarching aim to transform the world along humane principles that they associated with their faith. They were, in historian Carol Chin's assessment, "beneficent imperialists" preaching a universalizing strain of human rights derived from their North American and European homelands.[14]

Some missionaries renounced the idea of evangelization entirely in favour of the mutual progress of Asia and North America toward greater respect for human dignity. Take Toronto's Wilfred Cantwell Smith, later a leading scholar of comparative world religions, who wrote that he had discovered while preaching in Pakistan the good news that there were many paths to salvation, not just the Christian route.[15] Evangelization was turned on its head into the idea of two-way transmission.

Canadian missionaries played an outsized role in Asia, especially in Japanese-ruled Korea. In 1919, Korean nationalists launched a mass movement for independence "in the interest of the eternal and free development of our people and in accordance with the great movement for world reform based upon the awakening conscience of mankind." Painting their country as "a victim of the policies of aggression and coercion," they asked "how long have we been deprived of our right to exist?" The declaration drew from Christian, Confucian, and Indigenous Cheondogyo belief systems, combining local and global influences and responding directly to American President Woodrow Wilson's call for "self-determination." Korean nationalists travelled to the Paris Peace Conference, without success in having their case heard. "We shall safeguard our inherent right to freedom and enjoy a life of prosperity," they declared, linking their cause to the new spirit of humanity sweeping the world. "We have arisen now. Conscience is on our side, and truth guides our way."[16] This was no mere declaration. By Japanese accounts, more than a million Koreans joined protest marches. The Japanese arrested more than 47,000 Koreans.

Among the thirty-three signatories, though he is not named on the final declaration, was Canadian Presbyterian missionary Frank Schofield. He is the only foreigner to be buried in the patriots section of the Korean national cemetery. A statue of Schofield stands today at the Toronto Zoo, courtesy of former city councillor Raymond Cho and the Toronto Korean community. Arriving in Korea, Schofield was most concerned with conversion, but he himself was transformed by his experiences, becoming an ardent supporter of Korea's right to independence, despite Canadian missionaries' greater preference for Japan as a larger mission field and stabilizing force in the region. Schofield took an active part in drafting the declaration of independence, advised Korean counterparts on international reception of their work, photographed demonstrations, and carried the news of repression—and the message of Korean freedom—to global audiences.[17]

Missionary networks emphasized Japanese brutality against nationalists and Korean suffering. One Canadian Presbyterian highlighted "brutalities equal only to those committed by the Germans in France and Belgium," of schoolgirls having their hands chopped off, of civilians being bayoneted. An American supporter made links to the Armenian genocide, saying that Japanese soldiers "committed acts which were as far against the laws of humanity and civilization as the Turkish deeds in Armenia."[18] This account, penned by an army veteran and published by the Korean national association in the United States, was itself a testament to the collaboration between Korean nationalists in exile and North American supporters, a work of literature and information that echoes Gopal's case studies of those who wrote back against the empire from imperial centres.

Korean nationalists aimed at a global audience. "Korea proclaims to the nations of the world that the people of this land, with a history of 4,000 years, have now, in this age of world progress, asserted the independence and liberty of their nation," the announcement of the new republic went. Its draft constitution sang a hymn of rights: it guaranteed the universal franchise and the equality of men and women; promised freedom of religion, speech, association, movement, and the press; and abolished the death penalty. It also committed to health and sanitation, eliminated class distinctions, and declared education the government's primary responsibility.[19]

A language of rights emerged in the encounter of North American missionaries and Korean nationalists, who also remade Korean Christianity. The life of Sang-chul Lee provides an example of the mutual remaking of Korean and Canadian Protestant Christianity.[20] Born in Manchuria, Lee learned about rights not theoretically but through the lived experience of oppression. He described his experience of conversion to Christianity as authentically Korean: "It came to me that I was speaking not to some foreign God imported from Canada, but to my own God, who loved me." He aimed "to keep the authenticity of my original Christian experience, but . . . also to be fully a part of the real world."[21] He joined the Presbyterian Church of the Republic of Korea when it broke away from its more conservative parent and entered the world of minjung theology, the theology of the people, often translated as "liberation theology." The United Church of Canada, a product of church union at home, partnered with this more liberal wing of Canadian-inspired Korean Christianity.

Lee became "a Korean missionary to Canada" when he agreed to minister to a Japanese-language church in Steveston, British Columbia. He called himself fully Canadian, even arguing that "being a token is a ministry too."[22] It is worth underlining that Canada's embrace of multiculturalism came as the result of minority group activism, not as the gift of Pierre Trudeau. Lee himself wrote that he could teach Trudeau a lot about multiculturalism.

As South Korea sank into military dictatorship, Lee became an activist for the rights of his fellow Koreans from his new Korean church in Toronto. He cosigned the Korean Christian manifesto in 1973, spawned by a network of Koreans at home and in exile on the basis of human rights and dignity. He co-founded the North American Coalition for Democracy in Korea and quietly supported activists in groups such as Young Koreans United of Toronto willing to use public tactics. Lee became the moderator of the United Church of Canada from 1988 to 1990, playing a central role in moving the church toward inclusion of marginalized people, LGBT+ communities, Indigenous Peoples, and others among them. Others in the church such as Reverend Lois Wilson had similar perspectives but conceded that they were formed partly from the encounter with people other than European Canadians. Asian influences helped to shape the United Church and Canadian Christianity more generally.[23]

Rights and Constitution Making, 1945–59

Human rights appeared in the UN mandate as a result of pressure from non-governmental organizations (NGOs) and some smaller member states that forced an initially reluctant American government to consent.[24] The UDHR followed logically from this development. It was not a solely Western creation. Montrealer John Humphrey, as director of the small UN human rights division, wrote an early draft of the UDHR and stressed social and economic rights in a social-democratic tradition of rights, a far cry from the civil and political rights tradition that remains dominant in the United States and the West more broadly. This initiative was accepted with the support of Latin American delegations, with figures such as Hernán Santa

Cruz of Chile playing crucial roles.[25] Eleanor Roosevelt's deputy on the eight-person drafting committee was P.C. Chang of (the Republic of) China, who cited Confucian wellsprings of the definitions of human rights being developed. Although Western drafters outnumbered Asian drafters, the inevitable outcome of the composition of the United Nations during the late 1940s meant that Asian traditions also influenced the eventual text. For instance, Hansa Mehta of India drew from arguments about the rights of women first formulated in the 1930s within the Indian National Congress in her advocacy for women's rights at the United Nations, and Pakistan's Begum Shaista Ikramullah stressed women's equality both in her work at the United Nations and in drafting her country's constitution.[26]

South and Southeast Asian constitution making was a parallel process in the late 1940s with the writing of the UDHR, as Cindy Ewing points out in a discussion of constitution making in former South Asian British colonies. Constitutions are both legal documents and statements of principle. The entrenchment of human rights, and especially reference to documents such as the UDHR, sent important messages about the identities of new states as they drafted their constitutions. Both "contributed to a burgeoning global discourse of rights on a number of intersecting plans, national and international," Ewing writes. Seeing Asian constitution writing allows us to see the importance of the late 1940s as more than a false start in human rights history. Constitution making "offered a site for the materialization of a unifying rights discourse in Asia that first paralleled, and then intersected[,] with human rights projects at the UN."[27] These constitutions, written in the context of a British common law empire, laid out "fundamental" rights that the state could enforce alongside more aspirational rights and departed from the global mainstream in their guarantees for the rights of minorities, positing multi-ethnic states in ways that colonialism had undermined. Burma's constitution even guaranteed a right to secede.

We can build upon Ewing's discussion by adding the 1950s constitution-making processes in Malaya. Prime Minister of Malaya Tunku Abdul Rahman resisted reliance on British advice as the constitution for the Federation of Malaya was drafted in the run-up to independence in 1957.

Instead, he sought a Commonwealth advisory commission with representatives from Australia, Canada, India, and Pakistan, splitting "Old Dominions" from newer Asian states and cutting out the colonial power.[28] Canada struggled to find a representative but was keen to support Malaya's path. Unlike Burma, Malaya was happy to remain within the Commonwealth. It portrayed itself as the only genuine parliamentary democracy in Southeast Asia.[29] Its constitution followed India's by spelling out a list of fundamental rights and listing group rights, important in a federal state with no clear ethnic majority.

Canada welcomed Malaya's independence and saw itself as a mentor to the new federation. After all, as cabinet minister J.M. Macdonnell put it, Canada had "no record of imperialism or colonialism" and thus could mentor the newest Commonwealth member effectively.[30] Canada's first aid administrator, R.G. "Nik" Cavell, urged Canadians to "put our example before the South East Asian nations as one they might find it advantageous to follow." Indeed, he added, such was Canada's "duty."[31]

Yet Canada was not a teacher to the new Malayan pupil. Malaya's early UN initiatives stressed self-determination for Tibet and West Papua, a Dutch colony claimed by Indonesia. Canada stayed aloof from such questions. Malaya also joined the chorus condemning apartheid in South Africa, with Canada seeking a middle ground. There was little common ground between the two countries on human rights until Canada accepted the two human rights covenants and began, slowly, to change its own rights thinking.[32]

Bandung, the Philippines, and the Right to Self-Determination

Pro-Western Malaya was on the same page about the right to self-determination as more neutral or left-leaning Asia states. Here it joined a consensus forged at the Bandung conference in 1955 of twenty-nine Asian and African states, hosted by Indonesia. In Bandung, all participants agreed on the importance of international human rights, identified as one of its five main concerns.[33] The conference listed one collective right seen as the most fundamental of all rights: self-determination.[34] This was not new.

In 1950, for instance, Syria's UN delegate called self-determination "the essential pre-requisite of all other rights."[35] But Bandung established the right to self-determination as central in the Asian and African approach to human rights.

The conference's final declaration is crystal clear on the universality of rights, declaring "full support of the fundamental principles of Human Rights as set forth in the Charter of the United Nations and . . . of the Universal Declaration of Human Rights as a common standard of achievement for all peoples and all nations." Self-determination was "a pre-requisite of the full enjoyment of all fundamental Human Rights." Placing antiracism at the core of rights, it also deplored "the policies and practices of racial segregation and discrimination."[36]

Bandung put self-determination at the centre of the human rights agenda, a policy that countries of the Global South would follow consistently throughout the negotiations to turn the UDHR into two binding covenants. This was a struggle that they won: the right to self-determination is the first item in each covenant.

Bandung met with suspicion in most Western countries. Even Canada, the only Western country to send a note of greetings to the conference, opposed the idea that self-determination was a human right, arguing that it was "a collective matter rather than an individual right." Canadians worked to undermine a self-determination article in talks on the UN human rights covenants, in partnership with colonial powers (Britain, France, Belgium, the Netherlands, Australia, and New Zealand) and others (Sweden, Norway, Denmark, Turkey, and Brazil).[37] All of the independent states in Asia disagreed, and their view would prevail and ultimately help to convince Canada to reverse its opposition to collective rights. By the 1970s, the Canadian delegation to the United Nations thought that they could never vote against resolutions mentioning the principle of self-determination even if they disagreed with them.[38] Self-determination had become sacred to Ottawa, too.

The human rights themes set at Bandung—self-determination and racism—were central in the drafting of the two human rights conventions

(1966) and of the International Convention on the Elimination of All Forms of Racial Discrimination (1965).[39] Steven Jensen stresses this point in *The Making of International Human Rights: The 1960s, Decolonization, and the Reconstruction of Global Values*, which shatters 1970s-centric historiography by pointing to the drafting of these three instruments, and the final adoption of all three in a short span of time, in ways that showed the agency of the Global South. In his account, the appearance of the human rights covenants in 1966, and the Convention on the Elimination of All Forms of Racial Discrimination, stand at the centre. And thus so does the Global South. "In reality," Jensen writes, "what happened in the 1960s was that the states of Jamaica, Ghana, the Philippines and Liberia and others gave a master class in international human rights diplomacy to both the Eastern and Western actors embroiled in the Cold War."[40] His study does not highlight Bandung, but it is hard not to see continuities from Bandung's focus on racism and self-determination and the 1965–66 conventions—two opening with self-determination and one dedicated to racism. Although Jensen gives special attention to Jamaica as a pioneer in international human rights norms making, speaks less specifically about the Philippines, a country that gained its independence from the United States in 1946.

While remaining a close American ally, the Philippines played a more productive role on the UN Commission on Human Rights (CHR) than its former ruler. The Philippines was not, like India or Indonesia, a neutralist power. Nevertheless, it joined with neutralist rivals in Asia to use UN channels to push a "Third World project" in which the United Nations became the centre of the rights movement, allowing Asian states rather than Western ones to "punch above their weight."[41] As a CHR member in 1947–50 and again in 1963–73, the Philippines pushed the envelope on issues of racism and rights and consistently proved to be willing to challenge American opposition to international human rights norms setting. Whereas the United States under the Eisenhower administration dropped the UN human rights activism exemplified by Eleanor Roosevelt, the Philippines was among the voices, mostly from the Global South, that defended the UN rights project and shepherded the covenants to completion by 1966.

The Philippines was not a member of the drafting committee for the UDHR, though it sent multiple communications. Its views, however, were close to those of Lebanon's delegate, Charles Malik, who succeeded Eleanor Roosevelt as chair of the CHR.[42] These were Catholic-informed views that centred the dignity of the human person, in line with the thinking of French philosopher Jacques Maritain, but also placed high value on the traditions brought to the church by non-European parishioners, the gentes. This was not liberation theology, but it stressed cultural openness rather than fundamentalism. It has been dominant in the Asian Catholic-majority countries, the Philippines and Timor-Leste, which seek a middle path between traditionalists and the followers of liberation theology.

Post-UDHR, the Philippines became active in attempting to finalize the two human rights covenants and implementation measures that followed. One year after the passage of the UDHR, the Philippines criticized an American draft covenant for backsliding on the UDHR's economic and social rights clauses and in general failing to "convey the idea that the Covenant is to reinforce the Declaration of Human Rights." Along with Lebanon, the Philippines defended the existence of the Sub-Commission on Freedom of Information and of the Press, then under threat of dissolution, and made free information a campaign focus.[43] The Philippines supplied the UN special rapporteur on freedom of information, Salvador Lopez. It backed an American call for each country to make an annual report to the United Nations on its human rights performance but insisted that these reports not become substitutes for the covenants that the United States now opposed and advocated that the United Nations not simply "study" the reports but also take "action" on them.[44] The Philippines supported Poland's efforts to include the rights of the child in the human rights covenant(s), a topic that Canada opposed.[45]

The active role of the Philippines was recognized when Ambassador Felixberto Serrano became CHR chair in 1957. The same year the Philippines hosted the first UN regional human rights conference in Baguio. UN human rights division chief John Humphrey called the seminar "a great success, far exceeding my expectations," and used it as the template for regional conferences that followed.[46]

The main message from Manila was for the right to self-determination. In 1949, Philippine delegates pushed through a CHR resolution calling for the Trusteeship Council to consider the UDHR and for colonial powers to respect the rights laid out in the declaration, despite a French attempt to slow this by adding a reference to "progressive measures and appropriate procedures" over time.[47] The other priority was antiracism, with the Philippines a consistent advocate of a Convention on the Elimination of Racial Discrimination, making common cause with neighbouring neutral states despite its Cold War membership in Southeast Asia Treaty Organization and its bilateral defence ties to the United States. Special attention went to enforcement measures. In 1962, Philippine delegate Narciso Reyes called out UN members for "insufficient cooperation in the form of faithful compliance" with human rights standards. Finally, the Philippines joined Ghana to push successfully for provisions in the International Convention on the Elimination of All Forms of Racial Discrimination for the first ongoing monitoring body attached to a UN treaty, "one of the most important covenants ever adopted by the United Nations," in the words of John Humphrey.[48] It laid "the foundations for the international human rights system we know today."[49]

In comparison, Canada lagged behind. When the CHR completed drafting the two human rights covenants, Canada's UN delegation lamented that "the articles of the draft Covenant contained very serious defects." The lack of a "federal state clause" was "unacceptable to Canada," and the insistence, from Manila and elsewhere, that rights applied fully in colonized territories was "impractical" and "unworkable." Article 1 on self-determination was especially "inappropriate" and should also be deleted, Canadian officials argued.[50]

As Jennifer Tunnicliffe has demonstrated conclusively, Canada dragged its feet (at best) when it came to international human rights law. That changed only after the covenants were completed and Canada "transformed from a nation initially resistant to the notion of international human rights to one that eventually began to advocate for them" given global pressures and "growing public support for human rights at home and an active human rights movement."[51] Whereas Tunnicliffe concentrates on domestic debates, Andrew Thompson makes a related case for early Canadian complacency and the role of NGOs in his history of Canada and the CHR. Canadian commitment to "advance the international human rights agenda rather than hamper it . . . coincided with the rising influence of newly independent states," he writes.[52] Influence flowed, in this case, from the South to the North.

The clash over self-determination ended as the covenants came into effect and Western powers began to accept the reality of decolonization and at least pay lip service to antiracism. As Frantz Fanon quipped, "a veritable panic takes hold of the colonialist governments in turn. . . . Quick, quick, let's decolonize."[53] The fact that these two issues were key for "Third World moderates" in places such as the Philippines, Jamaica, Liberia, and the African "Brazzaville group" made it a virtual imperative for colonial powers and the United States to change course. Historian Steven Hugh Lee has pointed to Canada and its allies seeking and being forced to team up with "Asian moderates" in the Vietnam and Korean Wars.[54] This process continued during the Cold War as Ottawa, Washington, and other Western capitals backed "moderates" even as they worked to overthrow "radicals" in 1960s Indonesia, Ghana, and elsewhere. The price of working with the moderates may have been to accept their view of rights and self-determination.

Asian Canadians as Rights Builders

Canada entered the twentieth century with a rule of near exclusion. Asian and African migration was either banned (the Chinese Immigration Act, 1923, which tightened earlier exclusionary policies), politely but firmly prevented (the "continuous voyage" regulation, 1908), or diplomatically averted (the Canada-Japan "gentlemen's agreement," also in 1908). Public pressure dictated keeping Asians out, even painting them as a threat to Canadian liberties.[55] Men defined as Chinese were banned from employing women defined as white in 1912 in Saskatchewan, for instance, on the basis of the "danger" that they posed.[56] In 1907, whites rioted against Asians in Vancouver, an example of growing racism that echoed developments in the United States and Australia.[57]

During the Second World War, Canada's government deliberately and with full awareness violated the civil rights of Canadian residents of Japanese ancestry through forced displacement and property seizure. Racism was so high that "every man on a fish boat in the British Columbia coastal waters" was suspected of being "an Admiral in the Japanese navy," in the recollection of diplomat Hugh Keenleyside, one of the few in the government to resist the pressure to relocate Japanese Canadians.[58] These actions, ironically, spurred the growth of some of Canada's first human rights organizations.[59] The Japanese Canadian campaign for redress continued for decades and did not obtain one of the Canadian government's first apologies for rights violations until 1988.[60] The redress campaign was an example of a Canadian community of Asian descent organizing for its own rights. At the same time, it served as an example, a mirror that Canadians used to look at themselves prior to the age of truth and reconciliation.

In the wake of the war, Canada's exclusionary immigration policies increasingly embarrassed the country on the global stage. Canada wished to paint itself as a rights-respecting country and an advocate for the rights of those living under communism. Lester Pearson called for a token quota allowing some Asians to enter the country.[61] After John Diefenbaker became prime minister in 1957, he emphasized the role of rights rhetoric in Canadian domestic and foreign policy. The Canadian Bill of Rights was one step; enfranchising Indigenous people was another. If he was to advocate for "captive peoples" under communist rule, then Diefenbaker could hardly accept apartheid in South Africa.[62] Immigration policy finally removed race-based restrictions.[63]

With the opening of Canadian immigration to Asians, communities of Asian descent formed throughout Canada. In the same way that Sang Chul Lee advocated from Toronto for human rights in Canada, Canadian activists of Asian descent campaigned for rights in their own countries. Canadian churches formed a Canada-Asia Working Group with close ties to Korean

Canadian and Filipino Canadian communities that focused initially on centring human rights in Canada's foreign policy on South Korea and the Philippines.[64] Some Canadian activists would even be elected to their countries' post-dictatorship parliaments, as was Toronto's Albert Lin, a member of Taiwan's pro-independence Democratic Progressive Party.

Rights activism was aimed at Asian dictatorships and at Canada's foreign policy. Although Pierre Trudeau's government entrenched rights within Canada and built stronger links to Asia, it steadfastly refused to make human rights a guiding principle in its foreign policy. Trudeau aligned with leaders such as Lee Kuan Yew of Singapore and Indira Gandhi of India, not with rights activists in their countries. Rights advocacy was not an appropriate aspect of foreign policy, he insisted.[65] The historical record displays very limited evidence of rights advocacy overseas by Trudeau's government, despite the claims of some scholars.[66] It provides extensive evidence of the opposite. Canadian diplomats and policy makers flatly refused to advocate for human rights in the face of near genocide in Timor-Leste (East Timor). Even Cambodian refugees from the genocidal Khmer Rouge saw their stories reshaped to meet Canadian needs.[67] All of this echoed Trudeau's famous quip "Where's Biafra?" in the face of mass killings in a war of secession in Nigeria.[68] His successor, Brian Mulroney, promised to centre rights in Canada's foreign policy for the first time, echoing the advocacy claims of earlier Conservative governments and denouncing the Liberals for leaving human rights to the side.

The battle over trade versus human rights was joined most strikingly in the 1990s when Jean Chrétien's Liberals abandoned or rolled back many of the Mulroney government's human rights initiatives. High-growth China, and Asia more broadly, were firmly in Chrétien's sights as trade targets. His government opposed economic pressure to promote human rights. "Isolation is the worst recipe, in my judgment, for curing human-rights problems," Chrétien argued.[69]

Leading the opposition were Asian Canadian human rights groups and their supporters. Young Koreans United, the Canada Tibet Committee, Canadians Concerned about Ethnic Violence in Indonesia, and a host of other groups who advocated that Canada make human rights the centre of its approach to the country of their concern. Pressure built for rights to be integrated into foreign policy. That pressure flowed from Asian Canadian communities and then was embraced by church and labour circles in Canada. One coalition called for Canada to "apply additional pressure on China" at the United Nations; another called "the promotion of human rights just as important" as trade; and the list continues.[70]

Solidarity groups in Canada began to embrace the concepts of human rights generated by Asian and Asian Canadian activists in the course of their own struggles. Indonesia joined Malaysia, China, and others in preaching "Asian values" through the 1990s. East Timor, occupied by Indonesia since 1975, proved to be an especially attractive cause for many Canadians. Timorese resistance spokesperson José Ramos Horta declared that "human rights transcend boundaries and prevail over state sovereignty."[71]

Not by chance, this was the precise opposite of the Indonesian government's position on the rights debates of the 1990s. Picking up on collective and economic rights, the boosters of "Asian values" assailed Western governments much like the Soviet Union had done during the Cold War, criticizing their racism and stress on individual civil and political rights. The boosters argued that Confucian and Islamic cultures in Asia were more collective, more deferential to authority, more interested in basic needs and economic development than in individual civil liberties. Their claims peaked in the 1993 Bangkok declaration, in which they claimed that rights were culturally relative and thus effectively claimed an exemption from the type of pressure that they received from Western governments.[72]

Asian NGOs responded with their own declaration. They rejected both the notion that "Asian values" could override any aspect of the universality of human rights and the notion that human rights were Western in origin. Asia, they insisted, had much to teach on human rights, not only things to learn. This declaration influenced the language and concepts deployed by their Western NGO partners, creating a third position in the polarized debate over "Asian values." Asian NGOs rejected Asian government claims that national sovereignty came first, but they also stressed "solidarity rights." One call, for instance, was for Global North NGOs "to use the democratic space available in their societies to increase public awareness of how Northern control and domination of the international system curbs and curtails the basic rights of people in Asia."[73] Canadian groups took this to heart in their work.

Pro-Timor diplomacy is exemplified in the experience of Bella Galhos, the daughter of a family seen as pro-Indonesian living in Dili, the Timorese capital city.[74] Indonesian authorities selected her for a Canada World Youth exchange program, unaware that she had already started work with the underground student movement for independence. Once in Canada, she applied for refugee status in a dramatic escape from Indonesian minders that became the subject of a song by Winnipeg-based punk band Propagandhi. She joined the East Timor Alert Network and became one of Ramos Horta's team of young unofficial diplomats, working from Ottawa in tandem with another Timorese refugee, Abé Barreto Soares, in Toronto.

The two Timorese refugees substantially shifted the framings used by Canadian activists to emphasize the right to self-determination and a more collective view of rights. Both returned to Timor-Leste when it regained independence in 1999. Galhos worked with Canadian police on human rights training and then became the first woman in the country to come out as bisexual. She and her partner, Iram Saeed, a Muslim, India-born, development worker and rights activist, went on to found Arcoris, Timor-Leste's only advocacy group and shelter for lesbian, bisexual, and trans women. Galhos was also a co-organizer of the country's first Pride parade. She and Saeed have published research on violence against LGBT+ youth and advocated for an anti-violence emphasis within the international LGBT+ movement, in which they and other Timorese voices stress basic issues in contrast to Western activists who stress marriage equality. Galhos exemplifies, in other words, the two-way exchange of rights across the Pacific.

Conclusion

I have argued in this chapter that human rights were not a script written in Europe and modified with Canadian characteristics. They were not embraced as part of any sudden "revolution," in the 1970s or otherwise. Rather, rights diffused over time, and Canadian rights scripts were written in part by Asian hands, not only by European settler hands.

Rights flowed both ways across the Pacific. Whereas Canadian Frank Schofield sought to advance individual rights in Korea, Korean convert Sang-chul Lee also did much to move Canada's rights culture toward more collective and inclusive understandings. Although many retroactively paint Canada as a long-time crusader for human rights, it was in fact preceded by Malaya, the Philippines, Indonesia, and other Asian governments. Canada slowly came to embrace their perspectives on human rights, shifting away from full-throated opposition to the right to self-determination and toward reluctant acceptance and then whole-hearted embrace of that right. Asian Canadian communities and causes were important in advancing human rights understandings in Canada. This change eventually found its way into Canadian foreign policy.

When the National Association of Japanese Canadians received a redress settlement from the Canadian government as part of its apology to Japanese Canadians, it earmarked some funds to support First Nations struggles, identifying this as a duty to the original displaced people. Supporters framed the move as another step in the redress process. The association's Toronto chapter underlined the message in 2021: "In the Spirit of Redress, or that spirit of courage and tenacity in the face of horrible injustice, racism, ignorance and denial of the truth and of the past, let us stand together in support of residential school survivors, now."[75]

The guiding theme of Asian Canadian influences on Canada's rights culture, I think, can be summed up in the word solidarity. Canadians have been increasingly willing to accept collective rights and solidarity rights that draw from Asian traditions. Also, and it might not be coincidental, they draw from Indigenous traditions in what is now Canada—wherein Indigenous issues are the major challenge to Canadians' self-image as rights respecters today.

Notes

1 For a nuanced approach, see, for instance, Anthony Pagden, "Human Rights, Natural Rights, and Europe's Imperial Legacy," *Political Theory* 31, no. 2 (2003): 171–99. Although he places the genesis of rights in multiple religious traditions, the river metaphor comes from Paul Gordon Lauren, *The Evolution of International Human Rights: Visions Seen* (Philadelphia: University of Pennsylvania Press, 2011).

2 Brian Tierney, *The Idea of Natural Rights: Studies on Natural Rights, Natural Law, and Church Law 1150–1625* (Grand Rapids, MI: Eerdmans, 1997).

3 Samuel Moyn, "Human Rights in History," *Atlantic*, 11 August 2010, https://www.thenation.com/article/archive/human-rights-history/. Use of the term "human rights scripts" is inspired by the work of Marisa Ramos Gonçalves, including "Genealogies of Human Rights Ideas in Timor-Leste: 'Kultura,' Resistance and Memory," *Nómadas* 53 (2020): 51–67. See also Jack Donnelly, *International Human Rights* (London: Routledge, 2020); and Samuel Moyn, *The Last Utopia: Human Rights in History* (Cambridge, MA: Harvard University Press, 2012).

4 Dominique Clément, *Human Rights in Canada: A History* (Waterloo, ON: Wilfrid Laurier University Press, 2016).

5 Of course, all human rights history in Canada should start with Indigenous forerunners. Joan Sangster provides an exemplar. Her history of feminism in Canada opens coverage of the struggle for women's suffrage by noting how Indigenous women were first robbed of those rights as part of colonization. Joan Sangster, *Demanding Equality: One Hundred Years of Canadian Feminism* (Vancouver: UBC Press, 2021).

6 Ping-cheung Lo, "The Right of Self-Defense in Confucianism," *Canopy Forum on the Interactions of Law and Religion*, 14 July 2020, https://canopyforum.org/2020/07/14/the-right-of-self-defense-in-confucianism/; Lo Chung-Shu, "A Confucian Approach to Human Rights," sent to UNESCO in 1947, *UNESCO Courier* 2018, no. 4 (2019): 30–31; William Theodore de Bary, *The Liberal Tradition in China* (New York: Columbia University Press, 1983); Yong Li, "Confucianism and the Foundation of Human Rights," in *Human Dignity, Human Rights, and Social Justice: A Chinese Interdisciplinary Dialogue with Global Perspective*, ed. Zhibin Xie, Pauline Kollontai, and Sebastian Kim (Singapore: Springer, 2020), 19–32; Hans Ingvar Roth, *P.C. Chang and the Universal Declaration of Human Rights* (Philadelphia: University of Pennsylvania Press, 2016).

7 Priyamvada Gopal, *Insurgent Empire: Anticolonial Resistance and British Dissent* (London: Verso, 2019).

8 Lynn Hunt, *Inventing Human Rights: A History* (New York: W.W. Norton, 2007), 27.

9 See the voluminous literature on humanitarian and human rights movements such as Amnesty International.

10 Roland Burke, *Decolonization and the Evolution of International Human Rights* (Philadelphia: University of Pennsylvania Press, 2010); Eric D. Weitz, *A World Divided: The Global Struggle for Human Rights in the Age of Nation-States* (Princeton, NJ: Princeton University Press, 2019); Aryeh Neier, *The International Human*

Rights Movement: A History (Princeton, NJ: Princeton University Press, 2020); Moyn, *The Last Utopia*; Jovito de Araújo, presentations on truth and reconciliation in Timor-Leste, Sherbrooke, QC, 2019, and Dili Timor-Leste, 2020. For a summary of de Araújo's views, see https://reconciliationtim.ca/timor/reconciliation-as-process-not-project/.

11 Weitz, *A World Divided*, 8, 241.

12 A. Dirk Moses, Marco Duranti, and Roland Burke, eds., *Decolonization, Self-Determination, and the Rise of Global Human Rights Politics* (Cambridge, UK: Cambridge University Press, 2020), 1, 4–6. Related themes will be developed in Bradley Simpson's upcoming history of self-determination, *The First Right: Self-Determination and the Transformation of post-1941 International Relations* (Oxford University Press, 2025). In the meantime, see also Bradley Simpson, "Self-Determination, Human Rights and the End of Empire in the 1970s," *Humanity* 4, no. 2 (2013): 239–60.

13 Steven L.B. Jensen, *The Making of International Human Rights: The 1960s, Decolonization, and the Reconstruction of Global Values* (Cambridge, UK: Cambridge University Press, 2016), 13–14.

14 Carol Chin, "Beneficent Imperialists: American Women Missionaries in China at the Turn of the Twentieth Century," *Diplomatic History* 27, no. 3 (2003): 327–52.

15 Wilfred Cantwell Smith, "Work among the Moslems," *Presbyterian Record*, April 1942, 118–19. I explore this at more length in "Islam and Cold War Modernization in the Formative Years of the McGill Institute of Islamic Studies," *International Journal of Canadian Studies* 32 (2005): 15–43.

16 The text appears at https://en.wikipedia.org/wiki/Korean_Declaration_of_Independence. See also Erez Manela, *The Wilsonian Moment* (Oxford: Oxford University Press, 2007); Chong-sik Lee, *The Politics of Korean Nationalism* (Berkeley: University of California Press, 1965); Sheila Miyoshi Jager, *Narratives of Nation Building in Korea: A Genealogy of Patriotism* (Armonk, NY: M.E. Sharpe, 2003); and Hildi Kang, ed., *Under the Black Umbrella: Voices from Colonial Korea, 1910–1945* (Ithaca, NY: Cornell University Press, 2001).

17 Doretha E. Mortimore, "Dr. Frank W. Schofield and the Korean National Consciousness," *Korea Journal* 17, no. 3 (1977): 37–47; Frank Schofield, "What Happened on Samil Day, March 1, 1919," in *The Feel of Korea*, ed. In Hah Jung (Seoul: Hollym, 1966), 277–79; O.W. Nam, "The Transformation of Frank Schofield (1889–1970)," in *Opening Korea, a Hermit Nation in East Asia*, special issue of *Social Identities* 14, no. 2 (2008): 233–51; A. Hamish Ion, *The Cross and the Rising Sun: The Canadian Protestant Missionary Movement in the Japanese Empire, 1872–1931* (Waterloo, ON: Wilfrid Laurier University Press, 2009); John D. Meehan, *Dominion and the Rising Sun: Canada Encounters Japan, 1929–1941* (Vancouver: UBC Press, 2004).

18 Carlton Waldo Kendall, *The Truth about Korea* (San Francisco: Korean National Association, 1919).

19 Provisional constitution, in *Sourcebook of Korean Civilization, Vol. II*, ed. Peter Lee (New York: Columbia University Press, 1996), 435–36; and declaration of aspirations, printed in Kendall, *The Truth about Korea*.

20 This section is based on Sang-chul Lee and Erich Weingartner, *The Wanderer: The Autobiography of a United Church Moderator* (Winfield, BC: Wood Lake Books, 1989); Lois Wilson, *Turning the World Upside Down* (Toronto: Doubleday, 1989); *United Church Observer*, various issues; David Cragg-Kim, *Water from Dragon's Well: The History of a Korean-Canadian Church Relationship* (Montreal and Kingston: McGill-Queen's University Press, 2022); and personal communications, 1987–90.

21 Lee and Weingartner, *The Wanderer*, 58.

22 Lee and Weingartner, *The Wanderer*, 124.

23 Wilson, *Turning the World*.

24 Johannes Morsink, *The Universal Declaration of Human Rights: Origins, Drafting, and Intent* (Philadelphia: University of Pennsylvania Press, 2000); Jean H. Quataert, *Advocating Dignity: Human Rights Mobilizations in Global Politics* (Philadelphia: University of Pennsylvania Press, 2009); Neier, *The International Human Rights Movement*, 98.

25 Kathryn Sikkink, *Evidence for Hope: Making Human Rights Work in the 21st Century* (Princeton, NJ: Princeton University Press, 2018); Mary Ann Glendon, *A World Made New: Eleanor Roosevelt and the Universal Declaration of Human Rights* (New York: Random House, 2001).

26 Cindy Ewing, "Codifying Minority Rights: Postcolonial Constitutionalism in Burma, Ceylon, and India," in *Decolonization, Self-Determination, and the Rise of Global Human Rights Politics* ed. A. Dirk Moses, Marco Duranti, and Roland Burke (Cambridge: Cambridge University Press, 2020), 179–206; Glenda Sluga, *Internationalism in an Age of Nationalism* (Philadelphia: University of Pennsylvania Press, 2013), 102; Rebecca Adami, *Women and the Universal Declaration of Human Rights* (London: Routledge, 2019), 67, 114.

27 Ewing, "Codifying Minority Rights," 179, 180.

28 J.R. McKinney, Department of External Affairs (hereafter DEA), to Mel Carson, Canadian Trade Commissioner, Singapore, 16 July 1956, Library and Archives Canada (hereafter LAC), RG 25/6864/4457-D-40[1].

29 Malayan cabinet meeting with Prime Minister John Diefenbaker, 29 November 1958, LAC, RG 25/9799/20-CDA-9-PM-TOUR.

30 J.M. Macdonnell to John Diefenbaker, 11 September 1957, LAC, RG 25/4245/8250-C-40[1].

31 R.G. Cavell, speech to directors' meeting, Department of Trade and Commerce, 17 April 1956, LAC, RG 25/7337/11038-40[20.2]. On Cavell, see Greg Donaghy, "'Reasonably Well-Organized': A History of Early Aid Administration," in *A Samaritan State Revisited: Historical Perspectives on Canadian Foreign Aid*, ed. Greg Donaghy and David Webster (Calgary: University of Calgary Press, 2019).

32 Jennifer Tunnicliffe, *Resisting Rights: Canada and the International Bill of Rights, 1947–76* (Vancouver: UBC Press, 2019).

33 Roland Burke, "'The Compelling Dialogue of Freedom': Human Rights at the Bandung Conference," *Human Rights Quarterly* 28, no. 4 (2006): 947–65.

34 *Asian-African Conference Bulletin* 4 (19 April 1955), http://historybeyondborders.ca/?p=142.

35 Cited in Roland Burke, "Internationalism of Human Rights," in *Internationalisms: A Twentieth-Century History*, eds. Glenda Sluga and Patricia Clavin (Cambidge: Cambridge University Press, 2017), 287–314, quotation at 302.

36 "Final Communiqué of the Asian-African Conference," 24 April 1955, CVCE.eu, https://www.cvce.eu/en/obj/final_communique_of_the_asian_african_conference_of_bandung_24_april_1955-en-676237bd-72f7-471f-949a-88b6ae513585.html.

37 Tunnicliffe, *Resisting Rights*, 78.

38 A point made in numerous documents, for instance Canadian Delegation, New York, to DEA, 5 December 1978, LAC, RG 25, vol. 8587, file 20-TIMOR[5].

39 See https://www.ohchr.org/en/instruments-mechanisms/instruments/international-covenant-civil-and-political-rights; https://www.ohchr.org/en/instruments-mechanisms/instruments/international-covenant-economic-social-and-cultural-rights; and https://www.ohchr.org/en/instruments-mechanisms/instruments/international-convention-elimination-all-forms-racial.

40 Jensen, *The Making of International Human Rights*, 277.

41 Vijay Prashad, *The Darker Nations: A People's History of the Third World* (New York: The New Press, 2022). There are seventy human rights treaties and declarations negotiated through the United Nations. *Yearbook of the United Nations, Special Edition: UN Fiftieth Anniversary 1945–1995* (The Hague: Martinus Nijhoff, 1995), 285.

42 Philippine government comments, 16 January 1950, E/CN.4/353/Add.3.

43 Joint resolution by Lebanon and the Philippines, 17 March 1952, E/CN.4/SUB.1/173; statement by Ambassador Carlos P. Romulo, McGill University Archives, MG417/9/154.

44 Philippine comments, 15 March 1954, E/CN.4/690/Add.12.

45 CHR records, United Nations Archives and Records Administration, New York; Andrew S. Thompson, *On the Side of the Angels: Canada and the United Nations Commission on Human Rights* (Vancouver: UBC Press, 2017), 41, 66.

46 John Humphrey travel diaries, McGill University Archives, MG417/20/414.

47 "Au moyen de mesures progressives et de méthodes appropriée." Philippines draft resolution, 14 June 1949, E/CN.4/330; French amendment, E/CN.4/348.

48 Notes for 1964, typescript for book draft, McGill University Archives, Humphrey Papers, MG417/7/092.

49 Jensen, *The Making of International Human Rights*, 107, 121, 67; Thompson, *On the Side of the Angels*, 3.

50 UN division memorandum, 30 November 1954, LAC, RG 25/6380/4855-C-40.

51 Tunnicliffe, *Resisting Rights*, 7, 98.

52 Thompson, *On the Side of the Angels*, 13.

53 Frantz Fanon, *The Wretched of the Earth* (London: Penguin, 1967), 55.

54 Steven Hugh Lee, *Outposts of Empire: Korea, Vietnam, and the Origins of the Cold War in Asia, 1949–1954* (Montreal and Kingston: McGill-Queen's University Press, 1996).

55 Laura Madokoro, Francine McKenzie, and David Meren, eds., *Dominion of Race: Rethinking Canada's International History* (Vancouver: UBC Press, 2017); John Price, *Orienting Canada: Race, Empire, and the Transpacific* (Vancouver: UBC Press, 2011); Peter Ward, *White Canada Forever: Popular Attitudes and Public Policy toward Orientals in British Columbia*, 3rd ed. (Montreal and Kingston: McGill-Queen's University Press, 2002); Rita Dhamoon et al., eds., *Unmooring the Komagata Maru: Charting Colonial Trajectories* (Vancouver: UBC Press, 2019); Timothy J. Stanley, *Contesting White Supremacy: School Segregation, Anti-Racism, and the Making of Chinese Canadians* (Vancouver: UBC Press, 2011).

56 Constance Backhouse, "The White Women's Labor Laws: Anti-Chinese Racism in Early Twentieth-Century Canada," *Law and History Review* 14, no. 2 (1996): 315–68.

57 Julie Gilmour, "Interpreting Social Disorder: The Case of the 1907 Vancouver Riots," *International Journal* 67, no. 2 (2012): 483–95; Laura Madokoro, *Elusive Refuge: Chinese Migrants in the Cold War* (Cambridge, MA: Harvard University Press, 2016).

58 Hugh Keenleyside, interview with Peter Stursberg, 27 August 1980, LAC, Stursberg Papers, F-137-0-0-1, 108.

59 Stephanie Bangarth, *Voices Raised in Protest: Defending North American Citizens of Japanese Ancestry, 1942–1949* (Vancouver: UBC Press, 2008); Stephanie Bangarth, "Nikkei Loyalty and Resistance in Canada and the United States, 1942–1947," *Asia Pacific Journal* 6, no. 1 (2008), https://apjjf.org/-Stephanie-Bangarth/2649/article.html; Jordan Stanger-Ross, *Landscapes of Injustice: A New Perspective on the Internment and Dispossession of Japanese Canadians* (Montreal and Kingston: McGill-Queen's University Press, 2020).

60 Roy Miki, *Redress: Inside the Japanese Canadian Call for Justice* (Vancouver: Raincoast Books, 2004).

61 Patricia Roy, "Images and Immigration: China and Canada," *Journal of American–East Asian Relations* 20, nos. 2–3 (2013): 117–38.

62 Daniel Manulak, "Blood Brothers: Race, the Afro-Asian-Canadian Bloc, and South Africa's Expulsion from the Commonwealth, 1960–61," *Canadian Historical Review* 103, no. 2 (2022): 252–76; Linda Freeman, *The Ambiguous Champion: Canada and South Africa in the Trudeau and Mulroney Years* (Toronto: University of Toronto Press, 1997).

63 Robert Vineberg, "The Winds of Change: Ellen Fairclough and the Removal of Discriminatory Immigration Barriers," in *Reassessing the Rogue Tory: Canadian Foreign Relations in the Diefenbaker Era*, ed. Janice Cavell and Ryan M. Touhey (Vancouver: UBC Press, 2018), 227–46.

64 Anglican Church Archives, Toronto, Canada Asia Working Group Papers.

65 Asa McKercher, "Reason over Passion: Pierre Trudeau, Human Rights, and Canadian Foreign Policy," *International Journal* 73, no. 1 (2018): 129–45.

66 Dominique Clément, "Human Rights in Canadian Domestic and Foreign Politics: From 'Niggardly Acceptance' to Enthusiastic Embrace," *Human Rights Quarterly* 34, no. 3 (2012): 751–78; Costas Melakopides, *Pragmatic Idealism: Canadian Foreign Policy, 1945–1995* (Kingston: Queen's School of Policy Studies, 1998).

67 Laura Madokoro, "'Nothing to Offer in Return': Refugees, Human Rights and Genocide in Cambodia, 1975–1978," *International Journal* 75, no. 2 (2020): 220–36.

68 Stephanie Bangarth, "The Politics of African Intervention: Canada and Biafra, 1967–70," in *From Kinshasa to Kandahar: Canada and Fragile States in Historical Perspective*, ed. Michael K. Carroll and Greg Donaghy (Calgary: University of Calgary Press, 2016), 53–72.

69 John Stackhouse, "PM Defends Cautious Stand on Indonesian Abuses," *Globe and Mail*, 18 January 1996, A16.

70 "Open Letter to Canadian Prime Minister Jean Chrétien," 29 March 2000, https://www.dd-rd.ca/open-letter-to-canadian-prime-minister-jean-chretien/ provide accessed date; open letter to Asia-Pacific Economic Cooperation summit, 1994, document in author's possession.

71 José Ramos Horta, *Towards a Peaceful Solution in East Timor* (Sydney: East Timor Relief Association, 1996), 22.

72 Bangkok NGO declaration, April 1993, United Nations Digital Library, https://digitallibrary.un.org/record/170675?ln=en&v=pdf.

73 Bangkok NGO declaration.

74 This section draws from David Webster, *Challenge the Strong Wind: Canada and East Timor 1975–99* (Vancouver: UBC Press, 2020); Hannah Loney, "Speaking Out for Justice: Bella Galhos and the International Campaign for the Independence of East Timor," in *The Transnational Activist*, ed. Stefan Berger and Sean Scalmer (London: Palgrave Macmillan, 2018), 193–226; personal communications, 1993–2022.

75 "Support for Residential School Survivors," 1 July 2021, National Association of Japanese Canadians, Greater Toronto Chapter, https://torontonajc.ca/residential-school-survivor-support/.

Acknowledgements

This edited collection originated in a workshop held at King's University College in May 2022. The SSHRC-funded event brought together twenty-five scholars, both in person and online, for two days of enlightening and fruitful discussion about Human Rights. We are grateful for the generous in-kind and financial support provided by King's and Toronto Metropolitan University, which helped to make the event possible. We extend our thanks to all our participants and are so pleased to be able to showcase the work of such incredible scholars at various stages of their careers.

We would especially like to acknowledge Jason Chartrand, Carly Ciufo, Kyle Hammer, Michael Lynk, Laura Madokoro, Dominique Marshall, Deirdre McCorkindale, Rob Ventresca, and Nic Virtue for their vital contributions to the workshop and to the discussions that shaped this collection. We are also deeply appreciative of the invaluable assistance provided by undergraduate students Ben Koch, Elizabeth McKenzie, Wyeth Robertson, and Katie Carson, both during the workshop and in the development of the American Review of Canadian Studies feature that followed.

Many others have helped to bring this book together. We are so fortunate to have the team at the University of Manitoba Press to help guide us. Many thanks to everyone at UMP, including Barbara Romanik, Jill McConkey, Anoja Barham, Stephanie Paddey, Sarah Ens, and our meticulous copyeditor, Dallas Harrison. Thank you as well to Alexa Love for the cover design.

Lastly, we extend sincere thanks to the anonymous peer reviewers who both challenged and championed this work.

A Special Thank You

This book is dedicated to James W.St.G. Walker whose mentorship shaped not just this work, but the course of our lives. His wisdom, kindness, and unwavering belief in us have left an indelible mark. As former graduate students, we were profoundly shaped by his unwavering commitment to human rights scholarship and the example he set as both an intellectual and a human being. Jim taught us that history is never neutral, and that the responsibility of the historian is not merely to record the past, but to interrogate it with courage, clarity, and compassion. His pioneering work in race relations, equity, and human rights not only opened vital spaces within Canadian historiography but inspired generations of scholars to take up the difficult, necessary questions that justice demands.

More than an academic guide, he was a generous and principled mentor who challenged us to be rigorous in our research, honest in our analysis, and ethical in our pursuits. He never let us lose sight of the people behind the policies or the lives behind the legislation. With wit, humility, and a remarkable depth of knowledge, he taught us how to write, how to think, and how to care.

Jim also showed us what it means to be a truly impactful educator. He approached the classroom with deep respect for his students and a genuine appreciation for their curiosity, reminding us that teaching is not just about imparting knowledge—it can, at its best, be a powerful form of activism. Through his example, we came to see education as an important tool for challenging injustice and engaging with the world thoughtfully, purposefully, and with compassion.

Finally, beyond his role as a mentor, Jim has become a lifelong friend—one whose presence and support we cherish deeply. We are forever grateful for his guidance, his example, and his belief in the power of scholarship to make change.

—Jennifer Tunnicliffe and Stephanie Bangarth

Selected Bibliography

Abella, Irving. *Nationalism, Communism, and Canadian Labour*. Toronto: University of Toronto Press, 1973.

Abella, Irving, and Harold Troper. *None Is Too Many: Canada and the Jews of Europe, 1933–1948*. Toronto: Lester and Orpen Dennys, 1982.

Adachi, Ken. *The Enemy that Never Was: A History of the Japanese Canadians*. Toronto: McClelland and Stewart, 1976.

Adams, Catherine, and Elizabeth H. Pleck. *Love of Freedom: Black Women in Colonial and Revolutionary New England*. New York: Oxford University Press, 2010.

Adamson, Nancy, Linda Briskin, and Margaret McPhail. *Feminist Organizing for Change: The Contemporary Women's Movement in Canada*. Toronto: Oxford University Press, 1988.

Anctil, Pierre. "Interlude of Hostility: Judeo-Christian Relations in Quebec in the Interwar Period, 1919–1939." In *Antisemitism in Canada: History and Interpretation*, edited by Allan Davies, 135–65. Waterloo, ON: Wilfrid Laurier University Press, 1992.

Arnesen, Eric. "The Specter of the Black Strikebreaker: Race, Employment and Activism in the Industrial Era." *Labor History* 44, no. 3 (2003): 319–35.

Austin, David. *Fear of a Black Nation: Race, Sex, and Security in Sixties Montreal*. Toronto: Between the Lines, 2013.

Bangarth, Stephanie. "'Their Equality Is My Equality': F. Andrew Brewin and Human Rights Activism, 1940s–1970s." In *Taking Liberties: A History of Human Rights in Canada*, edited by David Goutor and Stephen Heathorn, 114–38. Don Mills, ON: Oxford University Press, 2013.

———. "'Vocal but not Particularly Strong'? Air Canada's Ill-Fated Vacation Package to Rhodesia and South Africa and the Anti-Apartheid Movement in Canada." *International Journal* 71, no. 3 (2016): 488–97.

———. "'We Are Not Asking You to Open Wide the Gates for Chinese Immigration': The Committee for the Repeal of the Chinese Immigration Act and Early Human Rights Activism in Canada." *Canadian Historical Review* 84, no. 3 (2003): 395–425.

Belanger, Yale D. "The Six Nations of Grand River Territory's Attempts at Renewing International Political Relationships, 1921–1924." *Canadian Foreign Policy Journal* 13, no. 3 (2007): 29–43.

Berlin, Ira. *Many Thousands Gone: The First Two Centuries of Slavery in North America*. Cambridge, MA: Harvard University Press, 1998.

Bialystok, Franklin. *Delayed Impact: The Holocaust and the Canadian Jewish Community.* Montreal and Kingston: McGill-Queen's University Press, 2000.

Boyd, John. "A Noble Cause Betrayed . . . but Hope Lives On: Pages from a Political Life." Socialist History Project. https://www.socialisthistory.ca/Remember/Reminiscences/Boyd/B3.htm.

Brodie, Janine. "Three Stories of Canadian Citizenship." In *Contesting Canadian Citizenship: Historical Readings*, edited by Dorothy E. Chunn, Robert Adamoski, and Robert Menzies, 43–66. Peterborough: Broadview Press, 2002.

Burke, Roland. *Decolonization and the Evolution of International Human Rights.* Philadelphia: University of Pennsylvania Press, 2010.

Callahan, Marilyn, and Christopher Walmsley. "Rethinking Child Welfare Reform in British Columbia, 1900–60." In *People, Politics, and Child Welfare in British Columbia*, edited by Leslie Foster and Brian Wharf, 10–33. Vancouver: UBC Press, 2007.

Camfield, David. *Canadian Labour in Crisis—Reinventing the Workers' Movement.* Halifax: Fernwood Publishing, 2011.

Cardinal, Harold. *The Unjust Society: The Tragedy of Canada's Indians.* Edmonton: Hurtig Publishers, 1969.

Chabot, Mélanie. "À la découverte de l'autre': Le mouvement de l'éducation des adultes au Québec et les questions des relations interculturelles (1945–1960)." In *Vers la construction d'une citoyenneté canadienne*, edited by Jean-Michel Lacroix and Paul-André Lintel, 171–86. Paris: Presses Sorbonne Nouvelle, 2006.

Clément, Dominique. *Canada's Rights Revolution: Social Movements and Social Change, 1937–1982.* Vancouver: UBC Press, 2008.

———. *Equality Deferred: Sex Discrimination and British Columbia's Human Rights State, 1953–84.* Vancouver: UBC Press, 2014.

———. *Human Rights in Canada: A History.* Waterloo, ON: Wilfrid Laurier University Press, 2016.

Cottreau-Robbins, Heather. "Searching for the Enslaved in Nova Scotia's Loyalist Landscape." *Acadiensis* 43, no. 1 (2014): 125–36.

Cuthbertson, Wendy. *Labour Goes to War: The CIO and the Construction of a New Social Order, 1939–45.* Vancouver: UBC Press, 2013.

Daschuk, James. *Clearing the Plains: Disease, Politics of Starvation, and the Loss of Aboriginal Life.* Regina: University of Regina Press, 2013.

Donovan, Kenneth. "Slaves in Cape Breton, 1713–1815." *Directions: Canadian Race Relations Foundation* 4, no. 1 (2007): 31–37.

Douglas, Lawrence. *The Memory of Judgment: Making Law and History in the Trials of the Holocaust.* New Haven, CT: Yale University Press, 2001.

DuBois, Alison. "Instruments of Policy-Making: Canadian 'Indian' and 'Aboriginal' Policy." In *Native Voices in Research*, edited by Jill Oakes, Rick Riewe, Alison Edmunds, Alison Dubois, and Kimberley Wilde, 233–42. Winnipeg: Aboriginal Issues Press, 2003.

Firpo, Christina, and Margaret Jacobs. "Taking Children, Ruling Colonies: Child Removal and Colonial Subjugation in Australia, Canada, French Indochina, and the United States, 1870–1950s." *Journal of World History* 29, no. 4 (2018): 499–532.

Fournier, Suzanne, and Ernie Crey. *Stolen from Our Embrace: The Abduction of First Nations Children and the Restoration of Aboriginal Communities*. Vancouver: Douglas and McIntyre, 1997.

Frager, Ruth, and Carmela Patrias. "Human Rights Activists and the Question of Sex Discrimination in Postwar Ontario." *Canadian Historical Review* 93, no. 4 (2012): 583–610.

———. "'This Is Our Country, These Are Our Rights': Minorities and the Origins of Ontario's Human Rights Campaigns." *Canadian Historical Review* 82, no. 3 (2001): 1–35.

———. "Transnational Links and Citizens' Rights: Canadian Jewish Human Rights Activists and Their American Allies in the 1940s and 1950s." In *Taking Liberties: A History of Human Rights in Canada*, edited by David Goutor and Stephen Heathorn, 139–65. Don Mills, ON: Oxford University Press, 2013.

Freeman, Linda. *The Ambiguous Champion: Canada and South Africa in the Trudeau and Mulroney Years*. Toronto: University of Toronto Press, 1997.

Gélinas, Xavier. *La droite intellectuelle québécoise et la Révolution tranquille*. Québec: Presses de l'Université Laval, 2007.

Gonick, Cy. *A Very Red Life: The Story of Bill Walsh*. St. John's: Canadian Committee on Labour History, 2001.

Goutor, David. "Constructing the Great Menace: Canadian Labour's Opposition to Asian Immigration, 1881–1914." *Canadian Historical Review* 88, no. 4 (2007): 549–76.

———. "A Different Perspective on the 'Labor Rights as Human Rights' Debate: Organized Labor and Human Rights Activism in Canada, 1939–1952." *Labor Studies Journal* 36, no. 3 (2011): 408–27.

———. "Drawing Different Lines of Colour: The Mainstream English Canadian Labour Movement's Approach to Blacks and the Chinese." *Labor—Studies in Working Class History of the Americas* 2, no. 1 (2005): 55–76.

———. *Guarding the Gates: The Canadian Labour Movement and Immigration, 1872–1934*. Vancouver: UBC Press, 2007.

———. "Standing by Our Principles: The Trades and Labor Congress of Canada and Immigration, 1933–1939." *Just Labour: A Canadian Journal of Work and Society* 11 (2007): 55–65.

Goutor, David, and Stephen Heathorn, eds. *Taking Liberties: A History of Human Rights in Canada*. Don Mills, ON: Oxford University Press, 2013.

Hall, Catherine, Nicholas Draper, and Keith McClelland. "Introduction." In *Emancipation and the Remaking of the British Imperial World*, edited by Catherine Hall, Nicholas Draper, and Keith McClelland, 1–33. Manchester: Manchester University Press, 2014.

Hinther, Rhonda L. "'Likely to Be Hampered and So She Prepared for the Worst': Far Left Women and Wartime Political Incarceration." In *Civilian Internment in Canada:*

Histories and Legacies, edited by Rhonda L. Hinther and Jim Mochoruk, 215–38. Winnipeg: University of Manitoba Press, 2020.

———. "'Thoroughly Impregnated with Bolshevik Philosophy': Annie Buller's Incarceration and Canadian Political Policing during World War II." *Labour/Le Travail* 94 (2024): 9–44.

Hooper, Tom. "Queering '69: The Recriminalization of Homosexuality in Canada." *Canadian Historical Review* 100, no. 2 (2019): 257–73.

Howard, Rhoda E. "Black Africa and South Africa." In *Human Rights in Canadian Foreign Policy*, edited by Robert O. Matthews and Cranford Pratt, 265–84. Montreal and Kingston: McGill-Queen's University Press, 1988.

Hunt, Lynn. *Inventing Human Rights: A History*. New York: W.W. Norton and Co., 2007.

Iacovetta, Franca. *Gatekeepers: The Politics of Citizenship in Cold War Canada*. Toronto: Between the Lines, 2006.

Jensen, Steven L.B. *The Making of International Human Rights: The 1960s, Decolonization, and the Reconstruction of Global Values*. New York: Cambridge University Press, 2016.

Johnson, Morgan Brie. "Settler Colonial Structures of Domestication: British Home Children in Canada." *Genealogy* 5, no. 3 (2021): 77–78.

Johnstone, Marjorie. "Settler Feminism, Race Making, and Early Social Work in Canada." *Affilia* 33, no. 3 (2018): 292–307.

Kinsman, Gary. *The Regulation of Desire: Queer Histories, Queer Struggles*. Montreal: Concordia University Press, 2024.

Lambertson, Ross. "'The Dresden Story': Racism, Human Rights, and the Jewish Labour Committee of Canada." *Labour/Le Travail* 47 (2001): 43–82.

———. *Repression and Resistance: Canadian Human Rights Activists, 1930–1960*. Toronto: University of Toronto Press, 2005.

Leslie, John, and Robert Maguire, eds. *The Historical Development of the Indian Act*. Ottawa: Indian and Northern Affairs, 1978.

Lindqvist, Sven. *The Dead Do not Die: "Exterminate All the Brutes" and Terra Nullius*. New York: New Press, 2014.

Lomawaima, Tsianina K., and Jeffrey Ostler. "Reconsidering Richard Henry Pratt: Cultural Genocide and Native Liberation in an Era of Racial Oppression." *Journal of American Indian Education* 57, no. 1 (2018): 79–100.

Lynch, Gordon. "Saving the Child for the Sake of the Nation: Moral Framing and the Civic, Moral and Religious Redemption of Children." *American Journal of Cultural Sociology* 2, no. 2 (2014): 165–96.

MacLennan, Christopher. *Toward the Charter: Canadians and the Demand for a National Bill of Rights, 1929–1960*. Montreal and Kingston: McGill-Queen's University Press, 2004.

Macleod-Leslie, Heather. "Archaeology and Atlantic Canada's African Diaspora." *Acadiensis* 43, no. 1 (2014): 137–45.

Madokoro, Laura, Francine McKenzie, and David Meren, eds. *Dominion of Race: Rethinking Canada's International History*. Vancouver: UBC Press, 2017.

Manzano-Munguía, María Cristina. "Conceptualizing Native Non-Government Organizations in Canada: An Ethnographic Approach." *International Journal of Interdisciplinary Social Sciences* 2, no. 4 (2007): 449–59.

———. "Mediating Aboriginal-State Relations through Native Non-Governmental Organizations and Aboriginal Leaders: An Alternative Model." PhD diss., University of Western Ontario, 2009.

Maracle, Sylvia. "The Eagle Has Landed: Native Women, Leadership and Community Development." In *Strong Women Stories: Native Vision and Community Survival*, edited by Kim Anderson and Bonita Lawrence, 70–80. Toronto: Sumach Press, 2003.

Maxwell, Krista. "Settler-Humanitarianism: Healing the Indigenous Child-Victim." *Comparative Studies in Society and History* 59, no. 4 (2017): 974–1007.

McCaskell, Tim. *Queer Progress: From Homophobia to Homonationalism*. Toronto: Between the Lines, 2016.

McCorkindale, Deirdre. "Weaponized History: The Underground Railroad's Mythologized Legacy in Canada." *American Review of Canadian Studies* 53, no. 1 (2023): 75–91.

McKercher, Asa. "Reason over Passion: Pierre Trudeau, Human Rights, and Canadian Foreign Policy." *International Journal* 73, no. 1 (2018): 111–31.

Mills, Sean. *A Place in the Sun: Haiti, Haitians, and the Remaking of Quebec*. Montreal and Kingston: McGill-Queen's University Press, 2016.

Momryk, Myron. "Ukrainian Internment during the Second World War." In *Civilian Internment in Canada: Histories and Legacies*, edited by Rhonda L. Hinther and Jim Mochoruk, 239–60. Winnipeg: University of Manitoba Press, 2020.

Moyn, Samuel. *The Last Utopia: Human Rights in History*. Cambridge, MA: Belknap Press of Harvard University Press, 2010.

Nelson, Bruce. *Divided We Stand: American Workers and the Struggle for Black Equality*. Princeton, NJ: Princeton University Press, 2016.

Ng, Wing Chung. *The Chinese in Vancouver, 1945–1980: The Pursuit of Identity and Power*. Vancouver: UBC Press, 2008.

Nworah, Kenneth. "The Aborigines Protection Society, 1889–1909: A Pressure-Group in Colonial Policy." *Canadian Journal of African Studies* 5, no. 1 (1971): 79–91.

O'Connell, Anne. "The Pauper, Slave, and Aboriginal Subject: British Parliamentary Investigations and the Promotion of Civilized Conduct (1830s)." *Canadian Social Work Review* 26, no. 2 (2009): 171–93.

O'Malley, Gregory E. *Final Passages: The Intercolonial Slave Trade of British America, 1619–1807*. Chapel Hill: University of North Carolina Press, 2014.

Palmer, Bryan. *Working Class Experience: Rethinking the History of Canadian Labour*. Toronto: McClelland and Stewart, 1994.

Parker, Roy. *Uprooted: The Shipment of Poor Children to Canada, 1867–1917*. Bristol: Bristol University Press, 2008.

Patrias, Carmela. "Race, Employment Discrimination, and State Complicity in Wartime Canada, 1939–1945." *Labour/Le Travail* 59 (2007): 9–42.

Pratt, Renate. *In Good Faith: Canadian Churches against Apartheid.* Waterloo, ON: Wilfrid Laurier University Press, 1997.

Rainville, Paul-Etienne. "'Un programme unique dans le monde entier': Le Congrès juif canadien et la lutte pour le droit à l'égalité 'raciale' et religieuse au Québec (1945–1950)." *Histoire sociale* 53, no. 109 (2020): 597–624.

Rooke, Patricia, and R.L. Schnell. "Imperial Philanthropy and Colonial Response: British Juvenile Emigration to Canada, 1896–1930." *Historian* 46, no. 1 (1983): 56–77.

Roth, Hans Ingvar. *P.C. Chang and the Universal Declaration of Human Rights.* Philadelphia: University of Pennsylvania Press, 2018.

Roy, Patricia. *The Oriental Question: Consolidating a White Man's Province, 1914–1941.* Vancouver: UBC Press, 2003.

———. *A White Man's Province: British Columbia Politicians and Japanese Immigrants, 1858–1914.* Vancouver: UBC Press, 1989.

Scott, Corrie. "How French Canadians Became White Folks: Or, Doing Things with Race in Quebec." *Ethnic and Racial Studies* 39, no. 7 (2016): 1280–97.

Swain, Shurlee. "But the Children . . . Indigenous Child Removal Policies Compared." In *Writing Colonial Histories: Comparative Perspectives*, edited by Tracey Banivanua Mar and Julie Evans, 133–43. Melbourne: RMIT Publishing, 2002.

Swain, Shurlee, and Margot Hillel. *Child, Nation, Race and Empire: Child Rescue Discourse, England, Canada and Australia, 1850–1915.* Manchester: Manchester University Press, 2010.

Tobias, John. "Protection, Civilization, Assimilation: An Outline History of Canada's Indian Policy." In *As Long as the Sun Shines and Water Flows: A Reader in Canadian Native Studies*, edited by Ian Getty and Antoine Lussier, 39–55. Vancouver: UBC Press, 1983.

Troxler, Carole Watterson. "Re-Enslavement of Black Loyalists: Mary Postell in South Carolina, East Florida, and Nova Scotia." *Acadiensis* 37, no. 2 (2008): 70–85.

Tunnicliffe, Jennifer. *Resisting Rights: Canada and the International Bill of Rights, 1947–76.* Vancouver: UBC Press, 2019.

Walker, James W.St.G. "Decoding the Rights Revolution: Lessons from the Canadian Experience." In *Taking Liberties: A History of Human Rights in Canada*, edited by David Goutor and Stephen Heathorn, 29–58. Toronto: Oxford University Press, 2013.

———. "The 'Jewish Phase' in the Movement for Racial Equality in Canada." *Canadian Ethnic Studies* 34, no. 1 (2002): 1–29.

Webster, David. *Challenge the Strong Wind: Canada and East Timor, 1975–79.* Vancouver: UBC Press, 2020.

———. "The Myth of Canada as a Voice for Human Rights." *Policy Options*, 4 March 2020, https://policyoptions.irpp.org/magazines/march-2020/the-myth-of-canada-as-a-voice-for-human-rights/.

Weitz, Eric D. *A World Divided: The Global Struggle for Human Rights in the Age of Nation-States.* Princeton: Princeton University Press, 2019.

Whitaker, Reg. "Official Repression of Communism during World War II." *Labour/Le Travail* 17 (1986): 135–66.

Whitfield, Harvey Amani. "The African Diaspora in Atlantic Canada: History, Historians, and Historiography." *Acadiensis* 46, no. 1 (2017): 213–32.

———. *Blacks on the Border: The Black Refugees in British North America, 1815–1860*. Burlington: University of Vermont Press, 2006.

———, ed. *Black Slavery in the Maritimes: A History in Documents*. Peterborough: Broadview Press, 2018.

———. *North to Bondage: Loyalist Slavery in the Maritimes*. Vancouver: UBC Press, 2016.

Young, Bryanne. "'Killing the Indian in the Child': Death, Cruelty, and Subject-Formation in the Canadian Indian Residential School System." *Mosaic* 48, no. 4 (2015): 63–76.